2003

To my Brother - Stanley

Hope you will enjoy this book - it will bring back old memmories since you were at the mill untill the last whistle blew.

Love you youngest sister
Lavin & Frank

The Oregon–American Lumber Company: Ain't No More

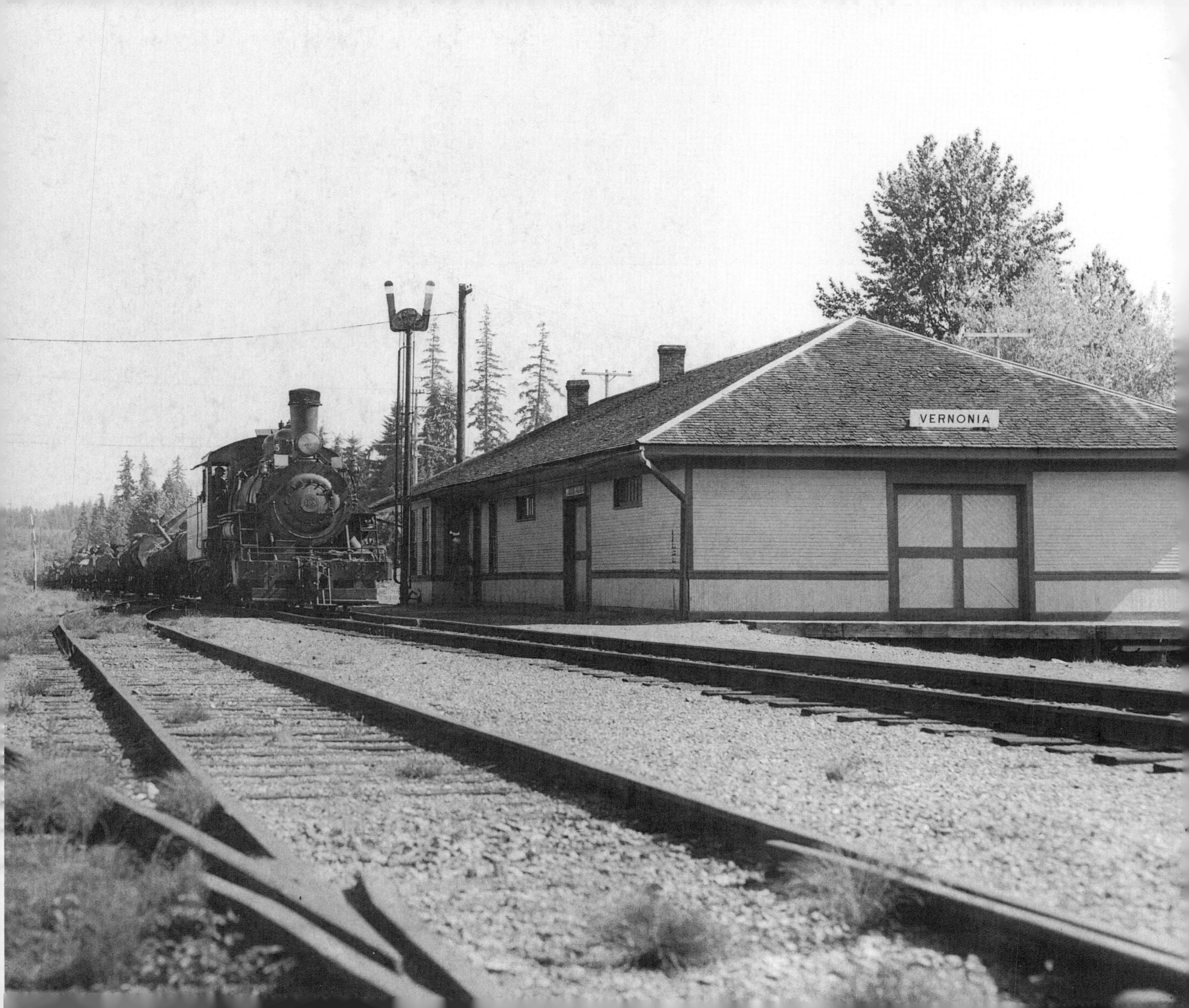
VERNONIA

The Oregon-American Lumber Company: Ain't No More

Edward J. Kamholz,
Jim Blain,
and
Gregory Kamholz

STANFORD UNIVERSITY PRESS

Stanford, California · 2003

Stanford University Press
Stanford, California

© 2003 by the Board of Trustees of the
Leland Stanford Junior University

Printed in the United States of America
on acid-free, archival-quality paper

Library of Congress Cataloging-in-Publication Data

Kamholz, Edward J.
  The Oregon-American Lumber Company: ain't no more/Edward J. Kamholz, Jim Blain, and Gregory Kamholz.
     p. cm.
  Includes index.
  ISBN 0-8047-4481-5 (cloth: alk. paper)
  1. Oregon-American Lumber Company—History. 2. Lumber trade—Oregon—History. I. Blain, Jim. II. Kamholz, Gregory. III. Title.
  HD9759.O74 K36 2002
  338.7´674´09795—dc21

                                      2002007735

Original Printing 2003

Last figure below indicates year of this printing:
11—10—09—08—07—06—05—04—03

Design and typography by Edward J. Kamholz

Opposite title page: O.A.L. 105 eastbound passing the Vernonia, Oregon depot in June 1953 with twenty-six loads of logs bound for the mill.

DEDICATION

Born in Kansas City, Kansas, by his eighteenth year, tall Judd Greenman had earned quite a reputation as a pitcher at Kansas City High School and with certain semiprofessional baseball teams. The company doctor for the Burns-Briggs Lumber Company of Edith, Colorado, offered young Greenman employment. The doctor, a high school friend of Greenman's mother, wanted the young man to pitch on a team that was sponsored for play among area mills and mining camps.

I have never known, Greenman once mused, *whether it was the Colorado climate and scenery or the lumber business that fascinated me.... Something did and I took a job in the mill and held one down in that and other mills for the next fifty-one years.*

Devoted husband and father of two, Greenman came to the Oregon-American Lumber Company as general manager of the Vernonia mill in 1925. During the next thirty-one years he secured a place among industry giants, both for the company as well as for himself. Never one to shy away from responsibility, a partial list of his accomplishments and contributions to society and industry include:

Appointed Chairman of the Welfare Committee of the State of Oregon by Governor Charles Martin.

Director, Northwest Oregon Forest Protection Association.

Member, West Coast Bureau of Lumber Grades and Inspection for nearly thirty years.

Trustee, Columbia Basin Loggers and Columbia Basin Sawmills.

Trustee, Lumbermen's Industrial Relations Committee, Inc.

Treasurer, West Coast Lumbermens Association, 1942–1945.

WCLA Vice President for Oregon, 1946–1953.

WCLA District Director, 1953.

Ex-Officio Director/WCLA Representative to National Lumber Manufacturers Association, 1954.

Member-at-Large, NLMA Board of Directors, 1951–1953.

NLMA First Vice President and member of Executive Committee, 1954.

NLMA President, 1955.

NLMA Chairman of the Board, 1956.

CONTENTS

The History Behind the History   ix

Foreword   xvii

Introduction   1

Constructing America   5

The Road to Vernonia   17

Boom Times Arrive   35

High Hopes and Dashed Dreams   89

Trials by Fire   121

From the Ashes   137

A New World   159

Lumber Goes to War   205

The Glory Years   243

The Last Stand   291

Epilogue   325

Appendixes
   A. *Comparison of Donkey Engine*
      Operating Characteristics and Performance   333
   B. *Mileposts*   335
   C. *Supplemental Notes on the Possible Cause*
      of the Salmonberry Fire of July 9, 1945   336
   D. *Elevations at Selected Points of Interest*   337
   E. *Major Tree Species of the Oregon-American*
      Lumber Company Timber Tract   338

Equipment Rosters
   Rod Locomotives   340
   Geared Locomotives   342
   Donkey Engines and Skidders   344
   Bulldozers and Graders   347
   Lumber Carriers   348

Research Notes   349

Index   355

THE HISTORY BEHIND THE HISTORY

The roots of *The Oregon-American Lumber Company: Ain't No More* are traceable to the authors' childhood days and before. Alfred "Paddy" Hughes, grandfather to brothers Greg and Ed Kamholz arrived in Vernonia, Oregon, in 1924, the year the O-A mill began operating, and he spent the next twenty-eight years of his life there, employed as chief electrician. Because the mill and company housing developments were powered by electricity generated by the on-site powerhouse, few details of the operation's inner workings escaped him. Doting grandfather that he was, he entertained Greg and Ed in his "office" at the sawmill as often as possible. His daughter, Amy, was herself a train fan and the boys' earliest memories revolved around their mom taking them to the nearby railroad yard to greet locomotive 105 whenever it brought in another train of logs bound for the mill. Their dad Marvin took every opportunity to show them as much as possible too. Over time the family took the boys on trips to the woods on the log train, drives to the camps, and made an afternoon ritual of chasing the train from Keasey or watching the crew dump logs into the millpond after school. Combined with tours of the sawmill and their own explorations, Greg and Ed developed strong boyhood impressions of the outfit. Little wonder that when the operation ground to a close in 1957 they felt the loss every bit as much as if there had been a death in the family. With so much yet to be learned and understood, the brothers would lament O-A's passing for nearly as many years as the company operated.

The brothers Kamholz openly hoped for the day some historian would take the time to research the company's rich history, but they were equally put off by the idea. They believed that without some factual written basis on which to base the story, the company's history would be unlikely to rise above a mere collection of anecdotes and a rehashing of newspaper articles. Although potentially interesting, neither anecdotes nor news clippings offered much insight into how the company came to be or what prompted its leaders to conduct the business the way they did.

About the same time Greg's and Ed's folks were steeping their boys in matters O-A, a similar situation was developing only about a mile away. Unbeknownst to the Kamholzes, the Blain family was making a ritual of leaving Southern California to vacation at Jim Blain's grandmother's home near Vernonia during the summer. Her place was conveniently located along Lone Pine Road, across from the SP&S passing track, where the daily O-A log train stopped to back its loads into the mill spur. Reminiscent of a Norman Rockwell setting, his grandma's place was a typical 1930s-style two-story mill house, complete with a hand-cranked telephone, single-bulb lights, a hand-pumped well, wood stove, barn, chicken coop, and outhouse. Jim

THE HISTORY BEHIND THE HISTORY

and his younger brother, Jerry, soon discovered the railroad tracks that ran just beyond grandma's pasture. Her back porch provided a commanding view of the SP&S freight traffic and O-A log trains.

The Blain boys' father, Marvin, grew up in Brownsville, Oregon, and had worked as a logger in the pre-Depression years. He longed to return to those roots following World War II. Determined to educate his boys in the fundamentals of logging and sawmilling, he began taking the family to Vernonia for summer vacations in 1948. Those annual visits were a highly anticipated family event that lasted through 1953. The Blain boys knew their dad's tutorial process would always include frequent trips to the O-A mill, train-watching trips to Keasey, the occasional foray to Camp Olson, as well as drives to the many abandoned logging sites that surrounded Vernonia.

Jim and Jerry spent many happy days watching the arrival and departure of the trains. Occasionally, their grandma sent the boys across the pasture to collect leftover grain from the empty boxcars for the chickens. If they timed it right, the chore provided a ringside seat for the afternoon log train's arrival. Rail fans can appreciate the scene. The 105's three-chime whistle blowing for the Lone Pine Road crossing, the passing of the heavily loaded train as it came to a slow, creaking stop, the anticipation of her engineer's whistling off to acknowledge the signal to begin backing into the mill spur and the sturdy Baldwin's struggle to get the train moving against the unfavorable grade. Likewise the sounds of the log train when it left early in the morning on the trip back to the woods, except the echoes of the 105's whistle on those frequent rainy mornings, were usually monitored by Jim from the comfort of the feather bed he occupied in the attic.

Jim's parents' Christmas gift in 1953 was a used 4 × 5 Speed Graphic camera. That year was momentous for another reason because, at age sixteen, he bore the badge of young adulthood, a driver's license. That last Vernonia summer Jim created his own lasting memorial of O-A: a photo collection. Yielding to his dad's lessons, many years of pleasant reminiscing followed, accompanied by the distant memory of the 105's whistle.

Thirty-two years later, those memories became the inspiration to record Oregon-American's history in a book. Jim visited the dean of Northwest short-line railroad history, John Labbe, to seek advice for the undertaking. John, ever helpful, fueled Jim's quest by providing him with numerous leads and sealed their friendship by putting his extensive O-A photo collection at Jim's disposal. Providentially, among Labbe's list of contacts was Greg Kamholz. Jim's letters to Greg requesting photographs and information remained unanswered until, at the urging of his younger brother, Ed, Greg replied. Finally, during the summer of 1989, Greg happened to visit Ed, who some years earlier had taken residence in the San Francisco Bay Area. Since Jim lived in nearby Scotts Valley, the eventual coauthors arranged to meet.

Perhaps skepticism being a particular family trait, Greg and Ed clearly recall leaving Jim's place after the first visit agreeing that while their new friend had a great photograph collection, how in the world could he expect to put a book together that would offer more than a superficial treatment of the company's story? Subsequent meetings led to a collaborative project, a silent videotape scrapbook of

Jim's photograph and movie collection. While the friendship deepened, it was difficult to overcome the feeling that Jim's quest for an inside look at Oregon-American was limited by time and the absence of primary research materials.

In the course of their increasingly frequent conversations, Jim advised that Oregon-American's company records had been donated to the University of Oregon's Division of Special Collections and University Archives, a part of the university's library system. Initial inquiries revealed it was a sizable collection that would take many hours to review. Occupational responsibilities, not to mention the remoteness of the collection from Jim's California home, put the company's records temptingly out of reach.

Matters drifted along until February 1991 at which time Ed found it necessary to pass through Eugene. He contacted the university and arranged to have a few boxes of the records available for his perusal. Fully aware of how anxious businesses of the current era are to rid themselves of old papers, not to mention how unlikely they are to commit anything to paper that might be controversial and potentially troublesome, he arrived expecting to see little more than sales orders.

Ed recalls of that February 8 morning that he had only turned the third page in the first box and lo and behold, there was correspondence about shay Number 116 that Oregon-American's parent company had sent to Vernonia briefly in 1926. That struck a chord for other than recalling mention of that locomotive by the long-deceased engineer of the Vernonia log train, this was the first instance of a written account of that locomotive's brief stint of duty. Every page seemed to uncover new revelations.

The Greenman Collection, the personal files of Judd Greenman, general manager and later president of Oregon-American, proved to be an amazingly rich chronicle of business correspondence penned by one of the old-growth Douglas fir belt's giant personalities. Not only did it contain the facts about how the company was run, but also the correspondence revealed the factors that influenced management to manage the way they did. In short, the body of information contained in the Greenman Collection represented a once-in-a-lifetime opportunity to write a lumber company history from a strategic, rather than an anecdotal perspective.

Ed describes diving into those first boxes:

> Five minutes into the first box and I was hooked. By the end of the day I was overwhelmed. Bits and pieces of puzzles Greg and I had pondered for decades were suddenly before me. For example, the correspondence not only told where and when they logged certain areas, it also told of the planning process behind those decisions. It was like Judd Greenman was telling the story personally. I couldn't wait to get on the telephone to tell Greg and Jim.

Exciting as this new information was, however, the practical matter of how to extract and organize the sheer volume of information began to sink in. Putting the Greenman Collection in a physical perspective gives some idea of what lay ahead. The documents, mostly carbon copies, were recorded on flimsy sheets of paper similar to tracing paper. Many had faded and were barely decipherable. That, however, was the least of the challenges. The collection, if stacked one document on top of the other, measured eighty-four linear feet, perhaps some 60,000 or more documents in total. Reporting back to Jim,

THE HISTORY BEHIND THE HISTORY

it became apparent the Greenman Collection represented the ultimate factual information basis on which to write the Oregon-American story. How to proceed?

Owing to a brief period during which both Ed and Greg had some flexibility with their work schedules, combined with Jim's willingness to make the book project a collaborative effort, the Kamholzes undertook to review the entire collection, tagging pertinent documents for reproduction.

Ed spent thirty-three days in Eugene between February and October, 1991, reviewing and marking documents. Greg took on the task of microfilming the selected documents and finished that phase of the project late in 1992. It took Ed until 1994 to prepare a searchable database suitable for keeping track of all the documents and two more years after that to complete a first draft. As word of the project spread, photographs began to surface so that by the time the work was ready to go to press, more than seven hundred images were available to the authors.

From 1985 to the present, countless doors opened and resources appeared, seemingly just when they were needed most. Many times the authors remarked that the project seemed blessed from the outset and their roles were merely attendant to some larger purpose. Certainly, something beyond the authors' mere desire to write a book was in play. Absent a more concrete explanation, perhaps this work responds to the collective sentiments and spirituality of those living and departed whose individual endeavors, woven together, were the fabric of Oregon-American's story.

ACKNOWLEDGMENTS

Between those early days of 1985 when this book was but a dream in Jim Blain's mind and the present, the authors have been truly blessed in their work to bring the Oregon-American story to life. Doors opened and key resources appeared like the parting of the waters. Along the way the authors made many new friends and renewed no small number of old family acquaintances. It's been a marvelous journey and merely acknowledging others' contributions fails to convey the true extent of gratitude.

The University of Oregon Library System, under which the Division of Special Collections and University Archives operates, proved to be more than simply a caretaker of its treasures. In particular, we must thank the Special Collections curator, Fraser Cocks III, for his early recognition of how large an undertaking we proposed when we began our research of the Greenman Collection. On the one hand, while making it clear that the university was in no position to provide document reproduction support, Fraser went to great lengths to facilitate our efforts to microfiche the documents. Without the university's assistance, we would have simply been unable to relate the Oregon-American story in any significant level of detail. In the end, we recorded nearly 16,000 documents on microfiche, totaling some 23,000 pages from the Greenman Collection, enough we think, to build the Oregon-American story from the ground up, and then some. For that, we are deeply indebted to our good friends in Eugene. Out of a desire to further enrich the Greenman Collection by providing it a visual perspective, we have donated prints and negatives from our extensive Oregon-American photograph collection to the university.

Significantly, one of the first and most successful authors to capture the spirit and flavor of railroad logging, John T. Labbe, the late dean of Northwest short-line railroad history, served as friend, mentor, and boundless source of inspiration, knowledge, and photographs. John got the log rolling with *Railroads in the Woods*, a book he coauthored with Vernon Goe in 1961, and provided those of us who aspire to write about logging railroad history with the benchmark against which all books since have been measured.

We are equally indebted to the late Rose Valpiani, Judd Greenman's longtime personal secretary, who, along with Mrs. Greenman, petitioned International Paper Company to have Mr. Greenman's correspondence files preserved and donated to the University of Oregon. Mrs. Valpiani facilitated that process and, years later, was a valuable source, both for photographs and insight into the personality of Mr. Greenman and others.

One of the greatest challenges we faced in this project was mapping Oregon-American's rail and truck road development. Through 1991, significant contributions to our knowledge bank of O-A and Inman-Poulsen operations were made by Don Devere, Dr. Dale Jost, and Harold Sandstrom. Without their research, cooperation, drafting, and encouragement, interest in the project might have lapsed. Discovery of the Greenman Collection breathed new life into this critical area, because it enabled us to plot property boundaries and spur development at specific periods in the company's life. Yet even this proved lacking because of the relative absence of maps in the collection. Only when we correlated written descriptions from the Greenman Collection to aerial photography found at the University of Oregon Map Library and the Oregon Department of Forestry were we able to re-create the period-specific maps that precede each chapter of *Ain't No More*. Still, it wasn't until we went to ground and physically located those long-abandoned rights-of-way that our perspective of the property reached the stage of true familiarity. And no one helped us achieve that familiarity more than O-A's former road construction man, George Lee. George and his uncle built, or had a hand in building, nearly every major Oregon-American right-of-way between the mid-1920s and 1953. A day in the O-A operating territory with George was like a tour of a 20,000-acre archaeological dig. Blessed with an incredible memory and the willingness to share his knowledge and experiences, he, more than any single living individual, put us in physical touch with the land we sought to learn about.

Significantly, our introduction to George Lee was facilitated by Robb Wilson, who, as curator of the Vernonia Museum of the Columbia County Historical Society, kept a constant vigil for information and resources in support of our research, and during his tenure helped organize several Oregon-American Old-timers' Picnics. These efforts provided the authors with many valuable contacts. Robb's predecessors, Bill Cavinee, John and Dorothy Stofiel, and Barbara Young also provided valuable assistance through their research of the *Vernonia Eagle* archives.

If George Lee was our savior in the woods, his counterpart on the mill side of the operation was Fred Roediger, who operated the horizontal resaw from July 20, 1936, until September 11, 1957, the entire time the sawmill operated after the Depression. Given his longevity, not to mention his experience during the Depression as a watchman, few had any better understanding of how the mill worked and where things were located than did Fred. For his boundless enthusiasm and for sharing his knowledge, we thank him.

THE HISTORY BEHIND THE HISTORY

Individual thanks are also owed to Forrest Beatty of the Oregon Department of Forestry's graphics department, Steve Waite, former O-A logging engineer, and Darrel DeVaney, whose efforts and contributions were instrumental in achieving our mapping objectives.

Our ability to convey details about the Northern Lines' negotiations with Central Coal & Coke, Oregon-American, and for the Portland, Astoria & Pacific and Nehalem Boom Companies were made possible by the generosity of John T. Gaertner, who provided the authors with relevant research notes from the Great Northern and Northern Pacific Railway Presidential Files that he used to write *North Bank Road*.

No less important were the many who provided us with photographs, stories, articles, technical assistance, leads, and hospitality. Collectively, their contributions represent the human interest and illustrative qualities of *Ain't No More*. Our thanks go to:

Gene Aherns; Jack Anderson and family; Kenneth Anderson and family; Dr. Leonard Arrington; Rick Aubin; Ethel Blackburn; Betty and Bob Blumenthal; Kent Boring, Stimson Lumber Company; Todd Bowerman; Clarence and Walter Bradford; Carroll Bradley; Nancy Burch, Vernonia City Librarian; Gary Canaparo; Glen Comstock; Barbara Diana Correia; Mary Cota; Jim Cox; Jean DeVaney; Bob Donkels; Alvin Elkins; Richard Engeman, University of Washington Libraries; Ivan Ergish; Herb Erickson; Mr. and Mrs. Oscar Farlin; Albert Farrow; Larry Fick; James Fox and Duffy Goble, Special Collections and University Archives, University of Oregon; Steve Gatke; Duke Gortler; Walter Grande; Martin Hansen; Steve Hauff; Glen Hawkins; John Henderson; Willis C. Hendrick; Jack Holst; Lee Hopkins, Kansas City Museum; Merv Johnson; Anne S. Jordan; Victoria Jones, Special Collections and University Archives, University of Oregon; George Kadelak; Carol and Ralph Keasey; Nora Keith; Fred Kepner; Kristen Kinsey, University of Washington Libraries; Stan Kistler; Dave Larson; Carol Lee; Dawn Lee; Larry Lee; James Lindsay; Edna and Walter Linn; George Martin; Ed Maas, Merritt Microfilming, Inc.; Dan and Linda Moore; Denise Morrison, Kansas City Museum; Curtis Nesheim; Lyle Noah; Carol and Bill Ostrander; Lloyd Palmer; Leston Peck; Gary Pennington, Central Coal & Coke Corporation; Emily and Erick Peterson; Margretta Pierce, Railway Negative Exchange; Dan Ranger; Mark Reed; Vivian Laird Reynolds; Doug Richter; Rosalie Roediger; Bill Roy; J. E. Schroeder, Oregon State Forester (retired); Tim Shiel, Stimson Lumber Company; Ken Schmelzer; Philip Schnell; Gary Schnoor; Robert H. Scott; Jim Shaughnessy; George Shore, Oregon Department of Forestry; Arlie Sliffe; Lyle Speers; Fred Spurrell, Suburban Photo; Ralph Swan; Faye and Bill Sword; Margaret Taylor; Ruth and Phil Taylor; John Taubeneck; Ken Tetzel; Kathleen and Don Tiffney; Lon Wall; Bert Ward; Fred Wenzel; Bob Wenzel; Lloyd White; and David Wilkie.

Institutions not otherwise mentioned in connection with specific individuals that contributed to the work include Delano Photographics and Northern Lights Studios, Fort Vancouver Historical Society, International Paper Company, Oregon Historical Society, Oregon State Archives, and Wy'east Color, Inc.

Special thanks are extended to Doug Decker, Director, Tillamook State Forest Interpretation and Education Program, Oregon Department of

Forestry; Ann Fulton, Ph.D., Portland State University History Department and Cultural Resources Management; and George Lee, Bruce MacGregor, and David L. Rygmyr, Oso Publishing Company for their time and trouble to review our manuscript drafts. Their insights and comments, some rather pointed, are deeply appreciated and were instrumental in achieving the finished product.

Finally, our endless gratitude goes to Norris Pope, Program Director—Scholarly Publishing, Stanford University Press. Norris championed our cause and guided us through the steps we needed to take to fine-tune the work so it would meet that venerable institution's benchmarks. Without him, this work might never have seen the light of publication. Our thanks also extend to Rob Ehle, Alex Giardino, Randy Hurst, David Jackson, Eleanor Mennick, Patricia Myers, Tim Roberts, and Ted Wagstaff of Stanford University Press for their work to produce this book.

FOREWORD

The old-growth Douglas fir lumbering era is pivotal in the current understanding of Pacific Slope development. Spanning the period from the late 1800s through the middle of the twentieth century, lumber enterprises served a twofold purpose. First, they created jobs that helped fuel the population migration to the West. Places such as Portland, Seattle, Tacoma, Aberdeen, Hoquiam, and Vancouver began as mere outposts and were the first stop-off points for those who heeded woods work as their calling. Overnight these places became boomtowns as sawmills popped up everywhere along the major waterways that served them.

Equally important, however, was that no sooner than these mills met the local demand for lumber than they responded to the call of distant markets elsewhere in the country. The promise of supplying building materials to a nation whose demands appeared infinite spurred the mills' growth and along with it swelled the employment in all phases of the business. Boomtowns grew into cities, and services and suppliers to the lumber industry evolved into growth industries in their own right. The ever-widening cutting circle required new ways to move logs and lumber to mill and market and gave rise to another growth industry—the railroad. Its arrival on the coast corresponded with that of the old-line lumber operators of the Upper Midwest and Deep South. Having depleted the lumber resources of those regions, the big names in the industry were anxious to find new operating territory of their own. This phenomenon ushered in the era of big-picture thinking, adventure, risk-taking, and no-holds-barred competition, the likes of which the region had never seen. Lumbermen made and lost fortunes, some several times over.

To most, the terms "lumberman," "lumberjack," and "logger," here used synonymously, conjure the image of some larger-than-life persona possessing a complex set of personality traits. Some descriptive words and phrases that come to mind include independent thinking, lusty, brawling, action-oriented, physically robust, rugged, profane, hard living, and the like. Much of that lore is true, as far as it goes.

Largely overlooked, however, was that lumbering in that era was very much a thinking man's profession. One need not spend much time listening to someone who made his living climbing trees, slinging rigging, setting chokers, or punching a donkey to realize that every tree cut and logged to the railhead presented a unique challenge. Everything changed every minute, so improvisation, job knowledge, alertness, and the ability to think on one's feet were not merely the hallmarks of a good logger, they were often the tools of personal survival. It was the same once logs arrived at the sawmill. Sawyers had to make instant decisions about how to cut each unique log and the grade recovery resulting from those decisions spelled the difference between

FOREWORD

profit and loss. Perhaps to a lesser degree, but not by much, every other occupation on the production line had as an occupational requirement some element of quick thinking and sound judgment.

With the passing of the old-growth forest, many have sought to immortalize the methods, sights, and sounds of that era. These authors have assimilated many accounts, anecdotes, articles, and firsthand recollections to capture the essence of those lively times. Any number of stellar works have recorded that legacy with promise of more to come, although that seems less and less likely as the ranks of those who lived that life diminish.

Yet the thinking man's analogy was not the exclusive domain of the hired help. The masterminds of the lumbering industry were businesspeople at heart. Their acumen in that arena was as much a necessity for survival as job knowledge was for those who made their living in the woods, sawmills, or, for that matter, any other form of business.

Here marks a clear point of distinction between this and other works about the lumbermen and the industry. Granted, we as authors are every bit as intrigued with every new story about loggers and sawmillers as we have been all along. But, has anyone ever wondered how these businesses got their start, how their owners approached the business, what their objectives and strategies were, why they managed the business the ways they did? The answers to these questions and many more like it have broad implications when viewed against the more tactical aspects of the business, those being the everyday processes of logging and sawmilling.

Where do we go to uncover answers to these questions? At the tactical level, logging and sawmilling occupations in the old-growth era required nimble bodies and strong backs, so out of necessity younger men occupied them. Although aging has taken its toll, enough of them survived to tell their stories and, to the extent other authors have recorded them, theirs is the legacy we read of today. At the strategic level, however, that is the story of the presidents, officers, and managers, many of whom were old to begin with and either had already succumbed or were about to when the old-growth era passed. Absent the forethought to preserve company records, that aspect of the lumberman's legacy has been buried and lost forever.

From the outset the authors had to face that very issue when undertaking to tell the story about the Oregon-American Lumber Company. Based on anecdotal sources alone it would have been a very incomplete story. Fortunately, in 1958, the year following the operation's demise, several insightful people convinced O-A's successor, the International Paper Company, that the personal files of Judd Greenman, longtime general manager and Oregon-American president, had significant historical value and warranted preservation.

Greenman's correspondence files spanned a period between 1917 and 1952 and touched on every significant issue the company faced during its life. The value of that correspondence becomes much more evident when one considers that this was an era that preceded the telephone, when written correspondence served as the primary method of communication. The collection is even more remarkable in that Greenman filed the documents in an era when fear of a court-ordered subpoena was not a constant consideration.

Had Oregon-American been just another "cut-out and get-out" operator like so many others of that period, the significance of Greenman's correspondence might wither under scrutiny. On the contrary, the roots of Oregon-American extended from two of the largest industrial concerns of the day. One of those companies was a key player in the development of a commercially feasible method to dry-kiln Douglas fir lumber, a feature that made economical shipment of the product to distant points of sale possible. Oregon-American also happened to own one of the finest stands of old-growth yellow fir, both as to volume and to quality. Further, as the company developed it formed a unique, quasi-partnership arrangement with the Northern Pacific and Great Northern Railroads. That relationship enabled it to market its output to the largest consumptive markets found more than 1,000 miles to the east. By most accounts, perhaps except total output, Oregon-American was a premier operator of the old-growth Douglas fir era.

As for writing this story from the company records, we have undoubtedly given it an editorial bias leaning toward the management view. In doing so, we stirred up more than one controversy when relating a story as told from the records to a veteran who experienced the same event but from a different aspect. Rather than apologize or gloss over these events, we have included statements from others as a counterpoint that we think will give the reader some clearer perspective.

Perhaps too, our extensive use of quotations contradicts conventional storytelling. However, we learned that paraphrasing also filtered out a large amount of emotional content so we decided to allow the original correspondent to convey the thought using his or her own words.

Now, having armed the reader with some insight about how and why we developed this work, we begin our story.

The Oregon-American Lumber Company: Ain't No More

INTRODUCTION

To the casual observer, the Oregon-American Lumber Company was, as Douglas fir–region lumbering operations went, like any other. But, if you asked any veteran of its logging camps, railroad crews, sawmill, or sales force, or the leaders of competing producers, or the members of industry associations of the era, every one of them would tell you—the O-A was something special.

Many would attribute it to the romance of the equipment, for who could deny the lasting impression made by its steam-powered skidders, donkeys, railroad, and mill as they logged, hauled, and sawed the trees into saleable form?

Others would point to the size and quality of O-A's own stand of old-growth yellow fir timber, widely regarded as one of the best ever known to modern man. Perhaps it was the oddity of locating such a large sawmill in the isolated community of Vernonia, Oregon, nearly 40 rail-miles from the closest major waterway; in doing so, it made the operation completely dependent on logs brought from close-by. Or maybe it was because O-A kiln-dried more of its lumber than any other producer in the Douglas fir region. To some, including those of us fortunate enough to see it operate before they exhausted the log supply, the fact that O-A was the last steam-powered "stump-to-the-boxcar" operation on the West Coast was reason enough to put it in a class by itself.

It had its distinct sounds too. Who could forget the rhythmic chunk of the faller's axe, or the groan of wire rope and bark of the Willamette two-speed yarder as it tightened slack on another turn of logs, or the thunderous roar of the little Baldwin Prairie locomotive as it backed yet another twenty-six sets of loaded, disconnected trucks into the mill yard, or the puff from the exhausts of the band mill's shotgun-feed carriages as they sawed another cant, or the mournful baying of the mill whistle announcing to Vernonia, the Nehalem Valley, and the surrounding hillsides, the start of another day?

To be sure, these sensory recollections would naturally be foremost in what old-timers relied on to describe what made the company stand apart. And why not? They were real, they were vivid. Even today, more than forty years after the last log went through the mill, mention an incident to one of the company's veterans and their memories return to the scene just like it was yesterday.

In all fairness though, if you questioned anyone who worked for one of O-A's competitors, wouldn't they use similar terms to describe what made their company stand apart? After all, didn't every other operator in the region use similar equipment and methods, log the same kinds of trees, and traverse the same sort of terrain?

So, if sensory recollections of O-A's operating methods don't quite support the premise that the company was special, what about the application of

INTRODUCTION

more "objective" criteria, such as who produced the most lumber, had the biggest mill, or the largest payroll? Although interesting, this approach falls short too because it fails to point out many of the company's defining features. But, if the Oregon-American Lumber Company was special, and it was more than just the trees, or the equipment, or the sounds, or the comparative statistics, just what was it that set it apart from the others?

The answer to that question requires a closer look into the company's strategic positioning, financial structuring, and ability to adapt to changing times that came into play during each phase of its history. These were the motivations, the ideas and plans of the people who defined and fulfilled O-A's purpose and mission. Only when you apply these to physical attributes, sensory recollections, and comparative statistics can you grasp what really made the Oregon-American stand out.

Surely, one distinguishing feature was the vision of David C. Eccles, who founded the company to develop a rail and lumber empire in one of the remaining and virtually untapped Douglas fir stands of the State of Oregon. Later, when Eccles's financial resources gave out, it was the singular drive of Charles Keith and the strength of his Central Coal & Coke Company seeking new operating territory to replace its depleted southern pine holdings that gave O-A much of its special character.

Keith built a fully integrated lumbering operation whose competitive position was defined not only by owning its own captive supply of old-growth yellow fir, but by establishing the means to convert it to high-grade finished lumber as well. Likewise, no small part of the operation's success can be attributed to his far-reaching plan to market the output of the mill to the major demand centers of the country that lay more than 1,000 miles to the east. Keith also forged important strategic connections with the Great Northern and Northern Pacific Railroads. These connections played a crucial role in O-A's success, first in establishing superior, though unconventional, transportation arrangements to move O-A's timber from the woods to Vernonia and beyond, but also by using the Northern Lines' financial resources to purchase raw timber stands for O-A to log and convert, thus greatly extending the company's life. This alliance was fundamental to the entire operation and was a key factor enabling Oregon-American to successfully establish its product in the large consuming markets of the Midwest.

Much credit also is due to the unwavering dedication and leadership of Judd Greenman, who, as Oregon-American's superintendent, general manager, and president from 1925 to 1953, led the company through boom and bust, natural disaster, war and peace, labor, social, and political unrest, industry upheaval, and eventually to the achievement of the potential Charles Keith saw in the company some thirty years before. Without Greenman's constant influence, Oregon-American would have never come close to realizing its full potential. For that matter, had it not been for the efforts of Greenman and others to keep creditors from selling the company's timber during the Great Depression, along with the help from the most catastrophic forest fire in Oregon's recorded history, it is doubtful the O-A would have survived at all.

Finally, you have to tip your hat to the people who came to the camps and Vernonia to labor for Oregon-American. They too set the company apart with the human spirit, dedication, and work ethic they brought to their jobs. Their purpose in life and pride in their work made buyers of lumber from Vernonia expect, and get, the best the industry ever had to offer.

Combined, these factors accounted for something larger than the sum of their parts and were the essence of what made this company special. That was the Oregon-American Lumber Company. This is its story.

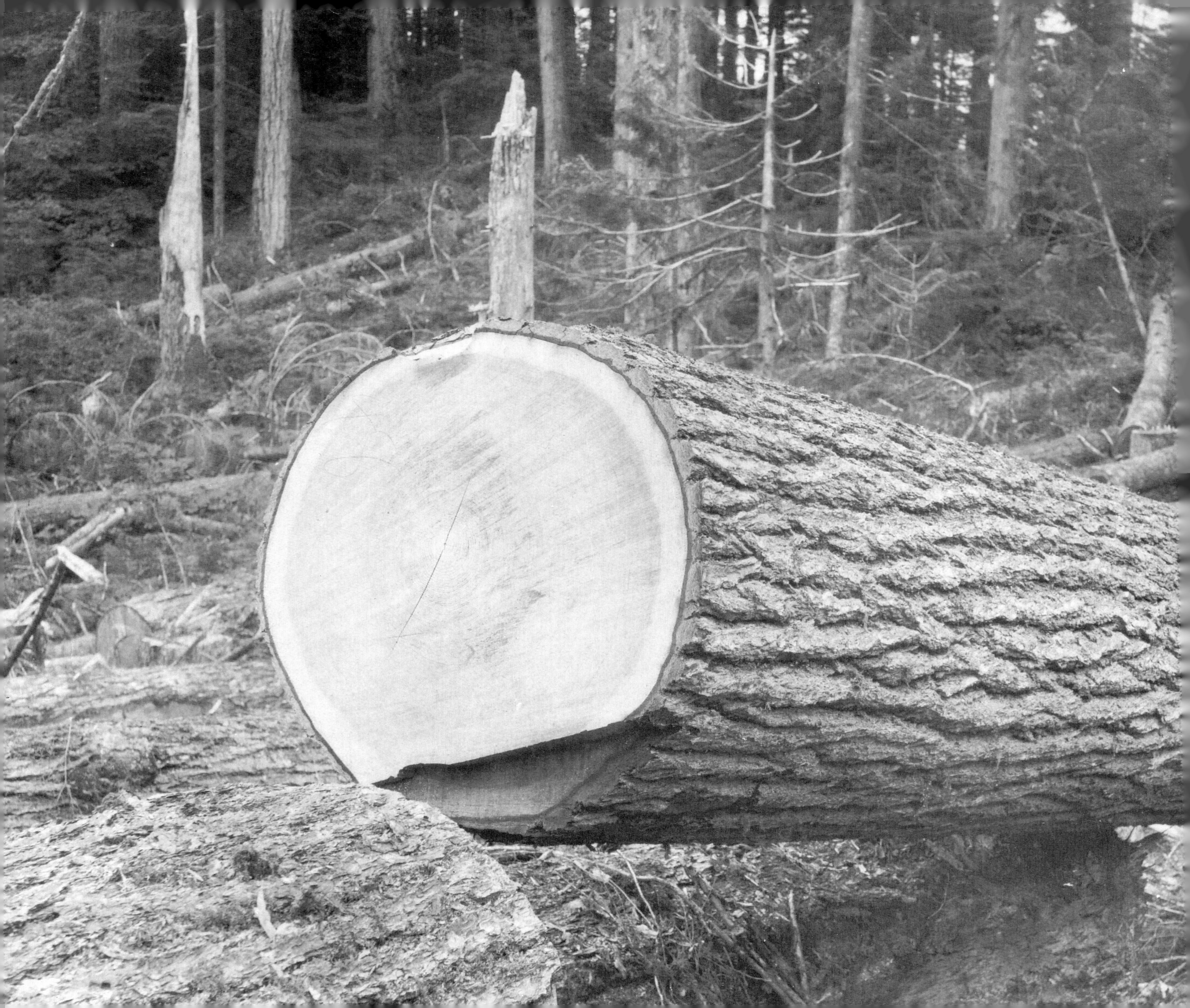

CONSTRUCTING AMERICA

The standard unit of measure used by the U.S. lumber industry is the board foot, representing the volume of a solid piece of lumber measuring 1 inch thick by 1 foot square.

Applying that yardstick to production that occurred between 1776 and World War II, no less than 2.4 trillion board feet of lumber were produced in the United States.[1] Rearranging the dimensions of the board foot slightly to give that production statistic a visual perspective, if all that lumber could have somehow been converted to a single board 1 inch thick and 1 mile wide, that board would have circled the globe three and a half times.

The rudimentary form of our domestic lumber industry took more than one hundred thirty years to produce half that theoretical board by 1909. The more refined form of the industry produced the remaining half in a mere thirty-four years. Moreover, this only accounts for the lumber produced, not the 450 million telephone and telegraph poles, the 11 billion fence posts, the 6 billion cords of fuel wood, nor the 150 million tons of wood pulp produced during the same period.[2] The lumber industry grew to play a dominant role in the U.S. economy by the early 1900s, eventually ranking second in employment, third in investment, and eighth in value of production. By then, more than 20,000 active sawmills were supplying 2,000 wholesale distributors and 20,000 retail outlets.

What forces were at play to drive that kind of production? Demographic developments, specifically the settlement patterns that took place while populating the land mass of the United States go a long way toward providing an answer.

In chronological order, these patterns fell into three distinct phases: the colonial and pioneering period of earliest settlements dating to 1830; the period of settlement in the Midwest and Far West from 1830 to 1880; and the period of industrial development and expansion from 1880 to beyond WWII.[3] A brief examination of some key features of each phase provides a foundation on which to tell the Oregon-American Lumber Company story.

THE COLONIAL AND PIONEERING PERIOD OF EARLIEST SETTLEMENTS, DATING TO 1830

Beyond providing materials needed for housing and fuel, early pioneers undoubtedly viewed the forest as equally a hindrance and a blessing. Before they could advance beyond mere subsistence living, they had to clear and convert enough forest land to crop land to grow food surpluses for winter survival.[4]

The process of making lumber, to the extent it developed at all, was hardly facilitated by the overabundance of hardwoods native to the eastern states. Not until settlers reached more northerly and inland regions did they find sufficient accumulations of the more easily worked northern white pine (and, to a lesser degree, southern pine to the south) to warrant some volume of lumber manufacture. This began to occur in the upper reaches of

Maine in the early 1800s and later spread to upstate New York. The combination of dense stands of soft, workable, but structurally sound trees, abundant water supplies to power milling facilities, and a budding rail and canal transportation system that provided a means to move the product between forest and population centers enabled the manufacture of lumber to become sufficiently widespread to remove it from the status of a specialty item into the category of a commodity. To the extent a center of lumber production and trade existed by 1850, that place was Albany, New York, located at the confluence of the Erie Canal and the Hudson River.[5]

Lumber production never exceeded more than 1 billion board feet per year during these formative years, an equivalent annual increment of 35 miles of our theoretical board around the world.[6] Absent more advanced manufacturing methods that would not appear for more than a half-century, large-scale production simply wasn't possible. Moreover, owing to the fact that lumber is also heavy and bulky, there existed only a mere canal system to transport the product any great distance. An overseas trade in ship spars and timbers notwithstanding, absent the infrastructure needed to easily transport products very far, lumber production and lumber consumption generally occurred in close proximity to one another during this era.[7]

THE PERIOD OF SETTLEMENT IN THE MIDWEST AND FAR WEST, 1830 TO 1880

This period was marked by dual trends. First, supplanted by a rapid increase in immigration, the population expanded beyond the Allegheny Mountains and into the Midwest.[8] Fueled by the same influx of immigrants, urbanization also began taking place.

For example, in 1830 only one in fifteen people lived in a community of 8,000 or more. By 1860 that number increased to one in every six, and by 1890 it stood at three in every ten.[9]

The geographic expansion was hastened by the development of the railroad network. The railroads moved people, facilitated trade and pushed the frontier westward. Between 1860 and 1890, populations of Philadelphia and Baltimore doubled, Detroit and Kansas City grew fourfold, Chicago tenfold, and Minneapolis and Omaha fifty times.[10]

Even though industrialization took root and made tremendous gains, agriculture still remained the nation's primary occupation. During this period, the number of U.S. farms tripled from 2 to 6 million and tillable acreage doubled.[11] Availability of construction materials was essential to support this expansion and demand for them fueled the growth of lumber as an industry.

This period also coincided with the arrival of the growing population at the edge of the great plains. Supplies of raw materials for lumber were, for the First time, no longer available at or near points of consumption.[12] The northern white pine forests of the lake states represented the nearest source, and soon the center of U.S. lumber production shifted to Michigan and Wisconsin, while Chicago, St. Louis, and Detroit became centers of both trade and consumption.[13]

It was during this era that the physics of steam power were applied to lumber production methods. The influence was profound, both as to scale and efficiency. The growing ability to produce in volume combined with an expanding rail network spurred the lumber business to grow exponentially.[14] Additionally, the natural transportation system in the form of the Mississippi River served as another outlet for logs from the northern white pine forests. The availability of waterborne sources of raw materials gave birth to many points of lumber manufacture between Minnesota and Missouri.[15]

An important and controversial facet of lumbering that haunted the industry for most of the next century arose during the lake states' reign of lumber production dominance. Despite their relative remoteness from centers of consumption, Midwestern northern white pine forests were thought to be so abundant that lumbermen utilized only the best parts of the best trees.[16]

From that time forward until the middle of the twentieth century, forest utilization and lumber prices followed one another so closely that given an abundance of manufactured wood products in the upper grades, lumber produced in the lower grades typically had to be sold at less than the cost of production, provided it could be sold at all. Given a choice between upper grades and those that were wormy, stained, or knotty, American consumers developed a strong resistance to buy anything but the best lumber. Once that mind-set established itself producers never found a way to break that vicious cycle. Manufacturing anything that fell short of those very high consumer expectations was to follow a paved road to ruin. Lacking some other outlet for wood products that were often the structural equal but that otherwise lacked in appearance, much of that lower-grade wood was simply left behind to rot on the ground. As long as lumbermen could turn to alternative raw material supplies located in the gulf states or the Far West to meet consumer preferences, the law of scarcity never came into play, and the underutilization phenomenon continued until most old-growth forests had been entirely consumed.

By the end of this period, lumber production had grown to about 18 billion board feet per year, an equivalent annual increment of about 645 miles of our theoretical board around the world.[17]

THE PERIOD OF INDUSTRIAL DEVELOPMENT AND EXPANSION, 1880 TO BEYOND WWII

The pace with which social and economic development occurred after 1880 became increasingly reliant on the efficient movement of goods of all types between suppliers and consumers, often over great distances. As rail hubs materialized in major urban areas it was only natural that trade and distribution centers developed there for all types of goods, including lumber.[18]

Yet throughout most of this period, the bulk of America's population resided outside cities (as late as 1920, for example, 60 percent of U.S. inhabitants still lived in rural areas).[19] Developments in that sector, particularly in the Great Plains farm belt, profoundly shaped the domestic lumber industry. Alone, the Homestead Act of 1862 and the additional 170 million acres of public land deeded to the railroads to give away as incentives failed to draw people to the plains. As beckoning was the opportunity to break ground on vast expanses of rich land that did not first require removal of trees, absent some way to overcome the isolation of living on the plains, the settlement of the territory west of Kansas City and Omaha did not take off until the railroads began laying rails into that region.[20] Once that began to happen, settlers flocked wherever the railroads went. The carriers brought the settlers and they hauled the fruits of the settlers' labor back to the population centers for consumption. On the heels of the settlers came merchants eager to provide goods.[21]

While the earliest settlers on the Great Plains made their domiciles of prairie sod, once they were able to convert their crops to cash they sought to improve their living conditions. Building a home made of lumber represented a major step in that direction. And, with the help of loans, farmers everywhere began mechanizing operations, as well as building barns, sheds, outbuildings, and windmills, all of it made of wood.[22]

More often than not, all the astute lumber producer had to do to capitalize on such opportunities was to load a railroad car full of lumber, ship it to the newest settlement on the line, and then open a retail yard to meet the demands of the locals. Once the product arrived, it sold itself.[23]

Owing to its development as a major rail hub combined with the concentration of lumber moving through its yards, Kansas City, Missouri, became the major lumber distribution center in the United States. Lumber jumped from only 1 percent of the city's wholesale trade in 1875 to 10 percent a decade later, and between 1890 and 1910, Kansas City was the leading city in the world for wholesale lumber sales. That city's booming lumber trade continued well into the twentieth century.[24]

A major reason for the Kansas City-as-a-lumber-hub phenomenon was due to the continuation of the expansionary farm era well into the 1920s. The period between 1909 and 1914 has been called the Golden Age of American agriculture.[25] The government encouraged farmers to plant as much grain as possible, and farmers were rewarded with dramatic rises in commodities prices during WWI. Farmers used those wartime profits to buy new land and equipment on the hope of expanding profits.[26] Great Plains farmers broke 32 million acres of sod between 1909 and 1920, and in the southern Great Plains portion alone, wheat acreage expanded 200 percent between 1925 and 1931, much of that on extremely marginal land.[27]

As that economic expansion equated to construction, construction equated to the need for building materials. As far as building materials were concerned, lumber enjoyed the preeminent position, at least in the farm belt and until the eve of the Great Depression.[28]

LUMBER AS AN INDUSTRY

Demand for lumber grew so fast that between 1890 and 1900, loggers depleted the virgin white pine forests of Wisconsin and Michigan to keep pace. New, larger, and more remote supplies had to be found. It became clear that only once the transcontinental railroad network was developed could the potential of distant forests be recognized.[29]

The period immediately leading up to the depletion of the northern white pine forests was notable because of the large accumulation of stumpage, or standing timber, by larger lumbering operators and timber-holding organizations. These new accumulations of raw timberlands first occurred in the remote southern pine forests of Arkansas, Texas, Louisiana, and Mississippi. Soon after, the same thing began happening in the vast and more distant Ponderosa pine and Douglas fir tracts of the Far West.[30]

The primary attraction that lured lumbermen south was the low cost of the land. Likewise, southern pineries were 1,000 miles closer to the consuming markets. By 1870, two-thirds of Louisiana's timber belonged to only sixteen corporate interest groups or individuals.[31]

Purchases of large timber tracts in these regions were marked by speculation. "Logging Chance," or the profitable conversion of standing timber to finished products, was only part of the story. Historically, few lumbermen ever made fortunes merely producing lumber. The big profits arose from acquiring undeveloped timber land cheaply and waiting for its value to grow. Usually, this did not occur until the railroads arrived to provide an economical way to move lumber to distant markets. Certainly this proved to be the case in the southern pineries after the Kansas City Southern extended its rails from Shreveport into the longleaf pine district of southwestern Louisiana in 1897.[32] This also held true in the Ponderosa pine and Douglas fir regions of the West although the process took somewhat longer and didn't begin overtake southern pine until 1920.

This era gave rise to the integrated lumbering operation in which timber owners also converted the raw material to finished lumber products and, to varying degrees, had a hand in marketing the output.

Although many of the industry's leaders were personally well-heeled, they needed outside sources of capital and financing to keep the wheels in motion. This became increasingly important as the center of lumber production migrated away from the logged-out forests of the upper Midwest and South to the untapped riches of the Pacific slope. The promise of great returns on money invested in the industry made the financial markets willing partners in the scheme. Consistent with the high-flying nature of the financial world during this era, many investments in the industry proved speculative at best.

Other industries showed their interest too, especially the transportation industry, and the railroads in particular. The lumber industry's need for economical means to ship its products to distant markets went hand-in-glove with the railroad companies' need for new sources of traffic. Favorable rates in return for guaranteed routings were the natural trade-off binding lumbermen and carriers. On the whole, this period was the dawn of big-picture thinking in the industry. It also set the stage for the lumber industry to account for 65 percent of the payrolls and 60 percent of the rail tonnage originating in Oregon and Washington.

By the fact that an integrated lumbering concern was based on depleting a resource, the entire financial underpinning of such operations had to be set up on a liquidating basis. The financial basis was therefore premised on the value and volume of the standing timber. The measurement to determine the volume of a body of standing timber is commonly called a "cruise." Developing a cruise was the process of systematically estimating the number of board feet growing in a specified area. In reality it was the process of scaling a sample of trees within a grid

A typical stand of longleaf pine as it appeared at Central Coal & Coke's Neame, Louisiana, operation around 1900. Larger trees, rugged terrain, and inclement weather called for big adjustments when Central moved its lumbering operations to the Douglas fir region. (Kamholz collection)

Table 1.1

Total U.S. Lumber Production

1909	1919	1929	1939	1945
44,510*	34,552	36,886	24,975	28,122

(Expressed in billions of board feet)
*Peak year of U.S. lumber production

Percent of Total U.S. Lumber Production

	1909	1919	1929	1939	1945
Southern pine	37	38	32	31	26
Douglas fir	11	17	24	26	22
Ponderosa pine	3	5	9	14	11
White pine	9	5	3	4	4
Hemlock	7	5	6	3	4
Oak	10	8	7	6	10
All other	23	22	19	16	23
	100	100	100	100	100[33]

U.S. Per Capita Lumber Consumption
1904 = 504 board feet (peak year)
1939 = 194 board feet[34]

defined according to accepted civil engineering methods and projecting that sample across a larger body of a tract. This became the standard method of determining value of timber stands within the lumbering industry and provided the yardsticks needed to buy, sell, and finance tracts and entire operations.

A brief glance at lumber production by period and species demonstrates statistically the development of the two great lumber-producing regions of the United States, the southern pine region and the region west of the Rocky Mountains, largely defined in terms of Douglas fir and Ponderosa pine production.

Products and Markets

Southern pine quickly rose to the dominant supply position by 1900. It emerged as a preferred material for flooring and trimmings because of its resistance to wear. Southern pine was also in great demand for ship work due to its high resin content and rot resistance. It gradually gained acceptance for use in home construction as well. Overall lumber production during the peak of the southern pine era was split with about 15 percent of the output in structural timbers, the balance in boards.

As structural softwoods were concerned, longleaf southern pine was highly regarded. Shortleaf pine was used mostly for construction, interior finish, sheathing, siding, flooring, and ceiling material as well as for boxes and crates. Having catered to the discerning tastes of a consuming public that demanded the highest-quality lumber possible, much of the southern pine lumber was produced as seasoned lumber, that is, lumber that was dried naturally or artificially to remove excess moisture, thus making it less likely to warp as well as making the product suitable for further processing such as planing for smoothness. Given lumber consumers' exacting standards, these added quality features ultimately set new standards for lumber made from competing areas and species.[35]

Generally, southern pine lumber found markets in all states east of the Rocky Mountains. About half the region's production shipped to destinations south of the Ohio River. States that led consumption included Texas, Ohio, Illinois, Pennsylvania, Indiana, Michigan, New York, Missouri, Louisiana, Oklahoma, Iowa, Kansas, and Nebraska.[36]

Two leading southern pine operators and main characters in the Oregon-American story, the Long-Bell Lumber Company and the Central Coal

& Coke Company, both of Kansas City, Missouri, exemplify how developments in the farm belt drove a substantial part of these two companies' lumber production, first in southern pine and later from Douglas fir.

Long-Bell began as a single sales yard in a remote Kansas crossroads in 1875.[37] Its first yard was so successful that thereafter, according to one of its founders, R. A. Long, *we just followed the railroads*.[38] Long-Bell added more yards until the enterprise grew large enough to consider supplying itself.[39] After a successful entry into manufacturing in a stand of southern pine situated in what would eventually become Oklahoma, the company began looking for additional raw material sources. Long-Bell managed to secure more than 130,000 acres in the southwestern Louisiana pine belt by 1902.[40] Additional tracts were added and by 1918 the company operated ten sawmills in the South. By virtue of its ability to control every aspect of its business from the stump to the sales outlet, Long-Bell was uniquely positioned to capitalize on the Great Plains expansion.[41]

Central Coal & Coke Company had also positioned itself to serve the needs of a growing farm belt except in its case it was producing and distributing coal. Like Long-Bell the Central Company quickly realized that coal could be sold the same way Long-Bell was selling lumber—by establishing sales outlets wherever the railroads went.[42] Central also discovered that as long as it had a sales network in place there was every reason to give that network more to sell and the commodity in greatest demand was lumber. Central's initial foray into the lumber business was the acquisition of an existing lumber production operation. Soon the company realized that nothing short of large-scale lumber production would adequately meet the demands of the Midwest farm belt expansion. Like Long-Bell, Central staked its claim on the future for lumber in the vast, undeveloped pine belt in southwestern Louisiana.[43]

The parallels between Long-Bell and Central Coal & Coke ran deep. For example, when R. A. Long decided that his company's rural Kansas headquarters was no longer fitting for a company of Long-Bell's stature in 1891, he set up shop in Kansas City, renting space in the Keith & Perry building, owned by and home of Central Coal & Coke. Long-Bell remained ensconced there until 1906 when it built its own office building in downtown Kansas City.[44]

Literally and figuratively, the elder lumber statesman R. A. Long and his young protégé and competitor Charles S. Keith cut a formidable swath in the southern pine lumber region and each in his

Central Coal & Coke Company had its headquarters in the Keith and Perry building in Kansas City, Missouri. In 1902, Central was the largest producer and distributor of coal west of the Mississippi. The company was also a large lumber operator in the southern pine region of Arkansas, Louisiana, and Texas. (Kamholz collection)

Charles S. Keith, president of the Central Coal & Coke Company. (Oregon-American Lumber Company, Special Collections and University Archives, University of Oregon)

own way established their respective operations as models for the industry.

Lumber demand grew to such an extent during the first quarter of the twentieth century that most of the old-growth southern pine stands were depleted by 1930. Thereafter, most of the southern pine output was in the form of second-growth production that was, almost by definition, smaller and less clear-grained.[45]

Foreseeing the eminent depletion of old-growth southern pine stands as early as the end of WWI, Long and Keith both had to answer the same fundamental questions. Could they simply close down their lumber empires once the southern pineries were gone? And if the answer was no, where would they go for more supplies?

Long and Keith were enlightened men and industry visionaries. Both were driven by the fundamental belief that expanding their businesses was a moral obligation that went far beyond accumulation of personal wealth. The notion that running out of timber meant going out of business likely never entered their minds, and so long before the end of the old-growth southern pine era, they were on the hunt for new places to make lumber. The huge untapped stands of far western forests beckoned, and Long and Keith focused their attentions there. And they had company. In fact, quite a number of operators whose names were associated with operations in the northern and southern pine districts eventually showed up in the West, including Weyerhaeuser, Pickering, Crossett, and C. D. Johnson, to name but a few.[46]

Having committed to find and exploit new reserves in the West, the more practical marketing challenge of how to meet the high expectations of buyers with a different kind of wood came into play, particularly when southern pine lumber would still be plentiful enough to represent a formidable barrier to entry by a competing material. These issues were of a pragmatic nature, however, and essentially boiled down to ensuring that lumber manufactured in the West had to be competitive with southern pine, as to price, availability, and quality.

Like in the south, the western lumber industry owed its beginnings to the transcontinental railroads. The carriers, to a large extent, accorded producers favorable shipping rates for lumber shipped to Minneapolis and Chicago. Still, western mills paid a higher basic freight rate per hundred thousand pounds than did their southern pine competition. However, these costs were offset to a degree by their lower cost of production, enough to allow them to place their output in the central states at competitive prices and, to a degree, states east of there as well. Even so, the marketing territory available to West Coast lumber of various species and grades was controlled by freight rates charged by the railroads resulting in the continued dominance of southern pine lumber east of the Mississippi.[47]

Douglas fir proved to be a versatile wood. It was stronger than pine, easy to make in many sizes and millable into a wide variety of items and grades that satisfied many different classes of trade worldwide. As a result of this broad array of marketing opportunities, the production of Douglas fir tended to be a much more complex manufacturing process than for most other woods. The typical large Douglas fir sawmill produced hundreds of different patterns of molding, interior finish and flooring, as well as many kinds and sizes of boards intended for use in ordinary dwellings, to ship and bridge decking, ceiling, siding and boards, dimension lumber of many sizes, large timbers for derricks, bridges, and other types of heavy construction, factory lumber, railroad ties, and many other items. Most of the fir mills also produced a number of by-products such as lath, and mills within reach of cities also enjoyed a ready-made market for much of their waste in the form of fuel, either as hogged chips or as sawdust. Douglas fir lumber was soon able to stand on its own merits in competition with southern pine and found considerable acceptance.[48]

The Railroads as Lumber Consumers

The railroads as consumers of lumber products had a key impact on lumber demand. It would be hard to find a better lumber customer than a railroad. An average main line mile of track, for example, required 3,000 wooden railroad ties, amounting to 111,000 board feet.[49] Add to that all the bridge timbers, piling, planking, not to mention all the decking, siding, and roofing lumber that was used in the construction of railroad cars, and it becomes quickly apparent why the carriers alone accounted for up to as much as 10 percent of all the lumber produced during this era. Railroads typically bought their ties and timbers from sawmillers located along the rail routes, and many mills existed solely for the business the railroads provided them.[50]

In fact, another name that is central to the Oregon-American story warrants mention here as a prime example of a lumbering operation that succeeded largely because of the market for railroad ties and structural timbers. David Eccles, who built a business empire radiating from the State of Utah during the late eighteen and early nineteen hundreds, started a lumber business in the Blue Mountains of eastern Oregon in 1883 primarily to supply railroad ties to the Oregon Short Line Railroad that connected Baker City, Oregon, and Ogden, Utah. Later, Eccles founded the Oregon Lumber Company at Baker City along with the Sumpter Valley Railroad, and for more than fifty years supplied railroad ties and timbers to the Union Pacific, which, by that time, had taken over operation of the Oregon Short Line. The company also produced some amount of board output and what production was not consumed by the railroad was either hauled back to Eccles's Utah retail outlet or sold as boxing material.[51] The Oregon Lumber Company's presence spread to the Douglas fir region in the Columbia River Gorge in response to the railroad company's demands for timbers that displayed greater tensile strength. Despite the fact that the Oregon Lumber Company held sufficient Ponderosa pine reserves accessible to the Sumpter Valley Railroad to keep the operation alive for decades, the quest for additional railroad business undoubtedly led Eccles's descendants to found the Oregon-American Lumber Company in the heart of Oregon's Douglas fir region.[52]

The Panama Canal

In the earliest days of the northwestern lumber industry, the primary markets were for piling used for ship masts along with other timbers used in ship building. Active markets also soon developed in California with the output shipping via the ocean. When the transcontinental railroads arrived, markets of the prairie states were made available to West Coast producers and served as an outlet for much of the lumber produced in the Douglas fir region.

In 1913, 78 percent of all Douglas fir lumber was consumed west of the Mississippi River. By 1940, this figure fell to only 50 percent, a shift brought about largely by the opening of the Panama Canal, which reduced sailing time from Puget Sound to northern Atlantic ports from seventy to twenty days. This reduced ocean shipping rates by about half, eventually forcing the railroads to reduce their rates in response.

All West Coast lumber producers with markets in the East benefited from the opening of the Panama Canal, but the ones who gained the most were the tidewater fir mills that produced unseasoned and unfinished common boards and dimension lumber. Because exposure to the wet ocean environment defeated the very purpose of seasoning lumber in the first place, higher lumber grades by necessity had to be shipped overland.[53]

Product Distribution

As the domestic lumber distribution system took form, the manufacturers produced the lumber, wholesalers helped the manufacturers sell lumber to retail yards or to industrial plants that used lumber as the raw material for their own products, and retail lumber yards provided the outlet for lumber needed by the general public for construction and other purposes. Until the 1920s, demand for lumber was steady and growing. All the sawmill man had to do was make the product; there was always someone there to buy it. The industry grew up in an era when the product sold itself.[54]

It wasn't until after WWI that competition among lumber producers materialized. In part this was due to inroads made by competing construction materials such as steel, bricks, and concrete. It was also a result of oversupply, brought about when large lumber producers were under great pressure to pay off the enormous debt they had incurred to set themselves up in the Pacific slope forests, and their belief that the only way to satisfy their creditors was to out-produce everyone else. By the time the Great Depression arrived, a distribution system had evolved to a point where manufacturers relied on one or a combination of several of the following selling arrangements.

Most all of the large lumber manufacturers maintained their own sales departments. A major part of the smaller mill operators depended entirely on the wholesale lumberman to do their selling and many of the big mills also depended on them to a lesser extent. Somewhere between 65 and 80 percent of the total lumber output was sold through wholesalers.

Wholesale dealers were generally of two classes, yard wholesalers and office wholesalers. There were two types of yard wholesalers, those who operated concentration yards and those who operated distribution yards. The concentration yard was a primary factor in regions dominated by smaller mills of the crudest type that were unable to produce anything but rough, green lumber. Concentration yards assembled the output of many mills and performed the finishing tasks such as drying and planing. The distribution yard generally was located in some city or center of lumber consumption where there was a local demand for small or large lots for prompt shipment. The distributing yard bought carload lots of seasoned, well-manufactured lumber from manufacturers of recognized standing, put the lumber in stock, and sold it to his trade. Wholesale lumber dealers took a particularly active part in the handling of intercoastal trade from West Coast mills to the eastern markets.

Commission salesmen occupied another tier in the lumber distribution system by performing services halfway between the wholesaler and a salaried sales force. Through them the manufacturer was able to maintain customer contact by direct invoicing, thus keeping the mills' identity before the customer. Commission salesmen sold lumber for the manufacturer on a predetermined sale-cost basis, for which they were paid a commission, generally 5 percent, but only on business acceptable to the manufacturer.

The commission man's stock-in-trade was salesmanship, knowledge of the markets, and close contact with a reliable source of supply. As a general rule, he lived in the district where he sold. Commission men generally represented two or more manufacturers of the same or different species, depending on the sources of supply needed to properly service the trade of their customers. The standard practice was for the commission salesman to keep in close contact with his regular buying trade, offering the stock available from his mill (or mills) at the prices fixed by the manufacturer. The commission man was recognized in the transaction as the representative of the manufacturer. Many mills depended largely or entirely on such salesmen for the merchandising of their output.

The retail lumber yard was the point of contact between the general public and the industry. This was also the source of supply of most building contractors. There were two kinds of retail yards. The single-yard type in which the owners were usually its managers and served only a single locale and the line yards, which were the most common type. Line yards were the chain-store type of selling applied to lumber retailing. These yards existed primarily in the middle western states and generally in small towns of agricultural sections. They had individual local managers but were controlled by a central office that established policies and prices and also did the ordering. Line yards began appearing immediately following the Civil War. Most were organized either by large manufacturers or by wholesalers who were seeking to establish dependable outlets. The opening up of the prairie country offered a made-to-order opportunity, because it presented a combination of vigorous demand from new homesteaders and a dearth of building materials in a thinly populated country, with little or no native timber from which lumber could be produced.[55]

Northwest Oregon and Principal Common Carrier Railroads near Vernonia, Oregon in 1922

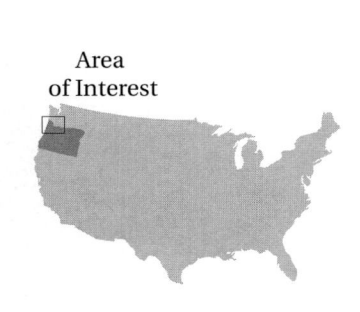

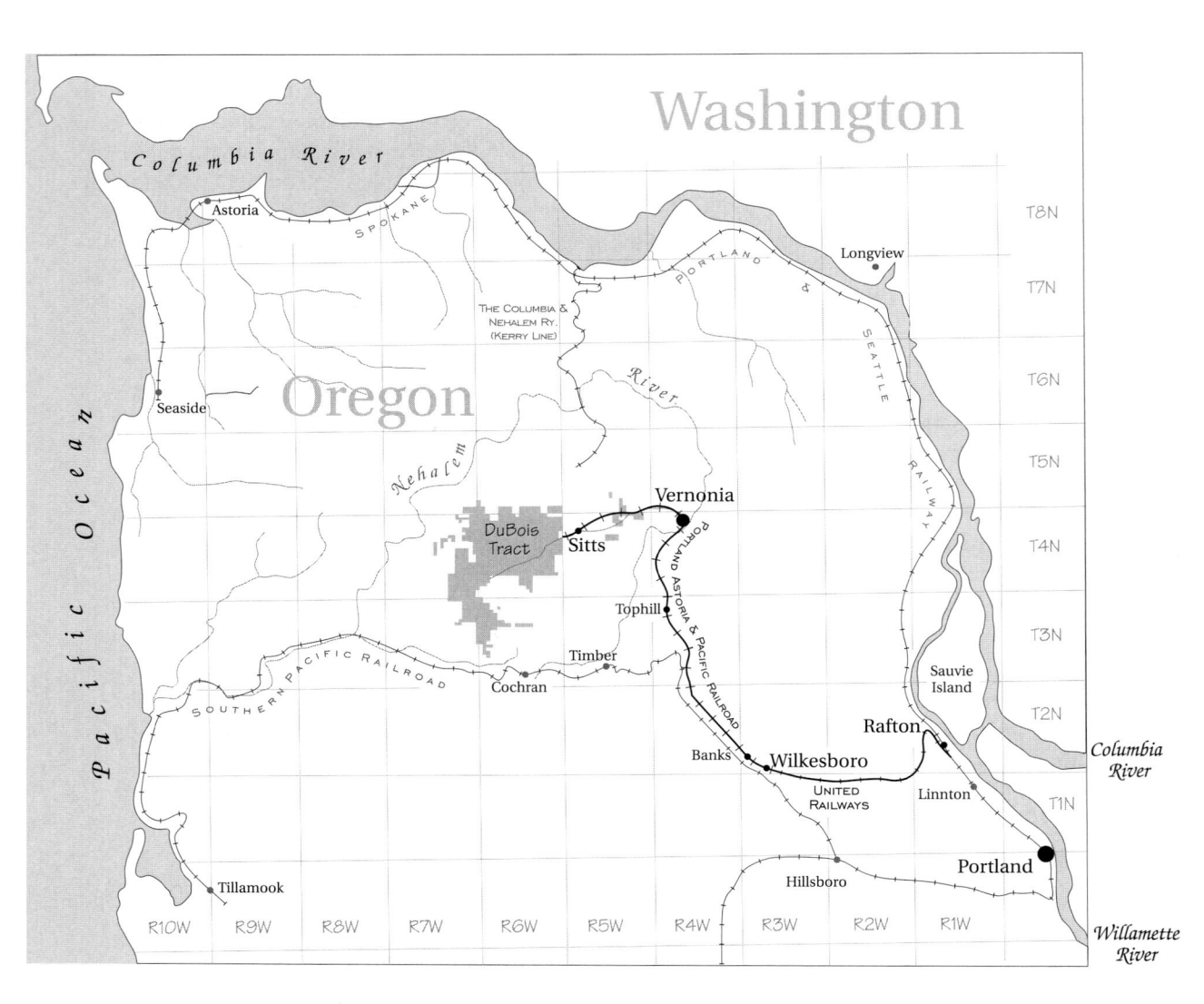

Drawn by E. J. Kamholz

THE ROAD TO VERNONIA

The tiny settlement of Vernonia, Oregon, was virtually unknown before 1922. Yet between 1893 and 1921 many events, which were set in motion by four nationally prominent industrial and transportation companies, conspired to change the term "Vernonia" from simply the name of an obscure village isolated in the northwestern corner of Oregon to a term that, when applied to Douglas fir lumber, stood for the best quality available anywhere in the world. In the process, it signaled Oregon's emergence as the leading producer of Douglas fir lumber in the nation.

Nestled in the Upper Nehalem Valley 32 air miles northwest of Portland, Vernonia's pioneers considered it the ideal place to settle and farm, for it offered a mild climate and the promise of a fresh start for anyone willing to clear the land of the large trees that blanketed the area.

Although its residents were aware of the forest's value to themselves for lumber and fuel, they probably did not fully realize the economic potential of one of the largest and finest stands of an old-growth yellow fir that ever existed—something only the richest and most powerful industrial concerns of the day could fully exploit. This tiny outpost's 150 residents, surrounded by Oregon's Coast Range and some 30 dirt-road miles from the nearest town of any consequence, could only dream of the day when modern transportation might arrive and bring with it the everyday conveniences enjoyed by their more urban neighbors.[1] It took the conglomeration of enterprises started by David Eccles of Ogden, Utah, the large coal and lumbering operations of the Keith family's Central Coal & Coke Company of Kansas City, Missouri, and James J. "Jim" Hill's Great Northern and Northern Pacific Railways to make a series of unrelated but converging strategic operating decisions that eventually created one of the most complex business alliances the lumber industry in the first third of the twentieth century had ever seen.[2]

DAVID ECCLES AND RELATED ENTERPRISES

A Scottish immigrant of the Mormon faith, David Eccles was the classical entrepreneur.[3] Beginning in the 1880s, he developed a vast network of lumber companies, sugar refineries, banks, railroads, and construction companies spread over seven western states and Canada.[4] At one time he was president of sixteen industrial corporations and seven banks and a director in another twenty-four enterprises.[5] His primary bases of operation were in Ogden, Utah, and Baker City, Oregon.[6]

Some of Eccles's many business interests became noteworthy in their own right. For example, by 1912, Utah Construction Company, of which Eccles was a major stockholder, had successfully completed construction of the 700-mile Western Pacific Railroad from Salt Lake City to Oroville, California.[7] Later, Utah Construction would play crucial roles

Opposite page: In 1922 the Portland, Astoria & Pacific Railroad was the newest common carrier tapping the forest riches of northwest Oregon. Intended primarily as an outlet for Oregon-American Lumber Company timber, the line soon became part of the United Railways and brought service to numerous loggers.

At its peak the Vernonia branch provided the Great Northern and Northern Pacific more originating rail traffic than any other in the State of Oregon.

David C. Eccles, president of the David Eccles Company, founded the Oregon-American Lumber Company in 1917. Later that year Oregon-American acquired the DuBois timber tract west of Vernonia. On it grew one of the best stands of old-growth Douglas fir known to modern man.

Eccles incorporated the Portland, Astoria & Pacific Railroad Company to transport O-A's logs from the woods to the Nehalem Boom Company, another venture he founded. The boom company eventually became the large commercial dump and log-rafting site on the Willamette River slough known as Rafton. (Utah State University Press)

in building the Hoover and Grand Coulee Dams.[8] Eccles was also instrumental in the success of Utah-Idaho Sugar Company, whose U and I Sugar brand became a familiar name on western states' grocery store shelves.[9] Although his business interests branched out into construction, railroads, mining, and sugar refining, Eccles considered himself primarily a lumberman as evidenced by his many ventures in that industry.[10] The largest of these enterprises was the Oregon Lumber Company.[11]

By 1912, the Oregon Lumber Company and related railroading operations had become major economic forces developing eastern Oregon timberlands near Baker City and the Sumpter Valley with others in the Hood River, Dee, Viento, Oregon, and Chenowith, Washington, areas.[12] Among these interests were the Mount Hood Lumber Company that operated a sawmill at Dee, Oregon, the Mount Hood Railway Company that hauled the Dee mill's lumber to Hood River and the Sumpter Valley Railway Company that operated out of Baker City, Oregon, serving the Oregon Lumber Company mill there.[13] The Sumpter Valley Railway Company, because of its heavy employment of Mormons, was often disparagingly referred to as the "Polygamy Central."[14]

David Eccles died unexpectedly in 1912.[15] Settlement of his large estate was a prolonged affair, not only due to the complexity of his holdings, but also because he had followed the church-condoned but state-condemned practice of polygamy that produced twelve offspring in his first marriage and nine more in his plural one.[16] So many members of Eccles's two families were involved in his business empire that division of his estate purely along family lines proved difficult.[17]

When Eccles's estate finally settled, its assets were divided five-sevenths to the primary family and put under the control of the David Eccles Company. David C. Eccles, the oldest son from that family, was named president.[18] The remaining two-sevenths of the estate went to the plural family and were placed under the control of the Eccles Investment Company. Marriner S. Eccles, the oldest son of that family, was named its president.[19]

As David Eccles's estate was largely comprised of stock, the respective holdings of the David Eccles Company and Eccles Investment Company largely reflected the five-sevenths/two-sevenths division of ownership in the total shares owned by the estate. As a result, the larger David Eccles Company largely controlled the destiny of the two families' fortunes.[20]

THE KEITH FAMILY AND CENTRAL COAL & COKE COMPANY

Richard H. Keith got his start in the coal business in Kansas City, Missouri, in the 1870s under the name of Keith and Hendry. In 1880, Hendry sold his interest to Keith and John Perry who joined forces as the Keith and Perry Coal Company. On April 16, 1893, Keith and Perry incorporated the business as the Central Coal & Coke Company.

While David Eccles was consolidating his empire, Richard Keith was building one of his own. By 1893, Central Coal & Coke had also entered the lumber business under the auspices of the Bowie County Lumber Company. It, along with the Keith and Perry Coal Company, formed the nucleus of the Central Company. Central Coal & Coke steadily grew by acquiring the Sweetwater Coal & Mining Company in Rock Springs, Wyoming, then the Kansas & Texas Coal Company and later the properties of the Tonty Lumber Company in Texas. More acquisitions eventually led the Central Company into the operation of coal mining and lumbering facilities in Wyoming, Missouri, Kansas, Arkansas, Oklahoma, Texas, and Louisiana. By 1904 Central Coal & Coke had established itself as the largest producer and distributor of coal west of the Mississippi River.[21]

Determined to establish Central as a major force in the lumber industry, the company expanded this part of its business from an initial mill in Texarkana, Texas, by establishing lumbering operations in Neame and Carson in Calcasieu and Vernon Parishes, Louisiana, with others in Houston, Montgomery, and Walker Counties, Texas.

By 1907, Charles Keith had succeeded his father in the business. However, unlike David Eccles who started many of the businesses he owned, once he graduated from Fordham University at the age of eighteen, Charles Keith went to work for his father. Keith advanced through Central's ranks, first as an accountant, then as an engineer and later by taking on increased responsibilities in the sales organization. He finally became president of Central Coal & Coke Company when he was only thirty-four years old.

Under Charles Keith's direction, Central Coal & Coke's southern pine operations in Louisiana and Texas continued to expand. By 1913, Central's various holdings needed additions and improvements. Among these was a mill for the Conroe, Texas, operation. These improvements required outside financing, which led to the formation of a wholly owned subsidiary—Delta Land & Timber Company. Delta Land & Timber Company took title to all of the Central's timber properties and sawmills. The additional capital generated through public financing fueled more growth and helped solidify Central Coal & Coke Company as a major operator in the southern pine lumber region.

Charles Keith rose to become a prominent leader in the southern pine lumber trade. When the Southern Pine Association trade organization was founded in 1915, he was elected its first president, a position he held for four terms. Robert A. Long, one of the most respected figures in the industry and a founder of the Long-Bell Lumber Company, once described Charles Keith as the best-informed lumberman in the country.

THE NORTHERN LINES

By 1908, Edward H. Harriman's Union Pacific and Southern Pacific Railroads had established a virtual monopoly on inbound and outbound rail traffic in the State of Oregon.[22] Even so, other

Central Coal & Coke's Neame, Louisiana, mill in 1902. The company also operated sawmills at Carson, Louisiana, and at Texarkana, Kennard, and Conroe, Texas. Many features of the Conroe mill were incorporated at the Oregon-American sawmill in Vernonia. (Kamholz collection)

major carriers found the lure of potential lumber, agriculture, and fishing traffic irresistible and undertook ways to reach these markets by building lines to Portland. In the 1880s the Northern Pacific Railway built a line from Pasco, Washington, to connect with the Oregon Railway & Navigation Company line over which the Union Pacific operated between Granger, Wyoming, and Portland. This gave NP only limited access, however.[23] NP later relinquished this route after it had constructed its own line from Pasco to the Puget Sound that allowed it to reach Portland via Tacoma.[24]

By 1895, James J. Hill, "The Empire Builder," and his Great Northern Railway had completed a competing line connecting Spokane and Seattle.[25] Soon after, Hill also gained control of the Northern Pacific. Yet even with a route connecting Portland to Seattle, the Northern Lines found it difficult to compete with the Union Pacific and Southern Pacific because direct access to Portland was only available through the Harriman-controlled Northern Pacific Terminal Company.[26]

Hill decided to remedy this situation in 1905 and had the GN and NP jointly fund an independent company to construct a line down the Washington side of the Columbia River to Vancouver.[27] To overcome the problem of reaching Portland, Hill planned to construct a direct line into Portland via

Vancouver.[28] As Hill operated the GN and NP independently, he had the two companies jointly build the connecting line, thus ensuring both entities equal and independent rights to operate over it.[29]

This independent concern, the Portland & Seattle Railway Company, was created in 1905. Its charter was to construct and operate railroad, telephone, and telegraph lines between Seattle, Portland, and Spokane along with branch lines as deemed necessary.[30]

In 1908, a year before construction of the Spokane to Portland line was completed, the GN and NP amended their arrangement and expanded the P&S's mission and operating responsibilities. This arrangement also changed the name of Portland & Seattle Railway Company to the Spokane, Portland & Seattle Railway Company.[31] Thus the SP&S came into being, satisfying Hill's objectives of a direct line west from Spokane to Portland and profits from the traffic riches Oregon offered.

THE OREGON-AMERICAN LUMBER COMPANY AND THE DUBOIS TRACT

As all astute lumbermen must, David C. Eccles began searching for his next timber stand long before consuming his present one. Having successfully gained a foothold in the railroad company marketplace for Douglas fir products through operations in the Columbia River Gorge, it was entirely logical for him to extend his holdings in the fir belt. Under the auspices of the Oregon Lumber Company, he negotiated purchase of an immense body of undeveloped timber in northwest Oregon located in the Rock Creek drainage system midway in a straight line between Portland and Seaside. The tract, owned by the DuBois Lumber Company of DuBois, Pennsylvania, contained more than 2 billion board feet of some of the finest old-growth yellow fir ever to exist.[32]

Far from an idle boast, the cruise of timber on this tract was truly impressive. Applying an old-growth Douglas fir–era yardstick helps illustrate that notion. Lumbermen then considered a stand superlative if it carried 100,000 board feet of merchantable timber to the acre. Timber does not grow uniformly, however, and its density on the ground varies according to age, growing conditions, terrain, sunlight, and moisture. While finding the occasional 100,000 board foot per acre in an overall good stand of timber was not unusual, maintaining that standard became increasingly difficult the larger the tract. The average old-growth Douglas fir forest in those days averaged about 55,000 board feet to the acre and ranged up to as high as 90,000 board feet to the acre in the most exceptional stands having a minimum size of 5,000 acres. By comparison, the average old-growth southern pine stand grew to a density of only 6,000 to 12,000 board feet to the acre, while the average old-growth Ponderosa pine stand typically grew to a density of between 14,000 to 25,000 board feet per acre.[33]

By contrast, the 22,000-acre DuBois tract had no fewer than ten entire sections (a section is 1 mile square containing 640 acres) that *averaged* more than 100,000 board feet to the acre. Based on minimum-sized subdivisions of 160 acres, the tract contained more than 9,000 acres that exceeded the 100,000 board feet per acre standard and, overall, averaged more than 90,000 board feet per acre across the entire tract. The edge of this tract lay only 11 miles west of Vernonia.

On June 20, 1917, brothers David C. and Royal Eccles, along with Charles T. Early, and M. S. Browning, former business associates of their father's lumber and banking enterprises, joined Joseph Scowcroft, husband of the Eccles brothers' sister, Vivian, and another brother from the first family, Leroy, to incorporate the Oregon-American Lumber Company in Weber County, Utah for purposes of conducting a lumbering business.[34] The Oregon-American Lumber Company contracted to purchase the DuBois timber tract on July 11, 1917. With the task of obtaining a large timber tract accomplished, the next step was to develop a transportation link to exploit it. Having successfully established the common carrier Sumpter Valley Railway Company, the Eccles naturally considered building their own railroad system. Doing so would not only tap Oregon-American's timber, it would also serve the needs of future operators on the line to and beyond Vernonia.

The Eccleses' operations were not strangers to this part of Oregon. A predecessor company to Utah Construction Company, Corey Brothers and Company, had undertaken construction projects for several different companies attempting to complete a rail connection between Astoria and Portland during the 1890s.[35] At one time, promoters in Astoria actively pursued a route connecting the two cities that was to traverse the Coast Range. This plan called for building a route south from Astoria to Seaside where it was to turn eastward up the Lewis and Clark River, crest the Coast Range through an 1,100-foot tunnel, then connect with existing rail lines west of Portland, in the Tualatin Valley, near the town of Hillsboro.[36] While its promoters had abandoned the plan once others had established a water-level grade along the Columbia River, the Corey Brothers and Company, now Utah Construction Company, undoubtedly used its familiarity of the territory in determining how best to move logs from the DuBois tract to Portland.[37] Armed with this knowledge, the Eccles turned their attention toward completing the line.

The United Railways

From its inception in 1906 the United Railways Company had been a struggling interurban rail line attempting to provide passenger and freight service between Portland and the Tualatin Valley.[38] James J. Hill purchased the United Railways in 1909 because it had potential as a source of traffic for the Northern Lines-owned Spokane, Portland & Seattle Railway.[39] By 1917, United Railways had completed a line via the Cornelius Pass tunnel connecting Portland with Wilkesboro, approximately 1 mile southeast of Banks, Oregon.[40] The United Railways Company offered, in Hill's view, a partially constructed route toward the port of Tillamook, Oregon, that gave the Northern Lines the opportunity to further compete with the Southern Pacific's line to Tillamook, then under construction.[41]

Hill delayed following through on his plan to extend the line to Tillamook and United Railways did little to generate traffic for SP&S in the years that followed.[42] Lumber demand increased during WWI. While many logging operators owning timber in the Coast Range requested United to extend its tracks beyond Wilkesboro, the Northern Lines resisted, claiming a road constructed solely for handling logs without any guarantee of moving the lumber produced from those logs eastbound from Portland, did not warrant further investment.[43] In fact, because potential for the United to generate revenue-producing traffic was perceived to be slight, sentiment ran high within the Northern Lines' ranks to sell the United line outright.[44]

In 1917 the American Land & Timber Company

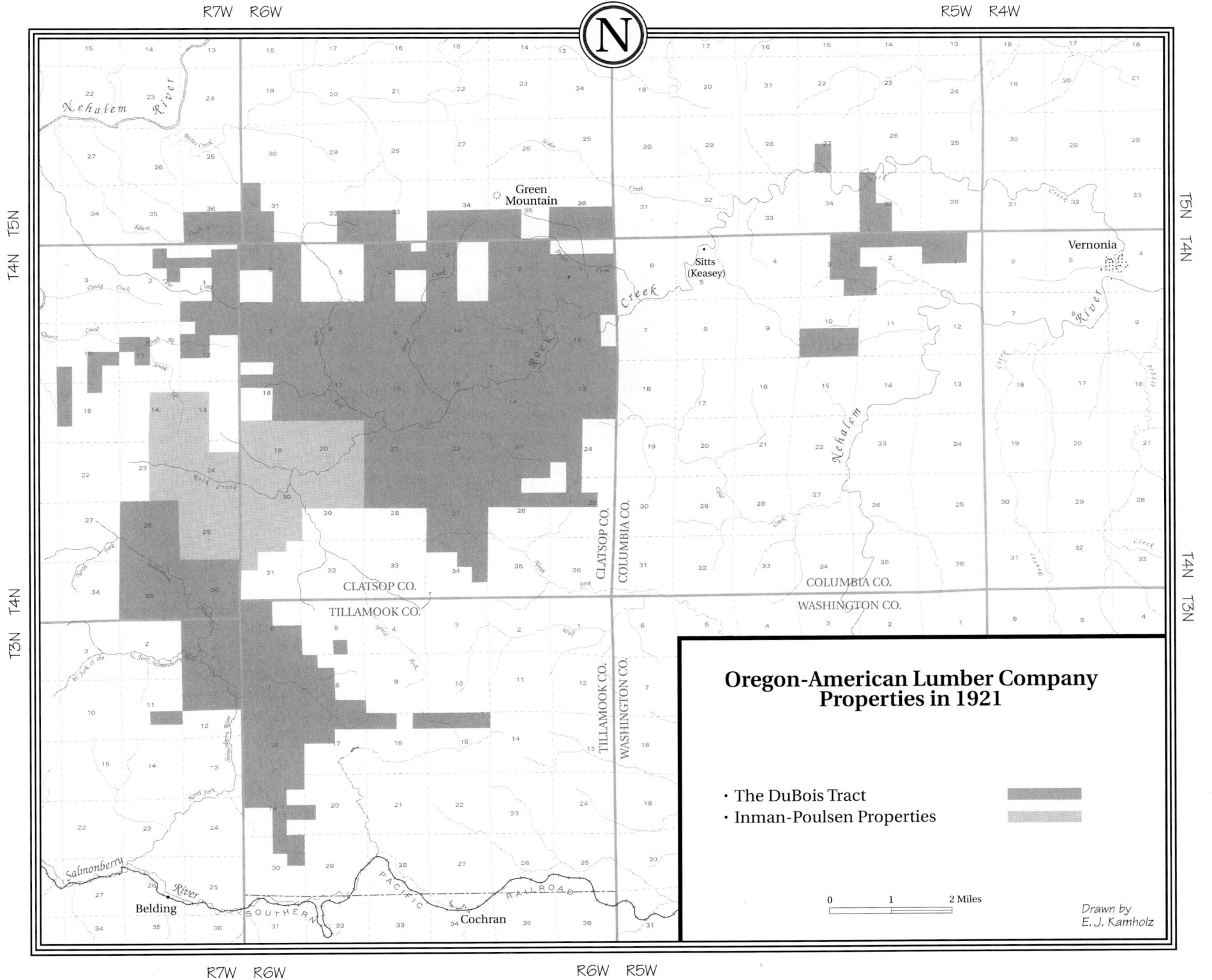

Oregon-American Lumber Company Properties in 1921

- The DuBois Tract
- Inman-Poulsen Properties

Drawn by E. J. Kamholz

Vernonia, Oregon, as it appeared in 1894. It was an isolated outpost of only 150 residents before the Oregon-American Lumber Company began constructing its mill there in 1923. Overnight the population grew to 1,500 and it was hailed as the fastest-growing town in the State of Oregon. (Columbia County Historical Museum)

incorporated the Gales Creek and Wilson River Railroad. The GC&WR built a line between the parent company's holdings west of Banks and Wilkesboro where it joined the United Railways. Once established, it provided access to Ruth Realty's proposed log dump site on the Willamette Slough at Burlington.[45]

The GC&WR eventually proposed buying the United Railways but the Northern Lines' $1 million asking price was more than the GC&WR was willing to pay.[46] A trackage agreement followed but even after the GC&WR began to operate in 1920, traffic was disappointingly low.[47] By then the Northern Lines were more anxious than ever to rid themselves of the United.

The Portland, Astoria & Pacific Railroad Company

Since Wilkesboro lay only 22 miles from Vernonia and another 11 miles from their timber, the Eccleses, like the GC&WR, investigated how best to capitalize on the existing rail line of the United Railways. The Portland, Astoria & Pacific Railroad Company was incorporated in Delaware on July 28, 1919.[48] Officers and directors of the transportation company were David C. Eccles, president; M. S. Browning, vice president; and Charles T. Early, secretary and treasurer. Marriner Eccles, from the plural family and president of Eccles Investment Company, joined them on the board along with Joseph Scowcroft.[49]

By September 1919 the Portland, Astoria & Pacific

Railroad contracted with Utah Construction Company to build the PA&P line from Wilkesboro to Vernonia and beyond into the Oregon-American Lumber Company timber holdings. Utah Construction Company was to complete the line by May 1920.[50] Befiting its interurban passenger service charter, the United Railways to Wilkesboro was electrified. Accordingly, when the Eccleses incorporated the PA&P they made that company's charter broad enough to operate using steam, electricity, or any other motive power.[51] The PA&P ultimately agreed to rent the United for $45,000 per year effective April 1, 1920.[52] United agreed to reduce the rental fee to the extent other users could be encouraged to use the line. Operating costs were to be based on usage.[53] In April 1920, PA&P contracted with A. C. Callan of Portland to buy 10,000 tons of railroad supplies including 3,000 tons of used 60-pound rail Callan was to obtain from the United States Spruce Production Corporation.

The Nehalem Boom Company

The Northern Lines, ever-mindful of the need for commerce to generate rail traffic for their branch lines and ultimately for themselves, were no strangers to the notion of offering enticements to encourage new businesses to develop along their routes. Acquisition of real estate for current and future development for themselves and potential customers was a mainstay tactic.[54] The SP&S's vehicle for this purpose was its wholly owned Ruth Realty Company that bought and developed real estate for itself and other business developers.[55]

The completion of the PA&P and the United Railways rental agreement promised Oregon-American the transportation link it needed to move its logs from Vernonia to the Willamette Slough. O-A needed two more elements to complete the master plan, however. First was a facility to unload the logs into the river. Oregon-American also needed a sawmill.[56] For unloading, the Eccleses incorporated the Nehalem Boom Company on February 10, 1920, to "conduct a general timber and booming business, to deal in timber and timber products and to construct and operate a railroad from United Railways to (Willamette) Slough."[57] The plan called for using part of the Ruth Realty Company's proposed industrial site at Burlington, close to the United Railways junction with the SP&S's Astoria branch line.[58]

Since SP&S officials also planned to use the Burlington facility as a boom site for other customers, they were concerned over the ownership vesting entirely with interests not connected with the railroad. So, in exchange for granting the Eccleses use of the Burlington site, SP&S took a half-interest in Nehalem Boom Company.[59] W. F. Turner, president of the SP&S, was named president of Nehalem Boom Company with Ray B. Early his vice president.[60] The boom company's location after that became known as Rafton.[61]

Plans for a sawmill never advanced beyond the Eccleses' vague promise that Oregon-American intended to build one somewhere along the lower Willamette River.[62]

THE DAVID ECCLES COMPANY'S FINANCIAL FAILURE

The United States economy entered a recession following WWI. By 1920, the lumber industry was suffering from a sharp downturn.[63] The lumber-based operations of the Eccleses proved especially vulnerable.

This period also marked a time of strife within

25

A prime specimen of *Pseudotsuga menziesii*, or Douglas fir. In its early stage of life lumbermen commonly called a Douglas fir tree red fir because of the reddish hue of its heartwood. As it gained height and the lower limbs fell from the bole, or main stem, the tree's diameter grew more slowly, adding a fine ring of new wood every year to the outside layer. Within the tree's first hundred years or so of life, a layer of highly prized, clear-grained wood encased the knots. Additional growth only enhanced its value. As the tree matured, the color of this outer layer developed a uniform yellowish color, hence the term "old-growth yellow fir." Typical trees in Oregon-American's stand were 300 to 600 years old. (Rose Valpiani collection)

and between the two Eccles families. Outwardly, it began when Leroy Eccles was ousted from his position as vice president and general manager of Amalgamated Sugar Company. Soon, trouble spread to the other entities in which David C. and Leroy were officers and directors and in which the David Eccles Company held large stock positions.[64] Other family members disposed of their stocks held by the parent David Eccles Company in exchange for various assets. In this way, the Eccles Investment Company gained control of the Utah Construction Company.[65]

Marriner Eccles, representing the second family and the Eccles Investment Company interests in the David Eccles Company, was among those dissatisfied with the performance of the latter company. In 1920 he presented its president, his half-brother David C., with a proposal to either sell out his interests in the Oregon Lumber Company or buy those of the Eccles Investment Company.

Rebuffed, the younger Eccles approached the Oregon Lumber Company directors representing the balance of the stockholders. He successfully gained their support and David C. Eccles was ultimately forced to buy out the dissident interests or lose his job.[66] Unable to obtain the cash to carry this out, David C. had to exchange bank stocks and minority interests in various other enterprises in which the David Eccles Company held minority interests. He was allowed to pay the balance in cash over a period of two years.[67]

By year-end 1920 the David Eccles Company found itself strapped for cash, its Oregon-American Lumber Company owing money on the DuBois tract and unable to begin logging it since there was no way to get the logs to market.[68] Furthermore, the PA&P had a rail line only partially completed and was under pressure to pay overdue bills. One of those bills was for three American Locomotive Company 2-8-2s that Alco had already delivered to Vancouver, Washington.[69] Additionally, construction costs owed Utah Construction Company were unpaid.[70] Matters worsened when the news arrived that Callan had spent the PA&P advance payment but could not produce the rail as promised. With the Eccles Company out of cash, railroad construction ground to a halt with only 15 miles of right-of-way graded and 4 miles of track in place.[71]

By 1921, the David Eccles Company's financial problems had grown to a point where it was insolvent. J. H. Devine was named the trustee in full charge of all its entities, including the Oregon-American, Portland, Astoria & Pacific, and the Nehalem Boom Companies. Utah Construction Company sued over unpaid invoices.[72] It became clear unless outside funding could be found, further development of the properties was impossible.

To raise cash, the Oregon-American Lumber Company sold a 3,200-acre subdivision of the DuBois tract to the Inman-Poulsen Lumber Company on January 21, 1921.[73] The agreement required Inman-Poulsen to move its logs to its Portland mill via the PA&P and United Railways, thus guaranteeing some level of traffic volume once the railroad was completed.[74] Still, the traffic provision was meaningless, for without a rail line connecting Inman-Poulsen to Wilkesboro, there was no way to generate any revenue to offset the rental for the United Railways.

Nor did the cash generated by the Inman-Poulsen sale solve the David Eccles Company's immediate financial problems. So, by spring 1921, the company had no choice but to sell the Oregon-American, PA&P, and Nehalem Boom Company holdings.

THE BIG MOVE WEST

Before the end of WWI, Weyerhaeuser, Crosset-Western, Long-Bell, Central Coal & Coke, and other substantial operators from the southern and upper Midwestern pine regions found their timber holdings largely depleted. The potential of the untapped western pine and Douglas fir regions along the Pacific Ocean shores beckoned and by 1920, many of these major lumber manufacturers had secured timber and started operations there.[75]

Charles Keith conditioned his search for new territory on the ability to produce lumber, not just logs. Since Central Coal & Coke had an already established distribution network for the output of its southern pine mills, the finished product of any new operation had to be marketable to Central's existing customers, the bulk of whom were in the Midwest and Great Plains states. Further, owing to the added distance between the Midwest and the West Coast, Keith had to consider how Central could price its products competitively relative to his existing southern pine trade given the additional cost of transporting lumber an extra 1,000 miles. Finally, the issue of quality came into play, for the Central Company had established a reputation with its customers for seasoned lumber.

This last condition had developed from Central Coal & Coke's practice of artificially drying much of its lumber production. The kiln-dried product gave customers the advantages of uniform-sized lumber, less subject to shrinkage and of a higher grade than green lumber. While kiln-drying was an established practice for seasoning pine lumber, there was no assurance the practice could be adopted to Douglas fir. So, unless Keith restricted his search to the western pine region, he first had to determine how to season Douglas fir artificially, a process many in the industry did not believe possible without suffering product degradation in the form of shrinkage, warping, and checking. Since Central's plan to move was predicated on diverting existing customers from pine to fir, this lack of a consensus was disturbing.

Central collaborated with the U.S. Forest Products Laboratory at the University of Wisconsin. Using the laboratory's design for a condition-controlled drying kiln, the company developed and tested a prototype to artificially dry green Douglas fir lumber. The experiment determined such a device could produce lumber that would meet the demands of the Central Company's trade.

Not only did the experiment prove it was feasible to kiln-dry green Douglas fir, it also gave Keith the plans for a commercially viable internal circulation kiln suitable for a mill installation. Central built two prototype kilns, one in Washington and the other in Texas. After more than a year's testing, the results were conclusive—green Douglas fir lumber could be artificially seasoned without suffering excessive degradation. Armed with this knowledge, Keith moved forward in his quest for new territory.

Central derived another benefit from the experiment, one that offset much of the added cost of moving products from the West Coast. Since the objective of seasoning lumber was to remove excess moisture content, thus offering consumers stability of the product, removal of moisture also reduced the product's weight, so while a shipment of dried lumber took up the same space on a rail car, it weighed less than green lumber and therefore could be moved farther for the same cost. Capitalizing on the resulting "underweights" enabled Keith's proposed operation to become increasingly competitive the farther his lumber was shipped, compared with those West Coast competitors who produced only green lumber. Keith now began his search in earnest. The plight of the Oregon-American/Portland, Astoria & Pacific/Nehalem Boom venture was a ready-made opportunity and his focus narrowed.

New Owners, New Life

On August 8, 1921, Central Coal & Coke took an option on the Oregon-American Lumber Company with a down payment of $500,000. Since Oregon-American counted among its assets the capital stock of both the PA&P and Nehalem Boom Company, the sale price of $7 million was inclusive of all three companies. It also included a $2.3 million mortgage for the DuBois tract.

While Central had operated common-carrier rail lines of its own, including the Missouri and Louisiana Railroad Company, it had no desire to continue the practice in Oregon.[76] Thus, a key condition of the sale required the PA&P be disposed of before the rest of the deal could be closed. Within days, Keith began to negotiate the PA&P's sale to the Union Pacific, even though the PA&P's lease agreement for the United Railways provided the Northern Lines a first option to buy the PA&P.

Unaware that Keith was attempting to sell the PA&P to the UP, Ralph Budd, president of the Great Northern, paid a visit to inspect the PA&P on September 2, 1921.[77] Central Coal & Coke's takeover of the Eccleses' interests was encouraging news to Budd and he began to appreciate the potential of the PA&P and United Railways arrangement. Not so much, however, that he saw any reason to buy into the arrangement until after the PA&P line had been completed.[78]

On September 21, 1921, the Union Pacific agreed to acquire the PA&P. That same day, Central Coal & Coke executed the agreement with the Eccles to buy the Oregon-American and the Nehalem Boom Companies. A major condition of the Union Pacific's purchase of the PA&P, however, required Oregon-American to build a sawmill on the PA&P line no farther east than Vernonia, thus guaranteeing the carrier shipment of lumber to Portland and points beyond instead of mere raw logs bound for the open market.

Central's deal with the Eccleses called for the sale of 80 percent of the Oregon-American stock, the balance of which was to remain in the hands of the David Eccles Company. For its stake, the David Eccles Company was to provide funding to complete the PA&P and to provide Oregon-American with a nucleus of personnel experienced in western logging operations.

Shortly after Budd returned from his inspection of the PA&P and reported his findings to Charles Donnelly, president of the Northern Pacific, both men became concerned that the potential of a line to the Oregon-American timber might attract the unwelcome attention of a competing carrier.[79] Still unaware that Keith had already negotiated the PA&P's sale to the UP, the Northern Lines offered to purchase the PA&P for essentially the same terms the Union Pacific had already offered Keith, namely for $2 million, provided O-A construct a mill of at least a 250,000 board feet daily capacity no farther east on the PA&P line than Vernonia.

Very soon after the Northern Lines made the offer Budd and Donnelly learned that Keith had already reached an agreement with the Union Pacific.[80] Faced with the prospect of losing the potential freight traffic to their fiercest rival, the Northern Lines exercised the option to purchase the line and, in doing so, agreed to buy the PA&P outright and uncompleted for $1,415,000. The carriers also agreed to assume responsibility for completing the line from Wilkesboro to the Columbia/Clatsop County line effective November 21, 1921.[81]

Central and the Northern Lines closed the sale on December 7, 1921. The Northern Lines also acquired Oregon-American's half-interest in the Nehalem Boom Company for $280,000.[82] Oregon-American, however, had to absorb construction debts amounting to $2.2 million that had been incurred constructing the PA&P, along with the three locomotives the Eccleses had ordered.

Having readily agreed to make Oregon-American a rail mill operation, Keith secured a trackage agreement from the Northern Lines granting Oregon-American the right to haul its log cars over the PA&P to his proposed mill site at a rate of only one dollar and twenty-five cents per train mile, empty or loaded. Further, in return for routing eastbound output from O-A's mill over the Northern Lines, the carriers provided Oregon-American the Portland basis rate of $12.75 per 1,000 board feet on eastbound lumber shipments plus favorable rates to tidewater locations for export and coastwise business.

Agreeing to put the mill near Oregon-American's timber was hardly a concession on Keith's part. While conventional mill-siting practice favored locating such facilities on major waterways that enabled operators to buy logs from many suppliers and to ship the finished products by water as well, there were exceptions, particularly when a mill operator owned sufficient timber to maintain the log supply needed to amortize the cost of milling facilities.

Keith's decision to make his manufacturing plant a so-called rail mill was determined by several factors. First, Central Coal & Coke, through its experience in the South, had found it preferable to put its mills nearer the timber to permit operating the timber using only one mainline locomotive. Second, it had proven cheaper to locate mills nearer the timber than to haul logs long distances. With the resulting lower cost of transporting logs, lumber was less costly to produce. To bear out the second factor, had

Keith opted to purchase the PA&P and operate the United Railways as David C. Eccles had originally planned, the annual fixed cost of transporting logs to the Willamette River would have been $435,000 per year versus only $16,200 per year required to haul the logs to his nearby mill. And while the decision to make Vernonia a rail mill could be justified for reasons of proximity and cost alone, the fact that kiln-dried lumber reabsorbed moisture when exposed to the elements virtually ruled out shipment by water, one of the fundamental reasons to locate a mill on a waterway in the first place.

Railroad Construction

As the Central Coal & Coke, Union Pacific, and Northern Lines negotiations for control of the PA&P unfolded in the distant Midwest, a flurry of events began taking place at the scene of construction beginning in August 1921. Buoyed by Central's down-payment for Oregon-American, the David Eccles Company lured Utah Construction Company back to work on the PA&P.[83]

About this time, Keith named his second-in-command, Frank Schopflin, general manager in charge of the new operation. Central also deployed its first employee to the proposed Vernonia operation in the person of William H. "Bill" McGregor. McGregor had been Delta Land & Timber Company's manager of logging and lands at Conroe, Texas. A forty-year veteran, he brought with him a vast knowledge of woods operations. He was also a seasoned hand at acquiring land and timber. McGregor set up shop in the Yeon building in Portland in the office the Eccleses had originally been using to operate the Oregon-American Lumber Company before its sale.

Chief Engineer of the PA&P was George Scoggins, who not only had been responsible for preparing the specifications for the rail line but was also supervising the work of Utah Construction. The primary hurdle Scoggins and Utah Construction faced in building the line was how to cross the first summit of the Coast Range at a place called, appropriately, Tophill, located 10 rail miles south of Vernonia, at an elevation of 1,033 feet. Scoggins's plan called for a 1,137-foot-long tunnel through a natural divide in the hills.[84] By September 1921 boring at the south end of the tunnel was proceeding at a rate of 6 feet per day.

Unfortunately, geologically unstable earth plagued the location chosen for the tunnel. First indications that the ground was unstable arose by October 3 when crews spotted noticeable evidence that timbers supporting the tunnel had begun to shift.

Anxious for completion so as to begin hauling logs, McGregor and Schopflin closely monitored progress on the PA&P. They were alarmed to discover that Utah Construction seemed intent to do the work as cheaply as possible. They noted, for example, that instead of backfilling every tunnel timber bent when installed as called for in Scoggins's specifications, such work had been done to only one in eight. Closer investigation made it clear that Utah Construction was disregarding the specifications in other areas too. They also developed a strong suspicion that Utah Construction was deliberately overcharging.

Doubts over Scoggins's ability to keep Utah Construction in line reached a head by October 18, 1921, when Schopflin reported continuing inability of PA&P to secure rail, his observation of "gross inefficiency" by Utah Construction, despite contin-

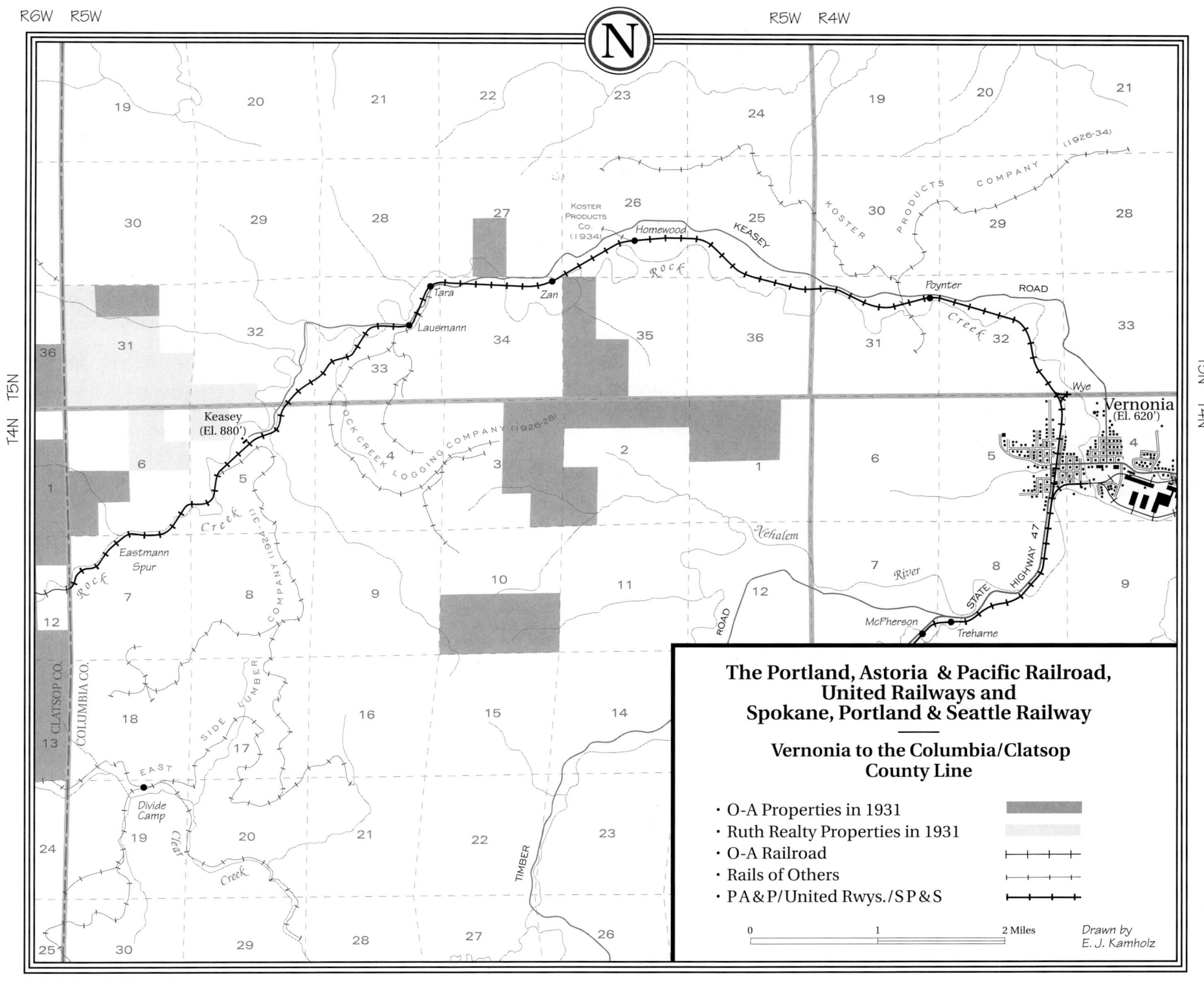

The Portland, Astoria & Pacific Railroad, United Railways and Spokane, Portland & Seattle Railway

Vernonia to the Columbia/Clatsop County Line

- O-A Properties in 1931
- Ruth Realty Properties in 1931
- O-A Railroad
- Rails of Others
- PA&P/United Rwys./SP&S

0 1 2 Miles

Drawn by E. J. Kamholz

ued optimism by PA&P forces who steadfastly reported that they would complete the line by December 1, 1921.

Keith, recognizing those delays in completing the line would would make it just that much longer before Oregon-American could begin producing logs wrote: *The progress is…certainly unsatisfactory, in fact it makes me sick to read of the situation that exists.*

To reduce delays once the PA&P was completed, the Central Coal-owned Oregon-American contracted with A. Guthrie & Company, a St. Paul, Minnesota-based construction company with offices in Portland, to clear, grade, and build a logging railroad from the terminus of the PA&P at the Columbia/Clatsop County line to the proposed site of Oregon-American's first logging camp, some 4.2 miles to the southwest. O-A retained G.V. Lintner, who, like the Guthrie Company, had enjoyed a successful working relationship with the SP&S on prior rail construction projects to supervise Guthrie's work.[85]

Concerned with Utah Construction's lack of progress on the PA&P, Oregon-American also commissioned Lintner to prepare an independent assessment of that situation. Lintner quickly determined that with Utah's present rate of progress, it would take five more months to complete the grading plus another month to finish laying the tracks.

Immediately after the Northern Lines' acquisition of the PA&P, the SP&S took charge of the construction supervision and replaced Scoggins with Lintner. By December 1921, Lintner's stronger direction led to sharp disagreements with Utah Construction Company forces and as work on the line halted due to winter storms, the Utah Company's involvement came to a close.

For that matter, this also marked the end of the David Eccles Company involvement in the Oregon-American venture, for despite its 20 percent stake in O-A, the Ecclese's defaulted on their obligation to finance completion of the PA&P. Keith's interests eventually had to make up the shortfall without ever regaining the stock.

By January 4, 1922, McGregor reported a foot of snow had fallen in Vernonia and that it became progressively deeper as the line moved into the higher elevations up Rock Creek. As he saw conditions, things would be going well if O-A could begin shipping logs by July 1922. Accustomed to the warm climate of the southern pine region, not to mention its flat terrain, Schopflin, having returned to Kansas City, replied, *I presume this is a sample of what we must expect during the winter months in this territory.*

The Tophill tunnel again began to develop trouble in early February 1922 when timbers in the south end began to shift nearly 3 inches per week. Some even began giving way. Lintner foresaw the need to retimber nearly 250 feet of the tunnel. Even so he remained optimistic that crews could lay track through it by April 1. By mid-February, however, soil movement had worsened, so it became a choice between even more retimbering or else day-lighting the tunnel. In the end, the retimbering option was selected, but it resulted in another delay of forty-five days or so.

Although the snow melted by the end of April, track-laying did not begin until May 26, 1922.[86] The SP&S hired A. Guthrie & Company to lay the track and exerted great pressure on the Guthrie Company's project manager, Natt McDougall, to complete the work quickly.[87] Forced ten-hour work days at low-wage rates soon began to take their toll on the Guthrie crews and men began to quit. McDougall, believing a reduction in working hours would reduce his labor turnover, shortened daily working hours to eight. In fourteen working days, Guthrie's crews laid only 3 miles of track against the 1.5 miles per day expected by the owners.

Schopflin, learning of McDougall's shorter work days, protested to Budd and Donnelly who placed even more pressure on the SP&S to speed McDougall along and promised Schopflin completion of the railroad by August 1, 1922.

By July 10, track-laying had improved to an average of 1,900 feet per day and it looked like Guthrie's crews might reach Vernonia by July 24, 1922. However, forest fires also plagued the region that summer and forced McDougall to raise labor rates to meet those of the firefighters.[88] McGregor figured this caused the Guthrie Company to lose between $800 and $1,000 per mile of track laid. Matters got worse when fires attacked several wooden trestles on the PA&P line causing even more delays while track crews fought the fires and repaired the damages. If McDougall did not have enough problems as it was, he experienced further interruptions when he had to repair inadequate grading and preparation work done by Utah Construction Company.[89] Despite the obstacles, Guthrie's track-laying crews finally reached Vernonia by the end of July and mixed-train service there began on August 3, 1922.[90] Finally, Saturday, August 19, the PA&P tracks to the county line were completed.[91] Vernonia was now a place on the map.

Oregon-American Lumber Company Logging and Railroad Development 1922-26

- O-A Properties in 1931
- O-A Green Timber in 1926
- Ruth Realty Properties
- Inman-Poulsen Properties
- O-A Railroad

0 — 1 — 2 Miles

Drawn by E. J. Kamholz

BOOM TIMES ARRIVE

Once the Oregon-American acquisition was completed and progress toward a logging program was underway, Keith focused his attention on organizational issues. Over the next several years constant activity between Central's Kansas City headquarters, the Northern Lines' home offices in St. Paul, Minnesota, and the financial districts of Chicago and Kansas City further shaped Oregon-American. Examination of the Central Coal & Coke and Oregon-American financial structures, the strategic alignment with the Northern Lines, and the method used to sell Oregon-American lumber provides a basis to understand how subsequent events shaped the venture's destiny.

THE THOMAS & MESERVEY CRUISE

Like most other debt-financed start-ups in the industry, Oregon-American's financial cornerstone was based on the quantity, species, and grade of timber it owned. Measurement of that inventory was determined by a cruise, or sampling of the timber. The cruise not only determined value but also established the basis of the venture's financial structure. Borrowing ability, the accounting system, equipment needs, and depreciation schedules each ultimately hinged on the cruise. If the cruise was accurate or even understated, the lumberman could expect a reasonable opportunity to pay off his debts and realize a profit provided he managed properly and the market for lumber held up. However, if the cruise was overstated, it diminished the chances of a happy outcome.

The firm of Thomas & Meservey conducted the Oregon-American cruise in 1921, and Keith relied on it to establish the price Central Coal & Coke paid for the company. Virtually every other key financial decision made following the purchase found its origin in the T&M cruise.

Despite publicly stated confidence in the cruise, Oregon-American retained Thomas & Meservey to conduct a check cruise of the timber that the company had logged between October 1922 and the winter of 1923. This was done as a precautionary measure but only fortified the belief that the original cruise had been conservative. In its report, T&M found that O-A had recovered 8 percent more timber than the firm had originally inventoried on the cutover lands in question. As the log scale was based on Columbia River Scaling Bureau standards, Thomas & Meservey's report further concluded:

> We are certain that an additional overrun would ensue if this timber had been milled by the Oregon-American Lumber Company. This is due to the fact that a great deal of timber must be left in the woods to meet the log scaling bureau standards. Considering [this] we recommend by a careful and economic operation you may expect a total overrun at the mill on our cruise of about 15% simply allowing for a degree of conservatism.

Opposite page: Oregon-American began logging in 1922 by clearing the area soon to be known as Camp McGregor. By 1926 the cutting circle had widened to encompass most of the main line and Spur 5.

O-A created its 36½-acre millpond at Vernonia by scraping the earthen floor and piling dirt and clay in berms around the perimeter to form a levee. The pond had a uniform water depth of 5 feet except in front of the unloading stations where it was increased to 12 feet. View overlooks the future train log dump. (Columbia County Historical Museum)

On the strength of this report and, for the sake of added conservatism, Oregon-American's timber account was set up at 8 percent more than the T&M cruise.

At the time Keith made no secret of the fact that he considered Thomas & Meservey to be the finest timber cruising firm in the region. The experiences of the next eight years proved far different from the expectations, however. Keith's faith in the cruise, not to mention the personal and professional trust he placed in the firm itself, proved greatly misplaced, the full extent to which is detailed in the next chapter.

FINANCIAL STRUCTURE OF THE CENTRAL COAL & COKE AND OREGON-AMERICAN LUMBER COMPANIES

Like most other operators making the move westward, Central Coal & Coke found it necessary to borrow money to buy its timber and construct the Vernonia mill. In 1922, Central and its bankers authorized a $7 million bond issue, only $4.5 million of which could be issued at the time because of a conflict in the company's financial directory. Since conversions from Central's southern pine operations were high, it was able to divert substantial revenues from the South to the West, offsetting the amount it was unable to borrow. Yet, by spring 1924 current operations could not meet the demands for cash, so Central issued the remaining $2.5 million in bonds. Nor was this enough, so overdue bills on the partially completed mill caused Central to overextend its bank loans.

To overcome the problem, Central's investment bankers proposed that Delta Land & Timber Company take title to the Oregon-American Lumber Company mill plant and lease it back to Oregon-American. Among the conditions of this arrangement, O-A had to pay all maintenance costs, insurance, taxes, and interest on the mill plus $3 per 1,000 board feet of mortgaged timber cut, sold, or otherwise disposed of. That plan also called for O-A to repay $1.80 per 1,000 board feet for noncompany timber manufactured at the mill. The latter provision was for additional security on the $7 mil-

Top: Construction crews used horse teams to grade the Vernonia mill site. The dry assorter building has begun taking shape in the background to the left. The company later constructed the office and a housing development on the elevated area to the right. View is looking west. (W. C. Alexander photograph; Martin E. Hansen collection)

§

Bottom: Locomotive 102 removing an empty gondola while crews prepared concrete foundations for the two rough lumber storage sheds. Temporary housing for construction crews is visible in the upper far right. (W. C. Alexander photograph; Bill and Carol Ostrander collection)

lion bond issue. Central, Delta, O-A, and the bankers set up this arrangement on March 1, 1924. Still, the start-up costs mounted and Central found it necessary to advance O-A additional working capital that, by March 31, 1927, amounted to another $2.5 million.

The DuBois mortgage fell due in July 1927 and when Central approached its bankers, they recommended Oregon-American issue bonds amounting to an additional $2.75 million, part of which was to pay off the DuBois mortgage with the balance to pay back Central for its advances. In addition, the balance of the amount still owed Central was to be

Top: Since Vernonia lacked facilities to house and feed the 200-man crew that built the mill, the company had to build bunkhouses and dining rooms for them at the west end of the mill site. (W. C. Alexander photograph; Bill and Carol Ostrander collection)

§

Bottom: O-A used its Industrial Works 40-ton-capacity locomotive crane to help construct the mill. The circular concrete structure in front of the crane was the refuse burner's foundation. Concrete pier blocks in the background marked the future site of the sawmill proper. The concrete slab at the far right was for the machine shop floor. (W. C. Alexander photograph; Bill and Carol Ostrander collection)

paid off by an issue of preferred stock to remove all debt from O-A's balance sheet except its bond issue. This agreement prevented O-A from borrowing any money from outside sources, instead making it rely on funds furnished by Central.

When all of the pieces of the financial plan were finally put in place, Central Coal and Oregon-American had outstanding bond issues totaling $7 million and $2.7 million respectively.[1] Central's bond issue was partially secured by Delta Land & Timber Company's title to the mill and other minor properties at Vernonia, along with all Central's stock in the Oregon-American (for example, all of its preferred and 80 percent of its common stock).[2] Oregon-American's bond issue was secured by its timber.[3]

Construction workers had started framing the dry assorter building by September 21, 1923. Staged materials are visible on either side of the floor. To the right is the stacker building, also under construction. (W. C. Alexander photograph; Bill and Carol Ostrander collection)

BUSINESS INTEGRATION AND THE OREGON-AMERICAN–NORTHERN LINES STRATEGIC PARTNERSHIP

The Oregon-American and Northern Lines business relationship was symbiotic. For their part, the carriers had the ongoing need to increase freight revenues enough to defray the cost of building tracks between population centers in the East and Midwest and the remote regions of the West. Oregon-American needed favorable freight rates to economically market its production in the distant Midwest.

The carriers perfected many tactics to achieve their objectives. They granted favorable rates to customers based on anticipated volumes of freight. They built branch lines to serve new sources of freight and sold natural resources from lands granted to them or obtained in right-of-way condemnation proceedings. Sometimes they invested in lands carrying natural resources that customers could later exploit. Finally, they developed commercial facilities to encourage businesses to locate on their routes.[4]

Charles Keith, through his Central Coal & Coke and Delta Land & Timber operations, was no stranger to developing close relationships with carriers. He had done so previously and through such arrangements the Central Company successfully opened markets for its southern pine lumber in the Midwest. This experience predisposed him to look to the rail lines as a resource to help him meet his business objectives.

Central's putting the Oregon-American mill in Vernonia and the Northern Lines' purchase of the PA&P served as the binding element to form a mutually beneficial strategic relationship between the companies. On the one hand, it helped the Northern Roads neutralize the lure of competing carriers and allowed them to substantially monopolize the handling of Oregon-American freight, both inbound and outbound. On the other hand, Oregon-American benefited greatly because the favorable rate on eastbound lumber shipments helped it overcome the disadvantage of being so distant from Central Coal & Coke's established market. The agreement allowing O-A inexpensive movement of

BOOM TIMES ARRIVE

Top: Eight days after the previous photograph was taken the dry assorter building's framing was all but completed. To the right of it stood a temporary sawmill. (W. C. Alexander photograph; Bill and Carol Ostrander collection)

§

Bottom: Shown is a December 30, 1923 construction scene of the Vernonia sawmill. Principal structures are, from left to right, the refuse burner, sawmill, Dutch ovens and powerhouse smokestacks, and fuel bunker.

Wood was the preferred construction material for sawmills in those days. O-A's sawmill proper was an oddity, for the company had it constructed entirely of concrete and steel to reduce the fire hazard. The insurance premiums savings were substantial. (Columbia County Historical Museum)

its own trains over the PA&P line between the woods and Vernonia was important too, because it fixed log-hauling costs at a minimum level.

In fact, Keith's quest to expand the Oregon-American operation and make it more efficient made the Northern Lines' top management realize that almost anything they did to help Keith achieve his goals was likely to increase their eastbound tonnage. Consequently, the scope of the Central Coal/Oregon-American/Northern Lines strategic relationship expanded as the operation grew.

RUTH REALTY COMPANY

For all the unique characteristics of the Oregon-American arrangement with the carriers, nothing more fully demonstrated the depth of that relation-

Top: Workers labored to complete concrete foundations for the dry kilns while the stacker building took shape in the background. (W. C. Alexander photograph; Bill and Carol Ostrander collection)

§

Bottom: By March 5, 1924, the sawmill complex had taken form. Company houses that employees rented are visible to the right.

Oregon-American generated its own electricity for the mill and company houses. Between 1928 and 1946 O-A also had a standby power arrangement with the city of Vernonia's electric utility. During that period the mill supplied a substantial amount of power to the city.

The person fishing in the foreground was optimistic, for the millpond had just begun to fill. (W. C. Alexander photograph; Bill and Carol Ostrander collection)

ship than the Northern Lines' acquisition of timber for O-A. Handled by the SP&S-owned Ruth Realty Company, lands thus acquired were held in reserve until Oregon-American was ready to cut the timber. This arrangement greatly extended the financial means of Central Coal & Coke and Oregon-American for, as a practical matter, it served as a loan without the normal security provisions typically required in transactions of this size. By 1930, Ruth Realty held some 12,000 acres of timber for Oregon-American, enough to extend the life of the Vernonia mill by one third.

Moreover, the Northern Lines considered expanding the venture even more by securing distant timber for movement to Vernonia. This was evidenced by a proposal to acquire the Hammond-

BOOM TIMES ARRIVE

Like the sawmill proper, O-A built the machine shop building with concrete and steel. (W. C. Alexander photograph; Bill and Carol Ostrander collection)

Winton timber tract in the Trask River and Wilson River watersheds, nearly 50 miles southwest by rail from Vernonia. To reach this tract would have required extending the Gales Creek and Wilson River line more than 22 miles west over the Coast Range. While the Northern Lines never acted on the proposal, the fact they even discussed it illustrates how Keith and the carriers viewed the potential benefit of extending their mutual timber holdings.

Little wonder Oregon-American officials often referred to the company's connections with the Northern Lines as a "quasi partnership"; the strategic alliance forged by Keith, Budd, and Donnelly afforded Oregon-American control over its products all the way from the stump to its wholesale distribution points. As a measure of how important this arrangement was to the Great Northern and Northern Pacific, by 1930 rail shipments from the Vernonia line became the largest single source of originating SP&S traffic in the entire State of Oregon.

MARKETING OREGON-AMERICAN LUMBER

Central Coal & Coke Company sold most of the Oregon-American Lumber Company output under the Central Coal & Coke brand and through the parent company's existing distribution channels. The Portland market, lumber sold at O-A's retail outlet in Vernonia, and a small amount of export trade accounted for the balance.

Under the supervision of Harry T. Kendall, Central's vice president of sales, the sales organization worked out of Kansas City and concentrated on moving the product through its network of independent lumber wholesalers whose territories spanned most of the country. Although choosing not to extend its distribution network strategy into

The 102's train crew paused during mill construction duties to pose for this photograph. Between 1924 and 1928, it served as the main line engine hauling logs from Camp McGregor to the Vernonia mill. Its long wheelbase was hard on the logging railroad between the county line and Camp McGregor though, and engine 105, a smaller Baldwin 2-6-2, eventually replaced it.

During the Depression-era shutdown, O-A used the 102 to supply steam to the mill's powerhouse so that electrical service could continue uninterrupted.

O-A sold the 102 in 1938. (W. C. Alexander photograph; John T. Labbe collection)

retail sales, an approach used by a few very large operators like the Weyerhaeuser Timber Company and the Long-Bell Lumber Company, the wholesaler network method proved an effective one, and Oregon-American used it until Long-Bell acquired the operation in 1953, four years before the timber ran out.[5] And, by virtue that all Oregon-American side lumber was kiln-dried, several advantages accrued to the Central/O-A marketing plan. First, it afforded an element of exclusivity in that it was a seasoned product versus the green lumber produced by much of O-A's West Coast competition. Second, due to the superior nature of the kiln-dried product, Central could command price premiums for much of the mill's production.

A RAIL LINE TO THE WOODS

Returning to events in Oregon immediately following the O-A acquisition, with delays in the PA&P's completion adding up to more than nine months, Keith and Schopflin were extremely anxious to commence logging operations as quickly as possible so they could temporarily sell logs to mills along the Columbia and Willamette Rivers. The need for revenue to offset the heavy carrying costs for the mortgage and property taxes until mill operations and lumber shipments could begin was a pressing one, particularly because of the heavy construction costs that lay ahead for the mill.

Construction

Unlike many logging outfits, O-A eschewed used machinery, wire rope, and motive power and bought most of its equipment new. Consistent with this philosophy, the company took no shortcuts when it came to building its railroad. Far from mak-

Top: A Willamette Iron & Steel Works Humboldt yarder swinging logs from its right to a "hot deck" in a multiple donkey haul. Once it hauled in a log turn crews reconnected the logs to another yarder's rigging. The distant machine relayed the logs another stage closer to the track-side landing.

Two- and three-donkey hauls up to three-fourths of a mile long were common before bulldozers became a fixture in the woods. The new machines helped Oregon-American build its railroad spurs closer to the logging, so the company needed fewer donkeys. (W. C. Alexander photograph; Bill and Carol Ostrander collection)

§

Bottom: When it came time to complete the rail line to Camp McGregor, O-A's Mikados proved too heavy for the unballasted rail, so the company leased the SP&S's ten-wheeler, Number 156, to finish the job. (Oregon Historical Society, DHR SP&S #156C)

ing the logging line a stump-jumper, the company professionally engineered the entire line, closely following policies that governed gradients and curvature. For example, with very few exceptions, grades did not exceed 6.5 percent and when they did it was always a favorable grade to the downhill movement of loaded log cars. These practices continued to be a standard throughout the company's thirty-five-year operating life. Even so, building the railroad at times proved a daunting task.

Under the supervision of Natt McDougall, the A. Guthrie Company handled all the work to clear, grub, grade, and prepare the right-of-way west from the Clatsop/Columbia County line. Since the PA&P had not yet reached the county line and lacked means to move heavy equipment to the scene, most of the work was done by hand. Guthrie did hire a subcontractor equipped with a small donkey engine but the machine was inadequate for the task. By mid-July, 1922, the Guthrie crew had completed the O-A grade to the point where the Inman-Poulsen line would begin, some 3.4 miles beyond the county line. Clearing and grading of log spurs commenced, as did work to prepare the O-A campsite, which was to be on the I-P mainline, nearly a mile southwest of the O-A/I-P rail connection. However, with only a partially constructed, single and narrow right-of-way available to move equipment, progress was disappointingly slow.

To begin logging immediately upon completion of the railroad, orders were place with Willamette Iron and Steel Works for additional yarding and loading donkeys beyond the four Willamette Humboldt-type yarders the Eccleses had purchased in 1918 and had turned over to Central Coal & Coke when it acquired Oregon-American. McGregor contracted with Willamette to have sled logs installed on the donkeys at the factory so O-A

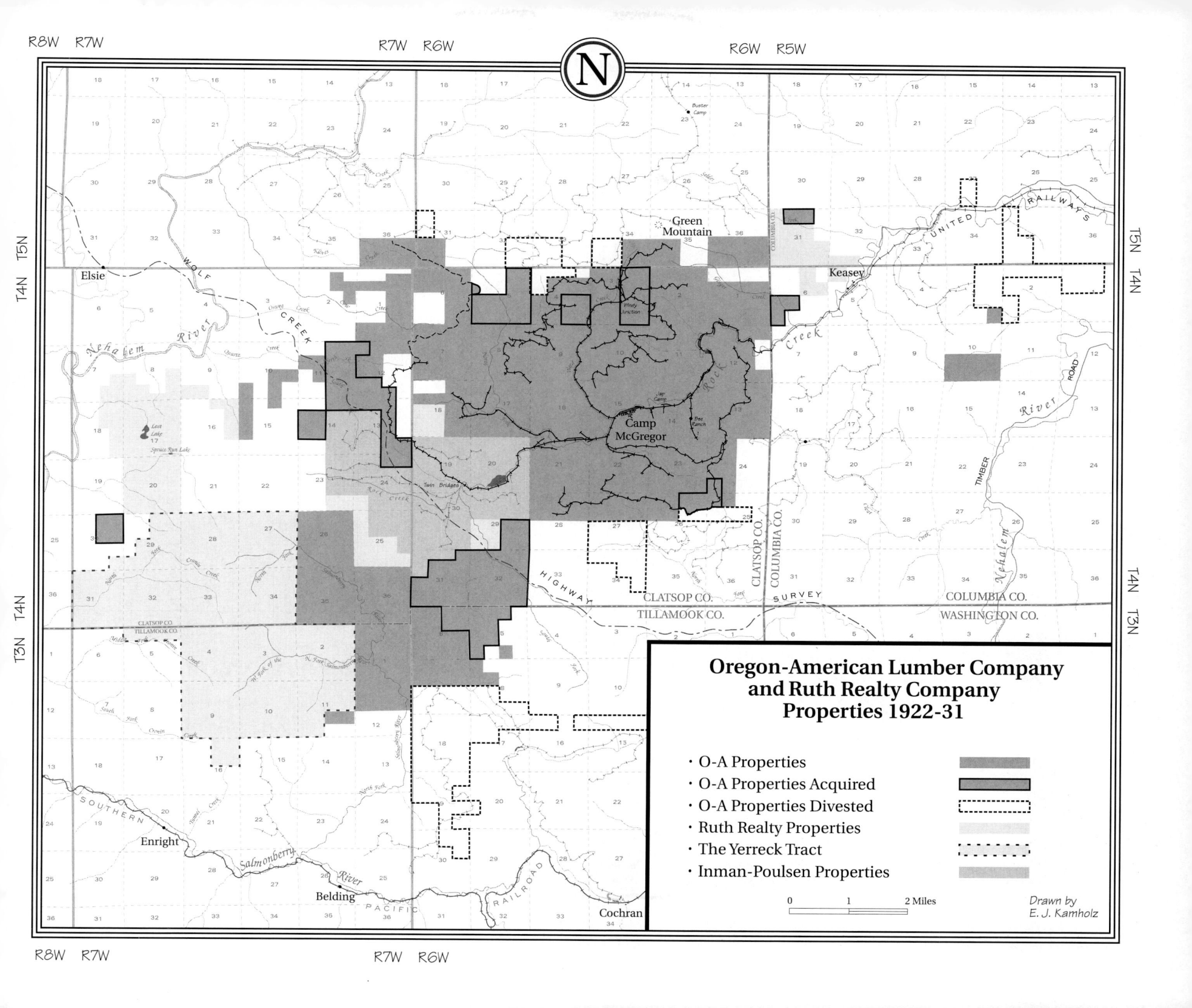

Oregon-American Lumber Company and Ruth Realty Company Properties 1922-31

- O-A Properties
- O-A Properties Acquired
- O-A Properties Divested
- Ruth Realty Properties
- The Yerreck Tract
- Inman-Poulsen Properties

0 1 2 Miles

Drawn by E. J. Kamholz

Keasey, Oregon in 1931

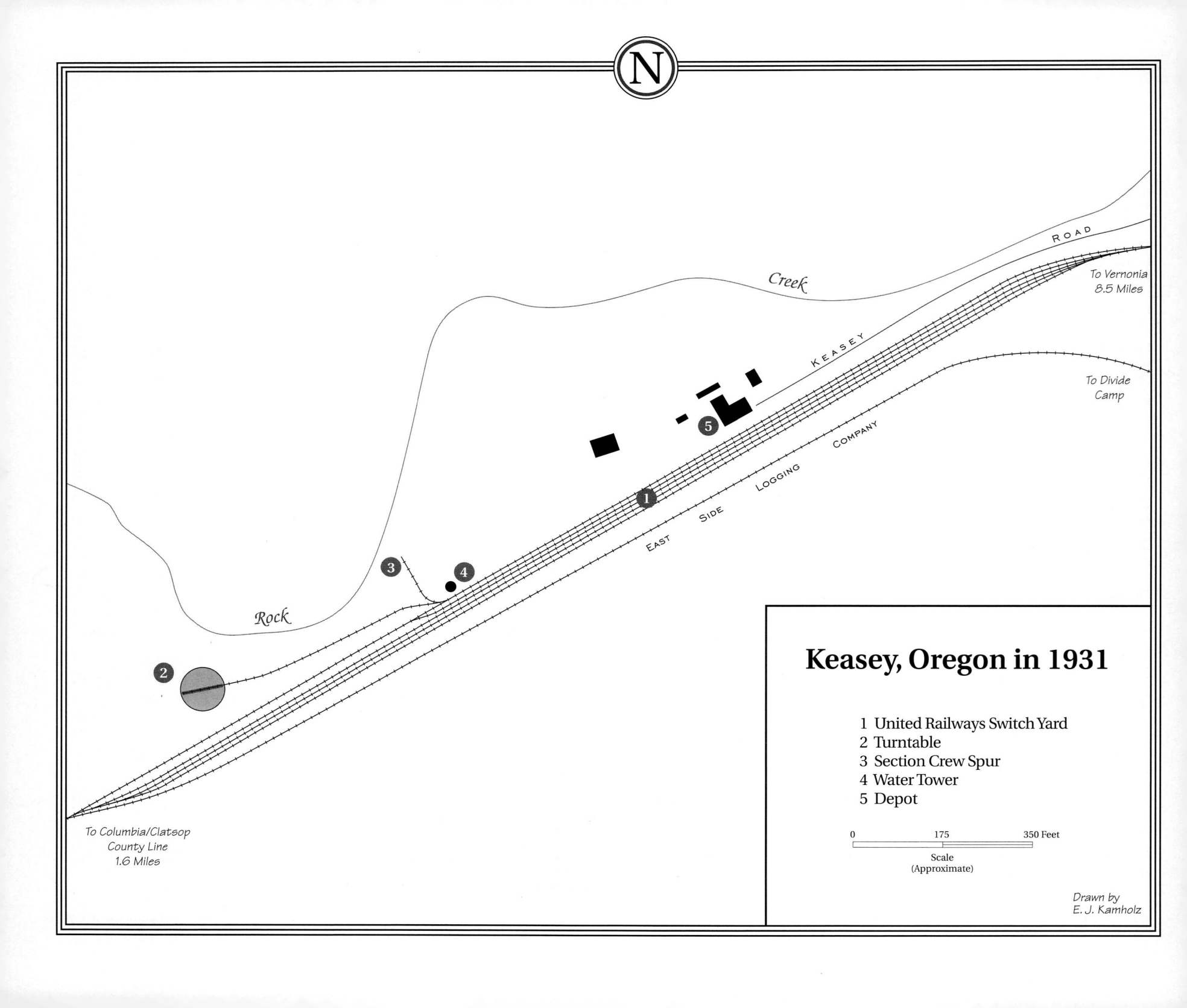

1. United Railways Switch Yard
2. Turntable
3. Section Crew Spur
4. Water Tower
5. Depot

To Vernonia 8.5 Miles

To Divide Camp

To Columbia/Clatsop County Line 1.6 Miles

Keasey Road

Rock Creek

East Side Logging Company

0 — 175 — 350 Feet
Scale (Approximate)

Drawn by E. J. Kamholz

Top: Oregon-American's initial logging cleared the main camp site in the fall of 1922. The company began building family houses at Camp McGregor in 1923. O-A named the camp after W. H. McGregor, who was a transplant from Central Coal & Coke operations in Texas. McGregor played a key role in O-A's purchase of Vernonia land for the mill and most of the after-acquired timber added to the original DuBois tract. (W. C. Alexander photograph, Margaret Taylor collection)

§

Bottom: Side view of one of the company's four Willamette Humboldt yarders. Oregon-American began logging nearly two years before the Vernonia mill opened. The company shipped raw logs over the United Railways line to Rafton and sold them on the open market. This provided a much-needed source of revenue while the mill was under construction. (W. C. Alexander photograph; Bill and Carol Ostrander collection)

could move them to the front and put them in service without delay. The United Railways, however, objected to the plan out of concern the assembled units would not clear the interurban electrical wires strung through Cornelius Pass tunnel.

After much arm-twisting on McGregor's part, United finally relented and allowed movement of two 11 × 13 loading engines mounted on sleds because, once on cars, their height of 18 feet, 4 inches above the rails cleared the interurban power lines running through the tunnel, although it was 7 inches less than the allowable clearance. The United did not acquiesce on movement of the larger donkeys, however, so O-A had to transport them

Left: A high-climber scales a future spar tree. All the timber in the new landing area has been felled. (H. Brown photograph; Rose Valpiani collection)

§

Right: The high-climber lopped off all the lower limbs on his ascent and has just topped the new spar tree. This was the most dangerous part of his job: if the trunk split when the top went over, he risked being crushed by his safety belt. (H. Brown photograph; Rose Valpiani collection)

Left: Once the top was felled and the tree stopped swaying, the climber could take a well-deserved breather. Next, he returned to the ground for a small pass block and line only to make the long climb back up the tree to begin rigging it with the heavier equipment needed for logging. (H. Brown photograph; Rose Valpiani collection)

§

Right: After the railroad and donkeys had moved in, crews finished rigging and began to log. (H. Brown photograph; Jim Blain collection)

An East Side Logging Company train at Keasey with a string of loaded disconnects bound for Rafton. Once dumped, East Side's logs were rafted up the Willamette River to its mill located under the east abutment of the Sellwood Bridge in Portland.

The curved spur to the left went to crew quarters for the United Railways' track workers. The middle spur led to a turntable used by the railway company's locomotives for their return trip. (Special Collections, University of Washington Libraries; photograph by C. Kinsey, Neg. 1063)

through the tunnel in pieces and add the sled logs later. By August 1922, McGregor had arranged to stage saws, axes, sledges, wedges, mauls, fuel, and oil at the initial landing sites. Crews rigged spar trees ahead of the donkeys' arrival so yarding could commence when they unloaded and moved the engines into position. The first logging site cleared an area for the main camp and logging headquarters. McGregor had falling crews clearing the site by September 1. Guthrie's nearby construction camp provided temporary living accommodations for O-A's woods crew.

With the arrival of the PA&P steel at the county line in late August 1922, the Guthrie crews developed an interchange yard at the Sitts ranch, located 1.8 miles east of the county line. This created a staging area for track crews to prebend rail and for O-A to store freight destined for the camp. Track-laying and ballasting on the O-A line beyond the county line began immediately.

O-A took delivery on its first logging locomotive, a new 70-ton, three-truck Lima shay, Road Number 103, in July 1922. Once the PA&P track-laying was completed, the shay departed for Vernonia under its own power. However, only 12 miles out of Portland, an eccentric blade failed, thus delaying the locomotive's arrival in the woods.

By September 20, O-A's twenty-man cutting crew had felled 1 million board feet of timber, and Guthrie had laid rails to the campsite. O-A established a rock pit on Turrish-owned property at the county line to supply ballast for the line. A loading

An Inman-Poulsen shay at Keasey with a load of logs bound for that company's Portland mill. Of all the logging operators in the Vernonia vicinity, Inman-Poulsen was the only one to use conventional skeleton and flatcars instead of disconnected trucks. (Special Collections, University of Washington Libraries; photograph by C. Kinsey, Neg. 1568)

donkey finished clearing the campsite before going to work on its first log-loading assignment on Spur 4, later to become the machine shop spur at camp. Oregon-American shipped its first train of logs to Rafton to dedicate the facility on October 10, 1922. Within three weeks, O-A had two logging sides in operation and daily log trains of twenty to thirty cars were moving to the river.

Disconnected Logging Trucks

Especially designed for use in hauling large logs of varying lengths, disconnected trucks were standard equipment on many private logging railroads in the Pacific Northwest. Their primary advantage lay in the fact they could transport logs longer than 40 feet, the upper limit of standard flatcars or skeleton log cars. Loads 100 feet long or more were feasible using disconnects because the weight of logs on the bunks provided the connecting force needed to keep loads from pulling apart. However, the fact that disconnects provided no means for connecting air lines meant that, apart from engine brakes, the only stopping power available was from brakemen walking the loaded logs from truck to truck, applying hand brakes on every two trucks in the hole between loads.

Another specialized feature of most disconnects was their low profile. Bunks, or the standards upon which the logs rested, were mounted closer to the rail than on common-carrier flatcars. Consistent with the low-profile design, most disconnect manufacturers mounted their couplers lower than the

Top and Bottom: Disconnected trucks allowed loggers to transport logs of varied lengths. The logs' weight kept the trucks from pulling apart. Couplers on disconnects were mounted lower than common-carrier equipment so locomotives needed adjustable-height drawheads. Due to the absence of air brakes, common carriers shunned handling disconnected trucks. To avoid the high cost of providing rigid-wheelbased log cars to loggers on the United Railways, however, the Northern Lines made an exception and became the only line in the Pacific Northwest, and perhaps the nation, to operate disconnected log trucks on a common-carrier line. Although conceding to the use of disconnects, United Railways drew the line on use of extended knuckles to connect couplers of different heights. In the woods, however, they were indispensable. Note the double-pocket drawhead.

Caulked boots worn by the brakies took an obvious toll on foot boards. (John T. Labbe photographs)

height of the bunks. This created misalignments when trainmen mixed disconnects with common-carrier equipment having standard-height couplers. The solution was to either use extended-length knuckles or install double-pocket drawheads on the common carrier equipment and switch couplers between the high and low pockets depending on the consist.

When word of O-A's plans to use disconnected trucks reached St. Paul, Budd and Donnelley advised that their use on the PA&P was unacceptable. That put SP&S officials in an awkward position: if the carriers denied O-A use of disconnects on the common-carrier line, then loggers would rightfully demand the railway company provide the necessary rolling stock to transport logs. The Northern Lines and their subsidiaries discussed alternatives at length and following a successful petition to the Interstate Commerce Commission on the matter, conditional approval for disconnects was granted. The provisions allowed use of disconnects on the United Railways west of Rafton but prohibited mixing disconnects with cars having standard-height couplers in the same train.

SP&S locomotives and cabooses in service on the United Railways/PA&P line were thus equipped with double-pocket coupler drawheads so they could couple with either type of car. United extended this arrangement to other log shippers along the PA&P including the East Side Logging Company, the Rock Creek Logging Company, and Beaver Creek Logging Company and to log shippers on the Gales Creek and Wilson River branch. By virtue of this arrangement the United Railways became the only common-carrier in the Pacific Northwest, and perhaps the nation, to allow regular operation of disconnected trucks over its rails.

O-A bought Willamette locomotive 106 in January 1927. Soon after it arrived, Clark Kinsey caught it, speeder 10, and Baldwin 105 at Camp McGregor. Caboose 367 shown behind the 105 is the original, long-wheelbased version built by the M. F. Brady Company of Portland. (Special Collections, University of Washington Libraries; photograph by C. Kinsey, Neg. 5378)

After Oregon-American began operating its mill in 1924, it reached more agreements with the Northern Lines. One provided for joint use of United Railways' tracks to Vernonia. Another called for joint maintenance on common track, telephone, and telegraph wires. Once O-A began hauling its logs to Vernonia, the distinction of using disconnects on the United Railways took an added dimension, for now a private operator was moving disconnects on a common-carrier line.

Railroad Activities Between the Woods and Rafton

When the Eccleses incorporated the PA&P as a common-carrier, their decision to acquire three 2-8-2s was consistent with the objective of hauling trains more than 40 miles to Rafton. However, once Central Coal & Coke took over and decided that concentrating solely on the movement of logs to the Vernonia mill better served its interests, it became evident the large, long wheelbased Mikados were miscast for their new role as woods engines. Alco had already shipped Road Numbers 100, 101, and 102 to Vancouver but the Keith-controlled Oregon-American refused to accept the 101. It was eventually resold to the Minarets & Western Railroad in Fresno, California, as that company's Road Number 101.[6] O-A did accept Numbers 100 and 102, however. The company rented the 100 to the SP&S during November 1922 but the engine saw little or no use after that. The 102 was pressed into service while the logging line was under construction. However, its weight proved too heavy to operate on the unballasted rail, so O-A had to lease the SP&S's Number 156, a 58-ton ten-wheeler, for work laying rail and ballasting.

O-A used the shay to haul logs and empty disconnects between the woods and Sitts and the 102 to haul equipment between Sitts and Vernonia.

53

Oregon-American evidently neglected to specify a road number when ordering the 104. Consequently, Baldwin christened it Number 1. Pictured at Camp McGregor, the factory paint striping is still visible. (Special Collections, University of Washington Libraries; photograph by C. Kinsey, Neg. 2518)

Nevertheless, even after ballasting the line to Camp, the Mikado was still too heavy and its wheelbase too long for low-maintenance service over the light rail and sharp curves beyond the county line. Number 100 was later picked up by the Weed Lumber Company of Weed, California.[7]

The SP&S provided the motive power on the United Railways/PA&P line and switched O-A's loaded disconnects at Sitts, along with those of the East Side Logging Company. Following the practice of other operators using disconnects, the railway company positioned the heaviest loads toward the front near the locomotive to reduce the likelihood of trains pulling apart. The consists were generally limited to between twelve and seventeen loads that were the most two consolidation-type engines could lift over the Tophill grade.[8] Once United dumped the loads at Rafton, the railway company returned empty disconnects to the woods the following day.[9] This became the standard operating procedure for handling disconnects over the United Railways between the county line and Rafton.[10]

When terms for the joint-use contract with the United Railways were established in 1924, Oregon-American was limited to moving a maximum twenty-six sets of trucks between the county line and Vernonia. United allowed the larger number because of the favorable ruling grade on loaded eastbound trains as far as Vernonia. Beyond twenty-six loads, however, the risk of cars separating became too great so that became the standard consist for the run.

For many reasons O-A's railroad start-up problems really never came under control until after mill construction was finished. Initially, track ballasting delayed log trains. Next, the United Railways often failed to schedule enough trains to guarantee a twenty-four-hour turnaround of disconnects between Sitts and Rafton. And, once the line between the O-A camp and its property was completed, Inman-Poulsen also began shipping logs to Sitts for interchange with the railway company. Further congestion was created when O-A contracted with A. Guthrie & Company to construct its Spur 5 system. That added even more inbound traffic, hauling rail, ties, ballast, and fasteners.

The Oregon-American and Inman-Poulsen trackage arrangement was an oddity in its own right. Established when Inman-Poulsen bought its tract from the David Eccles Company-controlled Oregon-American, it called for I-P to own the rail line west from what eventually would become Oregon-American's Spur 1. Accordingly, Inman-Poulsen owned the last mile of the main line to O-A's logging camp and the next mile or so beyond that to the border of the two companies' timber tracts. A further oddity arose after Central Coal acquired Oregon-American when Inman-Poulsen placed its headquarters camp on O-A's property, just a few hundred yards east of the property line.

The Inman-Poulsen upper camp and pond. Oregon-American bought the old track and negotiated a rights-of-way deed, allowing it to build new lines across Inman-Poulsen's property after I-P completed its operations in 1930.

When O-A reorganized following the Depression, one of the first jobs it undertook was to bypass the pond trestle that burned in the 1933 Wolf Creek Fire. The new line skirted the south perimeter of the pond to the right. (Special Collections, University of Washington Libraries; photograph by C. Kinsey, Neg. 1569)

While unclear why the Eccleses chose to sell Inman-Poulsen that particular part of the DuBois tract, the effect was to isolate the entire southwest segment of O-A's timber from the rest of its stand. Had Inman-Poulsen refused to grant Oregon-American a deed allowing unlimited right-of-way access over I-P's tract once they had logged it, it is highly unlikely Keith would have bought the property in the first place. While technically competitors, both companies had ample reason to coexist in harmony, first because they were guests on each other's property, and second because O-A had a future interest in I-P's cutover lands.

Oregon-American purchased a used, 40-ton Industrial Works wrecking crane from the E. T. Chapin Company of Spokane in September 1922. The company had the machine moved from Bovill, Idaho, to the SP&S shops in Vancouver for minor repairs before placing it in service. Its first duty assignment was to load gravel at the rock pit, but immediately following its arrival an operator accidentally dropped the boom, damaging it so extensively it had to be returned to the SP&S shops in Vancouver for repair.

No sooner had O-A's crane been fixed than Nehalem Boom Company's Rafton unloading crane tipped over into the Willamette Slough. At the urgent request of the SP&S, O-A lent the boom company its locomotive crane so log unloading could continue. While this kept logs moving to market, it also caused further delays in ballasting operations until the SP&S loaned its crane Number M-30 to replace O-A's while it was unloading logs at Rafton. Shay 103 also proved too heavy for the

Looking southwest over the Inman-Poulsen pond from the dam. I-P's upper camp is visible behind and to the right of the long trestle. I-P built the pond to stockpile logs during good weather to guarantee a steady winter supply for its Portland mill. (Special Collections, University of Washington Libraries; photograph by C. Kinsey, Neg. 1570)

poorly ballasted logging road and derailed, bending an axle in the process. That resulted in its return to the SP&S shops for repairs.

Because of the onset of the winter of 1922–23, O-A had to buy an additional 125 carloads of sand from the SP&S to complete the ballasting of its main line. The United Railways had its share of congestion to contend with too, for it had to ship some 250 carloads of sand from the St. Johns cut in North Portland to ballast its line between Wilkesboro and the county line.

Log deliveries were also delayed due to insufficient quantities of disconnected trucks. Only after operations were underway did it become apparent O-A needed the equivalent of three trainloads of trucks to maintain uninterrupted logging; one set loaded on the United Railways, one set loaded between the camp and Sitts, and one set of empties loaded at the donkey engines. Still, as logging operations continued expanding into 1926, even more trucks were needed until O-A had acquired a total of 135 sets.

O-A bought all its disconnected trucks from the Northwestern Equipment Company. Early shipments were equipped with bunks mounted rigidly to the truck frames. The bunks' inability to swivel their loads while the cars negotiated curves eventually caused them to fail and required the addition of kingpins and bolsters. Apart from this, the only recurring problem with the disconnects occurred when brakemen overapplied the brakes once loads were underway, thus causing flat wheels.

Given the large requirement for crushed rock needed for concrete mill foundations, plus that needed for additional ballasting on the expanding logging railroad, O-A purchased a new 120-cubic-yard-per-day–capacity rock-crushing plant in April 1923 and installed it on the Henry Turrish-controlled Appledale Land Company property located

Until 1922 the locals simply called it the Sitts ranch. The railroad arrived in August that year. By 1923 authorities had renamed it Keasey when a post office of that name was moved there from its former location, which was renamed Homewood. By 1924, the East Side Logging Company, shown here, had set up camp and was logging its way south.

Between 1922 and 1930, the United Railways, Oregon-American, Inman-Poulsen, and East Side accounted for as many as a dozen trains a day through Keasey. By 1933 it was all but shut down for the Depression. United Railways completely stopped passenger service on the line in 1934.

Oregon-American was the only outfit generating traffic to or from the place after resuming operations in 1936. O-A's last log rolled through on August 27, 1957.

Today Keasey is silent and largely grown over. Only small reminders survive to hint at its busy past. (Special Collections, University of Washington Libraries; photographed by C. Kinsey, Neg. 1054)

immediately west of the county line. Original estimates called for 3,000 cubic yards of crushed rock for foundations and ballast. However, after the machine had been in operation for three months, Schopflin and McGregor learned that total crushed rock requirements were nearly 10,000 cubic yards. So, only by double-shifting crusher operations and purchasing still more crushed rock from the railway company were those requirements eventually met.

The United Railways provided locomotive-turning facilities at Sitts in 1922 by installing an 80-foot turntable that had formerly been used at SP&S's Fallbridge (Wishram) yard.[11]

Once the Northern Lines took over the Portland, Astoria & Pacific and placed it under United Railways's control, there was no need to maintain its separate identity. So, on December 1, 1923, the United absorbed the assets and dissolved the PA&P.[12]

Other Logging Operators Using the United Railways in the Vernonia Area

Inman-Poulsen began shipping logs shortly after the line to its tract was opened in 1922. I-P owned a mill in Portland and was the only outfit served by the railway company west of Vernonia to haul logs on conventional flatcars equipped with air brakes instead of disconnects. Beaver Creek Logging Company (later to become Connacher Logging Company) began shipping logs to Rafton from Beaver Spur near PA&P milepost 17.7, south of Vernonia, in late October 1922. Shortly after that, Koster Products Company also began shipping logs to Rafton from Koster Spur near PA&P milepost 16.

Koster later built four more interconnecting spurs. The first of these, Koster Number Two, was at PA&P milepost 16.7. Another was at McPherson (PA&P milepost 20.1). Koster built two more spurs on the line west of Vernonia. The first one was near

BOOM TIMES ARRIVE

O-A began unloading logs in the Vernonia millpond on April 1, 1924, long before it was full of water. O-A initially used the locomotive crane before the Willamette electric unloading engine was installed. (Oregon Historical Society # OrHi 7854)

Poynter (United Railways milepost 40.6) and was built in 1927. Koster built the other at Homewood (United Railways milepost 43.2) in 1934.

When United Railways disbanded the PA&P in 1923, it changed mileposts to reflect mileages from United Junction (Linnton) instead of from Wilkesboro, thus adding 16.4 miles to the former company's mileposts. (See Appendix B for a complete list of PA&P, United Railways, and SP&S mileposts.)

In late 1923, the East Side Logging Company began setting up operations at the Sitts ranch yards for logging the Detroit Trust Company lands managed by the McPherson Brothers that lay to the south.[13] A year later, an East Side offshoot, the Rock Creek Logging Company, built a spur to the south of Lausmann (United Railways milepost 45.6) where it served logging operations there until 1926 when its equipment and steel were moved to East Side operations.

Sitts Ranch and Keasey

By July 1923 the O-A camp and the East Side staging area at Sitts ranch were home for hundreds of full- and part-time residents. Absence of postal services became a serious problem as the nearest post office was at Keasey, then at PA&P milepost 26.8.[14]

Supported by McGregor, Antone Lausmann, president of East Side Logging Company, successfully petitioned postal authorities to have the post office moved from Keasey to Sitts ranch. Difficulties were encountered getting the name changed from Keasey to Sitts, however, so they simply moved the old post office to Sitts and renamed the yards Keasey. The PA&P station at the "old" Keasey was renamed Homewood.

THE VERNONIA MILL

Locating the mill no farther east than Vernonia was a major consideration for the Northern Lines

Shortly after O-A installed the Willamette log unloader, the company replaced its original boom with the wrecking boom from the locomotive crane. (H. Brown photograph; Rose Valpiani collection)

when it came to terms with Charles Keith. While at first glance this demand might have seemed arbitrary, it had a practical side. Despite the fact that Vernonia lacked any size or infrastructure, it was the first place along the railroad east of O-A's timber holdings that offered enough flat land and an adequate water supply needed to support a mill of the required size.

Siting

Central withheld public announcement of the Oregon-American mill's location until February 1923, a deliberate ploy designed to help McGregor negotiate the lowest possible prices for land.[15]

Beginning in late 1921 McGregor, directly and through intermediaries, acquired a number of parcels situated between the southern and eastern city limits of Vernonia and the northern banks of the Nehalem River. Eager to have the mill in Vernonia, local government, civic, and business leaders strove to accommodate in every way possible to curry Oregon-American's favor and convince company officials to move there. The tactic to delay formal announcement that Vernonia would be the mill site worked for a while and the amount paid for land in town was pretty close to what the company had hoped to pay. Yet due to the obvious fact that someone was accumulating a large tract, the townspeople became thoroughly convinced by July 1922 that O-A was going to build its mill in Vernonia. Eventually, McGregor realized any advantage to keeping the company's plans secret had been lost, so he made the announcement official. McGregor was eventually able to block up 278 acres for the mill site and company housing developments in Vernonia and its outskirts.

Design

Plans for the Oregon-American mill were prepared in Kansas City during 1921 and 1922. Central

BOOM TIMES ARRIVE

The 105 started its career in the woods but worked the log-haul to Vernonia if the 102 needed repairs. Judging by its shiny appearance, this scene took place shortly after O-A took delivery on the little Baldwin in 1925 but before the company modified its pilot by adding full-length foot boards, making it more suitable for work in the woods.

The mill's wigwam-style refuse burner is on the right. Maintaining its appearance was difficult. Paint never proved satisfactory because it burned and left a white residue. In later years, O-A encircled the upper part with pipes and nozzles and pumped oil to the top to mist down the sides. That worked best of all. (H. Brown photograph; Vivian Laird Reynolds collection)

set a target completion date for summer 1924. Central retained John Monoghan to design the mill. During his career, Monoghan had developed a reputation as a peerless mill designer. Central hired Bill Atkins to manage the mill's construction. Like Monoghan, Atkins was regarded as one of the best mill builders alive.

While the mill was large by every measure, it was noteworthy for much more than its size alone. According to early issues of the local weekly newspaper, the *Vernonia Eagle*, the mill was the largest mill of its kind ever built, possessed the largest all-electrically driven planing mill in the United States, was the only sawmill in the Pacific Northwest constructed of steel and concrete, contained the most thoroughly equipped sorting shed in the country, and had the finest machine shop west of the Mississippi.[16] Except the fact the sawmill was unique for being constructed of steel and concrete, the rest of these claims were exaggerated. Larger mills either existed or were under construction then, both as to size and cutting capacity, including Long-Bell Lumber Company's two mills at Longview, Washington.

Even so the Vernonia mill was a large one, having a rated capacity of 350,000 board feet per eight-hour shift, with sufficient facilities beyond the sawmill to handle double-shift production. When running continuously at full production it could produce 180 million board feet of lumber annually. This placed the Vernonia plant in the elite ranks of the largest-scale lumber producers on the West Coast.

Perhaps of greater significance than size alone was

Top: Will Gibson, pond foreman, standing on the log slip. Once inside the mill, logs were trimmed to length and staged on the deck to await loading on the log carriages. Oregon-American's peak years of production occurred between 1926 and 1930 when the sawmill ran on a full, two-shift basis operating both head rigs. The company built cold decks to keep the mill supplied during winter months.

To the left at the east end of the pond is the Johnston & McGraw shingle mill built in 1925 to cut the company's cedar logs. The shingle mill burned in 1936 and was never rebuilt. (H. Brown photograph; Columbia County Historical Museum)

§

Bottom: The Willamette electric log-unloading engine. (Ken Schmelzer collection)

The Process of Making Lumber at the Vernonia Mill
(Indicates production flow only. See mill map for physical plant layout.)

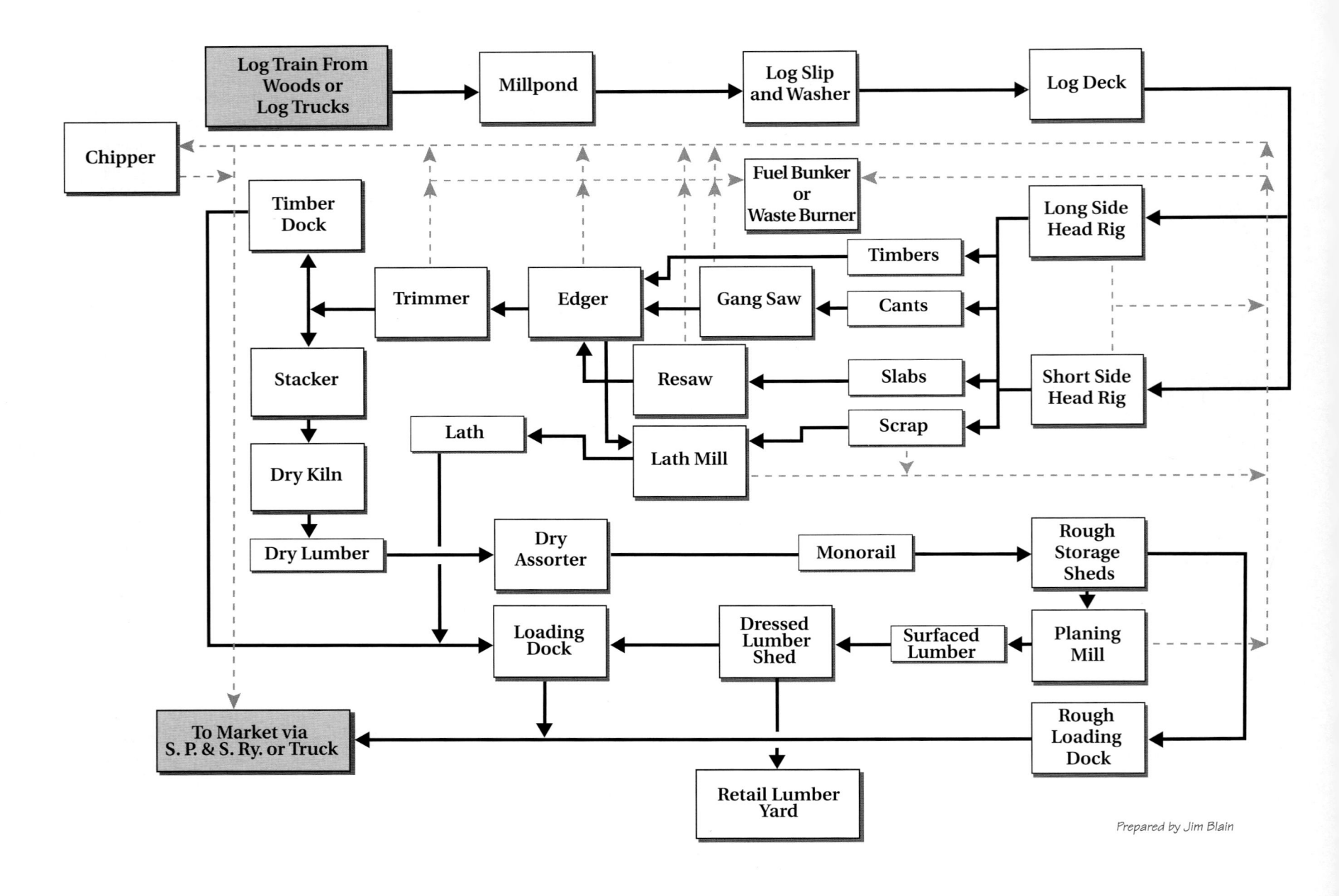

Prepared by Jim Blain

the fact it was a "rail mill," thus totally dependent on logs supplied from the immediate vicinity and on the single railroad that shipped its finished products to market. When viewed in light of the fact that most large sawmill operators chose to locate on major waterways to take advantage of logs supplied from many suppliers, the immensity of Keith's decision to locate the mill more than 40 rail-miles from the nearest open log market can be appreciated.

Many in the industry viewed the decision to construct the sawmill of steel and concrete instead of wood as near-blasphemy. This was done solely to reduce risk of loss due to fire. Despite the controversy caused by building the sawmill building with materials in direct competition with wood, the resulting savings in insurance premiums were substantial enough to rank alongside underweights as a key economic factor in the company's financial structure and provided sufficient advantages to offset any embarrassment created by the criticism of fellow lumber producers.

Another distinguishing feature of the mill was its

Once on the carriage, logs were squared and cut to desired dimensions on one of two Filer & Stowell head rigs. The photographer captured this one midway through the process on the long-side, right-hand rig.

The mill's two carriages were shotgun-feed types. A 16-inch steam cylinder propelled them back and forth. Power for each saw was provided by 240-horsepower electric motors. Head rigs cut only on the carriages' forward strokes. An offset on each carriage provided clearance for the return stroke. Set works were electrically operated, the dogs by air. A block setter rode the carriage and positioned logs according to hand signals given by the sawyer. The sawyer controlled the rate at which the carriage moved logs into the saw. (H. Brown photograph; Jim Blain collection)

The Oregon-American Lumber Company Mill at Vernonia, Oregon

1. PA&P /United Railways/SP&S Depot (Elevation 620')
2. PA&P /United Railways/SP&S Switchyard
3. Japanese Colony
4. Hindu Bunkhouse
5. Negro Colony
6. Filipino Colony
7. Mill Construction Camp
8. Public School
9. Lumber Storage Dock
10. Dressed Lumber Shed
11. Car Scale
12. Scrap Wood Conveyor
13. Rough Lumber Dock
14. Planing Mill
15. Monorail System
16. Rough Lumber Storage Sheds
17. Yukon Spur
18. Crane Run
19. Timber Ramps
20. Dry Lumber Assorter
21. Drying Kilns and Transfer
22. Stacker
23. Locomotive Shed
24. Locomotive Fuel Tank
25. Machine Shop and Car Repair
26. Refuse Burner
27. Sawmill and Sizer
28. Power House
29. Fuel Bunker
30. Log Slip
31. Pond
32. Drag Saw
33. Lock Decker
34. Water Treatment and Pumping Plant
35. Log Loader
36. Truck Log Dump
37. Train Log Dump
38. Johnston & McGraw Shingle Mill (1925–1936)
39. Office
40. O-A Hill (Company Housing Development)
41. Drinking Water Reservoir
42. Non-Potable Water Reservoir

Drawn by E. J. Kamholz

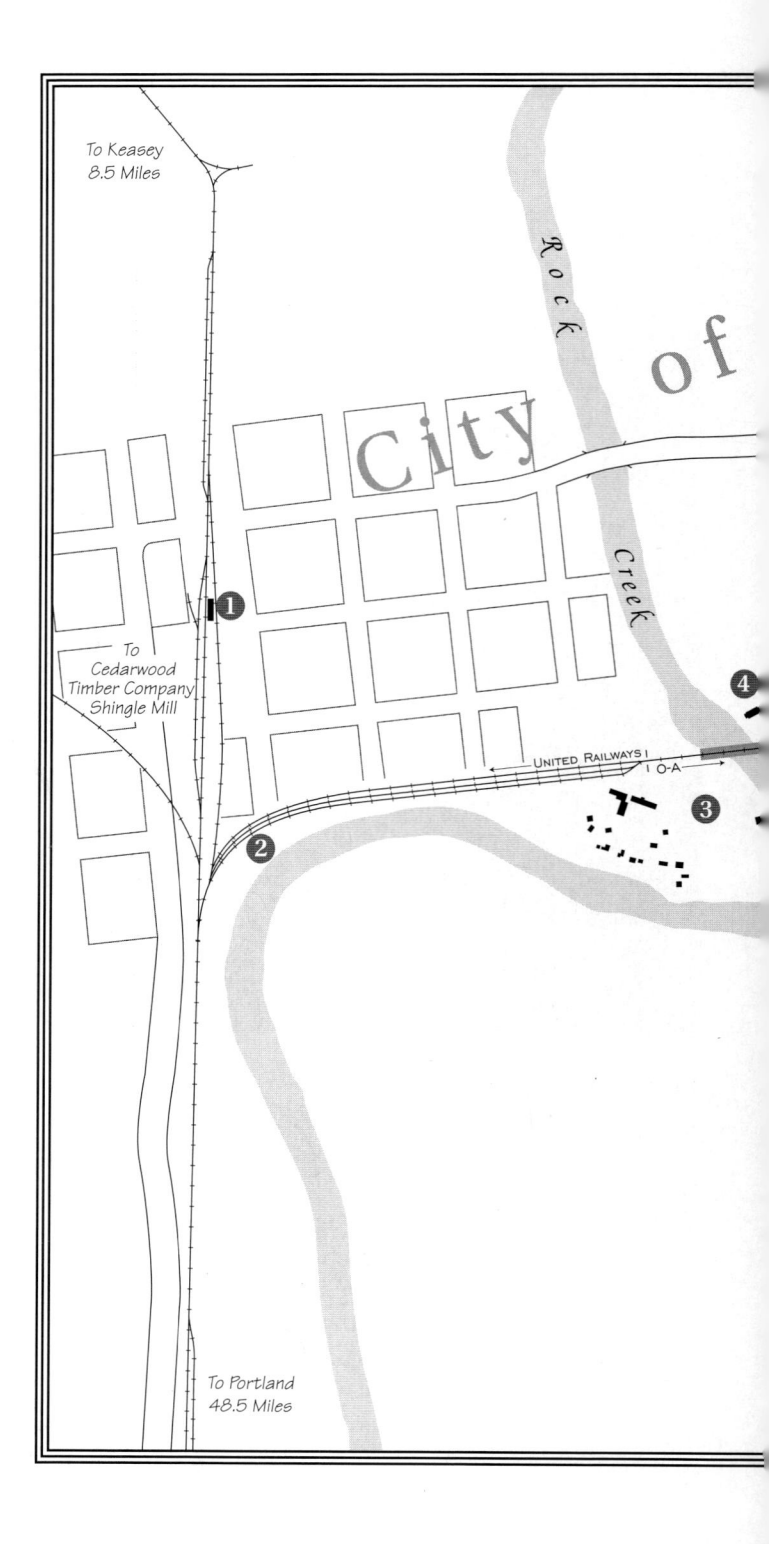

N

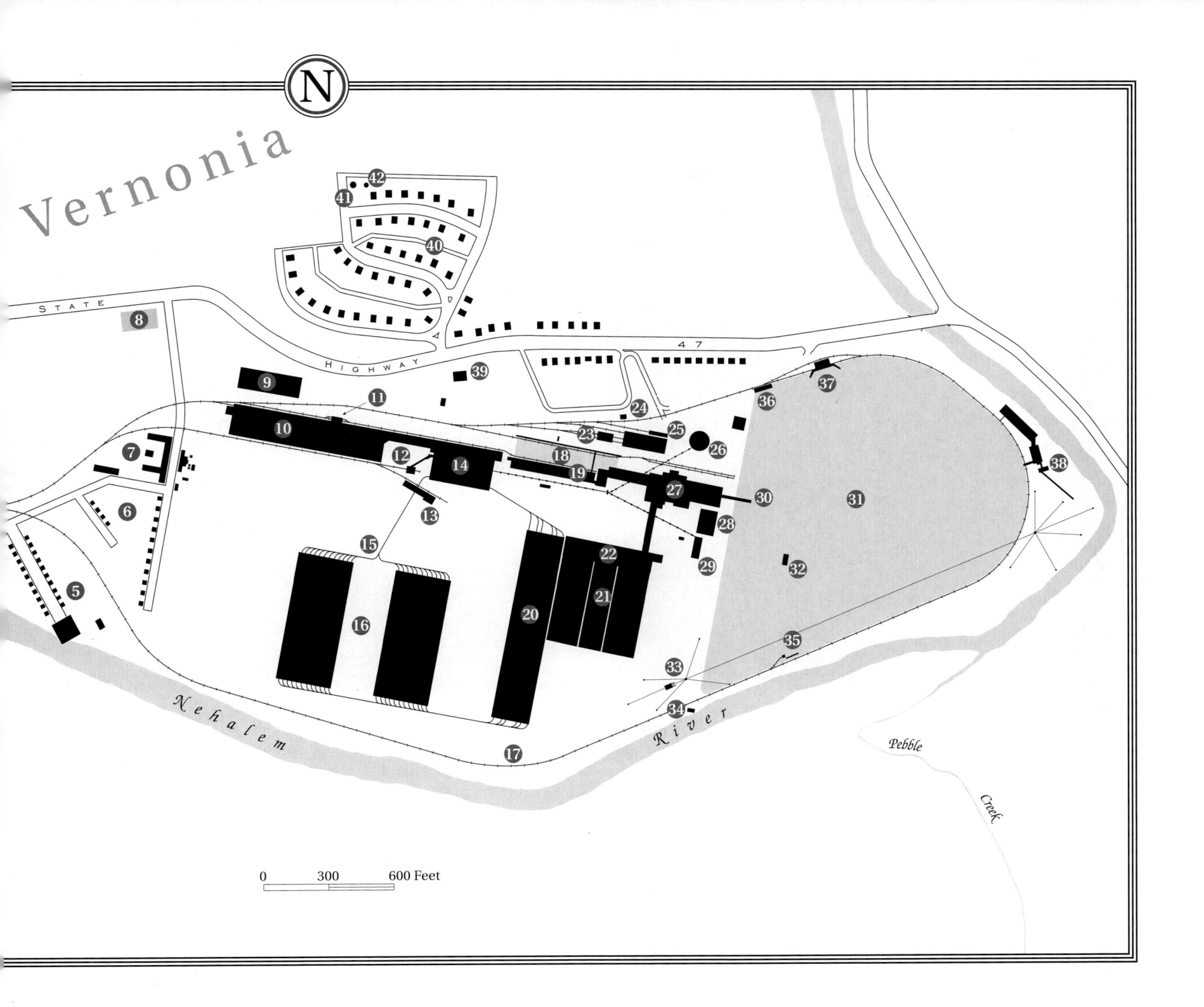

Vernonia

STATE

HIGHWAY 47

Nehalem River

Pebble Creek

0   300   600 Feet

BOOM TIMES ARRIVE

The short-side, left-hand rig had a bandsaw with a 10-foot clearance and handled logs up to 24 feet in length. Its long-side counterpart had a 9-foot saw and its carriage could accommodate logs as long as 40 feet. (H. Brown photograph; Rose Valpiani collection)

dedicated on-site power-generating plant, which not only provided sufficient electricity to meet the needs of the mill but also supplied all company houses with electricity. While Vernonia's privately owned electrical utility, the Vernonia Light and Power Company (which subsequently failed and was taken over by Oregon Gas & Electric Company) began serving Vernonia in 1923, for years the power company was unable to meet all the demands placed on it.[17] The utility therefore had to contract for surplus power generated by the Oregon-American plant as well as for back-up power when its own system went down.

The decision to electrify the mill had other implications too. The most notable was the decision to not use a stationary-wheel drive power arrangement from which other mill equipment was powered by belt-driven power takeoffs.[18] Instead, almost every phase of the Vernonia mill operation, except the band-mill carriages, kilns,

Table 3.1

Major Vernonia Mill Structures

Length and Width (in feet)

Structure	Dimensions
Sawmill	92 × 354
Powerhouse	82 × 116
Fuel Bunker	36 × 100
Timber Sizer	50 × 192
Timber Dock & Crane Run	76 × 511
Transfer to Stacker	30 × 237
Stacker	84 × 472
Front & Rear Kiln Platforms (2)	156 × 328 (each)
Dry Kilns (28)	11 × 110 (each)
Dry Assorter	180 × 888
Rough Storage Sheds (2)	258 × 594 (each)
Planing Mill	120 × 288
Dressed Shed	108 × 728
Car Loading Platform	80 × 1338
Machine Shop	70 × 200
Mill Pond	36.57 acres built with a uniform depth of 5 feet and equipped with three unloading dumps (two for rail, one of which was a backup, and one for motor trucks). Each dump well had a 12-foot depth.[25]
Monorail System	More than 5 miles in length.[26]

and other steam or air-driven equipment, were powered directly by electric motors, each with a capacity geared precisely to the needs of a particular operation.[19]

Y*ou know the farmer loads they used to sell at the retail lumber yard in Vernonia? Miscellaneous lengths and stuff? It was miscellaneous lengths alright, but it was all good lumber, not a knot in it. I paid eleven dollars a thousand feet for it. Built a house out of it. Good stuff.*

Not long ago I went down and bought a board and paid eight dollars and some cents for it. It was about 8 feet long, maybe 7 inches wide and pine. Pine's cheaper than fir. And the board had knots in it. Eight bucks for one board like that? And I bought a thousand feet for eleven dollars? Unbelievable! Down at Vernonia, they didn't sell junk like that. That was crap. They burned it in the burner.

George Lee, construction

Of course, the dry kilns were another major distinguishing feature. Other Douglas fir–region operators copied Oregon-American by installing kilning facilities of their own. However, based on seasoned lumber produced in comparison to total mill production, O-A consistently kiln-dried more of its total output than any other operator in the region.

As a final note on the uniqueness of the mill, no stone was left unturned in its design to mechanize operations and minimize labor content in the cost of manufacture. While perhaps not revolutionary in that respect, the mill was every bit as much "state-of-the-art" as the technology of the day would allow.[20]

After cants were sawed by the head rigs, they went to a 52-inch Wickes gang saw located in the center of the sawmill. There a crane stacked the cants on top of one another so that multiple cants could be gang-sawed at the same time. The two steam-powered cylinders above the machine pressed guide rollers on top of the stacked cants as they were fed through the saw. (H. Brown photograph; Jim Blain collection)

Construction

Atkins and his initial crew of twenty-five men arrived in Vernonia to begin construction in April 1923. The construction crew eventually grew to nearly 200. Since the town of Vernonia was unable to provide even rudimentary facilities to house and feed the workers, Atkins's first project was to build a bunkhouse, kitchen, dining room, meat and potato houses, and a cook's house. Atkins subcontracted this project to C. H. Bigelow who completed it early in May 1923.[21]

Once construction started, Central appointed E. E. "Edward" Hayes from Delta Land & Timber Company's Carson, Louisiana, plant as Oregon-American's first general superintendent.[22] Hayes was ideally suited for the task because he had earlier distinguished himself by getting the Carson mill rebuilt and running only eighty-three days after a fire had destroyed it.[23]

Atkins added other major contractors and suppliers including Whitten & Bryant, who cleared the mill site between August 1922 and the spring of 1923, and the A. Guthrie & Company, who built the railroad trestle across Rock Creek between the United Railways mainline in Vernonia and the mill site. Guthrie's crews also excavated the millpond. Milwaukee Bridge & Iron Company constructed foundations for machinery and heavy equipment, and Filer and Stowell of Milwaukee, Wisconsin, supplied much of the lumber-manufacturing equipment.[24] Pawling & Harnischfeger Company, also of Milwaukee, provided the monorail system used to transport bundled lumber to and from the kilns, rough sheds, rough dock, and the planing mill. North Coast Dry Kiln Company of Seattle constructed the dry kilns and Herbert S. Hare, landscape architect, laid out the company housing tract on what was to become known as the O-A Hill. A summary of major build-

Souvenir for
WITH NORTHEASTERN RETAIL LUMBERMEN'S ASSOCIATION SPECIAL

Old Growth Yellow Fir Timbers Car Material

ALL YARD STOCK KILN DRIED

VERNONIA, OREGON, MILL

CENTRAL COAL AND COKE COMPANY
KANSAS CITY, MO.

KILN DRIED DIMENSION

KILN DRIED COMMON BOARDS

Central Coal & Coke printed invitations to the July 10, 1924 dedication of the Vernonia mill on thin pieces of wood. (Kamholz collection)

ings and their dimensions shows just how large the mill, in fact, was (see Table 3.1).

The inner workings of the mill were no less impressive. A large conveyor, or "slip," transported logs from the pond to the sawmill deck. There, the logs were cut to length and distributed to either of two Filer and Stowell band mill head rigs. The "short-side," left-hand rig could handle logs up to 10 feet in diameter and 24 feet long. The "long-side," right-hand rig could cut logs up to 9 feet in diameter and 40 feet long.

"Cants," or the large pieces cut by the head rigs, were transported by a system of live rolls to the 52-inch Wickes gang saw or, after edging, to the timber dock. The gang saw could cut up to forty-four, 1-inch-thick boards simultaneously, and more if multiple cants were stacked and sawed at the same time. A horizontal resaw cut up to 4-inch thicknesses of lumber out of the rounded edge-slabs. A lath mill was located within the sawmill proper and further refined small slab wood scraps into lath strips.

Once edged and trimmed to length, boards were conveyed to a stacker and loaded on small railcars for kiln-drying. Central originally constructed the mill with twenty-eight North Coast Kiln Company forced-circulation kilns and one "Simmons," natural-circulation kiln. The Simmons kiln was the invention of R. A. Simmons, Oregon-American's chief engineer. An employee of Central Coal & Coke's southern pine operations, Simmons came to Vernonia in 1923 while the mill was under construction. His kiln design was a source of wide study in the industry, and a Booth-Kelly plant in Springfield, Oregon, later installed a number of them.[27]

Once dried, boards passed through the dry assorter for further segregation by dimension, grade, and length, then they were stacked and moved by monorail to the rough sheds for storage. Whether for stock

BOOM TIMES ARRIVE

The gang saw was adjustable for board width and operated on a 20-inch stroke. It could saw up to forty-two boards simultaneously from a block of stacked cants at a forward rate of 5/8 to 3/4 of an inch per stroke.

The feed rolls visible at the base of the saws propelled the cants forward and were steam-driven. (H. Brown photograph; Columbia County Historical Museum)

or to fill specific orders, monorails took boards from the rough sheds to either the rough loading dock for shipping or the planing mill for surfacing. The planing mill had eight planers and two molding mills. Once surfaced, boards were either stored in the dressed, or "slick" shed, or loaded directly on to waiting freight cars. Initially, workers transported finished products to railcars using hand-operated buggies. For large packages, they used horse-drawn carts. The company also constructed a retail lumber yard across the tracks from the loading dock to service the local lumber trade.

Power for the mill was generated by four 761-horsepower Sterling vertical-tubed, superheated boilers. The boilers operated at a pressure of 200 pounds per square inch and provided live steam to power the head rig carriages, air compressor, and dry kilns. Steam also propelled three General Electric generators. Two of the turbines had a 2,000-kilowatt capacity and a standby turbine had a 500-kilowatt capacity. Steam also powered the motor generator. Large "cyclones" blew mill waste from various parts of the mill to a concrete fuel bunker or the refuse burner. From the fuel bunker waste was conveyed to the powerhouse to fuel the Dutch ovens that heated the boilers.

With mill construction nearly complete, work commenced to fill the millpond during the spring of 1924. By early April Oregon-American ceased shipments to Rafton and began using its own trains to haul logs directly from the woods to Vernonia.[28] Thursday, July 10, 1924, "The Most Perfect Mill In the World," according the *Vernonia Eagle*, sawed its first log.[29] A special excursion train from Portland marked the dedication ceremonies. It carried many state and regional government officials along with an assortment of prominent business leaders. The train included two dining cars in the consist.[30] Quoting from the *Portland Journal* account of the event, the *Eagle* reported:

> The whistles blew at the magnificent new mill of the Oregon-American Lumber Company, Vernonia, the 225 men took their allotted places, the machinery was started by the electric power generated at the mill and the plant was put into operation for the first time. There was no fanfare or trumpets and no speech-making to inaugurate the new large scale enterprise. It just began to saw wood.[31]

The Lumber Contents of a Douglas Fir Log

This log might be cut in a number of ways. The purpose of the illustration is to show the portion of a log from which various items are cut.

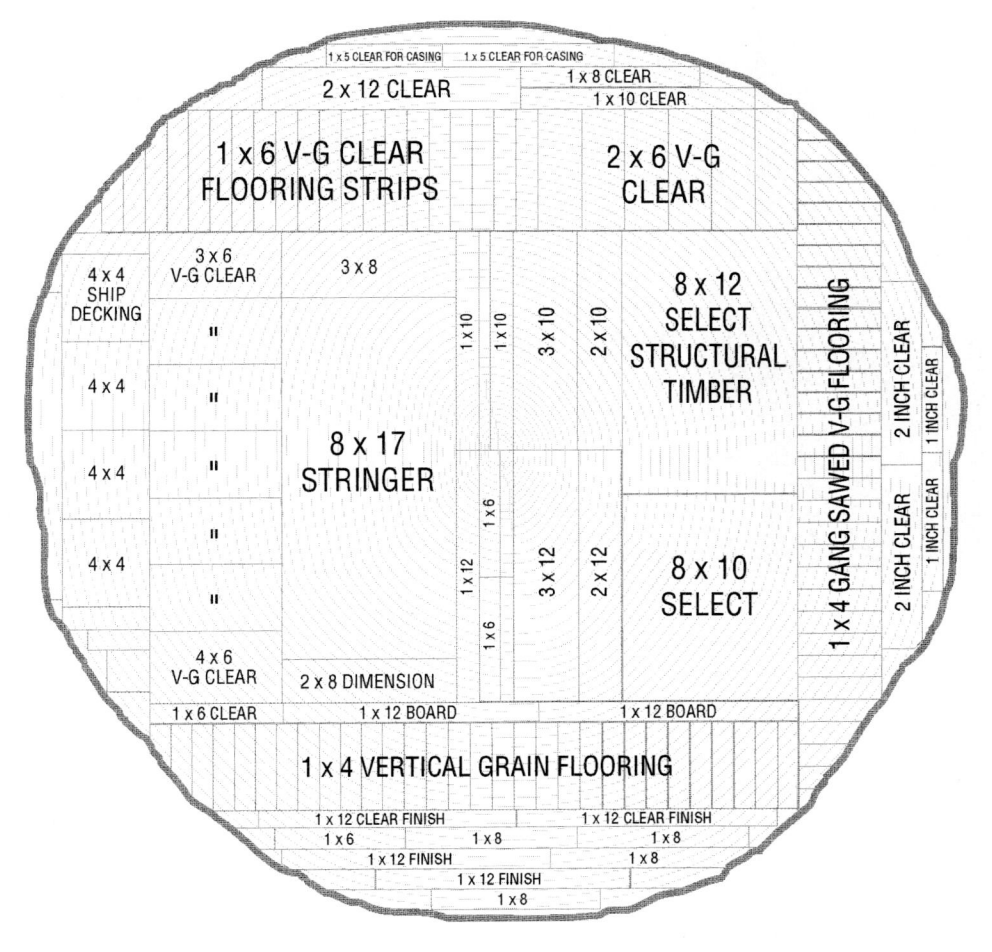

[Diagram of log cross-section showing the following labeled cuts:
- 1 x 5 CLEAR FOR CASING (×2)
- 2 x 12 CLEAR
- 1 x 8 CLEAR
- 1 x 10 CLEAR
- 1 x 6 V-G CLEAR FLOORING STRIPS
- 2 x 6 V-G CLEAR
- 4 x 4 SHIP DECKING
- 3 x 6 V-G CLEAR
- 3 x 8
- 1 x 10, 1 x 10, 3 x 10, 2 x 10
- 8 x 12 SELECT STRUCTURAL TIMBER
- 4 x 4 (×3)
- 8 x 17 STRINGER
- 1 x 12, 1 x 6, 1 x 6
- 3 x 12, 2 x 12
- 8 x 10 SELECT
- 1 x 4 GANG SAWED V-G FLOORING
- 2 INCH CLEAR, 1 INCH CLEAR, 2 INCH CLEAR, 1 INCH CLEAR
- 4 x 6 V-G CLEAR
- 2 x 8 DIMENSION
- 1 x 6 CLEAR
- 1 x 12 BOARD (×2)
- 1 x 4 VERTICAL GRAIN FLOORING
- 1 x 12 CLEAR FINISH (×2)
- 1 x 6, 1 x 8, 1 x 8
- 1 x 12 FINISH (×2)
- 1 x 8 (×2)]

This tree reached a diameter of 14 inches at an age of thirty years, at an age of one hundred years it was 27 inches in diameter, and at time of cutting was about three hundred years old and 42 inches in diameter. Its rate of growth decreased from an inch of wood in six years at an age of thirty years, to an inch of wood in twenty-five to thirty years at time of cutting.

This cross-sectional cutting diagram prepared by the West Coast Lumbermen's Association depicts the myriad of products that could be cut from a Douglas fir log. On a log-by-log basis, split-second decisions made by the sawyer spelled the difference between profit and loss. Sawmill operators highly prized good sawyers.

Between 1936 and 1957 two sawyers accounted for most of the Vernonia mill's cut: Earnest East on the long side, and Forest Blount on the short side. (Oregon-American Lumber Company, Special Collections and University Archives, University of Oregon; redrawn by Dan Moore)

After edging, live rolls moved the boards to the long- and short-side trimmers. This view shows the long-side trimmer. Boards were hand-fed to a table where a lugged chain picked them up and moved them from right to left into a bank of saws that cut each piece into desired lengths. The trimmerman in the elevated cage to the right controlled air cylinders that raised and lowered the trim saws. To the rear, lumber moved from left to right to the horizontal resaw (not shown).

The 8-foot resaw cut mostly 1- and 2-inch boards out of slabs, or the outermost parts of the log. Since these pieces contained a very high content of prized, clear wood the resaw operation was crucial for maximizing grade recovery.

After the mill went into operation O-A found the resaw's output overloaded the long- and short-side trimmers, so the company added a 100-board-per-minute capacity resaw trimmer (also not shown). (H. Brown photograph; Jim Blain collection)

Construction continued long after the mill went into operation. At its zenith, Oregon-American had, including dwelling units, 279 structures in Vernonia alone, representing 27.5 acres under roof.

MORE CAMPS, MORE EQUIPMENT

Once O-A began hauling logs to the Vernonia mill using its own train, it expanded its logging operations and had to purchase additional logging and railroad equipment. The most notable additions were the Willamette Iron and Steel Works tree-rigged skidder purchased in 1924 (at a cost of nearly $54,000 including wire rope and rigging, it was about twice as much as a new locomotive), followed by more donkey engines and another Baldwin Locomotive Works 2-6-2 Prairie-type locomotive.

O-A purchased the first of its Baldwins in 1923. The company used Road Number 104, a tank-type, primarily in the woods. The second, Road Number 105, was a conventional rod-engine equipped with tender. O-A purchased it in early 1925. Initially, the company used 105 in the woods, but it replaced the 102 on the run between the logging camp and Vernonia in 1928 because it was superheated and cost less to operate. It was also easier on the rails beyond the county line. The 104 also served as a standby engine to the 105 on the Vernonia run. Since they were used on the common-carrier United Railways

Top: Oregon-American was unique among fir mills in that every piece of lumber not made into a timber was kiln-dried. By 1926 structural timber orders declined to the point where the company had to add six more kilns to handle the resulting increase in board production.

While construction of the new kilns was under way, the log decker, in the house above and to the right of the kiln foundations, was busy moving logs back into the pond. To its right was the house for the pump that supplied water from the Nehalem River. (H. Brown photograph; Columbia County Historical Museum)

§

Bottom: After loading on kiln cars, lumber was ready for seasoning. (Betty Blumenthal collection)

between the county line and Vernonia, O-A maintained both Baldwins and the 102 to Interstate Commerce Commission standards.

By 1926, logging operations had progressed out of the Rock Creek valley floor to the Spur 5 and Spur 5 Switchback to the south. O-A also launched construction of a new line, Spur 17, by then. It followed Weed Creek to the north and served as the link to the company's next major logging campaign, the Spur 17 system. This major development, comprising four large arterial spurs, 17 North, 17 East, 17 South, and 17 West, provided the bulk of O-A's log needs through 1931 and eventually accounted for the removal of all timber

BOOM TIMES ARRIVE

lying to the north of the main camp that, by then, had been named Camp McGregor.

Refuse from the mill went into the top of the fuel house. Fuel for the furnaces came out the bottom on another conveyor. The fuel had to be caved onto the furnace feed chain by one man, sometimes two if it was packed hard. They risked their lives every day. The fuel had to be undermined to fall. We used potato forks and long, pointed poles to undercut the stuff. If you miscalculated you might be buried. We only had one man killed, fortunately. They found him standing with his left arm straight up. His name was Haymire. Real nice guy.

The fuel house supplied enough fuel for one furnace for two weeks when we were pulling only the lights. At the end of two weeks the floor would be visible and clean over nearly all its area. To take the mill off when we started up again, a small supply would be left in the northwest corner. This was mostly planer shavings and we had to use it efficiently because it burned up fast. If we misjudged we could have shut the plant down.

I worked in the fuel house for four and a half years and I was pretty sure hell would have been an improvement. We used beet forks to fill the house as full as possible. The damp fuel under us generated heat. The steel roof did likewise, and the planer fuel kept the air so full of dust it was hard to breathe. But $4.40 was important enough to keep us at it. I went home many, many times with my clothes stiff with salt. But, holy mackerel, I was in good shape.

I could have quit and hoped I'd get on in the woods. But that only paid $2.65 per day and I was in love and wanted to get my September bride a mansion with the $4.40 I was getting.

Todd Bowerman, powerhouse

As the logging area expanded, the transit time required to move loggers from Camp McGregor out to the logging shows had grown to the point where establishment of moveable remote camps became necessary. O-A established Camp Number 1 on the Spur 5 Switchback in July 1926 and Camp Number 2 was set up at Windy Junction on Spur 17 in 1928. Both had railcar-mounted cookhouses, dining rooms, and office buildings. Bunkhouses that the company had built on skids were moved from Camp McGregor to the remote camps and provided the living quarters.

By March 1928, O-A had removed almost all the timber from the Spur 5 Switchback and so moved Camp Number 1 to Spur 17 West. O-A later expanded the terminus of the four Spur 17 arterials at Windy Junction to include a makeup yard where loaded disconnects were prepared for their downhill journey to Camp McGregor.

As more logging equipment was placed in service, O-A again found itself short of woods motive power. The company needed more shays, one for use in railroad construction and another for use in switching between the landings and Camp McGregor where trains bound for Vernonia were made up.

As a stopgap, Central Coal & Coke shipped a 70-ton, three-truck shay from its Neame operation in Louisiana. Road Number 116 arrived in Vernonia in the spring of 1926 but it was in a poor state of repair and was of little value. By year-end it had deteriorated to the point where bolts securing the engine to the boiler had sheared. Considering its state of disrepair, the company decided to trade it for a new locomotive.

Unhappy with the service provided by Lima Locomotive Works for shay 103, O-A traded in the 116 for a new, 70-ton, three-truck, superheated Willamette shay-type locomotive instead. The company took delivery of this engine, Road Number 106, in January 1927. Since the 116 had been the property of Delta Land & Timber Company, Delta acquired the 106 so it could properly reflect the trade-in of the 116 in its accounting records.

By then, Oregon-American's need for additional

After lumber had been kiln-dried and graded it passed through the dry assorter where pullers removed individual pieces and assembled them in packages by dimension and grade. Monorails moved completed lumber packages to the rough storage sheds. (H. Brown photograph; Rose Valpiani collection)

rail spurs had prompted the company to establish its own railroad construction operation. Roughly thirty to forty Japanese laborers were hired for this purpose and a segregated bunkhouse, cookhouse, and dining room were built for them near Spur 8, about one-quarter mile east of Camp McGregor. Known as "Jap Camp," the camp's foreman and his wife ran it, the latter served as cook and operator of the bunkhouse. In 1928 O-A purchased a used, two-truck, 42-ton, Lima shay and pressed it into service for track-laying and maintenance purposes. The company assigned it Road Number 2, the same number it bore for its former owners.[32]

At its peak, Oregon-American woods operations employed between 250 and 300 men. The company strove to maintain first-class facilities for its woods crew and, as a part of this effort, encouraged loggers with families to settle there in company-provided housing. By 1930, forty families called Camp McGregor home. With the arrival of families came the issue of how to educate their children. Since the only way in and out of Camp was by rail and by virtue of the fact Vernonia lay nearly 16 miles away, the company built a school at Camp McGregor for grades one through eight. Clatsop County established School District Number 40 for that purpose and it was open almost continuously during Camp McGregor's operating life.

The Bee Ranch

One of the first annual plants to establish itself on cutover and burned-over timber lands was a phlox-like plant known as fireweed. This distinctively colored pink and purple plant grew heavily on logged-

Central Coal & Coke used a monorail system to transport lumber around its Conroe, Texas mill and adopted the same system at Vernonia. The O-A monorail system used more than 5 miles of track to move lumber between the dry assorter, rough sheds, rough loading dock, and the planing mill. Pictured are the four Pawling & Harnischfeger monorail cars and their crews. The operators rode inside. The hooker's job was hazardous because he had to ride the lumber packages up and down.

Pictured from left to right: Les Galloway, hooker; Jim Fluke, operator; Gerald Riley, operator; George Robbins, electrician; Mike Ludwig, rough dock and monorail foreman; Ivan Hess, hooker; Frank Worley, operator; Paul Wood, hooker; and Jim Newton, operator. (Wick Miller Men-at-Work Pictures; Columbia County Historical Museum)

off lands and served as one of nature's first methods of restoring humus to the soil. Once in bloom, the flowers from fireweed decorated the otherwise drab landscape with a riot of colors not unlike those that might occur during a fire, hence the plant's name. Aside from the natural benefits the plants bestowed on the soil, bees gathering fireweed nectar also happened to make the nectar into a particularly delicious form of honey.

Oregon-American, beginning in June 1928, rented its cutover lands exclusively to Lewis White, one of the Pacific Northwest's largest and best-known beekeepers. White built a small residence and production facility on the abandoned Spur 1 and pastured his bees on O-A lands during the summer growing seasons. The company provided White and his family with rail transportation and the "Bee Rancher" became a widely recognized fixture on the property. The fireweed honey that White's bees produced from O-A lands was a perennial winner of regional and national tasting contests.

LAND ACQUISITIONS AND EXCHANGES

From the outset it was clear the Vernonia mill would, if operated anywhere near capacity, consume the DuBois tract timber in little more than ten years. While O-A had a policy to purchase "farmer logs" from private operators in the Vernonia area, the volume of these logs was insufficient to provide more than a small extension of the mill's life. Acquisition of additional timber became, therefore, a top priority even before the mill had been completed.

Within the O-A tract there existed isolated pockets of timber owned by others that needed to be acquired and blocked up to assure efficient railroad and logging operations when the time came for O-A to cut timber in those areas. Parts of the DuBois tract were also isolated and impossible to reach with the railroad unless O-A obtained access across intervening lands. So, once logging operations had been set in motion, McGregor's efforts were directed to the acquisition of additional timber and to blocking up the existing tract into one solid body.

Since the Central-Delta and Oregon-American financing arrangements prohibited these entities from acquiring additional timber on their own behalf, Central formed the Rock Creek Timber Company as a shell company whose sole purpose was to sidestep those restrictions. It functioned as a transfer agent through which all subsequent land acquisitions and exchanges were handled.

The first major acquisition was the Yerreck tract, purchased in 1924 from A. S. Kerry, owner of the common-carrier Columbia and Nehalem River Railroad, or the Kerry Line as it was commonly known. As an aside, Kerry evidently intended to keep his ownership of this tract a secret, for "Yerreck," when spelled backwards and the letter "c" and one "e" left out, spelled Kerry.

Isolated as it was by O-A's land holdings, removing timber from the Yerreck tract to the north via the Kerry Line was unlikely. The Yerreck tract blocked up perfectly with O-A's Southwest Timber Unit that Inman-Poulsen's holdings isolated. The Yerreck tract also contained much more hemlock and allied species of thin-barked fir trees generally considered inferior to old-growth yellow fir.

Top: A monorail car delivering a package to the rough dock for shipment. A steel rod under each end of the load held the package together. Inside the rough sheds, monorail crews stacked individual bundles on top of each other. (H. Brown photograph; Jim Blain collection)

§

Bottom: Rough lumber was unstacked piece by piece then surfaced by the planers in the background. (H. Brown photograph; Columbia County Historical Museum)

Even so, the Yerreck tract purchase served a valuable strategic purpose, because buying it thwarted any potential threat from Inman-Poulsen to extend its operations in the area by acquiring more property. Further, the purchase opened the door for O-A to buy even more timber adjoining the Yerreck

BOOM TIMES ARRIVE

In the planing mill lumber was surfaced, restacked, and bound by hand into smaller bundles using twine. From there, lumber was moved either to the dressed shed for storage or directly to the loading dock for shipment. (H. Brown photograph; Vivian Laird Reynolds collection)

tract to the west and south. Rock Creek Timber Company subsequently deeded the Yerreck tract to Ruth Realty Company and it became the first block of Northern Lines' land held in reserve for Oregon-American.

O-A's first land exchange also occurred in 1924. It was driven largely by adverse terrain and inaccessibility to that part of its Southwest Timber Unit that extended west across the North Fork of the Salmonberry River. The C. H. Wheeler operation was the most likely candidate to remove timber on these lands since it was already operating in the vicinity. In return for O-A's timber, C. H. Wheeler deeded Oregon-American several of its own isolated parcels that happened to block up well to the Southwest Timber Unit.

O-A made other exchanges including several with the McPherson-controlled Detroit Trust Company interests that bordered the company's main tract to the south. These transactions were motivated by the adverse terrain O-A and East Side Logging Company encountered as their operations neared each other's. Some Detroit Trust Company timber was isolated due to extreme differences in elevation and the cost for East Side to construct a railroad to it was more than the timber was worth. That timber was readily accessible to O-A's Spur 5 Switchback that approached from a higher elevation. Likewise, O-A owned timber surrounded on three sides by McPherson holdings that was more easily reached by the East Side line. O-A and the McPhersons threw additional isolated subdivisions in other areas into the exchange for much the same rationale and the amount of timber involved.

As Oregon-American's logging moved north out of the Rock Creek basin, several opportunities to exchange parcels with the Knapp-Peninsula (K-P) Timber Company came about. K-P Timber Com-

This was one of two molding mills in the planing mill complex. (H. Brown photograph; Jim Blain collection)

pany was, by the late 1920s, operating an extension of the Kerry Line from Buster Camp to timber adjoining O-A's tract to the north. The two companies made several timber exchanges between 1926 and 1929. In each case it was of mutual benefit, either to overcome adverse terrain or to provide unobstructed access to otherwise isolated parcels.

INMAN–POULSEN LEAVES AND OREGON–AMERICAN TAKES OVER

Inman-Poulsen completed logging its tract by March 1930. Since, by then, Oregon-American had acquired the bulk of timber surrounding I-P's operations, I-P had little else to do but pick up its equipment and move out. I-P moved its remaining equipment to Zan siding on the United Railways in September 1932.

Oregon-American purchased Inman-Poulsen's mainline railroad beginning from the interconnection point east of Camp McGregor, including that part of the line that terminated near O-A's Northwest Timber Unit. This transaction for the rail line and some miscellaneous equipment was completed on March 29, 1930, for nearly $21,000. O-A designated that part of the Inman-Poulsen line past Twin Bridges as Spur 25.

Anticipating the need to develop timber in its Northwest Operating Unit, Oregon-American contracted H. S. Goodwin in June 1930 to clear, grub, and grade the right-of-way for the balance of Spur 25. Goodwin began where the Inman-Poulsen steel ended near the boundary with Oregon-American's property in the northwestern corner of Section 19, Twp. 4 North, Range 6 West. Shortly after that, O-A moved Camp Number 1 from Spur 17 West to its new home at the junction of mainline Spur 25 and Spur 25-1. By year-end 1930, the company disbanded Camp Number 2

Reminders of Oregon-American's Southern roots were everywhere. If one failed to catch the accents of former employees of Central's camps and mills, the street signs on the O-A Hill served the same purpose. (Kamholz collection)

and returned most of the structures to Camp McGregor.

JUDD GREENMAN AND OTHER KEY EMPLOYEES

Once logging and mill operations began, Central Coal & Coke brought in many people to staff key management positions. Many of those hired came from Central and Delta Land & Timber Company operations in the South.

Jack Baldridge was the first woods foreman and oversaw the buildup of logging operations. He was later replaced by Erwin Rengstorff, who served from 1927 to 1929 until E. R. "Pooch" Estey replaced him. Carl Davidson began as a purchasing agent but soon was appointed assistant superintendent working out of the Vernonia office.

E. A. Green was the first mill superintendent. Other notable key employees included Holly Holcomb, planing mill foreman; Hamp Roberson, sawmill foreman; Dave Marshall, master mechanic; Maynard Grunden, millwright; F. M. Ruhl, chief clerk; W. J. Lilly, stacker foreman; J. J. Grady, inspector of grades; and A. J. "Paddy" Hughes, chief electrician. Archie Knauss, who played a key role in the development of the kiln-drying process, was the first foreman of that department. C. L. "Connie" Anderson began as a shipping clerk when the operation started

After it was planed, lumber was stored in the dressed or "slick" shed, the center aisle of which is shown here. The uniform lumber length in each package suggests this scene occurred after 1939 when O-A installed double-end trim saws. (H. Brown photograph; Jim Blain collection)

and rose through the ranks to become general manager of the entire operation in its waning days.

However, no other new arrival had a more profound and long-lasting influence on Oregon-American operations than Judd Greenman did. A native of Kansas City, Kansas, and a graduate of its public schools, he began his career in the lumber industry when he was nineteen years old. In Greenman's own words, he went from Kansas City to play baseball and do a little incidental work for a sawmill in Edith, Colorado, owned by the Burns-Briggs Lumber Company and later by McPhee & McGinnity Company. He worked stints there and in a sister operation in El Vado, New Mexico, between 1904 and 1910. In between, he held various jobs at such places as the Crossett-Watzek-Gates lumber operation in Crossett, Arkansas, and at the *Kansas City Star* as a reporter. He also paved streets in El Paso, Texas, and worked for a short time in Temosachic, Chihuahua, Mexico, before migrating north in 1911 to go to work for the Union Mills Lumber Company in Union Mills, Washington. Greenman found his calling there and rose through the ranks of that company to become its general manager.

Although Hayes had done admirably as the Oregon-American general superintendent during the construction and start-up phases, the Vernonia mill

When the mill began operating, O-A used hand-operated buggies to transport lumber between the planing mill, dressed shed, and loading platform. (H. Brown photograph; Columbia County Historical Museum)

needed the leadership of a strong operating man.[33] Keith, under great pressure to realize the full potential of the mill because of the financial burdens incurred to get the operation started, found the thirty-nine-year-old Greenman to be the ideal candidate. He enticed him to come to Vernonia in April 1925 to make the mill produce.[34]

Greenman's many personal qualities undoubtedly persuaded Keith, for the man was brilliant, witty, decisive, an effective leader, personable, a talented negotiator, tough-minded, extremely knowledgeable, and yet, while opinionated, not so rigid in his thinking to make him unable to recognize his own mistakes and change as situations demanded. As proof of Keith's conviction that he had found the best person for the job, he hired Greenman at the highest salary ever paid for any mill man in two generations of Central's sawmilling experience.

Keith's hiring of Greenman marked two beginnings. The first was the friendship that developed between the two men that would sustain them and Oregon-American through troubled times that lay ahead. Second, Oregon-American began to take on a personality, for Greenman's influence was to become so embodied in every aspect of the operation that the company's identity became an extension of his own.

A car-loader passes a bundle of lumber to his partner inside the boxcar. Note the roller attached to the car door. O-A paid these crews according to how much lumber they loaded. The tallyman standing behind the stack of lumber kept track of the work.

The man to their right is using a wooden jack stand to lever boards into the storage bins. (H. Brown photograph; Rose Valpiani collection)

VERNONIA'S GROWTH

Arrival of the PA&P in July 1922 and mill construction crews in the spring of 1923 hastened Vernonia's evolution from an isolated settlement to Oregon's fastest-growing town.

Central Coal and Oregon-American officials did not follow the lead of some of their counterparts by building a "company town." Instead, they left the development of needed facilities to private parties.[35] This led to an influx of entrepreneurs and private developers to Vernonia. So, although the Oregon-American payroll fueled the local economy, residents of Vernonia were afforded substantial freedom of choice in almost every aspect of town life. Accordingly, many providers of goods and services moved in and established themselves.[36]

As a measure of how much the town developed, its population soared from less than 150 in 1920 to more than 1,500 by 1923.[37] Consistent with the large employee turnover so typical of many logging operations, Vernonia also was the host to a sizable transient population, particularly on weekends when loggers, their pockets full of money, came to town to "socialize."

By the end of 1924, Vernonia had a total of nine churches, two theaters (including one equipped with a $12,000 pipe organ), seven hotels, a bank, a newspaper, a telephone system, six modern auto-

Top: By 1927 O-A phased out lumber buggies and replaced them with motorized straddle carriers. The company's Gerlinger and two Willamette carriers are visible behind the grouped employees. The Gerlinger machine was on the left.

§

Bottom: These too were replaced by four, lightweight, Ford V-8-motored Gerlingers (three of which appear below) after the company reopened for business following the Depression. (Top: Special Collections, University of Washington Libraries; photograph by C. Kinsey, Neg. 2480) (Bottom: H. Brown photograph; Columbia County Historical Museum)

mobile garages, a dance hall, two whorehouses, four pool rooms, five bars and taverns, a department store, a lumber yard, three schools, an assortment of grocery and hardware stores, a jewelry store, four physicians, three dentists, and the usual assortment of allied businesses one would expect to see on any well-developed city's main street.[38]

Municipal facilities were established to serve the growing population. The Vernonia Light & Power Company was formed in 1922 and shortly afterward dammed Rock Creek between Keasey and the County line to construct a power-generating plant nearby to serve the area.[39] The city of Vernonia also built water-treatment and sewage-disposal facilities.[40]

Oregon-American sold most of its production through wholesalers. The company served the local trade through its own retail lumber yard located to the left of this storage building. (H. Brown photograph; Rose Valpiani collection)

A New Social Order

As new arrivals moved to Vernonia from other areas of the country, they also brought many diverse attitudes, beliefs, and values with them. By 1924 a plethora of lodges reflected this diversity and included the Masonic, Eastern Star, the Odd Fellows, Rebekah, the Woodmen, Grange, Relief Corps, Maccabees, Sons of Veterans, American Legion, Knights of Pythias, and the Ku Klux Klan.[41]

A weekly newspaper, the *Vernonia Eagle*, was founded in August 1922 and immediately assumed the role of the town's leading promoter, printing article after article about the many hopes, benefits, and needs of the community. Its founder and editor, Paul Robinson, touted the paper as the "mouthpiece of the Nehalem Valley" and went to great lengths to live up to his own billing. Almost every issue managed to simultaneously boast about Vernonia to itself and outsiders, point out opportunities for new businesses and services, and serve as a focal point for public opinion. In this latter role, the paper roundly praised and criticized the deeds of individuals and groups. The paper also assumed a moral stance, commenting on such varied topics as the evils of gambling, divorce, and alcohol consumption and to the "wisdom of landowners elsewhere in the State who sold land and gave jobs to Asians when even the Communists wouldn't."[42]

This kind of moralizing was, philosophically speaking, sympathetic to the rhetoric of the Ku Klux Klan. While the Oregon Klan's political theme was predominantly directed toward Roman Catholics, it implicitly carried over to racial and ethnic minorities as well. Ironically, the Klan's popular support in Oregon, like other states outside the South, seemed to grow most rapidly where it encountered the least opposition. For example, Roman Catholics comprised less than 8 percent of the state's population in the early 1920s. During this period, the number of Asiatics was actually declining. Likewise, fewer than 2,000 African Americans were residing in the state. From this one might conclude there was more tolerance of the Klan movement than wholehearted acceptance.[43] Further, when directly confronted, the Klan often proved less influential than its claimed membership might have suggested.

Klan activities in Vernonia bore this out. According to the *Eagle*, the KKK proudly called Vernonia one of its fastest-growing lodges. The paper routinely reported the Klan's activities and meetings held in Vernonia drew as many as 500 attendees from the town and surrounding areas.[44] Despite so much apparent support of the Klan in the Nehalem Valley, Oregon-American did not hesitate to carry out its plan to bring African American laborers formerly of Central Coal & Coke's mills in the South to Vernonia. The company also began hiring other racial minorities for work in the mill and for section gang work on the logging railroad.

O-A employed some minorities at skilled occupations in the sawmill such as trimmermen and edgermen. The company employed others at semiskilled and unskilled occupations. O-A paid all its minority employees the same as their white coworkers, however.

The company began laying groundwork for employment of African Americans while drawing up plans for the Vernonia mill. Segregated "Negro, Japanese, Filipino, and Hindu colonies" were constructed right along with the rest of the company's other employee housing.

The roots of Central's plan to employ racial minorities probably extended back to the coal mining part of its business. There, a long, contentious battle with the United Mine Workers had so seriously hampered the company's ability to control labor costs and manage the workforce that Keith had become convinced it would have been worth any price to keep that situation from duplicating itself in his West Coast lumber business.

On the one hand, Oregon-American's stated policy on minority employment was "to never employ other than white Americans except when continuous operation of the sawmill and logging camps required it." From a practical standpoint, however, "white Americans" having the same occupational skills as O-A's minority employees were no doubt widely available. It seems far more likely, therefore, that O-A consciously hired racial minorities out of the belief the company could exert sufficient control over them to discourage their aligning with the labor movement, assuming the unions had any desire to represent minority workers in the first place. Oregon-American's workforce finally unionized in 1936. The fact the unions after that maintained pressure to restrict the company's practice of employing racial minorities supports that conclusion.

Table 3.2
Race of Vernonia Mill Employees in 1929

	No. Employed	Per cent
Hindu	10	2
Japanese	35	7
African-American	39	8
Filipino	55	11
White	356	72
Total	495	100

A particularly blunt challenge to the company's decision appeared in a *Vernonia Eagle* article on June 5, 1925, that claimed, among other things, that Vernonia was a "white-man's town."[45]

A week later, however, E. E. Hayes, in one of his final activities in Vernonia, drew on his reputation as a civic leader and wrote a rebuttal article deploring the growth of a spirit of intolerance. He also reminded readers that denial of the privileges of citizenship because of race or color was not in the American spirit.[46]

Undeterred, Oregon-American followed through with its plan to hire and house racial minorities. While O-A was anything but a crusader for civil rights as we know them today, the practice of employing minorities continued for the duration of the operation, despite ongoing controversy. In fact, Oregon-American throughout its life was the largest single employer of African Americans in Oregon's lumber-manufacturing industry.

The brevity of the incident served as a measure of Oregon-American's growing economic and social influence in the community. It is also interesting that no more articles or editorials about the Ku Klux Klan appeared in the paper following the incident. Not long after, the *Vernonia Eagle* changed hands for the first of four times during its life and Robinson left the area.

The extent of O-A's minority hiring practices were evident from a 1929 summary of the company's payroll, broken out by race (see Table 3.2).

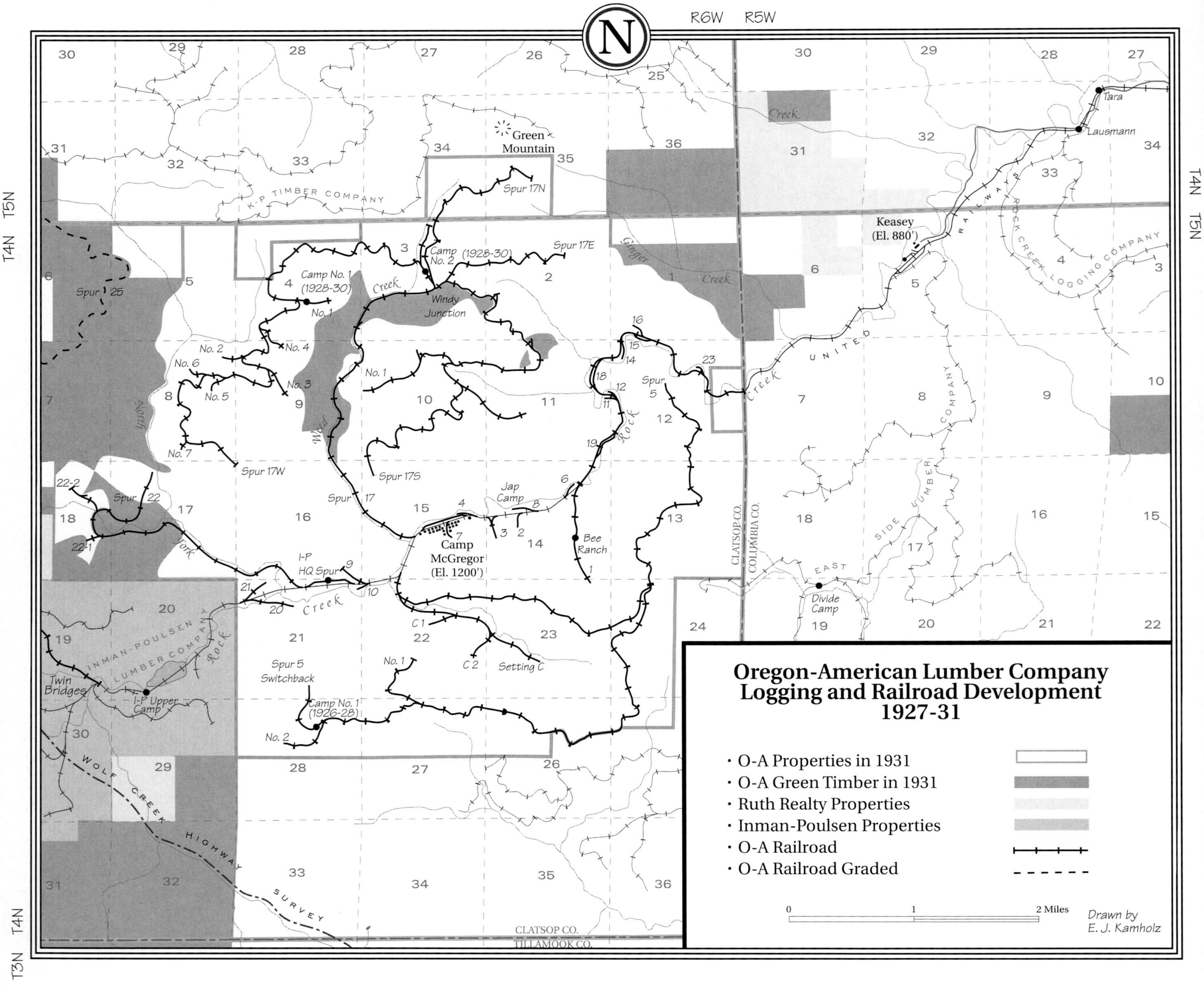

R6W
R5W
T5N
T4N
T3N
Oregon-American Lumber Company
Logging and Railroad Development
1927-31
O-A Properties in 1931
O-A Green Timber in 1931
Ruth Realty Properties
Inman-Poulsen Properties
O-A Railroad
O-A Railroad Graded
0
1
2 Miles
Drawn by
E. J. Kamholz
Green Mountain
K-P TIMBER COMPANY
Spur 17N
Spur 17E
Camp No. 2 (1928-30)
Camp No. 1 (1928-30)
Windy Junction
Spur 25
Spur 17W
Spur 17S
Spur 17
Spur 22
Jap Camp
Bee Ranch
Camp McGregor (El. 1200')
I-P HQ Spur
Keasey (El. 880')
Tara
Lausmann
RAILWAYS
ROCK CREEK LOGGING COMPANY
UNITED
EAST SIDE LUMBER COMPANY
Divide Camp
CLATSOP CO.
COLUMBIA CO.
INMAN-POULSEN LUMBER COMPANY
Twin Bridges
I-P Upper Camp
Spur 5 Switchback
Camp No. 1 (1926-28)
Setting C
WOLF CREEK HIGHWAY SURVEY
CLATSOP CO.
TILLAMOOK CO.

HIGH HOPES AND DASHED DREAMS

As an industry, lumber producers proved adept at conquering the logistics involved to uproot operations some 2,000 miles to the west. In fact, their efforts were so successful that by the early 1920s manufacturing capacity had grown far greater than the country's demand for lumber.

Lacking even the most rudimentary tools to measure changes in the market, the industry was slow to take stock of the fact that as the capacity to produce grew, per capita consumption of lumber, particularly structural varieties such as timbers, was actually declining. The decline was so significant that by 1930, total lumber consumption in the country was nearly 20 percent lower than it had been in 1910.

But, even after realizing that chronic overproduction was hurting all producers, unrelenting demand for financial performance from the industry's investors only served to worsen the situation. Lacking the mechanism and discipline needed to regulate production industry-wide, an individual operator's only means of survival often boiled down to increasing his production with the hope that by doing so it would offset the lower prices that were sure to develop as others followed suit.

Not surprisingly, by the mid-1920s there had developed a prevailing atmosphere of cutthroat competition among operators that ushered in a cycle of steadily eroding prices and corresponding efforts to increase production at ever-lower costs.

These conditions prevailed for the remainder of the decade and helped the industry earn its well-deserved reputation for "highballing" and for extracting everything possible from its workforce and equipment, often without regard to the human suffering that followed. Just as surely as the first half of the 1920s represented the contemporary zenith of the nation's lumber industry, events of the ensuing five years served to take it to its all-time low. The steady erosion in lumber prices continued until the 1929 stock market collapse, then they went into a free fall as investor confidence in all forms of construction evaporated.

Despite the best efforts of Charles Keith and other visionaries to right the ills of the lumber industry during these vexing times, the Central Coal & Coke and Oregon-American Companies fell victim to the tragic events of the Great Depression just like most other producers. Individual stories differed only in detail and suffering.

A TROUBLED INDUSTRY

By 1930, the National Lumber Manufacturer's Association and its affiliate, the West Coast Lumbermen's Association (WCLA), were calling for Congress to abolish existing antitrust laws out of a conviction that they stood in the way of the industry's ability to consolidate for a common good. Presumably through removal of antitrust restrictions, some in the industry believed acquisitions and mergers

Opposite page: Between 1927 and the 1931 Depression shutdown, Oregon-American finished logging the Spur 5 system and relocated operations north to Spur 17 and its arterials.

The road construction crew paused for the camera while grading Spur 22, the North Fork line, in 1928. The shovel is a gasoline-engined P&H model 206, one of two the company owned. Joe Wornstaff, shovel runner, stands on the track.

Wornstaff and his nephew, George Lee, graded many of Oregon-American's rail and vehicle rights-of-way between the mid-1920s and 1953. (Special Collections, University of Washington Libraries; photograph by C. Kinsey, Neg. 2456)

would help concentrate industry power in fewer hands and lead to more enlightened decision-making. Even so, such measures took time to carry out and offered little hope for immediate improvement.

Many options were considered during the WCLA's Del Monte Hotel Conference held on the Monterey, California, peninsula in the spring of 1930. Years later, Greenman mused philosophically about that conference, writing that he

> ...rubbed shoulders with the "Giants" of the industry who, to get out from under their debts, tried to effect a merger which would have made Big Steel look like a corner grocery store. For the welfare of the common man and more particularly in light of present tax laws it probably is well that providence and people who didn't owe very much money intervened and put a halt to the industry nonsense.

As more operators began to take stock of the situation, the industry made other abortive attempts to "self-regulate." One particularly heavy-handed measure was the so-called Del Monte program, named after the above-mentioned convention, in which a faction within the WCLA successfully gained the backing of most West Coast operators to ban all second-shift mill operations—a form of forced curtailment.

On June 1, 1930, the National Lumber Manufacturer's Association named a special committee for "Securing Orderly Control of Lumber Production and Distribution." This blue-ribbon task force featured some of the biggest names in the industry, including Charles Keith, John W. Blodgett, John W. Watzek, and F. E. Weyerhaeuser. An equally impressive committee on "Retail Cooperation" was formed and was

The Japanese track gang and shay Number 2 pictured at "Jap Camp" shortly after O-A purchased the 2-Spot in 1928. (Special Collections, University of Washington Libraries; photograph by C. Kinsey, Neg. 2477)

chaired by Harry T. Kendall and included Edward Hines as a member.

These committees recommended voluntary production curtailment and development of consumptive forecasts of demand as a basis for setting output levels. Yet as relevant as their objectives might have been, they proved too little and too late to have any impact. Still, the attitude of many producers was to ignore what was going on around them and continue producing as they had been all along out of the belief that "the other guy" should make the sacrifice.

Taken as a whole, nothing of substance materialized to stem the chronic oversupply condition. Eventually the market for lumber became so oversaturated that by late 1931 demand for lumber fell to its lowest level since 1869. Few industries suffered more as the nation's worsening economic problems ushered in the Great Depression.

THE ROAD TO DEFAULT

Oregon-American's fortunes fared no better than the rest of the industry as far as finding markets for its output was concerned. A cursory examination of the company's order file, for example, clearly illustrated the glut of construction materials in the market: between 1924 and 1931, O-A's structural timber orders fell from nearly 27 percent of its overall business to less than 12 percent. This shift in demand prompted O-A to add six additional North Coast drying kilns in 1926 to accommodate the resulting increase in board production.

As the Vernonia mill entered only its third year of operation, dwindling lumber demand made it more difficult to run anywhere close to capacity. In subsequent years, the mill never produced at more than 85 percent of its rated output.

Greenman, recruited for his operating know-how,

Japanese track laborers unloading ties on the Spur 17 system. (Special Collections, University of Washington Libraries; photograph by C. Kinsey, Neg. 2519)

lived up to his reputation, and the mill achieved substantial gains in productivity. Oregon-American cut 153,520,334 board feet at Vernonia in 1926, the peak production year in its entire operating life. Between 1926 and 1929, average sawmill production per man hour increased steadily from 33,000 board feet per man hour to nearly 40,000, despite a reduction in total sawmill output to 141,000 board feet in the latter year.

Logging efficiency improved dramatically during this period too. Production per side reached 195,630 board feet per day in April 1930. Log costs equaled $10.70 per 1,000 feet that month of which labor accounted for only $3.21 of the total. The following month, production had increased to an average daily output of 225,000 board feet per side. Greenman commented he knew nothing approaching this in the way of logging performance in his previous experience nor had he heard of *but mighty few instances where anything like this production was maintained over any considerable period of time.*

The decline in the lumber market was accompanied by similar problems in the demand for coal. Coupled with depletion of Central Coal & Coke's reserves in its coal and southern pine forests, the parent company found itself on thin financial ice and the Vernonia operation's performance became all the more critical.

Timber that Never Existed

If the deteriorating market situation failed to provide sufficient cause for alarm, the discovery that Thomas & Meservey's cruise of the DuBois tract was overstated certainly did. Suspicions arose initially during the 1924 C. H. Wheeler timber exchange when an independent cruise of the O-A parcels reported 20 percent less timber than Thomas & Meservey claimed in their 1921 cruise. As O-A gained more operating experience these early suspicions were born out more fully. The situation greatly worsened the company's financial woes; since the quantity of recoverable timber on uncut lands was overstated by 20 percent, not only was the recovery accounting system on which it was based equally overstated but also correspondingly less money was available from future sales to repay Oregon-American's bond issue. Accordingly, this meant a reduction in Central Coal & Coke's revenues too, thus limiting its ability to repay its own bonded indebtedness.

Following a meeting with Keith in February 1926 in which he reported the discrepancies to Thomas & Meservey, the firm recruised 3 square miles in the main tract. It also conducted an inspection of cutover lands to determine if logs had been left behind that otherwise might have been recoverable.

T&M's recruise showed only 3 percent less than their original cruise and their final report concluded that since Inman-Poulsen's operation was experiencing an overrun against its part of the original 1921 cruise of the entire DuBois tract, the only plausible reason for O-A's 20 percent underrun against the same cruise was due to a failure to log all the merchantable timber on the land. T&M also attributed some shortfall to more defect and breakage than originally accounted for in the 1921 cruise, but went on to express confidence that that particular problem was an isolated one not likely to occur over the remaining tract.

In July 1926, O-A deployed its own scaling crew to sample some of the same 40-acre parcels of cutover lands recruised by T&M and found only number-three-grade hemlock left behind. Number-three-grade hemlock was, in fact, largely unmerchantable, even during the best of market conditions. Such logs were generally left on the ground as they were not worth the effort to bring them to the mill.

As time went on, the discrepancy between cruise and actual recovery proved consistent. By February 1927, Greenman wrote to Keith:

> I am about to come to the conclusion that there never was as much timber on the lands we have

A falling crew posed after completing the undercut on a prime Douglas fir. The men are standing on springboards so they can make their cut above the tree bole's swell. The position of the undercut determined where the tree would fall. (Kamholz collection)

HIGH HOPES AND DASHED DREAMS

After the fallers finished the undercut they attacked from the other side with their crosscut saw. They drove wedges in the kerf to keep the saw from binding. A few more saw strokes and a few taps on the wedges will send this grand specimen to the ground where buckers will cut it into desired lengths. (Special Collections, University of Washington Libraries; photograph by C. Kinsey, Neg. 2493)

logged as was cruised, even after every tree and snag and pole and the anticipated growth in the next 25 years had been included. I don't like to say this for it may be that the cruise on lands to be logged in the future is understated but I am just as positive as can be that in 1926 we did not leave 30% of the original stand on the ground, counting culls, poles, and everything else.

In February 1930 he added:

I repeat here what I have said before a good many times. In my opinion our recovery policy is as nearly right as we can get it and we are using every reasonable means to keep it right. We use a check scaler in the woods to follow up after logging is complete and reports show only three-fourths of 1% of logs being left on ground that should have been brought in. I too will repeat what I said the other day, namely, that we are bringing to the mill logs which should be left in the woods right now.

The same month, concluding an investigation into Inman-Poulsen's recovery experience against the T&M cruise Greenman wrote:

I-P used the Macklin cruise which was 91.7% of the T&M cruise. Lowell Young [I-P's logging superintendent] said I-P's recovery on the entire tract was 93% of the Macklin cruise which should make their recovery 85.7% of the T&M cruise. Young also said if they had the job to do over again, they would leave considerable timber that they took and found unprofitable.

This revelation ruined Thomas & Meservey's reputation with Keith and Greenman. Unfortunately, the damage had already been done.

Making Something Out of Nothing

Faced with a shrinking market and the prospect of converting 20 percent less timber than originally counted on, Keith and his top managers struggled to find ways to make up the difference. Kendall, displaying the marketing genius that would earn him national prominence in the industry, proposed establishing a brand preference for Central's lumber,

A crew took time for Clark Kinsey to take their picture beside a Humboldt yarder. Kinsey made his living photographing scenes like this and selling the prints to those who posed.

Seated third from left was E. R. "Pooch" Estey who was O-A's logging superintendent between 1929 and 1937. (Special Collections, University of Washington Libraries; photograph by C. Kinsey, Neg. 2449)

built on the product's kiln-dried properties. The cornerstone of this program was the application of the CC&CC trademark to every piece of lumber shipped from Vernonia so to create brand awareness and preference for the Central product by wholesalers, retailers, and end-users. The program also made much of the fact that Central Coal & Coke lumber came from Oregon-American's own stand of old-growth yellow fir, thus assuring buyers of a uniformity of product quality unattainable from open-market mills.

The company instituted a corollary program in which O-A began grade-marking its output according to WCLA-established guidelines. Greenman personally involved himself in the WCLA's establishment of grades and served on the association's grading committee during the critical stages of the program's development. Other, promotional schemes were developed to increase brand preference. One included the practice of shipping Christmas trees in each loaded boxcar ahead of the holiday seasons. Another involved a program of shipping customers miniature toy wooden trucks, each loaded with CC&CC branded lumber. That program's popularity was enhanced by painting the name of the retail purchaser on the side. Kendall, over Greenman's strenuous objections, went as far as to conduct a trial program of manufacturing prefabricated hog-feeder houses at the Vernonia mill for sale to Midwestern farmers. This program barely went beyond the initial planning phase, however.

The tree-rigged skidder weighed 160 tons and was originally equipped with four-wheel trucks under each end. O-A was concerned the unit's weight was poorly distributed and it was likely to tip over when crossing soft fills during moves. So, by late 1927, the company replaced the original trucks with an eight-wheel truck under the boiler and a six-wheel truck in front.

Note how the chassis was lashed to the spar tree. Jacks were used to raise and level the skidder and, once in position, cribbing was put under the car to further stabilize it. (Special Collections, University of Washington Libraries; photograph by C. Kinsey, Neg. 2512)

While striving to make the Central product line stand out in the eyes of buyers, another program was initiated to find a market outlet for lower grades of logs that, until then, had been left in the woods because of their marginal value. The original DuBois timber stand, while known for its content of old-growth yellow fir, also contained lesser but substantial amounts of western red cedar and hemlock. Approximately 4 percent of the stand consisted of cedar and another 9 percent or so was hemlock.

When logging operations started, O-A recovered the cedar and sold the logs on the open market. Recognizing the potential additional conversion possibilities it offered and the advantage of furnishing finished cedar products under the CC&CC brand, O-A leased a parcel of land adjoining the eastern edge of the Vernonia millpond to the Johnston & McGraw Shingle Company in late 1925. Johnston & McGraw built a mill capable of converting cedar logs at a 15,000-board-foot-per-day rate and began producing shingle and shakes from cedar logs brought to the Vernonia millpond.

The profitable conversion of hemlock logs presented a different challenge. First, hemlock was generally considered an inferior wood for lumber and could not command the same price as fir. Second, handling it was difficult. Hemlock logs were prone to sink in the pond and were difficult to mill.

The cedar was generally interspersed within the timber tract as a whole. Hemlock, however, proliferated at some higher elevations in the O-A stand. Once logging operations fanned out from along Rock Creek Basin and moved up into the hills to the north and south of Camp McGregor, they encountered greater concentrations of it. Sometimes, individual logging sides encountered much greater proportions of hemlock than any other species, thus disrupting the supply of the more marketable yellow fir to the mill. The economics of tying up rail and logging equipment by leaving the hemlock behind and then returning to recover it during more favorable times could not be justified. Accordingly, O-A logged it as it was encountered and the product mix suffered as a result.

The company also experimented with recovering broken hemlock logs and treetops, bringing them to Vernonia and chipping them for the pulp market. However, the lack of suitable logging equipment needed for economical removal of small pieces, the absence of rail cars capable of handling such items, and the cost of installing chipping equipment at the mill doomed this project almost from the start.

The raw materials mix problems presented by hemlock were made even more pronounced by virtue of one of the few major errors made during the design and construction phase of the Vernonia mill. Before plotting the physical plant on the Vernonia tract, Central Coal & Coke surveyed nearly twenty other West Coast operators to decide how large to build the millpond. Estimates from this survey suggested 1 acre of millpond would hold 600,000 to 1.2 million board feet of logs. Wanting a log inventory in the pond sufficient to keep the mill supplied during months when inclement weather curtailed logging, O-A mill planners used the smaller estimate and plotted a pond of 36.5 acres next to which they constructed the rest of the mill. Once the pond was filled with logs, however, it would only hold 457,000 board feet per acre.

The Willamette tree-rigged skidder in operation on a setting on Spur 17 East. Camp Number 2 was just over the hill behind the skidder. Spur 17 South is barely visible in the tree line to the left.

The self-contained "unit," had three sets of engines. In front, the loading engine operated the loading boom. The skidding engine swung logs into the landing via a skyline. The remaining engine rigged the next skid road while the skidding engine was busy logging the current one. (Special Collections, University of Washington Libraries; photograph by C. Kinsey, Neg. 2516)

A steam side in operation. Between its tree-rigged skidder and eighteen steam donkeys, Oregon-American could operate four logging sides simultaneously.

The company bought all its logging equipment brand new when it began operating. (Special Collections, University of Washington Libraries; photograph by C. Kinsey, Neg. 2484)

If logging in northwestern Oregon had been a year-round affair, this alone probably would not have presented an insurmountable hurdle. But, since elevations in the Coast Range above 2,000 feet were subject to snowfall from December through April, something had to be done to assure a continuous supply of logs for the mill during winter months.

By then it was too late to enlarge the pond since it was bounded on two sides by the Nehalem River, one side by the mill, and the rest by facilities needed for unloading logs. Consequently, O-A was forced to remove logs from the pond and cold-deck them along the pond's south levee, a practice started in 1924 and continued annually until 1929. Cold decks ranged in size from 12 to 15 million board feet. A Willamette 200-horsepower, electric-motor driven, log-decking donkey engine was installed to handle this chore.

The cold-decking engine presented problems of its own, for it lacked the power needed to move the larger-than-average logs sent to the mill in early years of operation. And, since the smaller logs it could handle ran predominantly to hemlock, the company was forced to mill an inferior raw material during some winter months. Unable to maintain lumber production in many desirable types and grades, O-A's profits suffered.

With unrelenting pressure to improve conversion, O-A was also forced to log marginal raw material to the mill. The yield was Number 3 Common lumber that, even when kiln-dried, proved inferior in the eyes of the consumer. Even so, it grew to account for nearly 13 percent of the mill's cumulative output from 1924 to 1932.

By August 1930, unsold stocks of Number 3 Common had grown to immense proportions in the Vernonia mill storage sheds. Greenman complained to Kendall:

> Sometimes I think the industry would be infinitely better off if it would collectively take this Number 3 Common out of its sheds, run it over a trimmer, dump it in a wood box, sell it as fuel, and quit accumulating it. But I don't mean that this should be done simply because Number 3 Common and poorer is today valueless when considered in competition with other woods, but I mean that it

should be adopted as general practice for all time to come.

I am very much convinced the Fir industry has suffered extensively by reason of its effort to save too big a portion of what is really a worthless product.

Later, replying to a CC&CC salesman's complaint over the difficulty of selling Number 3 Common and, after running out of room to store lumber required putting 600,000 board feet of the stuff outdoors at Vernonia, Greenman wrote:

> You point out these items are a source of constant annoyance [to you]. So is practically all the other lumber we have these days. The lumber in our rough sheds is really more of an annoyance to us than this lumber on the carrier dock and while it may not be annoying you very much, it is causing us so much concern that we are only running the sawmill to about 60% of capacity because of its presence there.

By December 1930, the unsold inventory had grown so much Greenman wrote Kendall:

> If the transcontinental railroads out here would let us take our stock of 2 × 4's Number 3 Common and lay them end on end along their tracks, they would reach from Vernonia to Williston, North Dakota, on the GN; to Glendive, Montana, on the NP; to Laramie, Wyoming, on the UP, or down to where the bathing beauties and date palms grow at Los Angeles on the SP.
>
> If we could transfer the whole lot of these 2 × 4's Number 3 Common over to Kansas City (which, in my opinion would be a very desirable disposition of them) and then started out from Kansas to lay them end on end...to the east they would reach to Philadelphia.
>
> Our stock of 2 × 4's Number 3 Common laid end on end would be 944.8 miles long.
>
> This letter is written merely to show how little is going on at Vernonia.

So, in a real sense, Central Coal & Coke and Oregon-American were twice-victimized by prevailing market conditions—first by overproduction and second by efforts to increase realization from its raw materials base by producing inferior grades of lumber.

THE CENTRAL COAL & COKE RECEIVERSHIP

Despite its assets of $25 million, Central Coal & Coke found it increasingly difficult to generate sufficient cash flow from its declining lumber and

Skagit MAC 4-40 speeder Number 10 making a delivery at a landing. Later, O-A added an enclosure to the bed to protect passengers and goods from the elements.

The company used the double-tonged "hayrack" boom system until the Depression. After that, O-A used the heel-boom loading method to avoid making royalty payments to the inventor of the hayrack loading system. The heel-boom also reduced the cost of labor required to handle an extra set of tongs. (Special Collections, University of Washington Libraries; photograph by C. Kinsey, Neg. 2522)

THE BIG TREE

	Top Diameter	Length	Scale
First log	90"	24'	9,514'
Second log	87"	24'	8,929'
Third log	82"	32'	10,580'
Fourth log	71"	32'	7,724'
Fifth log	55"	48'	7,312'
		160'	44,049'

No story about a logging outfit working in some of the biggest timber in the world would be complete without a story of its biggest tree. While larger specimens of old-growth yellow fir certainly existed, few achieved the notoriety of Oregon-American's Big Tree felled in August 1929.

Greenman, describing the tree to Charles Keith, wrote:

> This was quite a remarkable tree. It was about 10 feet in diameter at the ground and was 8½ feet in diameter breast high when it was severed from the stump. The tree was about 230 feet in length over-all but only 160 feet of it could be recovered as the top was very coarse and heavy limbed and broke to pieces at the 55 inch diameter when the tree was felled.

> The full scale content of the tree must have been in the neighborhood of 60,000 feet. It was not possible for us to scale any of the top above 55 inches but the full scale of the recovered logs was:

The tree was remarkable in other respects. The surrounding forest consisted entirely of trees of medium size and from three to four hundred years of age. This hoary monarch, as shown by a count of annular growth rings, was 838 years old.

Twelve distinct fire scars were apparent in the rings accumulated during the first four hundred years of the tree's growth, while no serious fire scars were found in the sections of growth occurring during the last half of the tree's life.

Thus, we have an accounting for the fact this tree stood alone in a forest half its age. Recurring fires, doubtless lightning caused, wiped out its fellows of like age but for some unaccountable reason this giant, Phoenix-like, reared its head at least twelve successive times from the ashes of its contemporaries.

In the past four hundred years, nature softened her blows at the patriarch, permitting it to stand in peace and in freedom from fires, while a new generation of youthful progeny, scarce half its age, grew up around it. Whether this four-hundred-year freedom from fire resulted from changing climate conditions, or from a discontinuance of the Indian custom of burning out the forests every so often to improve their hunting surroundings, or merely whether a kind chance intervened to spare the aged one and his younger brethren, we of course do not know.

Suffice it to say that even a roughneck lumber jack, schooled in the Paul Bunyan style, must have some qualms of conscience at terminating an existence that had its beginning when Godfrey of Bouillon was organizing the flower of European chivalry for their first Crusade against the wily Saracen.

The chronological history of outstanding events occurring during the life span of this one great tree reads like a statement of major recorded accomplishments of the Anglo-Saxon race. As I said above, this remarkable specimen of *Pseudotsuga Taxifolia* was struggling up to find its place in the sun when old Godfrey went in search of the Grail and in confusion of the unspeakable Turk.

The tree had reached the ripe old age of 124 years, was more than 2 feet in diameter, and must have been 100 feet high when the English barons wrested the Magna Charta from King John at Runnymede and laid the sixty-three chapters of its pattern before all future democracies in 1215.

By the time Christopher Columbus discovered the land in which it stood, our tree was more than 4 feet in diameter at the stump, had, through those mysterious processes which baffle scientists, converted the chemicals of the soil and the air into a carload of lumber and had passed through twelve successive forest fires, which while leveling its neighbors, succeeded only in leaving their scars on its massive bole for kind nature to heal and record as but passing experiences in its eventful life.

The tree reached its prime about the time of the American Revolution. Could it have been cut and put to mankind's use while Washington and his armies trod the forests that sloped to the ocean lapping the opposite shores of the continent, or even as late as when Lewis and Clark roamed the cathedral woods of the very county in which it stood, more and better lumber could have been recovered from our tree.

A serious streak of rot extending throughout the entire length of the body of the tree and affecting about a third of its total cubical content, will materially reduce the aggregate recovery of lumber when the logs are sawn and will impair the value of much of the lumber that is recovered. However, we should be able to produce from this one tree a good big box car full of clear lumber. If the harvest has been delayed, and the crop somewhat damaged, thereby, it is nevertheless an important garnering and, as in other crops, better a late harvest than one too early.

The butt logs of this tree are so large we will probably have to split them before sawing. We will hold them here for you to see on your next visit. Anything that calls for as much verbosity as we have indulged in here certainly should be seen.

News of the Big Tree spread rapidly. The National Lumber Manufacturer's Association picked up the story and submitted an article to the *New York Times* that featured it in that paper's October 19, 1930, issue.

Pieces of the tree were kept for posterity. O-A sent a small piece to George L. Hathaway of Northville, Michigan, for use in "The American Goodwill Table." This table included pieces of wood from the Washington Elm, U.S.S. Frigate *Constitution*, Parent Naval Orange Tree, the White House, Old Kentucky Home, and many other unusual sources.

(Looking east over Rock Creek at Camp McGregor in the late 1920s. The two large buildings in the foreground were schoolhouses. Operating as School District Number 40, grades one through eight were taught there. Behind the schoolhouses were forty family houses built by the company.

After the Wolf Creek Fire destroyed Camp McGregor in 1933, O-A rebuilt it in 1936. The school reopened in 1939. (Special Collections, University of Washington Libraries; photograph by C. Kinsey, Neg. 2520)

coal-mining operations to service the debt issues it had created to finance the Oregon-American venture. As a result, Central was unable to report a profit after 1924.

But as lumber prices plummeted after the stock market crash, Central Coal & Coke's financial position deteriorated quickly, so Keith, by mid-November 1930, had to instruct Greenman to put mill operations on a four-day per week or less basis until after the first of the year. He wrote, *I do not want to do this but as I see it, we cannot do anything else. Business has simply dried up.* By then, prices had fallen so low lumber was selling for 25 percent below its cost. Running out of cash, Keith turned to the Great Northern and the Northern Pacific for financial assistance.

Near the end of his rope, Keith wrote Greenman on January 13, 1931:

> Our cash position is in such shape that it is just impossible to start operations unless we can arrange to get some funds.... We are not in a position to help our men out because we cannot do it.
>
> Last week I thought we had it in position where we could be refinanced. Under present conditions, it is impossible to do any public financing. In the absence of having some of our friends like the NP or GN or others coming to our rescue, we are out of luck and it can not be done. In the meantime we will simply have to wait and see what we can work out with the banks. The company may be forced into a receiver's hands....
>
> I would have shut down long ago if it had not been for the question of paying interest, and so long as we could get some conversion out of the raw material, the company was better off operating than shut down.

Out of options and trying to preserve its remaining assets, the Central Coal & Coke Company and the Delta Land & Timber Company turned to the courts for protection on January 24, 1931. The court appointed J. M. "Joseph" Bernardin the receiver for the two companies on January 26, 1931.

Downtown Camp McGregor looking west. Inman-Poulsen's mainline was the clear track to the right over which Oregon-American operated for several miles. Spur 7 curved off to the left through the middle of camp. The white buildings in the distance were the schoolhouses. (Special Collections, University of Washington Libraries; photograph by C. Kinsey, Neg. 2450)

Bernardin had been a former member of the Central Company's board of directors and was a member of the Federal Reserve Board for the 10th District. Although Keith did not put Oregon-American into receivership the company was directly affected since it was leasing the Delta Land & Timber Company-owned mill.

Bernardin's first task as receiver was to gain financial control of the Central-Delta properties and to sort out which parts to close down and which parts to continue operating. Of chief concern was Oregon-American's bond issue interest payment due in April 1931. O-A still held considerable finished lumber inventories at the mill and a large quantity of felled timber in the woods. These represented a potential source of badly needed cash that could be applied to the bond interest. Consequently, Bernardin first reduced salaries to minimum levels, ordered layoffs of all nonessential personnel, then authorized logging and sawmill operations to continue only to the extent necessary to dispose of the inventory.

Recognizing the hardship reduced wages would have on employees, Greenman lobbied for and was granted permission to reduce rents on all company houses. Keith wrote to Greenman on February 10, 1931, *The Receiver has named my salary reduction (70%) and there is nothing for me to do but take it. I agree with you that (reducing salaries cannot overcome the lack of business.).... God knows what is ahead of us but it is certainly not encouraging.* Consistent with salary reductions ordered for personnel at Vernonia, Greenman reduced his own monthly salary from $675 to $300 per month.

To facilitate sale of its existing finished lumber inventory, Greenman recommended a plan for a limited sawmilling operation to replenish missing stock items. *By proper sawing and selling the two million feet of usable lumber that will result will mean that for every foot thus produced it will help us sell 4 feet we otherwise will only sell with great difficulty.*

He was also concerned for the recovery of 23 million board feet of downed timber that was subject to deterioration if left in the woods for an

As O-A's operations moved steadily farther away from Camp McGregor, the company established two movable camps to reduce travel time to and from work. Camp Number 1 was first put into operation on the Spur 5 Switchback in 1926 then was moved to this location on Spur 17 West in 1928. It operated there until 1930 when O-A moved the camp to Spur 25. The Depression forced the company to shut down logging before the camp was ever reopened on Spur 25. The 1933 Wolf Creek Fire destroyed it. (Special Collections, University of Washington Libraries; photograph by C. Kinsey, Neg. 2444)

extended period, not to mention the potential fire hazard it represented. A limited logging program using one high-lead side and the skidder was approved. Supplementing this program was the removal of logs along the railroad right-of-way using the locomotive crane.

A committee of the Central and Delta creditors was formed shortly after Central sought protection from the courts. This group, the Central-Delta bondholders' committee, represented the interests of those two companies' bondholders and was allowed considerable say-so in ongoing activities after that. The committee viewed keeping Oregon-American operating favorably as long as sufficient business could be conducted to meet interest payments on the O-A bonds due April 1, 1931. The Central-Delta bondholders' committee thus approved loaning Oregon-American sufficient working capital to continue operations through that period. O-A's lumber inventory at the Vernonia mill secured the loan.

As logging the downed timber progressed, Greenman was told to curtail this operation to a four-day-per-week basis. That he was able to continue operating five days per week was influenced by his analysis of the problems that a shortened workweek in the woods would create: *The logger is working for $3.20/day and working only 4-days per week will give him earnings of only $12.80 per week against our charges for board, bed and doctor which amount to $9.75 per week, leaving the gentlemen $3.05 per week to buy clothing, tobacco, whiskey and the other necessities of a logger's life.* The logging program was finally curtailed on May 1, 1931, leaving only a small amount of felled and bucked timber on the ground. Picking up the right-of-way logs with the locomotive crane continued,

The interior of a rail-mounted kitchen car at Camp Number 2. (Special Collections, University of Washington Libraries; photograph by C. Kinsey, Neg. 2498)

however. The Camp McGregor cookhouse was closed and the commissary sold goods on a cash basis to those few men still employed. The company allowed families to continue living in their houses at Camp rent-free, provided they obtained their groceries elsewhere.

In mid-July 1931, the company halted the right-of-way log recovery program, effectively ending all operations in the woods. O-A confined its sawmill operations to logs delivered to the Vernonia millpond by independent contractors. By then, the market was so depressed the operating policy shifted to one in which the preservation of capital assets became the most important consideration. Since the most valuable O-A asset was its timber, there was more financial benefit in leaving it standing than by logging it. And, as the lumber market failed to show signs of improvement, the Central-Delta bondholders' committee decided against continued financing of the mill-operating program. That forced O-A to stop purchasing logs from independent suppliers.

Lacking a supply of raw materials the sawmill was shut down completely on August 8, 1931. The kiln-drying and dry assorter departments followed suit once transit lumber had been handled and stored. The planing mill and shipping departments continued operating, however.

Following closure of the sawmill, Bernardin authorized O-A to permit employees living in company houses at Vernonia to continue residing in them rent-free provided the tenants paid for maintenance and upkeep.

To balance its remaining stock of finished lumber on hand, O-A purchased out-of-stock finished lumber items from other manufacturers and paid to

HIGH HOPES AND DASHED DREAMS

This page: Oregon-American put Camp Number 2 into operation on Spur 17 at Windy Junction in 1928. It operated there until 1930 when the company returned most of the buildings to Camp McGregor where the 1933 Wolf Creek Fire consumed them. (Special Collections, University of Washington Libraries; photograph by C. Kinsey, Neg. 2488)

§

Opposite page: One of O-A's Willamette Humboldt yarders on the 100-ton steel donkey-moving car en route to a new landing. Befitting the highball pace of logging, the donkey was kept under steam during its move. (Special Collections, University of Washington Libraries; photograph by C. Kinsey, Neg. 5374)

have it hauled to Vernonia. Lumber so purchased was then used to fill out orders on hand. In December 1931, more than 12 percent of O-A's total lumber footage and nearly 18 percent of its shipments were derived by lumber purchased from outside sources. The few orders Kendall's forces were able to book frequently called for items O-A did not have in stock. As a result, a great deal of rework had to be done to previously finished lumber. Greenman wrote, *For the present, the situation with respect to planing costs is so uncertain I confess I don't know how to arrive at them. Some of this lumber is being almost worn out in the processes of making it into salable form and that increases planing mill losses and costs substantially.* By December 1931 the difficult task of reworking existing stocks led to concern over losses incurred in the planing mill. Greenman wrote:

Our direct planer loss in the months of October and November 1931 averaged 13.2% against 11.81% for the year 1930. Our planing mill loss is being influenced very materially by our policy of attempting to sell something we do not have and to produce that something out of something else. This situation will tend to become worse instead of better as our stock assortment deteriorates.

You appreciate, I am sure, that of the 10,741,000 feet of total lumber inventory we had on December 1, 1931, 6,696,000 or 62% is dressed lumber that has been through the planing mill and on which no further loss will be created unless we sell it in some other form than the present.

The market situation continued to deteriorate so much that on March 12, 1932, Kendall wired

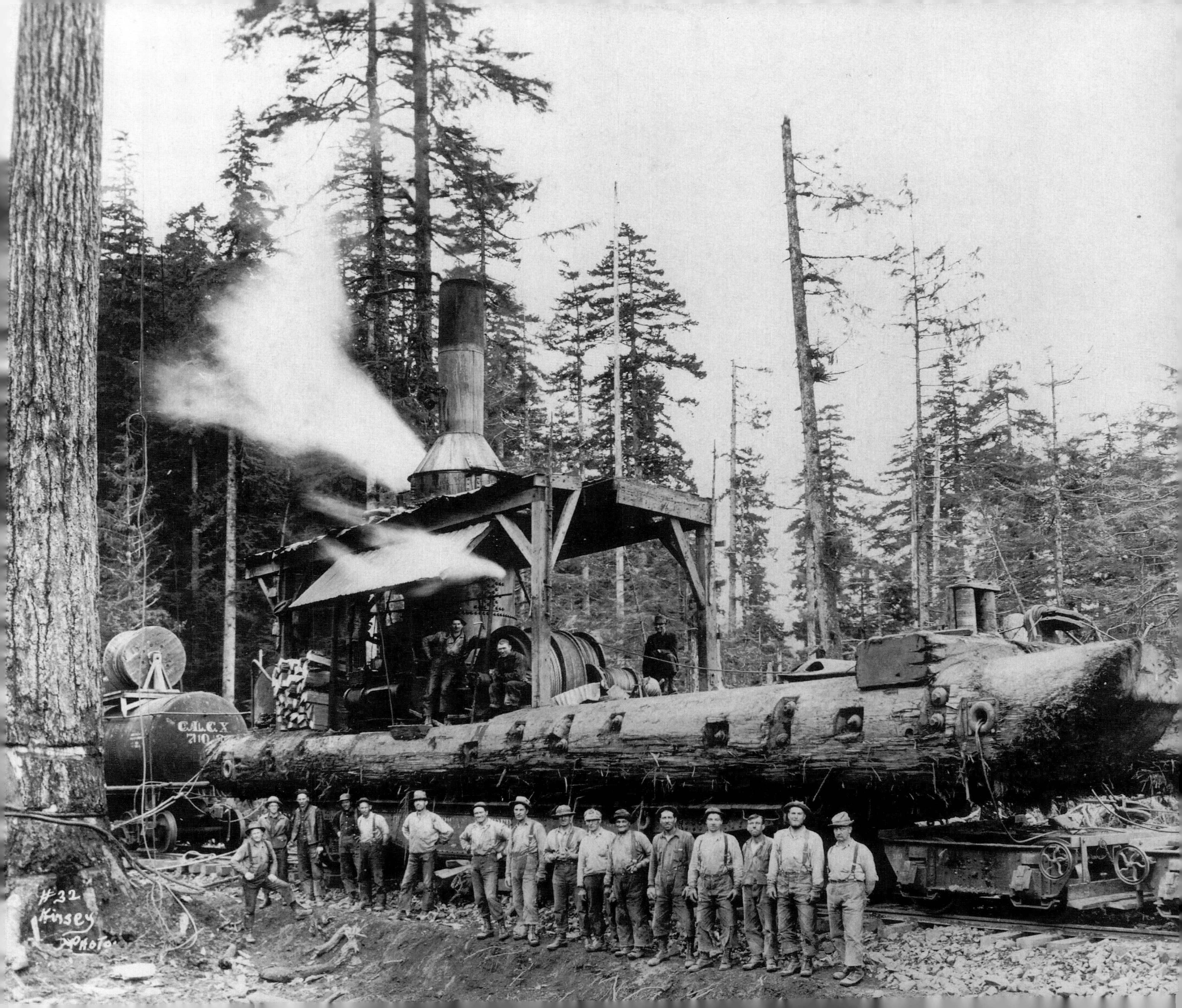
C.L.C.X
#32
Kinsey
Photo.

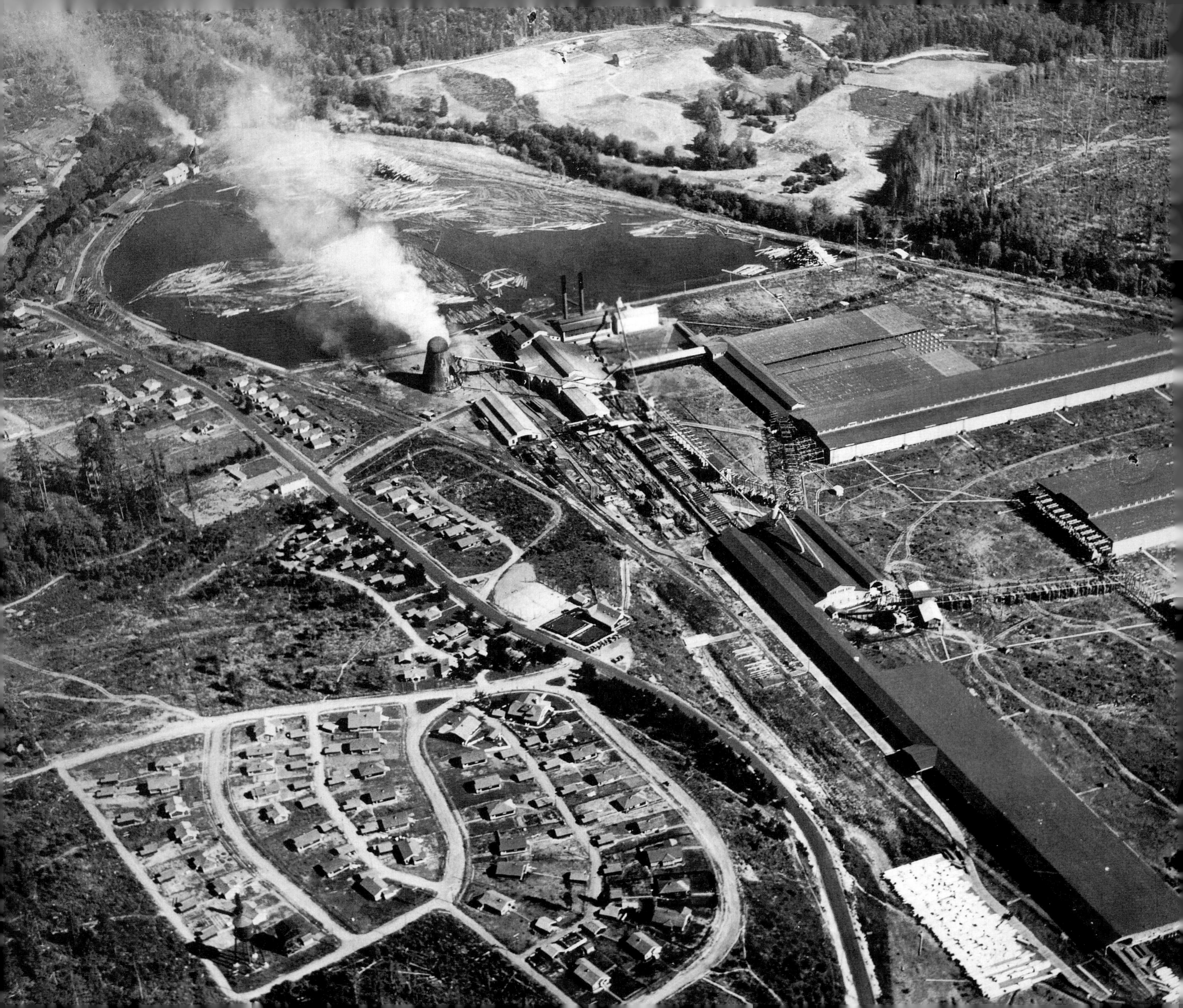

Greenman to turn down an order from the J. W. Copeland Yards for 42,000 board feet of car siding at $4 per board foot, FOB Mill for all grades ... *turn this order down—it is too cheap. ... We have got to stop somewhere. ... A reasonable reduction from our prices is satisfactory, but not 50% or more from the prices we have on our list.* O-A sold the remaining 5.5 million board feet of lumber to the M&M Woodworking Company of Portland in April 1932. With this transaction, the planing mill and shipping departments were closed down completely on June 17, 1932.

It took M&M Woodworking nearly eleven months but finally on May 8, 1933, they shipped the last of the inventory leaving the dressed shed completely empty and, according to Greenman, *looking just like we had just built it to commence the storage of lumber.*

Following sale of the lumber to M&M, only a skeleton staff was retained for plant protection purposes. There were two such crews. One consisted of approximately thirty men employed by the Central-Delta Receiver. They provided plant security and some small level of maintenance capability for the Delta Land & Timber properties in Vernonia. The actual headcount varied as work was shared between as many employees as possible. The other crew, employed by Oregon-American with funds supplied by the Central-Delta Receiver consisted of Greenman, F. M. Ruhl, an office manager, a janitor, a barnman to care for the company's livestock, and a caretaker for the Vernonia guest house. Locomotive 102 remained fired up most of the time to provide steam to the mill powerhouse turbo-generator. It also provided the power needed to keep fire pumps operable.

Another small contingent was kept on the O-A payroll to look after Camp McGregor and the timber holdings. It consisted of E. R. Estey, logging superintendent, a speeder driver, and the part-time help of Paul L. Thompson, logging engineer. The receiver put Greenman in charge of the Central-Delta forces and also those on the O-A payroll.

WHO OWNS THE ASSETS (AT LEAST THE ONES THAT CAN BE SOLD)?

When Central Coal & Coke sought receivership from the courts to protect the company from its creditors, Central's secured creditors, the ones holding the Central-Delta bonds, formed a bondholders' protective committee whose seven members consisted of the bond issues' underwriters and major holders. Chief among them were Edward C. Cronwall, president of Cronwall & Company of Chicago; Sigmund Stern, president of Stern Brothers & Company, Kansas City, Missouri; and Robert C. Schaffner, who chaired the committee and represented A. G. Becker & Company of Chicago.

The Central-Delta bondholders' protective committee wasted no time asserting the position that their interests took priority over all other creditors. The committee premised their position on the theory that Central had pledged its Oregon-American capital stock as security for issuing the bonds in the first place. The fact that Delta Land & Timber Company held title to the Vernonia mill and Oregon-American and was merely leasing it only fortified the Central-Delta bondholders' resolve.

Confident in their rights and desperate for some measure of payback on their investment, the Central-Delta bondholders sought to recoup what little they could by selling the most liquid asset available—the Oregon-American timber. As one

Opposite page: The Vernonia mill as it appeared in 1927. The Company housing development on the O-A Hill is visible to the lower left. The two rough storage sheds are at the extreme right. That long building complex in the front center consisted of, from right to left, the dressed shed, loading dock, and planing mill. Note the monorail system used to transport lumber between the dry assorter, rough sheds, planing mill, and loading dock. An open storage area for finished lumber is across the tracks from the loading dock. The company built a roof over it soon after this photo was taken. Below and to the right of the open storage area was the retail lumber yard. Buildings in the lower right-hand corner housed and fed construction crews while they built the mill. The Johnston & McGraw Shingle Mill stood at the far east end of the millpond at the top of the photo. (Delano Photographics and Northern Light Studios/Brubaker collection, Portland, Oregon)

When loggers needed draws on pay to finance purchases at the camp commissary, O-A issued token currency. Construction of the Wolf Creek Highway in 1939 provided residents of Camp McGregor easy access to the outside world and the importance of company brass diminished accordingly. (Willis Hendrick coin collection; Jim Blain photographs)

measure of their desperation, had their efforts to sell O-A's timber been successful, they would have disposed of the future supply of raw material for the Vernonia mill, thus rendering it valueless.

Nonetheless, representing the committee, Cronwall traveled to Portland in the summer of 1931 where he sought the personal assistance of none other than M. C. Meservey of Thomas & Meservey to find potential buyers of O-A timber. Through his own actions Meservey, conveniently choosing to overlook the loyalty owed Charles Keith, openly betrayed his former client by preparing a list of prospective buyers. Meservey's list included Henry Turrish, a major owner of timber lands in the Nehalem Valley, the Clark & Wilson Lumber Company, whose operations were moving toward Vernonia from the Scappoose area west of the Columbia River and was logging a substantial part of the Turrish timber, Eastern & Western, Inman-Poulsen, and the J. A. Byerly family, owners of the K-P Timber Company whose operations lay immediately north of the O-A timber tract.

Since none of the other prospects showed any interest, many in fact reacting in disgust to the proposal, Cronwall focused his attention on the Byerly's K-P Timber Company. He finally prompted some action when on August 5, 1931, Oliver Byerly, the senior Byerly's son and manager of the K-P Timber Company operations, called Greenman to express specific interest in a block of Oregon-American's timber served by the partially completed Spur 25 system. This block, later to become known as the "Northwest Unit," consisted of approximately 340 million board feet of timber, essentially 40 percent of O-A's remaining stand and the best of what remained uncut from the original DuBois tract.

To his credit, Byerly also admitted some discomfort over this inquiry given the good relationship that had built up between the two companies over the years. He was also quick to point out that he had only made the call at the vigorous urging of the Central-Delta bondholders' committee.

The Byerlys subsequently prepared a part-cash and part-cutting contract offer on the O-A timber and presented it to the Central-Delta bondholders' committee. The committee, although finding the offer

In one of its promotional efforts to capture sales in the era leading up to the Great Depression, the company gave its good customers toy trucks similar to this one. The trucks were loaded with pieces of miniature lumber. O-A even painted the name of special customers on the side. (Kamholz collection)

wanting, summoned Bernardin and Keith and sought to have Bernardin visit the Northern Lines and see if he might work out something better, presumably on the theory that if the Byerlys did buy the timber, they would move it over the common-carrier Kerry line to the Columbia River, thus denying the Northern Lines any benefit of the traffic.

Bernardin declined to make this overture. However, he had no objection to the committee's doing so, which it did, but without success. Bernardin was mindful that when and if market conditions improved, sufficient security existed to recover the equity of creditors and stockholders alike. He therefore found little justification to agree to any sale on a basis such as that offered by the Byerlys. Further, he questioned the propriety of selling any Oregon-American assets because of the fact O-A was bound to default on its own bonds.

Negotiations between the Central-Delta bondholders' committee and the Byerlys continued into the winter of 1932. However, as conditions in the lumber market further declined, and public sentiment against disintegration of the Oregon-American properties mounted, the Byerlys developed cold feet and began to backpedal.

THE OREGON–AMERICAN LUMBER COMPANY RECEIVERSHIP

Oregon-American failed to pay interest on its bonds due April 1, 1932, and defaulted the issue. Bernardin petitioned the courts to have his receivership extended to Oregon-American properties in the State of Oregon. In a parallel development to the Central-Delta situation, the Oregon-American bondholders' protective committee was formed and George R. Birkelund, a vice president of Baker, Fentress & Company, a Chicago underwriter of the O-A bond issue, was named chair-

Declines in the market for structural items notwithstanding, timbers were always a substantial part of the mill cut. After 1936 O-A modified the mill to handle timbers up to 4 feet square. Before WWII many of these so-called Jap Squares were exported for remilling.

Crane tracks for the timber dock are visible to the left. The large, elevated pipe to the right carried planer shavings to the refuse burner. Another carried sawdust from the sawmill to the fuel bunker. A system of "cyclones," or large blowers, visible at the burner and the fuel bunker, moved the refuse. The cyclone nearest the planing mill (not visible) was powered by a 400-horsepower electric motor, the largest in the mill. It had to move all those shavings a long way. (H. Brown photograph; Kamholz collection)

man. The Oregon-American bondholders' committee objected to Bernardin's receivership being extended to Oregon-American properties in Oregon. It did so citing potential conflicts that would arise between the O-A bondholders' interests and the interests of those represented by Bernardin in the Central-Delta receivership and that his appointment might prejudice or delay efforts by the Oregon-American bondholders' committee to recoup their investment. Judge John H. McNary of the U.S. District Court for the District of Oregon was sympathetic to this objection and on June 4, 1932, appointed Aubrey R. Watzek of Crossett-Western as receiver for Oregon-American.

O-A was faced with delinquent taxes amounting to nearly $250,000, so Watzek, at the urging of the Oregon-American bondholders, petitioned the court to disaffirm Delta Land & Timber Company's lease of the mill to O-A, on the theory that its provisions requiring Oregon-American to make lease payments based on timber processed through the mill or otherwise disposed of, presented an insupportable burden in his ability to liquidate timber to pay the taxes. Watzek, in his role to protect Oregon-American assets, sought not to sell timber outright. Rather, if released from the provisions of the Delta lease, he favored a plan of logging O-A timber to the Columbia River, trying to realize sufficient profit from such sales to pay the property taxes.

The Central-Delta bondholders objected to the petition to disaffirm the lease claiming it constituted a lien on substantially all Oregon-American property, thus serving as a prior lien ahead of the mortgage securing the Oregon-American bonds. The Northern Lines, wanting to protect their interests, filed a claim through United Railways that its contract with Oregon-American also established a prior lien on the O-A timber. The Oregon-Amer-

The general manager's home on the O-A Hill in Vernonia. Judd Greenman resided there from 1925 until he retired in 1955. (H. Brown photograph; Rose Valpiani collection)

ican bondholders, out of concern that a court ruling might establish the lease as a prior lien, responded by petitioning the court to foreclose the mortgage securing the Oregon-American bonds.

From the Background, the Voice of Reason

While the creditors sought to dismantle the Vernonia properties, Keith and Greenman, having no authority of their own, found these proceedings unsettling at best. Greenman, voicing his frustration, wrote:

> The parties at interest here in my opinion might just as well face the facts now as ever and realize that nobody in the world can liquidate Oregon-American stumpage as economically and as efficiently as we can right here in this sawmill in Vernonia.
>
> ...no alternative of disposal of the timber for conversion in other channels will bring the owners and security holders as much money in conversion here in this mill will bring.
>
> There isn't any use in the Central or Oregon-American bondholder kidding himself into believing that he is going to get out with a whole skin by selling Oregon-American timber to somebody that will have to pay a lot more to convert it into lumber than we will have to pay.
>
> That is a violation of economic law that even a school child can perceive.

On February 27, 1932, Keith wrote Greenman, *We are in the hands of the bondholders' committee, who in fact are nothing more nor less than a wrecking crew and if allowed free hand they will certainly destroy us.* Keith, on Bernardin's appointment as the Central-Delta receiver, was named general manager of Central and Delta and reported directly to Bernardin. Greenman continued to report to Keith. Once Oregon-Amer-

The Vernonia mill office as it appeared in the 1920s. A survivor of at least three serious fires, the building is now the home of the Columbia County Historical Museum. (H. Brown photograph; Columbia County Historical Museum)

ican went into receivership, however, their formal reporting relationship was effectively severed and after that, Greenman reported directly to Watzek.

The change in formal reporting did nothing to diminish the strong personal relationship between Keith and Greenman. Instead, it served to strengthen it as they corresponded frequently and at length, each advising the other of events in their respective camps. Bernardin and Watzek, by contrast, maintained a more arm's-length relationship that was understandable given the different interests they represented.

The lengthy Central-Delta receivership gave Keith an extended opportunity to have Bernardin's ear. Oregon-American's afforded Greenman the same opportunity with Watzek. This, coupled with the fact both Keith and Greenman were commanding personalities in their own right, gave both men many opportunities to influence the thoughts of their respective receivers.

Writing Greenman in February 1933, Keith said:

> It seems to me that it is up to us to persuade the court, in any event, that the lease should not be voided and it is an economic question as well as a question of law. We must be prepared to meet the issue and if it is at all possible, you and I should be thinking together. I would not ask you to violate your conscience or agree with me in my thought unless you are actually persuaded that I am right. If the conclusion should be reached that there is no economic value in the Oregon-American timber, or the Delta mill property, it will be just too bad for everybody. Personally, I think now as I have heretofore thought that there is value in both, but under present conditions no value can be secured

through conversion. However, I believe the time will come in the not very distant future when it will be possible. As to just when this will occur, I can not tell and I do not know, but I do know that the country is not decadent; values will be restored and business will come back again in greater quantities, with lesser opportunity to satisfy it than we have had in the past. I am sorry I can not sit down and talk it over with you. The alarming thing, as I see it, in the lumber industry, is the hopeless attitude they are taking. We at least must shake ourselves out of it, if the others do not.

Greenman's response read in part:

I am just as firmly convinced of the soundness of your views on the basic questions underlying the lumber industry as you are and am even more opposed than you are, if that is possible, to any move that will result in divorcing our timber from the mill property....

I have the feeling the courts will look on this matter (of timber disposal) rather broadly. It will need to be pointed out that if this timber is separated from the mill, it will doubtless go into "cold storage"...and the local taxing agencies will suffer if the proposed yield tax prevails, as it doubtless will sooner or later.

I have been frankly disappointed in Mr. Watzek's attitude toward the proposal to separate the timber from the mill. I think he is motivated by an honest concern for the holders of the first mortgage on the timber. He has very firm convictions on constitutional property rights...and I believe he is influenced much more by them than by any underwriters....I believe he places the obligation created

After operations commenced the company realized its millpond would not store enough logs to keep the sawmill supplied when bad weather shut the woods down in winter. To keep things running during years of heavy production, O-A built cold decks on the pond's south levee. A Willamette Iron & Steel Works electric log-decking engine was used for this until 1930. It was in the small house just to the left and behind the deck. The electric decker lacked sufficient power to handle large logs and production suffered accordingly. Cold decks made after reorganization were either built by the locomotive crane or the tree-rigged skidder. (H. Brown photograph; Rose Valpiani collection)

HIGH HOPES AND DASHED DREAMS

Some office staff were on hand to pose on January 9, 1928. From left to right: F. Merle Ruhl, chief clerk; Phil Taylor, tallyman; Charles Richardson, stenographer; Judd Greenman, general manager; J. Vernon McAllister, statistics clerk; Walter Wolff, agent; Herb Hollyfield, bookkeeper; Carl E. Davidson, logging superintendent; Frank B. Crosby, paymaster; and Ulas Scott, assistant paymaster.

Davidson was a former member of the AAU championship basketball team from Kansas City. He quit Oregon-American during the Depression to attend law school. He graduated from the University of Oregon with the highest honors and later distinguished himself through his work to overhaul the Oregon State tax statutes. (H. Brown photograph; Columbia County Historical Museum)

by the bond above any other consideration, and I respect him for it. The thing we will have to do, of course, is convince the court that in these times even mortgage obligations must be waived unless the country is to go to pot.

Later he added:

I know you will protect me in these matters. There is some question of the propriety of my acting as intermediary (between Watzek and Bernardin) in these exchanges of correspondence and opinions. I shall not, of course, violate any confidence imposed in me and I pass these matters to you only when I feel no confidence has been violated.

By early 1933, lumber prices began to show signs of improvement. Greenman, at Keith's request, submitted a plan to operate the Vernonia mill on purchased logs on May 6, 1933:

I think the plant should be started as soon as there is even a promise that it can be run and pay its direct expenses. I think that time is here, or at least, is fast approaching. The desirable way to run, of course, would be on our own logs but I think that it is a good ways off. I believe the O-A crowd is afraid to risk their security through milling operations, even if the complicated questions of priority of claims on conversion assets could be amicably settled. I think a small, successful operation on purchased logs will go a long way toward winning them over to permit integrated operations. I believe it is perfectly natural the O-A crowd should hesitate to put their trees into an operating experiment on today's lean markets. Once cut, their security is gone.

The Central-Delta bondholders and other creditors are in a different position. Their security will be improved by operating.

But, like Seward, I think the way to resume is to resume.

The prospect of improving markets in concert with the Keith and Greenman lobbying effort began to take hold, and on June 8, 1933, Watzek wrote Bernardin:

It is my personal feeling…that if the [WCLA "Code of Fair Competition"] results in sufficient increase in selling price without an unreasonable increase in cost of production, it may be possible to operate the Vernonia mill on O-A logs.…If we conclude it is not possible and Mr. Greenman can work out some plan to operate the mill on purchased logs, that may be desirable as an alternative.

Bernardin replied:

I am in sympathy with any plan that will permit the Oregon-American to liquidate some of its timber through the Vernonia mill, and would lend my assistance to the extent of a sympathetic consideration of at least a temporary reduction in the rental…[and] also any assistance compatible with our bank account towards financing the operation…[the bulk] of the problem of raising most of the working capital would fall upon [O-A] shoulders.

Mill department heads posed in front of the mill office on March 29, 1928. Among them were: Archie Knauss, dry kilns, second from left; R. A. Simmons, chief engineer, third from left; A. J. Hughes, chief electrician, fourth from left; Walter Wolff, agent, sixth from left; Judd Greenman, general manager, ninth from left; Holly Holcomb, planing mill, tenth from left; Dave Marshall, machine shop, thirteenth from left; C. L. Anderson, shipping clerk, fourteenth from left; Carl E. Davidson, assistant superintendent, fifteenth from left; Frank Crosby, paymaster, sixteenth from left; and Earl Blieile, shipping, twentieth from left. (H. Brown photograph; Columbia County Historical Museum)

Later he added:

> It is entirely out of the question to count upon the funds of the Central-Delta Receivership for a complete financing of lumber operations at Vernonia, and this regardless of whether the operation is to be conducted by you, by me, or by both of us.
>
> Now the question as to whether or not we can get any assistance from our several trustees and bondholders' committees is one which I cannot answer at this writing. I think it would depend upon our convincing them that the probabilities for loss were remote and that the operation would be of benefit to the estates.
>
> Whether you should lease the mill and use it to cut up the O-A timber with the idea you could sell the lumber to the Central Company in order that you might have the advantage of their trade name makes a strong appeal to me. I am in favor of a plan involving the use of the mill for cutting lumber.
>
> I wonder if you realize how much a voice the trustee and bondholders' committee will have in the subject which we are considering?

On June 25, 1933, Greenman wrote Keith describing Watzek's intentions to log Oregon-American timber to Rafton:

> I believe Mr. Watzek has made up his mind to institute such an operation even though it meets with objection from the other interests involved including the Central-Delta and the carriers. I don't know anything about it but I should say offhand the Court might be pretty likely to permit him to operate even over the objection of the other parties on the ground that he needs money for taxes and such an operation will be in the public interest as far as employment is concerned.
>
> The answer to this is to have Mr. Bernardin try to work out some kind of mill operating plan with Mr. Watzek that involves a considerable degree of cooperation, and possibly some sacrifice, on the part of both of them. I have suggested operation to Mr. Watzek along the following lines and the suggestion has never been ridiculed....
>
> Mr. Watzek is fully aware that all the hazard of integrated operations will be centered in the mill operation of any operating plan...and has indicated to me no desire to avoid sharing those hazards.
>
> I believe Mr. Watzek is fearful of mill operation, feeling that he should not undertake it for his estate because of legal and financial complications that might arise from his operation of the mill property. On the other hand, I believe he would much prefer to put O-A timber through the Vernonia mill than sell it on the open market. I am satisfied he would go a long way, maybe even more than half way, to meet Mr. Bernardin in an operating plan that gave reasonable assurance, at least until the tax situation is cured, of a stumpage return for his interests.
>
> I don't know how to handle the situation but there ought to be some way to bring these two men together and let them discuss an operation in which all the factors would be so distributed as to put neither of their estates in jeopardy through the hazards incident to operations.
>
> You are the logical person to handle this.

On July 8, 1933, Watzek formally proposed an operating plan to Bernardin designed to meet the primary urgent need for funds with which to meet the most pressing tax delinquencies. He added, *If you and I can agree on a program to recommend to both Committees, the chances of success with them are much greater than if a different plan is submitted to each Committee.... Mr. Greenman and I shall await with interest the reaction you and Mr. Keith have to our suggestions.* On July 25, 1933, Bernardin replied:

> You as Oregon-American's Receiver and I as the Central Receiver are both interested in the preservation of the timber, and are united on the proposition that in some way money must be obtained for payment of some threatening taxes. As Receivers, we think the money can be obtained by operating the properties. If the two bondholders' committees don't accept our judgment that an operation will provide the necessary means, then I think they owe it to the creditors whom they represent to suggest some better plan.

But for the hand of fate, a neighboring logger's negligence, the New Deal, and a healthy dose of intervention by Mother Nature, the stalemate might have continued indefinitely.

1932 Fires and the Wolf Creek Fire

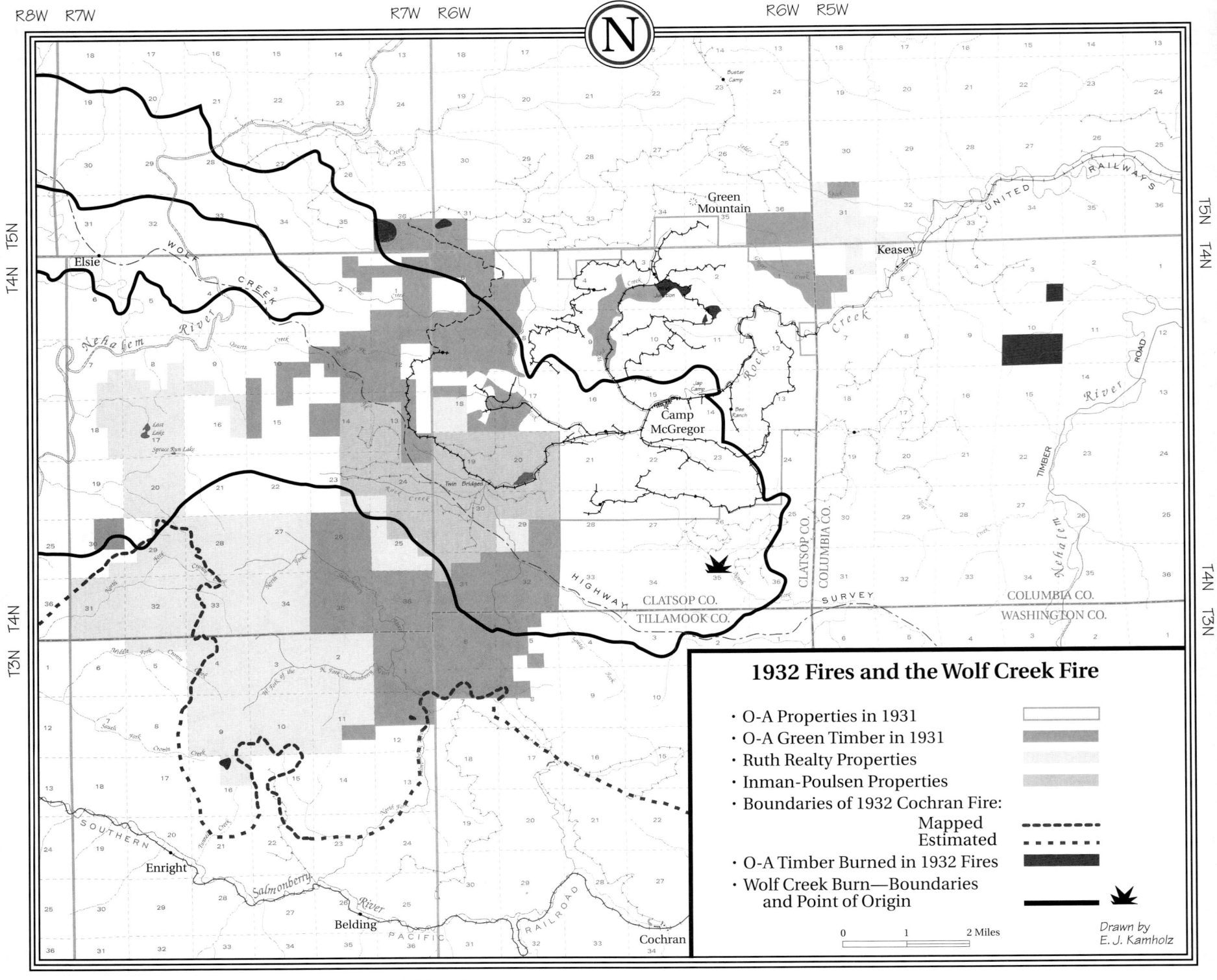

- O-A Properties in 1931
- O-A Green Timber in 1931
- Ruth Realty Properties
- Inman-Poulsen Properties
- Boundaries of 1932 Cochran Fire:
  - Mapped
  - Estimated
- O-A Timber Burned in 1932 Fires
- Wolf Creek Burn—Boundaries and Point of Origin

0   1   2 Miles

Drawn by E. J. Kamholz

TRIALS BY FIRE

In sharp contrast to the fiercely independent competitiveness lumbermen displayed in the marketplace, they universally cowered at the prospect of forest fires and the losses from them. Still, the individual methods different operators used to handle these crises were striking and spoke volumes about their operating practices, if not their character.

EARLY FIRES AND FORESTRY STATUTES

By the 1920s, the State of Oregon had developed a body of forestry statutes regulating the prevention, control, and suppression of forest fires. Various cooperative regional protective associations had been formed to identify and reduce fire hazards before they could develop into actual fires. These so-called patrol associations also regulated slash burning and governed the mobilization of fire-fighting efforts once fires, regardless of their cause, broke out.

One key part of the forestry laws read that the spread of a fire from one member-owner's property to another's did not automatically make the owner of the property on which the fire started liable for damages that occurred after the fire spread. Injured parties had to prove negligence by someone, either concerning the fire's start or by failing to take reasonable precautions to prevent its spread.

Like other operators, Oregon-American experienced numerous fires during its existence. Events following some of these fires not only culminated in the first court tests of the Oregon forestry statutes concerning liability, they also had broad implications for Oregon-American, the Detroit Trust Company, owners of the McPherson-managed holdings lying immediately to O-A's southern flank, and the East Side Logging Company.

Slashing

Once an area has been logged and left cluttered with unmerchantable debris, burning this so-called slashing is about the most effective tool the logger has to reduce fuel content and its hazards.

If left unburned and under the right conditions of low humidity and wind, slashing is easily ignited. If it is dried out and concentrated on the ground, it has all the qualities needed to burn fast and hot. Allowed to burn unchecked, slashing fires can easily spread to standing timber and thus present a sizable risk.

Early on, operators developed the practice of purposely setting fire to slashing on logged-off lands as soon as possible after logging was finished and equipment had been moved elsewhere. This practice continues today. Typically, operators burn slashing in the fall, ideally during cooler days and just before the arrival of the rainy season—added measures of precaution taken to guard against such fires getting out of control.

Opposite page: Ruth Realty Company holdings in the southwest tract were seriously damaged by fire in 1932. The Wolf Creek Fire of 1933 killed even more along with 40 per cent of Oregon-American's remaining stand of green timber.

TRIALS BY FIRE

The K-P Timber Company Fire of August 31, 1928

On August 31, 1928, a fire originated at 11:00 A.M. on K-P Timber Company lands near O-A's Spur 17 West, about one-half mile from O-A's Camp Number 1. O-A's crew from Side Number 1 was heading for dinner at Camp Number 1 behind locomotive 106 when the alarm was sounded. The crew immediately went to the fire scene and started building trails to prevent its spread. E. H. Rengstorff, O-A's logging superintendent, learned of the fire shortly after it broke out and ordered the skidder crew from Side Number 3, the section gang, locomotive 103, and a water car to the fire.

Winds propelled the fire around the fire trails, so part of the O-A fire-fighting crew retreated to prevent the fire from crossing Spur 17 West and from reaching Camp Number 1. The remainder fought to keep the fire from crossing an abandoned skid road. Crews failed to check the fire, however, and it burned over Side Number 1 that afternoon.

During this time the K-P logging crew nearest the fire did what they could to protect their own equipment. Some resentment arose from the fact that the crew from another K-P logging side operating nearby continued logging for some time before joining the fire-fighting effort. According to Rengstorff, K-P men did not leave their jobs and begin fighting the fire until two to three hours after it broke out.

O-A's losses from this fire amounted to some 4 million board feet of downed timber. The fire also claimed some rigging and caused serious damage to Humboldt yarder engine Number 1985.

The Oregon-American Fire of September 21, 1928

On September 18, 1928, Oregon-American started a slashing fire at 8:00 A.M. in the same vicinity as the K-P fire that burned over into O-A's holdings. This was in the area between Spurs 17-W-7 and 17-W-8. The fire was set as a preventive measure to burn slashing that remained on O-A property following the K-P fire of August 31.

The September 18 O-A fire got away, however, and on September 21 spread to K-P Timber Company lands, causing damage to logs, one donkey, an oil car, and two crew cars.

The apparent lack of concern and potential negligence by K-P Timber Company for making only a token effort to prevent the spread of its August 31, 1928 fire caused McGregor to retain the Pinkerton Agency to investigate for Oregon-American. By September 28, 1928, Pinkerton had assigned one of its operatives to hire on at K-P. The agency instructed the man, identified in his reports only as "D. C.," to investigate the origin of various K-P fires, including the one that damaged O-A. Pinkerton also instructed him to determine what means K-P took to prevent fires and to obtain names and addresses of knowledgeable parties. D. C. gathered evidence until October 26, 1928.

Representatives of Oregon-American and K-P Timber Company warily discussed settlement of potential claims each had against the other arising from the two fires. No definitive conclusions were reached, however, and the issues remained unsettled through the next year.

The Oregon-American Fire of May 21, 1929

Oregon-American's Side Number 3 was operating in an area about 1,500 feet north of Camp

McGregor, moving logs to the railhead on Spur 17 South. Around 2:30 P.M., a strong north wind carried sparks from a yarding engine into the top of a snag, causing it to ignite. Fanned by the wind, burning debris from the snag blew all over the logging area lying to the south, creating many spot fires that quickly spread beyond the logging crew's ability to contain them. By 3:00 P.M., the spot fires had joined to present a front nearly one-half mile long, threatening Camp McGregor and the area beyond it to the south.

By 5:00 P.M., the main part of the fire had burned over O-A's new Willamette 13 × 14 yarder, Number 2504. The loggers prevented the fire from reaching the swing and loading machines operating on that side, however. O-A deployed all available men to keep the fire away from green timber on Spur 17 South. To the south of the point of origin, however, the fire jumped Rock Creek and the railroad mainline, surrounded Camp McGregor on three sides, then rapidly spread farther south toward the former site of Camp Number 1 on the abandoned Spur 5 Switchback. To the south of that lay the East Side Logging Company's logging area.

O-A's loggers were barely able to control the fire's northern flank, let alone prevent its spread to the south. Accordingly, Greenman dispatched locomotive 105 with a crew of forty-one men from Vernonia to join the ranks of firefighters. Greenman also telephoned Antone Lausmann, president of East Side Logging Company, at his home in Portland to warn him of the fire and that O-A could not spare men to prevent the fire's advance to the south. He requested Lausmann put East Side men out to check the fire's spread along the old Spur 5 Switchback right-of-way. Greenman offered to pay the East Side costs of fire fighting if Lausmann would do so. Lausmann agreed to personally look the situation over and put a crew of East Side men on the fire if he felt it was necessary.

Lausmann telephoned Greenman at 10:00 P.M. that night. He advised the fire was not as bad as he had expected and that East Side crews would fight the fire once it reached its own railroad right-of-way with the expectation of checking its progress there. Greenman repeated his offer to pay for Lausmann's fire-fighting costs without accepting responsibility for East Side property damage because O-A was not negligent or indifferent to the fire but did feel a neighborly interest in preventing damage to East Side's property.

On May 22, O-A advised Inman-Poulsen of the threat the fire presented to its operations. Unlike East Side, I-P agreed to build a fire trail on the west end of the fire and its crews did so the next day. This was done at O-A's request and expense.

At 12:15 P.M. on the 23rd, Lausmann called Greenman, requesting O-A send several crews of buckers and fallers to stop the fire's progress before it reached a strip of green timber on the north edge of the East Side operation. Greenman relayed Lausmann's request to Carl Davidson, assistant superintendent to Greenman, who was overseeing the fire-fighting effort from Camp McGregor. When Davidson called Lausmann to advise that no men could be spared, Lausmann objected to shutting down his operations to deploy his crews to the fire. Both men agreed if O-A could not spare any men by the next morning, Lausmann would shut down his logging operation and put his crew on the fire. Davidson agreed to send O-A's shay Number 2 to the East Side camp the next day to help shuttle water cars.

At 4:00 P.M. that afternoon, the fire broke over to the East Side logging operation and destroyed 12 million board feet of downed timber and a donkey engine. Rain began falling on the evening of the 23rd. It extinguished the fire, but only after some 4,000 acres of O-A and Detroit Trust Company lands had burned.

On May 29, Lausmann visited Greenman to advise that East Side had suffered insured losses of $27,000, uninsured losses of $11,000, and fire-fighting expenses totaling $5,000. When asked what O-A's position would be toward payment of East Side's uninsured losses and fire-fighting expenses, Greenman replied that Oregon-American had done everything possible to keep the fire from reaching East Side property. He had promptly notified Lausmann of the fire and the probability it would reach East Side. Greenman also made it clear that in all matters concerning the fire and its spread to others' property, Oregon-American had conducted itself according to the laws. Greenman's notes following this meeting read in part:

> The dictates of common sense and neighborly courtesy [would lead to the conclusion that]...O-A should assume no responsibility for any of the East Side losses excepting as to the uninsured portion of East Side's fire-fighting expense and the cost of reinstating East Side's fire-fighting insurance policy.
>
> ...The fact East Side elected to continue logging on May 22nd and chose to wait until the fire reached East Side before fighting it put a little different aspect on the matter than it would have carried had (East Side) quit logging and made an effort to stop the fire on O-A property instead of their own.

Oregon State Forestry Statutes Put to the Test

By year-end 1929, East Side presented O-A its bill for uninsured fire-fighting costs. O-A agreed to pay the bill but only if East Side and its insurance company would execute a release preventing the insurance company from pursuing O-A further. Greenman also made it clear the payment, once made, did not constitute an admission of liability. The insurance company refused to agree to Oregon-American's terms so O-A declined the claim.

Shortly afterward, East Side Logging Company and its insurer, North River Insurance Company, sued Oregon-American for damages amounting to nearly $30,000. In the complaint, East Side and North River claimed their damages were caused in part by Oregon-American's negligence for failing to burn slashing created during its previous four years' operations on the Spur 5 Switchback rail line lying immediately north of East Side's timber and operating area.

In its defense, Oregon-American claimed its Camp Number 1 and one-half its logging operations were along the Spur 5 Switchback between July 1926 and March 1928. Exposure of its property to fire precluded it from burning slashing in the area during that time. And, while authorities had granted O-A a permit to burn its slashing in September 1928, the same authorities revoked the permit after East Side Logging Company complained the burning of O-A's slashing represented a hazard to East Side's operation.

Oregon-American's counsel, the Portland firm of Wilson & Reilly, expressed concern that while little question existed that O-A had acted within the legal framework of the Oregon statutes governing forest operations, the statutes had yet to be tested in the courts. The outcome of the trial was, therefore, not a sure bet by any means.

The *East Side/North River* lawsuit made it awkward for Oregon-American to resolve its claims against the K-P Timber Company arising from the fires of August and September 1928. While neither O-A nor K-P had taken legal action to collect their claims against the other, a precedent created by an East Side victory in its case against O-A would have offered one company a much stronger legal basis on which they could pursue the other for damages. For this reason Wilson & Reilly were instructed to proceed with filing a suit against K-P Timber Company for loss and damage suffered in the fire of August 31, 1928, which originated on their property. Greenman, explaining the situation to Keith, wrote:

> There is an interim period of about 30 or 40 days subsequent to August 31, 1930, during which [K-P] might file suit against us for damage from a fire which they allege started on our property....
>
> The statute of limitations runs against our claim on August 31, 1930, and [if] we did not file our suit, and [K-P] files theirs, we would simply be out of luck. Our claim in this matter amounts to about $75,000, but we will file for double damages under the negligence statute, as that is another matter that we do not dare to do, for if we filed for simple damages, and they sued us for double damages, we would be out of luck again....
>
> Of course, we feel that the prosecution of this suit will depend entirely on the decision finally rendered in the case of the East Side Logging Company against ourselves. That is, if we beat the East Side suit, in our opinion there is no chance of recovering anything from the K-P Timber Company. On the other hand, if the East Side Logging Company does recover against us, then I should say that we would have a very good chance of recovering from the K-P Timber Company.

Oregon-American filed suit in U.S. District Court against the K-P Timber Company claiming $136,000 in damages.

The K-P Timber Company and its insurer immediately countersued Oregon-American for $164,000 in damages K-P claimed it suffered when Oregon-American's September 21, 1928, slashing fire spread to K-P's property.

The *East Side/North River vs. Oregon-American* case went to trial in late July 1930 in U.S. District Court. In early December, the judge delivered his verdict deciding completely in favor of Oregon-American. In advising Keith of the victory, Greenman wrote:

> We won a complete verdict in the East Side Logging Company fire suit on the facts which makes it extremely unlikely they will attempt an appeal....
>
> ...in my opinion, a notable victory was won and the logging industry of the Northwest has been benefited by Judge Bean's decision.

James Wilson, Oregon-American's attorney who successfully defended the case, later wrote Keith:

> The position taken...by the loggers with reference to [the forestry statute] is that they have been contributing annually so much per acre to the fire patrol associations for the very purpose of relieving themselves in case of fire from damages should a fire on their lands get out of control.
>
> The loggers and their attorneys have been

watching the East Side Logging case very carefully…Judge Bean's decision will have a lot to do with quieting the mass of litigation that has arisen over forest fires since the East Side Logging Company started the ball rolling.

I have no fear the case can be upset on appeal.

East Side and the insurers did not appeal Judge Bean's ruling and, subsequently, Oregon-American and K-P Timber dropped their respective lawsuits against each other.

THE FIRES OF 1932

While economic events of the Great Depression played out, parallel developments in the heart of the Douglas fir belt set the stage for what was to become a defining moment in the industry's history—one that also became a major rallying point that ultimately helped lead the lumber industry in the region to recovery from its economic woes.

The near-complete shutdown of the industry and the scarcity of funds to complete housekeeping tasks required to reduce the threat of forest fires created conditions in northwestern Oregon that, in the years following 1930 and 1931, were similar to the construction of a natural form of time bomb, simply waiting for the right moment to set off a chain-reaction of destruction.

The convergence of time and conditions occurred first in 1932. At the beginning of northwestern Oregon's fire season that year, fire patrol authorities and operators had a general feeling that curtailed logging operations would greatly lessen the overall risk of fire. Even so, there existed a very real concern that the extremely high level of unemployment in the area might, by itself, encourage those desperate enough for work to set fires on purpose for the sake of the jobs those fires might create.

As the season progressed, however, those concerns seemed groundless, and it proved to be one of the mildest periods of summer weather ever recorded. Little fire activity of any kind took place. Still, with such great quantities of accumulated slashing on the ground carried over from prior years' logging, there was a strong desire to dispose of this material. So, when weather forecasters predicted heavy rains beginning on September 19, 1932, various fire patrol associations lost no time interpreting this as the signal to proceed with many simultaneous slash burns on the assumption that the early season rains would serve to keep matters from getting out of hand.

The storm predicted for September 19 never materialized and by the following day, skies began to clear. Still, conditions for slash burning remained very good and so, for the next week, authorities continued the general program.

On September 27, however, everything changed. First the skies cleared and temperatures soared into the nineties. The humidity dropped into the twenties, and strong east winds developed that served to dry things out even more. On October 4, a slashing fire near Wedeberg responded to these conditions and got out of hand. It burned the town of Cochran and created widespread damage. Five separate fires including the Cochran fire attacked Oregon-American and Ruth Realty Company properties between September 14 and the onset of rains on October 10.

The Vernonia/Keasey Fire

This fire was the work of an arsonist and was set in the western suburbs of Vernonia on September 10. Heroic efforts of townspeople and patrol associ-

The West Oregon Lumber Company logging works as it appeared following the Cochran Fire of 1932. The incline railroad, visible at the bottom-right center, was used to lower loaded log cars down the steep canyon wall to the Salmonberry River and a connection with the Southern Pacific.

The Cochran Fire also burned much of the Ruth Realty timber stand that lay northwest of this scene.

Oregon-American bought the remnants of this tract in 1940. It blocked up perfectly with its own holdings. (Oregon Department of Forestry)

ation employees saved that part of the town lying south and west of the United Railways tracks. The fire eventually burned more than 10,000 acres of lands previously cutover by Koster, Van Vleet, Rock Creek, and East Side logging operations. Setting a backfire along the East Side Logging Company railroad right-of-way finally stopped it, about 8 miles west of Vernonia. Isolated stands of timber in Sections 3 and 10 in Twp. 4 North, Range 5 West owned by Oregon-American were seriously damaged by the fire. Owing to the poor stand of timber on these parcels, however, economic loss resulting from the fire was considered inconsequential.

The Tideport Fire

The Tideport Logging Company set this fire on September 12 to burn slashing created by that company's logging operations. Tideport started its fire on the NE ¼ of Section 35, Twp. 5 North, Range 7 West and it spread into Oregon-American Lumber Company lands in the NWSW corner of Section 36 5/7. This fire joined the fire started by K-P Timber Company on its lands that also spread over into Oregon-American holdings. Ground and crown fires that developed killed outright or seriously damaged a total of about 90 acres of green standing Oregon-American timber.

127

Camp Number 1, Spur 25 following its total destruction by the August 1933 Wolf Creek Fire. Pictured in the foreground are bunkhouse sleds and bed frames. (Martin E. Hansen collection)

The K-P Timber Company Fire

This too was a slashing fire ordered by the fire patrol association on September 19. K-P intended it to clear up about 2,000 acres of unburned debris that it had accumulated during more than three prior years of logging on Sections 29, 30, 31, and 32 in Twp. 5 North, Range 7 West and on the south ½ of Section 36 in 5/7. It burned fitfully on the rain-dampened slash for a week, accomplishing less than authorities hoped it would. That fire also flared up when the weather changed on September 27. In the face of the east winds, the fire attacked Oregon-American green standing timber on a 3-mile front across Sections 5 and 6 in Twp. 4 North, Range 6 West, Section 31 in 5/6 and Section 36 in 5/7, all lying north and west of O-A's Spur 17 system. Effective trailing by K-P firefighters minimized the damage to O-A timber except in Section 36 5/7 where the fire joined the Tideport fire already in progress.

Much of the damage O-A suffered to its timber in this fire was along its partially developed Spur 25 right-of-way. The K-P Timber Company lost fifteen trestles aggregating 3,700 feet, along with a considerable amount of logging equipment in this fire.

The Oregon-American Fire

Greenman and logging superintendent, E. R. Estey personally set this fire on September 19 to dispose of 50 acres of slashing created by operations in 1930 and 1931 in Sections 2 and 11 in Twp. 4 North, Range 6 West, along Spur 17 South. They spent the 19th and 20th starting and restarting the fire with kerosene while rains fell. The fire loafed along doing less than desired until the weather changed on September 27. This fire flared up and

Twisted metal was all that remained of the Camp Number 1 saw filer's shed following the Wolf Creek Fire. Warped saws in the debris provide stark testimony to the fire's intense heat. (Martin E. Hansen collection)

Estey's small crew soon lost control of it. Most of the fire-fighting effort was made to protect logging equipment, the railroad, and its trestles, an effort that was successful. Meanwhile, however, the fire spread rapidly and threatened O-A's mainline and Camp McGregor before jumping Rock Creek and heading south toward the Spur 5 Switchback and lands cutover by the East Side Logging Company. This fire also joined the K-P fire to the north and eventually spread over about half O-A's cutover lands, covering some 5,000 acres in the process. Apart from consuming a small amount of standing timber along Spur 17 South this fire did little damage, but given the large area it covered, the fire proved expensive to contain. One measure of how much debris was left on the ground following logging was that some areas covered by this fire had burned as many as three times previously since O-A began logging in 1922.

The Cochran Fire

Of the five fires that affected Oregon-American in 1932, the Cochran fire was the most destructive. Fire Patrol Association authorities started it on September 19 and, like the others, it generally burned less than hoped for. However, once charged by the change in weather, it spread over thousands of acres and burned towns, farms, logging camps, railroad structures, and a large amount of timber. The fire so extensively damaged several tunnels on the Southern Pacific's Tillamook branch line that it interrupted rail service for a month.

Oregon-American's losses from this fire were both direct and indirect. Severe crown fires developed on company timber in Sections 7 and 8 in Twp. 3 North, Range 6 West and Section 12 in 3/7. The location lay in the extremely rugged Salmonberry River canyon territory on the south-

TRIALS BY FIRE

The right-hand Twin Bridge at the confluence of Rock Creek and Military Creek following the 1933 fire. Originally constructed by Inman-Poulsen and taken over by Oregon-American in 1930, O-A rebuilt the trestle after the company began rehabilitating the Spur 25 system in 1936.

Today the area is heavily grown over but the close observer can still find a couple of bridge bents from the replacement and the original left-hand twin that I-P built in the early 1920s. (Martin E. Hansen collection)

ern flank of O-A's Southwest Timber Unit. The fire killed nearly 80 percent of the timber on those areas that burned. At the height of the fire on October 10 and 11, Estey reported he could plainly hear the roar of the fire from Camp McGregor, 7 miles away.

By far, the most severe damage to Oregon-American interests occurred after the Cochran fire swept more than 16 miles north and west from its point of origin, down the Salmonberry River canyon to its confluence with the Nehalem River. At this point the fire turned north along the Nehalem River. Then it spread east into the headwater canyons of the North, Middle, and South Forks of Cronin Creek, all on the western part of Ruth Realty's holdings. The terrain in this area was the most rugged of all the combined O-A and Ruth lands. The origins of the South and Middle Forks of Cronin Creek, for example, begin at elevations of about 3,000 feet but fall to only about 400 feet by the time they join the Nehalem, less than 5 miles away. Another fifteen lesser creeks, each divided by sharp ridges in the area, speak further of the broken terrain in the tract.

This area had also seen previous forest-fire activity, the last occurring in 1907. Between the accumulation of dead snags, rough topography, and hot, windy weather, the Cochran fire found every reason to spread into the Ruth stand, which it did with abandon. In fact, clear evidence showed the fire not only burned eastward into the face of prevailing winds, it burned downhill almost as readily as it burned going up.

In total, 2,084 acres of Ruth Realty lands burned. Ninety-two percent of the timber on those parcels, nearly 79 million board feet, were killed by the fire.

Direct losses to Oregon-American's green timber arising from the 1932 fires were comparatively light,

The long trestle that crossed the Inman-Poulsen log pond following the Wolf Creek Fire. O-A bypassed the trestle on land to the south when it began rehabilitating the rail line in 1936. (Martin E. Hansen collection)

accumulating only one and seven-tenths of the remaining cruise, of which that part consumed in the Vernonia fire was considered practically worthless to begin with.

Describing the damages to Keith, Greenman concluded:

> There is nothing very pretty in this picture. About the only saving grace, if any, lies in the fact this fire burned what, in my opinion, is the least desirable of the Ruth timber. It is the poorest stand; the least accessible and stands on the worst ground. There is considerable question in my mind if the timber on [Section] 31, 4/7, for example, has ever had any conversion value at any market prices that have [been] obtained since we owned the property.

He added, *Had unfavorable weather continued for a week or so more, there would have been no timber worthy of the name left in Clatsop, Tillamook or Washington Counties. Only good fortune and Nature and certainly nothing man did or could do saved the stand.* In fact, many believed that had the hot and windy weather prevailed another week, the fires would have burned all the way to the Pacific Ocean.

THE WOLF CREEK FIRE OF AUGUST 1933

Sobering as the 1932 fires might have been, they were only the opening acts to the greatest single economic and ecological disaster in the recorded history of northwestern Oregon—the 1933 Tillamook Burn.

The Tillamook Burn has been widely studied and reported. Yet obscured and ignored by countless articles, books, and the passage of time is the fact that while the infamous Tillamook Burn of 1933 raged, another large fire, one completely separate and distinct, burned just to its north. This fire, officially known as the Wolf Creek Fire, itself was a disaster of no small means. Between August 24 and mid-September 1933, it burned an area of more than 47,000 acres. Of particular interest to this story, the Wolf Creek Fire, not its more widely recognized counterpart, the Tillamook Burn, was responsible for burning the main tract of Oregon-American's timber stand. Equally overlooked is what started the Wolf Creek Fire. Unlike the Tillamook Burn, the cause of which was clearly determined, authorities never determined what actually started the Wolf Creek Fire, although some believed it to be the work of an arsonist.

The Fire

The Wolf Creek Fire began at 4 P.M. on August 24, 1933, near the center of Section 35, Twp. 4 North, Range 6 West. The fire originated in unburned slashings created by the East Side Logging Company in 1929 and 1930 on lands owned by the Detroit Trust Company.

Authorities immediately dispatched men and equipment from Vernonia and their efforts kept the fire from progressing through the remainder of the day. But, around 1 A.M. on the 25th, the wind suddenly shifted. Now blowing from the northeast, the wind steadily picked up velocity until it reached gale proportions. The wind drove down the humidity and soon pushed the fire past its bounds. On-the-scene firefighters immediately sent for reinforcements that arrived during the early morning hours. Authorities also made calls for 300 Civilian Conservation Corps men but since they were encamped near Mt. Hood, nearly 100 miles away, they did not arrive until late that afternoon.

In the face of the strong wind, the fire quickly advanced. Updraft from the fire picked up burning

They had those CCC boys and everybody they could find in the country working on that fire. It was just going crazy. The day after it started I was up on the spur at Twin Bridges that curved around a little knob. Dad dropped me off in the middle of the day then he and the rest of them went up the North Fork. We had 300 beehives at Twin Bridges and I went up to build a fire trail around them. Two hives of bees burned up there. I was 17. I did everything that I could and then started back down toward the other bees on the North Fork.

The wind changed. It had been coming from the east then it shifted so it was coming out of the west so it made the fire turn back on itself, toward Camp McGregor. I got to the Inman-Poulsen Upper Camp and the pond when the fire came back again. The CCC boys was all gone. They'd thrown their shovels and grub hoes down and down the railroad track they'd gone.

All the fire had was the dead fireweed and its kind of a fibrous material, y'know, the stalk of it. The stalk was laying on the ground. And this was what was actually burning.

When I got to the long trestle it was on fire. I was trapped and couldn't get out. That's when I went to that

pond. In the upper part of the pond there was a bunch of alder trees and I was out on a sawgrass point. I guess I'd been there about three hours when a roving fire warden came by. We went up to the bunkhouses in camp and got two mattresses each, regular single mattresses. We layed one of them out on the mud and then we took the other one and soaked the top of it in the water and then we crawled in between them when the fire went over.

The mattresses caught fire. I didn't know that. I slept right on through it but this fire warden said he got up and put the fire out in the mattresses, soaking the tops of them again. We were there at the pond it seems to me like 32-34 hours.

If somebody had torn up the plank walks they had between the houses they'd have saved McGregor, 'cause the fire just went house to house on that walk. That walk was just like kindling.

When they started hauling those families out of there was when the CCC's tried to push the women and kids off the train. They were scared. Most of those kids were from back on the East Coast.

McGregor was the last thing to burn.

Lloyd White, son of Lewis White, the bee rancher

debris and cast it high in the air. Once airborne, the strong east wind propelled the flaming refuse west, sometimes miles ahead of the ground fire. Directly in the path of this airborne debris lay the main body of Oregon-American's green standing timber. When the burning debris fell there, it ignited the bone-dry foliage and, fanned by the same east wind, created immediate crown fires. Those fires cast off even more burning debris that created yet more spot fires, all of which soon combined into a solid front, consuming everything in its path. These events unfolded so quickly and in such magnitude that firefighters never had a chance to head off the crown fire, much less do anything to control it.

In contrast, spot fires landing in cutover areas of Detroit Trust and Oregon-American lands advanced slowly so authorities deployed all available forces to forge trails to prevent the fire from spreading to East Side's equipment and camp and to Camp McGregor and O-A equipment that it had scattered about its land. Firefighters accomplished much effective trailing the remaining part of August 25 and on into the following day.

However, like an afterthought, the wind, at 5 P.M. on August 26, suddenly reversed its direction and, at hurricane velocity, began blowing the fire from the west toward Camp McGregor. Firefighters fell back to protect Camp McGregor and for a while it looked like they would be successful. That is, until a burning snag fell and severed the pipeline that carried the camp's water supply.

Facing a hopeless situation, authorities ordered four families, other residents of the camp, and the CCC firefighters, a total of nearly 300 persons, to quickly board a train waiting to move them to safety. In their panic to escape, and mistakenly thinking there was no room left on the train, some of the CCC crew reportedly tried to throw families off the cars. Within an hour, Camp McGregor succumbed to the flames. Although the most extensive damage caused by the Wolf Creek Fire occurred within two days of its outbreak, the fire continued burning until rains finally began on September 5.

This fire crowned whole sections of timber; it spotted ahead as much as 2 miles at one jump and burned downhill and against the wind, so you know it did an enormous amount of damage. We never had a chance. Ten thousand of the best men that ever wore calks could only have done as we did—stood and watched her go. We had about 300 CCC boys in the camp at the time it burned but they were worse than useless.

Judd Greenman

The Damage

Camp McGregor's destruction was complete, right down to the wooden sidewalks that connected the bunkhouses. Camp Number 1, which had been moved from Spur 17 West to a clearing on Spur 25-1, met the same fate. Assessed damages for both camps totaled nearly $140,000, for most of which O-A carried insurance.

The Willamette skidder, two locomotives, and two oil cars stored at Camp McGregor survived unscathed. O-A had scattered its donkey engines around its property and periodic efforts to maintain bare ground around them prevented their destruction. Firefighters waged a hard but successful battle to save three donkeys on Spur 22.

Assorted rigging, a couple of speeders, and some railcars were lost. The company insured none of the logging equipment.

Except one small trestle heading into Camp McGregor from Keasey, all losses to the railroad lay west of there. The trestle on Spur 17 nearest Camp McGregor suffered minor damage. Two trestles on Spur 22 were lost along with twenty more on the mainline between McGregor and Camp Number 1. Fourteen of those were carryovers from Inman-Poulsen, however, and would have needed rebuilding in any event. Railroad ties along the entire line west of Camp McGregor were nearly a total loss, because of the fire and rot.

Greenman added a firsthand impression of the Wolf Creek Fire when he wrote W. H. McGregor to inform him of the news. By then, McGregor had retired and returned to Texas.

> I am sending you a set of pictures of Camp McGregor taken after the fire of August 24–28, 1933. The pictures speak for themselves as to the damage done to this fine camp. Camp 1, which you will possibly remember was located in the SW1/4 of Section 7 4/6 on about 40 acres we had cleared for the site, is equally flat and distressing looking....
>
> This fire started in about 450 acres of unburned slash left by the East Side Logging Co. On the N½ of Section 35 4/6 way down in the NENE corner of the township. It traveled nine miles in two hours, burning in a northwesterly direction and finally burning over 45,590 acres of timbered and cutover land. About two thirds of the burn, or 30,000 acres, was timbered....
>
> In addition to the two camps, this company had involved in the fire about 365 million feet of timber

in Twps 3/6–4/6 and 4/7 in addition to about 170 million of Ruth Realty timber. I estimate the killed timber on our holdings and contract stuff at 40% of the stand in addition to which I think 15 or 20% is badly damaged by heavy ground fires and doubtless will die in the Spring. This fire crowned whole sections of timber; it spotted ahead as much as two miles at one jump and burned downhill and against the wind, so you know it did an enormous amount of damage. We never had a chance. Ten thousand of the best men that ever wore calks could only have done as we did—stood and watched her go. We had about 300 CCC boys in the camp at the time it burned but they were worse than useless.

In addition to the timber and the camps we have lost 5,400 feet of bridges chiefly on the old I-P line where they were about obsolete anyway. A pile driver and one loading donkey burned over but were not seriously hurt. There was no damage to locomotives but we did lose our water tank; one oil tank and about all the wooden frame cars we had including all 10 camp cars which were stored at Camp McGregor and burned when the camp did.

All in all, it's a pretty sick mess and I imagine, wipes out any possibility of equity the stockholders ever did have. In my opinion, the property will do well now to pay its debts and, lacking compromise, may not even be able to do that.

The Blame

If anyone connected with Oregon-American had an opinion on the cause of the Wolf Creek Fire, it was never committed to correspondence, at least any that survived with the company's records. The company maintained that the cause was unknown. Nevertheless, as to conditions that enabled the fire to take hold and spread, Oregon-American had very definite conclusions, supported by strong evidence.

The East Side Logging Company had repeatedly ignored instructions issued annually by regional fire patrol association authorities and the State Forester to dispose of slashings it had created during logging operations conducted in 1929 and 1930. These slashings lay in Sections 25, 27, 34, 35, and 36 of Twp. 4 North, Range 6 West. Each time authorities issued those orders, East Side responded by saying that burning its slashings would endanger its logging and railroad equipment and the company's financial condition prevented it from moving or otherwise protecting its equipment. East Side's failure to dispose of its slashings was in direct violation of Oregon Forest Laws.

By 1933, title to all of East Side's assets had been removed from the company and transferred to the L&M Holding Company owned by East Side's principal stockholders, Antone Lausmann and Frank Miller. As receiver for Oregon-American, Watzek quickly sought a legal opinion. It clearly supported a cause of action arising from the failure of East Side and Detroit Trust to dispose of slashings. However, given the muddied waters of ownership of East Side's assets and a similar problem obtaining the names of people who were members of the Detroit Trust Company syndicate, collection of damages was anything but a sure bet and Watzek took no further action.

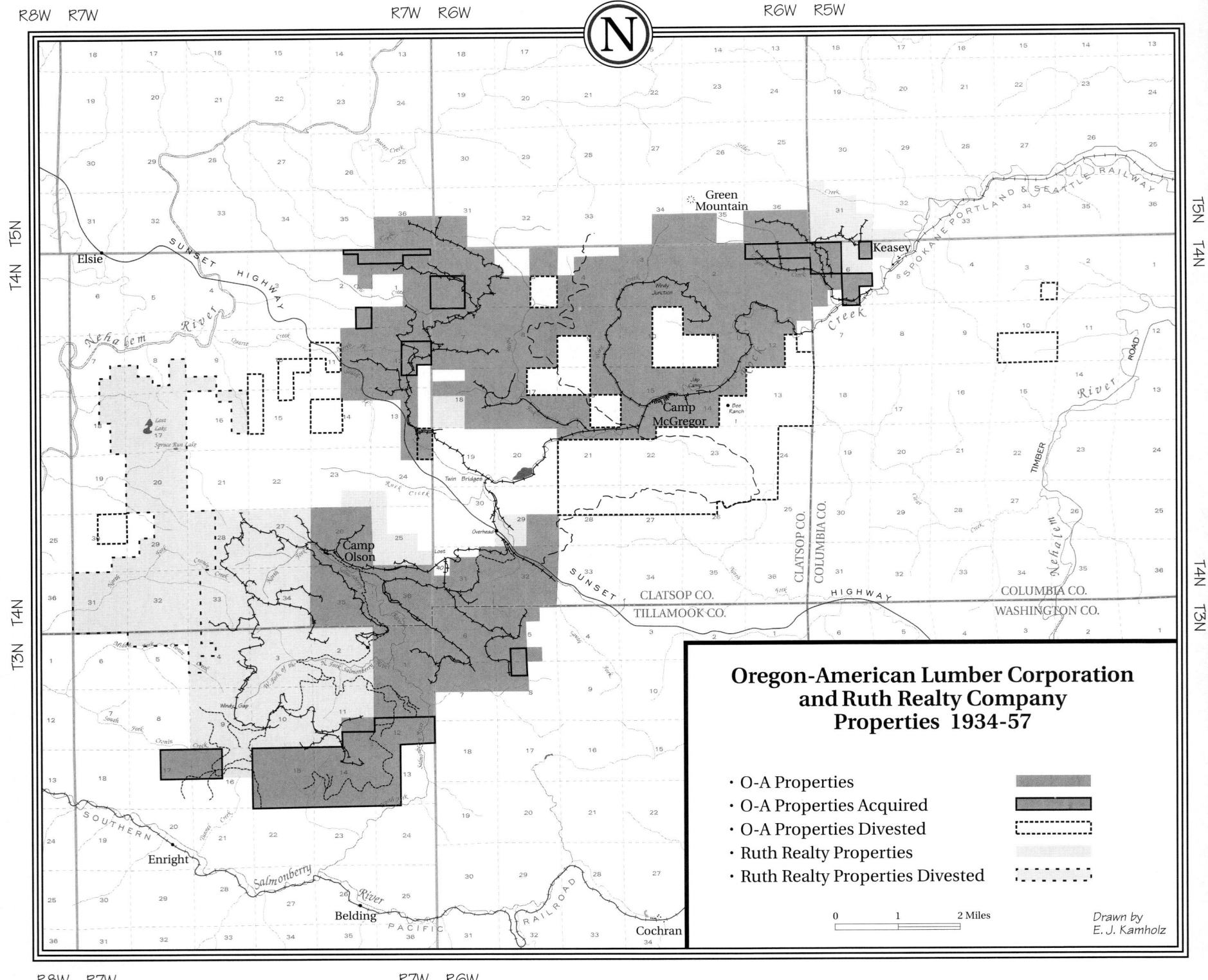

Oregon-American Lumber Corporation and Ruth Realty Company Properties 1934-57

- O-A Properties
- O-A Properties Acquired
- O-A Properties Divested
- Ruth Realty Properties
- Ruth Realty Properties Divested

0   1   2 Miles

Drawn by E. J. Kamholz

FROM THE ASHES

Once the 1933 fires cooled, work began to assess the damage. The prospects were daunting. From inside the burned areas all one could see was an endless tableau of smoldering, broken land that only days before had been blanketed with towering, lush, green trees. Now all that remained was a graveyard of blackened dead snags. The trees, stripped of their foliage remained standing as if to bear witness to man's folly and nature's unmerciful counterpoint. Even where the fire had not crowned and had remained on the ground the damage was severe, giving promise of only greater losses to come as the trees' burned trunks gradually failed to sustain life.[1]

The Tillamook and Wolf Creek Burns together consumed some 311,000 acres, an area of nearly 500 square miles. The fires destroyed 12.5 billion board feet of green timber, enough to build one million, five-room houses, timber that would have kept Portland and other mills supplied for twenty years. Monetary losses created by the disaster were enormous. Future payrolls estimated at $200 million were lost, not to mention potential tax revenues the counties and state would never realize. At depressed, pre–WWII prices, the direct loss of timber to the fire was more than $20 million.[2]

As for Oregon-American's losses, the Wolf Creek Fire killed a total of 404,061,000 of the remaining 1,022,448,000 board feet based on the original Thomas & Meservey cruise, or nearly 40 percent of the company's remaining uncut timber. The fire also killed untold thousands of board feet of timber along the Ruth Realty tract's northern extremes. Without question, the fires of 1933 changed the economics of the Northwest lumber industry forever.

As the chilling news sunk in, however, there also grew the conviction that operators could realize much profitable salvage, provided the price for lumber went up enough to warrant the undertaking. Time was critical, however. Loggers could harvest Douglas fir and cedar trees of average size with very little loss to insects and fungi, provided they salvaged them within one to two years. Larger trees offered even better hope. They could also salvage hemlock if they acted immediately, although to a lesser extent and probably not at all if it was left unlogged beyond two years.

Salvage logging was not without its costs, however. The loss of sap made trees brittle and more likely to break up when felled. That and the loss of the cushion provided by the foliated tops reduced the recoverable volume. As the effects of boring insects and rot accumulated, proportionately less of the tree was recoverable. Logging under these conditions became even more dangerous.[3] Meanwhile, as the industry realized that salvage opportunities were substantial, the lumber market itself cast some ray of hope on matters as it began improving.

Other positive signs appeared in the months immediately following the burn, most notably in a

Opposite page: To create workable operating units, expand timber reserves and dispose of burned and logged lands, Oregon-American and Ruth Realty made many changes to their holdings after the Depression.

collective approach to recovery by the lumber industry itself. Still, as operators began realizing the potential advantages of immediate salvage, they were also cautious because a surge in production could easily upend the fragile lumber market if no steps were taken to harness production consistent with demand, the very problem that led to the collapse of the industry during the Great Depression.

In the period leading up to the fires the federal government, keen to establish mechanisms and programs to restore the economy, encouraged the industry to craft a so-called Lumber Code designed to regulate output. Authorities immediately considered losses caused by the Tillamook Burn as they worked out provisions of the code. The resulting increases in allotments granted Columbia River mills were a large impetus for operators to combine their salvage efforts to recover as much from the burn as quickly as possible. Fellow operators in the area drafted Aubrey Watzek, his own Crosset-Western holdings on which the Tillamook Burn had originated, to represent them to the secretary of agriculture in Washington, D.C. He was directly involved in the achievement of increased Lumber Code allocations for Columbia River mills.

So, in a cruelly ironic way, the staggering losses to Northwest Oregon forests resulting from the Tillamook and Wolf Creek Burns provided the very catalyst needed to put sawmills back in operation. Thus began the slow process of economic recovery.

Salvage provisions effectively barred Oregon-American from shipping logs to river mills because it had ceased shipping to those markets in 1924. However, as sawmill capacity, or the lack of it, was a principal factor governing the rate at which salvage in the burn could proceed, authorities granted Oregon-American its own allocation, provided the company cut its salvaged logs at Vernonia. It was therefore doubly ironic that the Wolf Creek Fire brought the battling bondholders' committees to the bargaining table to figure out how best to recover their investment, and that any plans they developed required O-A's timber be milled at Vernonia.

REORGANIZATION

In those uncertain months following the fires the receivers, particularly Watzek, recognized they would have to provide leadership to all parties claiming interest in Central Coal & Coke and Oregon-American. That Bernardin and Watzek had reconciled themselves to a plan to log O-A timber to the Vernonia mill even before the 1933 fires occurred, it was only natural, given Watzek's involvement in obtaining lumber code allocations, for him to take the lead in developing an operating plan to get things started. His proposal, that Oregon-American timber be cut at Vernonia under the direction of the receivers, was submitted to both bondholders' committees in November 1933.

The prospects were not appealing. As a firsthand witness to the destruction, Greenman underscored the direness of the situation and wrote to Keith:

> I believe this very Tillamook County timber constitutes a threat to timber, log and lumber values for years to come.... [The need for rapid disposal] will serve to establish values for some time to come and, because of the handicaps from which it suffers, the values will be low.
>
> I know that I told Mr. Watzek when he had uncovered the extent and severity of the burn, that

I felt the equity had all been burned out of the property.... In my opinion, the only way in the world the stockholders will ever get anything out of the property will be acquiring additional timber, under favorable marketing conditions. It is my firm conviction they will never realize a dime on the conversion of the presently owned timber and, in fact, I am dubious about the ability of the property to pay off its proposed debt with the limited assets it will have.

And it may be that I am all wrong and that there are vastly more possibilities in the situation than I can see. As I have written you before, my judgment is warped and distorted by my experiences during the last few years to the point where I can see but little good in anything. I am truly ashamed that I apparently do not have your courage, when you really have so much less reason to be courageous than I do.

Failing to fully comprehend their limited choices, the bondholders committees' reacted coolly to Watzek's operating plan.

However, while traveling between Portland and Washington, D.C. on lumber allocation business in late January 1934, he proposed another meeting with the bondholders' committees. At this meeting in Chicago, George Birkelund, chairman of the Oregon-American bondholders' committee, submitted his own plan of reorganization that addressed the underlying issues of asset ownership, the key point of disagreement between the parties. Birkelund's plan broke the impasse, and after a brief series of negotiations both bondholders' committees adopted the plan. Principal features of the proposed reorganization are shown in Table 6.1.

Table 6.1

Reorganization

Of the two unpaid bond issues, Oregon-American's issue totaled $1,720,800 and Central-Delta's was $2,076,200.

Recognizing the need for outside working capital funds to rehabilitate the company's properties, the plan sought to secure a loan of approximately $700,000 for this purpose, giving it a prior mortgage over all other interests until paid off.

The plan called for a new bond issue—income mortgage bonds—secured with a second mortgage, with distribution as follows:

Debt

To O-A Bondholders, par for par	$1,720,000
To CC&CC and Delta Land and Timber Company, 50 percent of former Interests	1,038,000
Total	$2,758,000

Equity

To O-A Bondholders, one stock share for each $100 par value of bonds	17,208 Shares
To CC&CC Bondholders and Central Equity (Formerly 100 percent of O-A Preferred and 80 percent of Common Stock)	25,100 Shares
To Reorganization Compensation, Management and Contingencies (including the remaining holders of O-A Common Stock)	7,692 Shares
Total Equity	50,000 Shares

Stockholders were to surrender their shares for deposit in a voting trust controlled by five voting trustees, two appointed by Oregon-American bondholders, two by Central-Delta bondholders, and one by equity.

Claims and counterclaims between the two bondholders' committees were to be withdrawn. Unsecured creditor claims were to be written off.

This represented a major concession by the Central-Delta bondholders, because it essentially reduced that group's claims by one-half, in return for a substantial future equity position in the reorganized company, the interests of which could not appear until that company's operations had redeemed the first and second mortgage bonds, or in ten years, whichever came first.

On learning of the proposed reorganization plan, Greenman wrote to Watzek on February 3, 1934:

> While I am glad to know that it is possible for all our interested people to sit down and discuss reorganization without flying at one another's throats, it is naturally distressing and discouraging to learn that a reorganization plan is being considered which, in my opinion, puts the property right back where it has always been through the saddling on of a debt load it can never hope to carry to the end of the road.
>
> The proposed control set-up seems to be fair and equitable. I don't know how efficiently a committee of five can run a lumbering operation for I never had any such experience. My offhand guess would be that they would be just about one-fifth as efficient as individual control, but that again may be my pessimism cropping out.
>
> I have not dropped the ideal of getting your operation started even if you and the Trustees and the Committees and everybody else has. To me, it just don't make sense to turn from the practical possibilities of a receiver's operations to the will-of-the-wisp of reorganization. The trouble is, I guess, that it don't have to make sense to me.

When more than a month elapsed after the Chicago meeting without further progress, Watzek grew impatient and urged the committees to speed things up. Feeling obligated to pay off some of the property tax liability, he began applying pressure on the committees and gave them a one-month deadline, after which he threatened to petition the court for authority to either begin salvage and liquidation of company property or postpone liquidation with consent of all parties.

Bernardin agreed with Watzek but not without noting that he lacked the ability to apply further pressure by following through on a joint operation of the mill. Still, the practical and legal difficulties of achieving a unified plan of reorganization proved slow to resolve and matters dragged on into the spring of 1934.

Greenman, completely frustrated by the reorganization's snail-like pace and his own sense of helplessness in the matter, gave serious thought to resigning for a position in the federal government's National Recovery Administration. Keith, while naturally disappointed, wrote to Greenman:

> I do not think I have any right and I certainly have no desire to stand in your way of doing something to better your situation. Any other position on my part would be selfish and a poor reward to one who has been as loyal as yourself. I would greatly

like to have you, in case you do go with these people, tell me if we do get to the point of operations, that you will take charge of the operation there in the future as you have in the past.

Later he added:

I have been informed [a reorganization plan is nearly completed and if, when so translated into a formal agreement] production will go ahead at Vernonia without waiting for the whole program to be carried out along the line suggested by Mr. Watzek.

Undoubtedly, if the plant at Vernonia operates you are the man to operate it. Whether I will have any connection with it or not, I do not know. You may be assured of that, and without any qualifications, they have got to have somebody to run the plant and somebody who knows how to do it. Certainly nobody in the group of bankers or the receivers has the ability.... You are the only one I know of that stands in the picture, so in that matter, you may be assured, without hesitation on my part, this will be a fact.

On June 19, 1934, Oregon-American's directors filed a bankruptcy petition in U.S. District Court in Missouri. The filing was made under provisions of the revised bankruptcy laws that had recently been passed by the McKeown Act. The directors filed the bankruptcy petition to consolidate all the attendant issues in the same jurisdiction. Watzek, by then fed up with the situation and thwarted in carrying out an operating program to best serve his estate, was clearly of the mind that the petition was meant to undermine the proposed reorganization. He wrote Greenman of his conclusion, *If there is to be a wrangle,* *I shall not accept the trusteeship, and it is quite likely I may not do so even though all parties finally get together on an agreed reorganization plan.* He need not have worried, for the next day, the U.S. District Court for the Western Division of the Western District Court of Missouri approved the Oregon-American bankruptcy petition, appointed Bernardin as trustee, and directed Watzek to turn over to Bernardin all property of the Oregon-American Lumber Company in his possession, thus ending Watzek's duties as receiver.

On July 9, 1934, the financial interests submitted a plan of reorganization for the Oregon-American Lumber Company to the court that largely reflected the plan they had agreed to in January. George R. Birkelund of the Oregon-American bondholders' committee, Robert C. Shaffner of the Central-Delta bondholders' committee, and J. M. Bernardin, trustee, were designated the Reorganization Committee.

As to Watzek's term as Oregon-American's receiver, Greenman commented to Keith:

I know from talking to Mr. Watzek that, because of a press of his own affairs largely arising out of plans the Crossett-Western and Blodgett people have to operate in their burned Wilson River timber, he is anxious to be released from further responsibility and work in connection with our affairs as promptly as possible.

If there are to be any ancillary or subsidiary trustees for the Oregon-American in Oregon, I sincerely hope we can get some one who will be as fair and as friendly as Mr. Watzek has been. We have all learned, I think, that our interest can not be safely trusted to everyone who would like to have the job.

Keith, in response, wrote:

I have been informed that I am to be in the picture in the reorganization. In what capacity, I do not know. Without any question of doubt, if I am in any capacity, I will need you and want you badly. I have every confidence in your ability, integrity and loyalty. We have a fight ahead of us and I don't know of any better associate that I could have than yourself.

Greenman, by this time, had reconciled himself not to leave the situation as it stood. Responding to a job offer he wrote:

I am more or less obligated to see this thing through to some kind of a conclusion; first, because of the very high regard I have for the people with whom I am associated and second, because about all the stake I have been able to accumulate is tied up in this business. So far as the stake is concerned, I could probably leave that to the tender mercies of my successor and the fates, but I can't so easily get rid of the other obligation. Charles Keith, who brought me here at the highest salary he had ever paid any mill man in two generations of sawmilling, has been much more than a boss to me. He is in bad trouble now. Maybe I can help him out. If so, I certainly owe it to him and to his friends and associates to do so.

The reorganization plan of O-A is still in the "nebulous" state. The Federal Courts have approved them, a majority of the creditors are satisfied with them and it only remains to be seen if the proper amounts of working capital to put the property in operation can be secured. If they can..., I would not be at all interested in your proposition....

On the other hand, if this property cannot be put in operation fairly early this year, I will be looking for a job. Some time ago I made up my mind that I would not sit here and look at $5 million worth of empty buildings through another winter. I am nearly 50 years old and, as you know, sawmillers wear out fairly early in life.

Still apprehensive of the future, Greenman wrote to Keith of his misgivings: *It must be apparent to anyone that long-range recovery will do us no good. We must have lumber profit-making possibilities in the next five years to help us any. We only have 8–9 years' supply of timber at the best, if we run at half capacity, and it is entirely conceivable to me that we will exhaust our own supply in 6–7 years.* Casting his personal misgivings of the long-term prospects aside, Greenman prepared his best estimate of Oregon-American's remaining timber. He presented his findings on September 10, 1934, a summary of which is presented below. As a practical matter, these assumptions would serve the same function as the Thomas & Meservey cruise had for the predecessor company:

1. Recovery in unburned stands will practically coincide with our experience to date, which has been 80.24% of the original cruise.
2. We will suffer a loss in logging the burned timber of 30% of the recoverable green *stand* (not the green cruise).
3. Hence, that the recovery on burned-over lands will be 56% of the original cruise, making the underrun against the original cruise on burned lands 44%. Twenty percent because of overcruising and 24% because of damage to the timber by fire.

I have assumed, as have all the authorities of

which I know, that the thin-barked species—Hemlock, Larch, White Fir, etc.—and the thin-barked specimens of Douglas Fir, which are the small trees included in the cruise, will be a total loss. If we get on the land in time to salvage some of these easily destroyed species and specimens, fine and dandy. If we are delayed, for any cause, they will be valueless.

I can't make too plain to all concerned that these estimates of recoverable quantities of fire-killed timber are *guesses*, pure and simple. There is no formula by which the damage to the fire-killed timber can be even approximately calculated.

On November 26, 1934, the court approved the Oregon-American Lumber Company Plan of Reorganization with minor modifications to the capitalization structure originally proposed in January of that year. These changes resulted in the creation of 44,079 shares of stock.

The press release announcing the reorganization plan stated:

> [The reorganization] provides that the first mortgage bondholders of the Oregon-American Lumber Company and of the Delta Land & Timber Company will exchange their securities for income bonds in a new corporation to be presently formed, the O-A bondholders getting dollar for dollar in the exchange and the Delta Land & Timber Company bondholders getting an arbitrary amount of bonds agreed on in advance as representing the worth of the Vernonia property owned by that company and covered by its separate mortgage.
>
> Bondholders and stockholders of the old company will receive voting trust certificates for capital stock in the new company as their interests appear.
>
> Certain unsecured claims have been waived and others, very small in amount, will be paid. Control of the new company will rest in five voting trustees to be selected from the various groups of security holders....
>
> This action marks the first step in efforts looking toward rehabilitation of the Vernonia property and resumption of logging and milling operations. A vast amount of work remains to be done before the certainty of operations is assured. Working capital must be provided from outside sources; the details of formation of the new company must be worked out; transfers of property from the old company to the new must be accomplished and new securities must be exchanged for old ones before there can be any certainty about resumption of operations. After all of this has been done, and a definite decision to operate has been reached, much time must be spent in rehabilitating the logging property before operations can be started. It is impossible at this time to make any estimate of the date of resumption of operations. It is not even certain as yet that all of the efforts to set the new corporation on its feet will be successful.

The sentence *Bondholders and stockholders of the old company will receive voting trust certificates for capital stock in the new company as their interests appear* was an understatement if ever there was one. First, the shares were designated "no par value," so on the simple accounting principle that if liabilities equal assets, no equity existed. On the face of it, the Oregon-American Lumber Corporation was, at the time of its birth, as thoroughly debt-ridden as it could possibly be; only through retirement of all its bonded indebtedness was there the faintest hope of the enterprise's ever having worth to its so-called owners.

On December 14, 1934, the new organization filed to incorporate in the State of Oregon. With the formation of the Oregon-American Lumber Corporation on that date, the torch passed from the failed dreams of Charles Keith and his Oregon-American Lumber Company to the hope and promise of a brighter future.[4]

With this symbolic gesture came new owners, new senior management, a vastly changed social, political, and business environment, and a decidedly different, and scaled-down, vision of the company's future. Nevertheless, it was a beginning.

The New Management

The voting trustees and directors of the Oregon-American Lumber Corporation resembled participants in a shotgun wedding. The reorganization plan's requirement for balanced representation of the debtors and competing creditors literally forced former protagonists together. A rundown of the players illustrates this notion.

Voting Trustees

The voting trustees were: George Birkelund of Baker, Fentress & Company, Chicago and former chairman of the Oregon-American bondholders' committee; R. R. Clabaugh, former member of the Oregon-American bondholders' committee; Robert C. Schaffner of A. G. Becker & Company, Chicago and former member of the Central-Delta bondholders' committee; Paul H. Saunders of Saunders, Son & Company, New Orleans, and former member of the Central-Delta bondholders' committee; and Charles S. Keith, former president of the Central Coal & Coke, Delta Land & Timber, and Oregon-American Lumber Companies.

Directors

The board of directors, appointed by the voting trustees, was no less an interesting mix. Membership included E. C. Cronwall, who was president of Cronwall & Company, Chicago and a former member of the Central-Delta bondholders' committee. As a side note, Cronwall's efforts to sell O-A's timber to the Byerly interests no doubt remained fresh in Greenman's mind. The man's appointment must have been like a nightmare come true for Greenman, who earlier had written Keith: *I notice by the papers that our friend Cronwall has been made chairman of the Long-Bell reorganization committee. I hope when the time comes for reorganization of the Central that we can escape the fate of falling into the clutches of a committee headed by that cold-blooded eel.* Cronwall's presence proved invaluable, however, for through his many contacts in the financial community, particularly with the Reconstruction Finance Corporation, the company managed to secure its working capital loan.

Fred R. Olin, a seasoned, thirty-two-year veteran of the Hammond Lumber Company was the only "neutral" party in this select group. Having no previous involvement with Oregon-American or its creditors, Olin was undoubtedly chosen because he represented an impartial viewpoint. Owing to his neutrality and because of his strong financial background, Olin was also named president and treasurer of the new corporation.

The third director, Henry F. Chaney, was a vice president of Baker, Fentress & Company and worked out of that company's Portland office, thus serving to move the seat of operating control closer to Vernonia. Chaney was also elected chairman of the board of directors.

Omar C. Spencer, partner with the Portland law firm of Hart, Carey, Spencer and McCulloch, was appointed secretary. Coincidentally, the firm was also counsel for the SP&S, a situation no doubt viewed favorably by the new management given O-A's long-standing close relationship with the railway company.[5] Coincidentally, Spencer grew up in Vernonia and his father sold Oregon-American the property on which the company built employee housing, this area having become known as the "O-A Hill."

Greenman, though indispensable, was not made a director. The new board, however, appointed him vice president and general manager of the entire operation and, as a practical matter, he was made the operating head of the business.

By June 15, 1935, the legalities to establish title to the properties were completed and on that date Bernardin executed the deed transferring all the Oregon properties to the new corporation. Attention soon focused on taking advantage of the recently passed Oregon State Legislature bill, the so-called Burned Timber Tax Compromise Law, and O-A filed petitions with Columbia, Clatsop, and Tillamook Counties for substantial reductions in past-due property taxes. Olin and Greenman successfully negotiated these tax compromises by early November 1935—just before public opinion had sufficiently jelled against such practices. In so doing, they obtained reductions in overdue property taxes through 1935 of 30 percent in Tillamook and Columbia Counties, and 35 percent in Clatsop County, where most of the company's burned timber was. Total tax relief amounted to more than $85,000. The counties also waived an additional $75,000 in overdue interest.

NORTHERN LINES AGREEMENTS

Oregon-American's bankruptcy and rebirth as the Oregon-American Lumber Corporation effectively voided all contractual arrangements that existed between the old company and others, including the agreements with the Northern Lines.

Yet the strategy underlying many arrangements between the old Oregon-American and the carriers remained as valid as ever. Accordingly, the companies renewed many prior agreements including those governing traffic and maintenance provisions. The railroads even liberalized some, granting O-A the freedom to move tools and equipment between Vernonia and the county line in regular log trains not subjected to regular tariffs. Notably absent, however, was the renewal of any agreement obligating the new Oregon-American to repurchase Ruth Realty timber held for the old Oregon-American.

Although the desirability of acquiring the Ruth timber was unquestioned, three factors stood in the way of committing to it. First, as it assured the earliest possible means of repaying debt, the Oregon-American Lumber Corporation's reorganization plan was premised on liquidating company-owned timber as early as possible. Second, committing to the Ruth timber, except where scattered parcels of it lay mingled with O-A holdings, would have saddled the company with more debt. Already obligated to repay bondholders of the old company and faced with the added debt for a working capital loan, the new Oregon-American was unable to further burden its delicate financial structure. Finally, and largely a practical matter at that, most of Ruth's holdings lay miles from O-A's existing logging railroad development and would not be within reach for years to come.

Recognizing that nothing had changed the original premise underlying Ruth Realty's purchase of the timber (for example, the Northern Lines' desire for the freight traffic it represented), Oregon-American provided the carriers no more than a verbal assurance of its intention to acquire the timber some time in the future.

Still there remained the more pressing issue of how to salvage the thousands of acres of Ruth timber burned in the 1932 and 1933 fires. But for a small parcel surrounded by O-A holdings, most of the burned Ruth timber was hopelessly far removed. Recognizing its inability to undertake salvage logging outside its own burned timber, Oregon-American recommended Ruth sell its burned timber to independent loggers and helped facilitate that process.

THE RECONSTRUCTION FINANCE CORPORATION LOAN

As matters progressed, the new board's attention focused on the last major objective needed to commence operations, obtaining the working capital loan. By then Greenman had begun seeing rays of hope and confided to Keith, *I believe the directors are making progress in arriving at an understanding of what is ahead of them. I was very discouraged at their attitude at first, so much so that I was on the verge of throwing the whole thing up several times. However, I believe that I begin to see a slight change in their philosophy which is naturally encouraging.* As Cronwall and others cleared the path for the Reconstruction Finance Corporation working capital loan, the task of preparing the application itself fell to Greenman. His correspondence to the board and excerpts from the application itself revealed a great deal about the plan to restart operations.

Herewith preliminary draft, or "dummy," of the RFC loan application....

This application merits your serious study. It contains many opinions; a little philosophy and some promises, as well as the facts and figures. The opinions, philosophy and promises are all mine so long as the application remains in our hands, but once it is fully executed and turned over to the governmental agency, they become yours. For this reason I suggest that you acquaint yourselves with the documents quite thoroughly.

While this is so far my baby, or very largely so, it is now deposited on your doorsteps for such treatment as you see fit to give it. You will not hurt my feelings any if you conclude we should start all over again and have another child. Or, if you want to shear its locks, or circumcise it, or otherwise operate on it, please do not hesitate on my account. What we want is this money and any ideas on how to get it will certainly be welcome.

[The plan] contemplates a single shift operation of the mill running 40 hours per week to be supplied with logs from two sides and a rig-up. The logging operations would be conducted for approximately one year at this rate in timber available to Spurs 17 and 22, about 2/3 of the timber from Spur 17, where the timber is practically all green, and 1/3 from Spur 22, where the timber is all burned. Assuming a recovery against the cruise of 80% in the green timber and 56% in the burned timber, there would be available in these two locations requiring a minimum of railroad rehabilitation, approximately:

54 Million feet of green timber on Spur 17
19 Million feet of burned timber on Spur 22
During the year in which the timber was being

removed from Spurs 17 and 22, Spur 25, to which there is tributary some 300 Million feet of cruise, could be rehabilitated.

I believe that, if logging operations are conducted before worms get to working in the heartwood of the killed trees, we will get a very much better grade recovery from burned logs than we ever have had from green ones. We will recover from the fire-killed stands only the very best logs out of Douglas Fir and Red Cedar trees. The inferior species and the tops of the Douglas Fir and Cedar trees will, of necessity, be left in the woods for they are already worthless or non-recoverable. In other words, the estimated shrinkage in recovery against the cruise will occur in the least desirable species and in the least valuable portions of the Douglas Fir and Cedar trees. This may well tend to considerably improve our estimated realization.

It will take from four to six months, depending on the season when work is undertaken, to get logs coming out of the woods. Hence, granting the necessity for carrying one month's production of logs in the millpond, it will take from five to seven months to get the mill started after a decision to operate is reached and from eight to ten months after such decision is reached to build a lumber inventory up to the point where as we may expect to handle the kind of business available today.

O-A filed the RFC loan application on September 4, 1935. Immediately, company officials turned to their political allies, urging them to exert what influence they could bring to bear on the RFC for speedy approval of the loan.

Charles Donnelly, president of the Northern Pacific, encouraged the RFC to approve the loan on October 14, 1935:

The two Northern Lines have been deeply interested in this Vernonia mill operation from the time when the plant was first constructed about ten years ago, and during the period of its operation the Great Northern and Northern Pacific received more than 2.5 million dollars in revenue from the movement of the lumber product of this mill.

I do say unhesitatingly—and I feel sure Mr. Kenney [president of the Great Northern] will agree with me—that there are few enterprises in the Pacific Northwest whose resumption of business we could more gladly welcome than that of the Oregon-American Lumber Corporation.

The RFC approved the loan on October 28, 1935. The agency made its first funds disbursement on January 8, 1936, and proceeds from it were appropriated as shown in Table 6.2.

Table 6.2
RFC Loan Distribution

For Delinquent Taxes	$253,200
For Rehabilitation of Plant and Logging Properties	136,100
For Extension of Railroad	23,500
For Payment of Reorganization Fees	31,000
Balance, Solely for Operating Purposes	256,200
Total	$700,000

In parallel with Oregon-American's reorganization, a similar program was underway to revive Central Coal & Coke. Sigmund Stern, of Stern Brothers & Company, Kansas City, Missouri, represented a substantial interest in the Central-Delta bond issue and therefore played a major role in the reorganization of that company. It too was renamed during the reorganization to Central Coal & Coke Corporation. In the process, Stern came to control the Central Company. The new management relegated Charles Keith, though still representing Stern's interests in Oregon-American Lumber Corporation through his duties as a voting trustee, to the sidelines when it came time to set forth the new operating programs for the Central and O-A.

REHABILITATION

Restoration of Oregon-American's property largely fell into two categories—rebuilding the dwellings and common facilities at Camp McGregor, and repairs to the railroad. While the Wolf Creek Fire's damages demanded most of this work, specifically the rebuilding of camp structures, trestles, and the burned-out part of the railroad, the railroad also required a significant amount of repair overall. Largely, this was because the line to Camp McGregor and beyond had not been maintained. During the shutdown, the only service over the rail lines had been by speeders, operating daily runs between Camp McGregor and Keasey for supplies and mail.

West of Camp McGregor the railroad almost had to be rebuilt from scratch. Fire had damaged or destroyed virtually every trestle along this part of the line, a summary of which appears in Table 6.3.

Owing to the lengthy Oregon-American shutdown and the resulting lack of traffic over the United Railways, the SP&S had only maintained the line as far as Poynter on the Keasey line. The railway company kept that portion of the line repaired to serve the Koster Products Company logging spur there. A small amount of track work had also been done as far as Tara to accommodate another Koster Spur put into operation near Homewood in 1934. However, by 1936, the United Railways line between Keasey and the county line was in such bad shape that a speeder could barely move over it.

Table 6.3

Trestles Damaged by Fire West of Camp McGregor

	Number of Trestles	Aggregate Length
Mainline from County Line to Spur 25	14 of 16 total	3,494 Feet
On Spur 25	4 of 4 total	1,344
On Spur 22	4 of 4 total	640
On Spur 17	1	130
Total	23	5,608 Feet

Once reorganized, and while Oregon-American was anticipating its RFC working-capital loan, Keith requested the Great Northern initiate repairs to the Keasey line. However, nothing came of this. A proposal to remove the East Side Logging Company equipment from the area had failed to materialize, and the official line from the SP&S remained noncommittal until definite word about when Oregon-American would commence operations. Once the RFC funds began flowing, however, officials of the Great Northern and SP&S visited the line to find out the extent of repairs necessary to put it back into operating order and authorization to rehabilitate the line immediately followed.

Oregon-American, unable to safely use a locomotive on the line, began hauling lumber with speeder Number 10 between the Lindsay mill in Vernonia and Camp McGregor, completing three and a half trips of up to 3,000 board feet per trip daily. Greenman expressed hope that if the SP&S decided not to make temporary repairs to their bridge spans, they would at least agree to hold up the major repairs long enough to allow speeder transport of materials O-A needed to complete its own work.

Meanwhile, the company started constructing prototype bunkhouses at the Vernonia mill. Likewise, to get a jump on early operations, O-A purchased some old camp cars Inman-Poulsen had been storing at Zan siding. By adding a second shift and a trailer to the speeder shuttle, crews delivered something more than 30,000 board feet of materials daily to the O-A side of the county line. O-A also began rehabilitating "Jap Camp" to house a thirty-five-man construction crew.

Replacement of railroad ties on the county line to Camp McGregor route was delayed while considerable work was done to clear brush and open cuts along the right-of-way. Little or no such work had been done for more than five years.

As the end of February 1936 approached, O-A employed various independent contractors to build fifty-odd bunkhouses on the mill's shipping platform. Meanwhile, the SP&S began accumulating materials needed to replace bridges 49-6 and 49-9 above Keasey, a process that, while enabling O-A to accumulate its own materials and put "Jap Camp" in condition to house the construction crew, was disappointingly slow.

In order to make up for lost time, Greenman proposed movement of the rehabilitated I-P camp cars and about twenty-five bunkhouses to Keasey on April 5, 1936. His plan was to push the bunkhouses out on the high trestle immediately above Keasey and line them across to the 2-Spot shay operating from the opposite side of the trestle. However, on learning of the plan, SP&S officials embargoed that part of the line above Keasey, citing unsafe condition of the bridge trusses. Even so, O-A started timber cutting-crews by April 21 with the hope that logging could commence by May 15.

The SP&S was unable to complete its part of the rehabilitation until May 28. While this enabled O-A to complete all its bridge work, except the replacement of the span on its bridge Number 3, a task that could not be completed until the SP&S had lifted its embargo, delays continued to mount. By the time all railroad rehabilitation was finally completed, however, both O-A and the SP&S had restored their respective tracks to a comparable condition. As such, a common speed limit of 10 miles per hour for loaded trains and 15 miles per hour for empty trains was established between Camp McGregor and Vernonia.

Delays resulting from the closure of the United Railways line, primarily due to the replacement of two bridges above Keasey, required Oregon-American to apply for a supplemental loan of $100,000 in August 1936, a request that the RFC granted in October of that year. Logging finally commenced on a single logging side basis on Spur 17, and the first loads to the Oregon-American Lumber Corporation mill were put on cars on June 24, 1936. Two days later, the new company unloaded its first logs in the Vernonia pond.

Greenman, summarizing the rehabilitation of O-A's line, wrote:

> The job of fixing up our railroad has been a terrific one and has far exceeded our original estimates, both in cost and length of time necessary to do the work. We have put more than 15,000 ties in the

The Great Depression and haggling creditors kept the Vernonia operation closed for more than four years between 1932 and 1936. Reorganized as the Oregon-American Lumber Corporation and given a breath of life by a Reconstruction Finance Corporation loan, the company began rehabilitating in early 1936.

O-A hired independent contractors to build replacement bunkhouses on the mill's loading dock. (Betty Blumenthal collection)

railroad between the County line and Spur 22 and from Spur 22 westward over Spur 25. I think we will have to replace every tie as that is the old I-P track and is in worse condition than our own was. However, some of the other items of our estimated cost of rehabilitation has taken less money than we had figured so that on the whole we will, I think, come out fairly close to the estimate.

The SP&S delayed us very greatly, making it impossible for us to get materials and equipment into the woods to do our work with.

This assessment did not include the cost of rebuilding the main line and Spur 25 from the former I-P log pond dam and beyond to the former site of Camp Number 1, a distance of 5 ⅓ miles. The cost of this alone was more than $40,000.

Inman-Poulsen had constructed its mainline on a trestle across the southern bank of its pond. The 1933 fire burned the trestle so Oregon-American opted not to rebuild it and instead rerouted the line along the pond's former south boundary.

Fortunately, and itself a measure of the esteem former employees held for the company, Oregon-American was able to rehire more than 85 percent of its former workforce, both at the mill and in the woods. In some departments, like the mill's stacker force, every man rehired was one who once held a similar job with the company. This proved extremely helpful getting restarted and minimized lost motion and training. Connie Anderson, according to Greenman *the best lumberman in the organization,* was among those who returned. O-A rehired Anderson as mill superintendent, and it fell to him to get the mill up and running.

While property rehabilitation was still underway, O-A focused attention on how to sell the new venture's production. Olin traveled east during April and May of 1936 and reestablished selling connections at nearly all the principal lumber-consuming centers where Vernonia lumber had been sold in the past. In many instances, he engaged the same firms and individuals who formerly had sold the product under the Central Coal & Coke name. To

Claiming it was unsafe, the United Railways embargoed the high trestle immediately west of Keasey until repairs could be made. This delayed the rebuilding of Camp McGregor.

When the line reopened, the bunkhouses were loaded on disconnects and hauled to Camp. (Kamholz collection)

manage this network, Oregon-American hired J. Walter Vaughan as sales manager in June 1936.

With sufficient log inventory floating on the Vernonia pond, O-A started the long-side band mill on Monday morning, July 20, 1936, and for the first time in five years, life in Vernonia again fell in step to the sawmill's cadence. The sawmill cut 106,000 board feet that first day. Within a week, the long-side was producing half the mill's anticipated production and the short-side was put on line. By August 6, the mill was running full blast.

ORGANIZED LABOR COMES TO VERNONIA

If rehabilitating Oregon-American's operation had taken place under conditions that existed before the Great Depression, the task would have been monumental in its own right. However, many New Deal policies governing business practice forced employers to adopt different methods of operating. As far as the lumber industry was concerned, no other new government policy had a more profound effect than that which legitimized the organized labor movement.

The seeds for labor unrest in the lumber industry were sown years before the Great Depression. Low wages and long hours combined with harsh, unsafe working conditions all served to breed discontent in the hearts and minds of the industry's labor force. Formation of the Industrial Workers of the World, the IWW, or "Wobblies" as they often called themselves, was a first attempt by workers to present a united front against the power held by employers. As early as WWI, the IWW began flexing its muscle, and employers, fully aware of the threat organized labor represented, retaliated vigorously.

Lumber demand during WWI was great. The threat of lost production resulting from strikes prompted the federal government to intervene and form the Loyal Legion of Loggers and Lumbermen, or the "4L." With patriotism used as its central theme, the 4L provided a forum for labor to air its concerns and demands to management and served to quiet the violence that often characterized labor-management confrontation.[6] Largely, however, the

4L did little to improve the workers' lot and employers continued exercising their near-absolute powers as before.[7]

The economic collapse that brought on the Depression effectively equalized the balance of power between labor and management. Passage of the Wagner, or National Labor Relations Act, legitimized the union movement and spawned creation of the American Federation of Labor (A F of L) and a spinoff from that umbrella organization, the Committee for Industrial Organization (CIO).[8]

While the underlying discontent present throughout the industry undoubtedly had found its way to Vernonia, the first indication of trouble arose in the summer of 1930 when the Clark & Wilson Lumber Company, responding to declining market conditions, imposed a 6 percent wage reduction on its loggers.

Oregon-American, citing the uncooperative position taken by Clark & Wilson toward Charles Keith's efforts to bring about an industry-wide curtailment of lumber production, refused to go along. Greenman, writing Keith about the Clark & Wilson plan, observed, *I think this action by Clark & Wilson may have some far reaching effects in the long run.* Responding, Keith noted, *Personally, I think it is a mistake to reduce wages unless it is done concertedly. Furthermore, I do not believe that any reduction in wages would be to the benefit of any one but that it would hurt. In the first place the reduction of wages might cause our labor to organize.* These sentiments were not isolated. The Western Operators Association Bulletin of July 13, 1930, reported:

> [The period of extended shutdown in logging camps] has been attended by an increase in radical activity in all sections, with radical leaders successfully capitalizing this unemployment condition, and unquestionably recruiting many members to swell the ranks of discontented.
>
> The spirit of unrest has been agitated by (wage adjustments) and there is a sullenness that is very evident in many of our concerns at the present time.

Even the 4L bulletin of July 24, 1930, added: *The organized labor movement is being extended in the face of and because of existing conditions. Wage cuts to extreme lows provide convincing arguments for revolutionary organizers, leaders and agitators.*

Their distaste over wage cuts notwithstanding, competitive pressure forced Keith and Greenman to follow Clark & Wilson's precedent and they implemented a similar reduction for O-A's loggers. On August 8, 1930, Keith wrote Greenman, *Generally speaking I am opposed to cutting wages under present conditions. However, if our competitors do it what is there left for us to do?* O-A was similarly forced to lower wages by 10 percent at the mill on November 17, 1930.

Recognition that most employers were cutting wages and fear of outright job loss probably served to quell any thoughts of a backlash from the ranks of labor. The seeds of unrest finally began to germinate when those fears turned into reality and the industry closed its doors during the Depression.

Following passage of the Wagner Act, Greenman commented on July 20, 1933:

> There is no question but that labor, including the 4L, is going to feel its oats for a while. They are invited to feel them by the Industrial Recovery Bill and would be less than human if they did not

exhibit the sense of power they must feel as a result of the passage of this legislation.

Between labor and taxation, the path of industry is not to be strewn with roses, at any rate, for some time to come. I am pessimistic about the whole affair.

Greenman's sense of foreboding was justified. On June 12, 1934, he wrote Keith:

> We have had very definite and acute labor troubles right here in the Valley. There is an activated local of the Timber Workers department of the A F of L right here in Vernonia and within the last 60 days it succeeded in closing down Clark & Wilson's camp for nearly three weeks. So far as I know, none of our employees belong to this union but if we reduce their wages, in the face of higher scales in the industry generally, we may be reasonably certain that they *will* belong and that trouble will result.

And while efforts were underway to reopen Oregon-American, Greenman wrote E. C. Cronwall on May 25, 1936:

> I believe it is not entirely optional with us, as you have apparently assumed it is, to support or not support the logging operators of the Columbia Basin in their effort to work out a livable working agreement with the Union.
>
> I am confident that organized labor would not permit us to operate this property if we were ready and willing to do so. There are five or six hundred idle men from surrounding logging camps in and around Vernonia. The Sawmill & Timber Workers Union local in Vernonia has a membership of about 900 persons. All of these men are idle excepting those employed by us and by one or two very small logging operations in the vicinity.
>
> We are already beginning to hear rumblings of discontent from these idle men because of the fact that we are continuing employment for our people while they are unable to work. We have answered this complaint by the statement that in working our people we are merely putting our property in the same condition in which the Clark & Wilson property, for example, was when it shut down.
>
> This fact must be taken into consideration for I am reasonably confident that any effort to ship logs out of Camp McGregor would result in prompt picketing of the operation. If this followed, our men, although they are loyal people, would have the same reluctance to pass through picket lines as has been displayed elsewhere in the region.
>
> We are in a hotbed of Unionism here in Vernonia and we must take it into account in every move that we make.

Merely one of the union's efforts to impose conditions of employment was clearly illustrated in Greenman's reply to a Sawmill & Timber Workers Union, Local 2557, demand that Oregon-American not employ racial minorities:

> It has been in the past, and will continue to be in the future, our policy and purpose to employ only white Americans when competent men of this race and nationality are available for doing our work. We have never employed other than white Americans except when continuous operation of our sawmill and logging camp necessitated it.
>
> We expect to pursue this policy in the future, but we do not want to be handicapped by an outstanding promise that we will not employ persons

of other nationalities or Americans of the Negro race if we find it necessary to do so in order to maintain continuous operation of our property.

You may be assured of our cooperation in the effort to make as many jobs as possible available for white Americans. Our people have been here a long time, too, and we have as much interest in the welfare of this nation, of this state, and of this community as any member of your organization possibly can have.

On July 23, 1936, three days after the mill resumed operating, Greenman wrote to Keith,

> The labor situation is literally *HELL*. These greenhorns of the logging and milling industry know so little about true labor organization that they make themselves as much of a nuisance as possible. I suppose they will settle down after awhile but they certainly are the nuts now

And a few days later, commenting on getting the operation underway again:

> The biggest handicap we will be under, in my opinion, is the one arising from the fact that the industry is so completely unionized now that it is impossible to run a logging camp or sawmill according to the dictates of economy and good management but rather it must be run to the dictates of some walking delegate of the Union.

And finally, commenting on the one issue that would come to act as the single most divisive topic characterizing Oregon-American's labor relations throughout much of its remaining operating history, Greenman advised Keith on August 17, 1936:

> I will of course use the greatest possible effort to see that we do not have a closed shop either in the mill or the woods. We are not going to admit that we have it any where, but in fact, we do have a closed shop in the woods today. I think every man up there with the possible exception of the superintendent and the logging engineer belong to the Union.

Later, he added,

> It's a great life—if you can stand it. Well, I hired out for a tough guy and it appears I am going to have to live up to my reputation.

Employers, realizing many issues at hand were industry-wide, began organizing themselves into negotiating units, both to provide support and services to one another in collective bargaining and to ensure consistency between themselves with respect to wages, benefits, and so forth. Accordingly, Oregon-American appointed the Executive Committee of the Columbia Basin Loggers to represent the company for this purpose. Operators created a sister organization, the Columbia Basin Sawmills, to handle the task of negotiating with sawmill workers' union representatives on issues that were common across that phase of the industry.

Writing Harry Kendall, now with the Weyerhaeuser Timber Company, Greenman also observed:

> The trouble with our labor relations in this little area in northwest Oregon, which is the only part of the Fir region that is experiencing serious labor difficulty, is that we have in the area, I believe, a more radical class of people working in the camps and mills than elsewhere. Locally, our troubles were

created when the loggers of the Clark & Wilson Company moved into Vernonia several years ago following the transfer of the seat of their operations to the Nehalem Valley.

Clearly the days when the employer could dictate employee policy were over, and the challenge of running the business intensified. Yet for all the apparent problems the union movement presented Oregon-American as it struggled back to life, the stiffest challenge from organized labor was yet to come.

A FOOTNOTE TO OREGON-AMERICAN'S REBIRTH

When Sigmund Stern took control of Central Coal & Coke it faced similar debt repayment issues as Oregon-American. Stern adopted the singular operating policy of repaying the debt to the exclusion of much else—particularly anything related to expansion. This hand-to-mouth, pay-as-you-go approach carried over to Oregon-American and every capital expenditure had to pay for itself in short order. No one, at least in the early going, gave much thought to extending the life of either company beyond such time when the debts had been repaid. This "self-liquidating" policy weighed heavily on every operating decision made after reorganization and continued well into the 1940s when O-A could evidently not only repay its debts but operate profitably.

Clearly, this was a sharp departure from the Charles Keith operating philosophy and Keith's dissatisfaction was obvious when he wrote Greenman:

> The Central plan has been approved and it should not take long now to complete it. I am not very happy over the plan because I do not see anything in it. They could very easily put this property on a basis where it could pay off its debt in 6–7 years and have it free, but it takes money to do it. I have not been able to convince them that they should put the money up.

Under the circumstances, Keith had little meaningful reason to continue his association with the Central. The beginning of the new enterprises' lives marked the end of their "expansionary" period under Keith. And so, on September 3, 1936, he chose to resign.

On learning of Keith's resignation, Greenman wrote:

> I am inexpressively shocked by the news in your letter of September 4 in which you say you have severed your connection with the Central Coal & Coke Corporation and are moving away from Kansas City.
>
> It seems to me that a great moral injustice has been done by action which makes it seem necessary or desirable for you to disassociate yourself from these businesses which you and your father founded and conducted for so many years.
>
> I know that you will soon find something to do that is worthy of your vast capacity and ability. I am not worrying about that part of the matter at all, but I do feel greatly concerned over the action of your creditors which apparently required you to feel that you could no longer be associated with your own companies.

Friends in Kansas City wrote Greenman the following month that *[Keith's] family seem to know he has simply quit. He moved to Keytesville, Missouri on the 30th of September, went to bed and has been in bed ever since.*

Waxing philosophically in his 1936 Christmas greeting to Greenman, Keith wrote,

> The Year 1936 has recorded much history. Kings have been dethroned, and established governments have been endangered. Personal liberties have been both increased and restricted. The World moves. "Divine Providence moves in a mysterious way" It is never wrong. Its ends are always justified.

By early 1937, Keith began to show signs of recovery, however. He started making overtures to old industry friends and associates for some kind of employment. The question of "What can the industry do for him?" became a profound point of personal and professional embarrassment to many, for as Col. W. B. Greeley of the West Coast Lumbermen's Association wrote to M. B. Nelson, president of the Long-Bell Lumber Company:

> Knowing Mr. Keith as both you and I know him, I just cannot picture him taking a subordinate, especially a semi-clerical place in an association or lumber office. I think that sort of thing just won't do.
> I assume that Mr. Keith's need is real; and I don't want to go on regretfully declining his request for a job without undertaking to find an answer.

Commenting on Greeley's suggestion that Keith's friends in the industry arrange a modest stipend worked out through the auspices of the National Lumber Manufacturer's Association, Greenman wrote:

> I think the plan you suggested to Mr. Nelson would be ideal, provided it can be worked out without Mr. Keith's knowledge.
> I don't know just what Mr. Keith's circumstances are. I think he is flat broke and so heavily debt-ridden personally that he never will be able to work out. At the same time I believe there is money in the Keith family, which is a large one, so that he will never suffer want or privation. Of course this does not answer the problem, because Mr. Keith, like any man of spirit, wants to stand on his own feet, or at least come as near to standing on them as circumstances will permit.
> If the situation was somewhat different with Mr. Keith's old companies, they should and doubtless would take care of him without calling on any outside assistance. However, you know the circumstances there well enough to realize that both the Central and this company are purely liquidating operations with no other ultimate objective than satisfaction of creditors.

Times were tight, however, and the industry was unable to mount anything material to help Keith. Finally, by October 1939, he began working for some reciprocal insurance companies in Kansas City that had long been active in the lumber industry.

In January 1940, Kansas City, Missouri, appointed Keith interim mayor, a position he held only several months. In April of that year, he wrote Greenman advising that his son Bill had gone to work for Union Wire Rope Company and asked for favorable consideration of that company's products, adding, *When you help Bill, you help me.* However, as O-A had previously stocked up heavily on wire rope during a temporary price war for the product, Greenman was little able to help, even with Stern's urging.

On Tuesday, October 9, 1945, Charles S. Keith died at age 72 following a long illness. Among the observations made by *The Kansas City Times* in his obituary, the paper wrote:

> Charley Keith, a lad with a quick mind that took him rapidly through Fordham University to graduate at 18, went up in the corporation to head and dominate it after 1907 until it sank into a receivership in the days dark for lumber in 1931.
>
> Charles S. Keith never got back into lumber or coal in any important way, nor regained his fortune. He emerged to public notice in 1940 by accepting the mayoralty of Kansas City for the three months interim between the time Bryce B. Smith left the City Hall in disgust and the inauguration of Mayor Gage and the new citizens' group in April 1940.
>
> In the weeks while he was mayor, Mr. Keith was not noticeably pushed around by the machine that had named him when it found itself in desperate need of a couple of good names.
>
> He was dubbed a rugged old individualist… and never became happily accustomed to being ordered around.
>
> Years ahead of the big blow that leveled most of the lumber giants in the 1930's, Keith saw the menace and put most of his time into a vain effort to unite West Coast lumber interests. Perhaps he never got his picture dark or vivid enough. Later he was called lumbers' unsung Paul Revere.
>
> Keith saw the storm coming, but couldn't escape. He had no private cyclone cellar. His personal fortune went. The old Keith & Perry building, once a downtown symbol, came into gloomy red-ink years.

Greenman undoubtedly spoke for many in the industry when he observed:

> I feel that I lost a close personal friend when Mr. Keith died because he meant much more to me than a boss would ordinarily be to a fellow. I always was charmed by his personality and one of the great regrets of my life is that it was not possible for this Company to do more for him in his declining years than could be done under the circumstances.

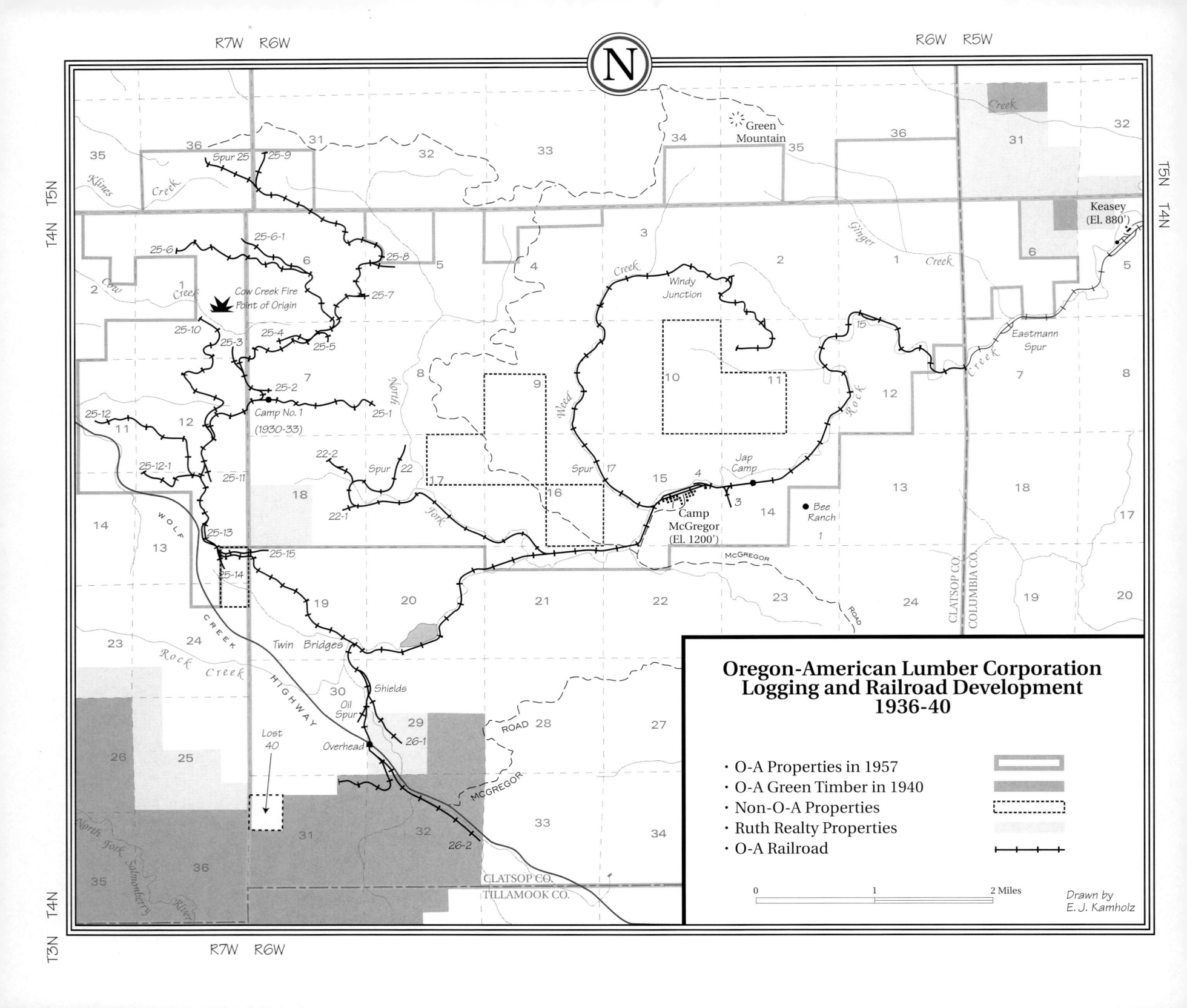

**Oregon-American Lumber Corporation
Logging and Railroad Development
1936-40**

- O-A Properties in 1957
- O-A Green Timber in 1940
- Non-O-A Properties
- Ruth Realty Properties
- O-A Railroad

0   1   2 Miles

Drawn by E. J. Kamholz

A NEW WORLD

The post-Depression New Deal policies of the Roosevelt administration marked a period of vast change in the business world. These changes, mostly compressed into the last half of the 1930s and coupled with the financial restrictions facing most lumber operators, presented the industry with unprecedented challenges. Unsteady markets, demands of old and new creditors, the promise of new technologies, government regulations, and labor unrest all served to keep industry leaders on their toes. The way they handled these challenges often spelled the difference between success and failure. The manner in which Oregon-American met these issues going forward did much to establish the company's unique character.

CLIMBING OUT OF THE HOLE

When the Oregon-American Lumber Corporation resumed operations, management premised the entire venture on a race to see if company-owned timber reserves could hold out long enough to pay down the company's debt. The financial future of the Central Company, now headed by Sigmund Stern, was greatly dependent on the operating performance of Oregon-American. As a practical matter, Central's stake in the venture was much greater than its mere 57 percent ownership of Oregon-American's stock, for O-A had to pay off not only its RFC working-capital loan but all of its second mortgage bonds before any value could accrue to the stock. With so much at stake, therefore, Stern's influence generally prevailed when O-A had to make any important financial decision. As such, the Oregon-American Lumber Corporation adhered to a tight budget approach in every phase of its business.

One striking example of the new Oregon-American's austerity measures began when O-A started rehiring in 1936. The company put many positions that had formerly been salaried on a day-wage basis, including those of all mill foremen—a practice unheard of in the industry. Accordingly, the payroll for managerial and general supervisory personnel, officers, and directors accounted for less than 2½ percent of sales, an unprecedented low level, even by the meager standards of the day.

However, despite universal agreement on the need to minimize costs, no such consensus was reached on how far to expand production. Oregon-American's sales organization, largely a concoction of former Central Coal & Coke independent wholesalers was, in the minds of Olin and Greenman, barely sufficient to handle the 75 million board foot output projected for the first year of operations. Still, the mill had barely sawed a log before the voting trustees began mounting pressure to expand sawmill output by adding a second shift. However, once it became evident the expense of gearing up for additional output would require an investment in inventory and facilities beyond the corporation's immediate financial means, the voting trustees backed away from that notion.

Opposite page: Most of Oregon-American's logging between 1936 and 1940 was salvaging fire-killed timber tributary to Spurs 22 and 25. The balance came from a small amount of green standing timber on the Spur 17 system spared by the Wolf Creek Fire.

A NEW WORLD

Oregon-American incurred a net loss of $267,451 for the shortened 1936 operating year. On the positive side, however, the lumber market continued to improve, and as the year closed, sales volume had increased substantially. By the end of 1937 a definite sense of optimism prevailed. The lumber market's upswing had continued and mill production climbed to 62 million board feet, allowing the company to accelerate its debt-service payments.

Recovery of burned timber ran close to expectations. Hemlock and other thin-barked species had proven unrecoverable and were left standing. The company also experienced considerable losses with fir as tops broke up badly in falling. However, this left only the best part of the logs, so grade recovery improved as a result.

After reviewing the 1937 annual report, Bernardin wrote to Greenman,

> I have not received any letter in a long time that pleased me more than yours.... The balance sheet is a real joy to look at, it reflects much credit on the management which if left alone will, with half a chance, work the company out with a fair return to the bondholders, which I think is about all any of us thought could be done.

Conditions warranted a sense of optimism in Vernonia. By April 10, 1939, O-A had reduced the original balance on the $800,000 RFC loans to less than $300,000, more than $140,000 in advance. In addition, the company had redeemed more than $150,000 of its second mortgage income bonds at a cost of only $43,000, less than twenty-nine cents on the dollar.

The low redemption price suggested how little confidence the financial markets had for Oregon-American's long-term prospects. For O-A, however, it was a windfall because for every dollar repaid, the company retired more than $3 in bonds.

Reflecting its improved financial posture, O-A altered the makeup of the board of directors on April 8, 1940. With Cronwall's role in the RFC loan arrangement finished, Lester Roth replaced him. Since the Central-Delta bondholders were next in line for repayment, Sigmund Stern was elected to the board. No doubt because of the company's operating results, Greenman was also named a director then.

November 1940 marked a major milestone in the Oregon-American Lumber Corporation's recovery, because the company repaid the remaining balance of its RFC loan that month, more than one year early. Consistent with the company's rising fortunes, the market for second mortgage income bonds, now in first mortgage position, had risen to more than $47. With a modest 1940 profit of nearly $67,000, O-A was, for the first time since starting in 1936, able to make interest payments to its bondholders.

If increasing production by adding a second shift at the mill was not feasible at first, maximizing the mill's single shift output was, as Greenman urged Anderson on March 19, 1937:

> Our average board measure production per day for the first 14 working days in March have been 342,000 feet. If this rate is continued for the remainder of the month, we should make a total of 7,869,000 feet of lumber in March. This is by far more than the mill ever made in any month on a single shift basis.
>
> Without desiring to appear avaricious at all, I would like to see production stepped up for the

remainder of the month if possible so that we will make a total of 8,000,000 feet or over during March. Possibly a word to the boys and a little adjustment of your operating program would result in such a fine operating record I would consider quite remarkable.

On March 15, 1938, the sawmill cut 422,220 board feet, the largest single-day, single-shift production up to that time. Announcing the achievement, Greenman, still the pragmatist, added ruefully, *The next job we have facing us is of course to find somebody that will buy 422,000 feet of lumber from us in one day.*

THE DETROIT TRUST COMPANY LAWSUIT

Earlier, considerable attention was given to the May 29, 1929, fire that escaped Oregon-American's boundaries and damaged property of the East Side Logging Company, including timber that the company had under contract from the Detroit Trust Company. Also discussed was East Side's unsuccessful lawsuit claiming Oregon-American had acted negligently and how East Side's failure to win its case established a precedent supporting Oregon State forestry statutes. Ironically, the roles of the protagonists reversed in the 1933 Wolf Creek Fire. But, unlike in 1929 when there was a decided absence of evidence supporting negligence on O-A's part, there was, in the 1933 Wolf Creek Fire, very substantial evidence supporting negligence on East Side's part, both as to cause and to the extent of damages arising from the Wolf Creek Fire once it spread beyond the Detroit Trust Company holdings. Immediately following the 1933 fire, Greenman personally obtained statements from witnesses familiar with the circumstances. But the company took no action until 1935 when, coincident with Oregon-American's reorganization of that year, the statute of limitations dictated the matter be pressed or dropped.

The largest sawmill cut that I can remember was about 1949–50 and totaled 471,000 feet in an eight-hour shift.

Fred Roediger, resaw

A major impetus to sue arose from the outcome of the *Silver Falls Timber Company vs. Eastern and Western Lumber Company* case in which the court awarded the plaintiff a sizable judgment based on the defendant's negligence when it left unburned and illegal slashings contrary to the direction of fire-control authorities. As this was the first instance in the state where an operator had ever been awarded substantial recovery based on a forest fire negligence claim, the Oregon-American board's resolve stiffened and they pursued the lawsuit.

So, in 1935, the Oregon-American Lumber Corporation, on behalf of its predecessor company, sued Detroit Trust Company and East Side Logging

Table 7.1
Claims Against Detroit Trust Company

	Damages Claimed
Oregon-American	$731,221.89
US Epperson	123,375.15
Aetna	14,705.65
Hammond Lbr. Co.	106,167.50
Hammond/Tillamook	200,860.00
Total	$1,176,330.19

A NEW WORLD

This mobile camp was home to right-of-way construction workers who built the Spur 25 off-spurs after the company reorganized. It is pictured at the junction of main line Spur 25 and Spur 25-6. In the background stands yet-to-be-salvaged, fire-killed timber from the 1933 Wolf Creek Fire. This photograph was taken in 1938. (George Lee collection)

Company. The Hammond Lumber Company, which suffered losses from the same fire, and both companies' insurers, joined O-A. Collectively, the plaintiffs sought to recover damages listed in Table 7.1.

By the time O-A sued, the East Side Logging Company had long-since disbanded so, for practical purposes, the Detroit Trust Company became the primary quarry.

Individuals owned the Detroit Trust Company properties operating through syndicates. These individuals were largely residents of the State of Michigan. The syndicate had trusteed the lands to Detroit Trust Company for administrative purposes and the latter held title to the lands. Jack and George McPherson handled actual administration of the trust.[1] Unsure as to the ability of the syndicate to pay, Oregon-American's attorneys, Wilson & Reilly, traveled to Michigan to investigate the financial condition of individual syndicate members. Once they learned that syndicate members were indeed solvent, the matter was pressed vigorously.

After a lengthy period of legal maneuvering, representatives of the Detroit Trust Company approached Oregon-American with a settlement offer and finally, on November 25, 1938, the day before the trial was to begin, the parties reached an out-of-court settlement for $175,000. Of that total, Oregon-American's share was nearly $92,000. While

The loggers called it the "Japanese skidder" because O-A's pre–WWII section crew consisted of Japanese laborers. Actually it was a Clyde track layer O-A bought from the Tideport Timber Company in 1936. The company disassembled it at the Tideport camp and rebuilt it at Camp McGregor on an old flatcar. It paid for itself many times over. (John T. Labbe photograph)

far short of the original claim, the settlement offer came at a time when the O-A was short of cash. The prospect of a long and expensive trial, coupled with an uncertain outcome, prompted company officials to accept the settlement. Oregon-American applied $70,000 of its proceeds to redeem second mortgage income bonds at a price of $35.

THE SHORT ROUTE TO THE SEA

The popularity of the northern Oregon beaches was well established and growing by the late 1920s. However, with access limited to Southern Pacific and SP&S passenger trains or, to a torturous and roundabout drive via Astoria, vacationers' demands for a shortened motor vehicle route prompted the Oregon State Highway Department to investigate a direct, state-of-the-art highway linking Portland to the coastal resorts. The Highway Department proposed two routes. The first was a "Vernonia-to-Hamlet" route, an 86-mile, $4 million route through Scappoose and Vernonia that was to follow the gentle grades of the Nehalem River Valley. The second was the "Wolf Creek" route, a 79-mile, $4.5 million undertaking that went directly over the rugged Coast Range.

Voters from the Portland area clearly favored the Wolf Creek route. However, due to the fact it would have traversed undeveloped timber holdings

A NEW WORLD

Anxious to please Portland voters and provide new jobs, the State of Oregon announced plans to build a "short route to the sea" in 1932. Construction of the Wolf Creek Highway (later rededicated the Sunset Highway) was highly unpopular with logging outfits like O-A whose properties the road divided.

In the spring of 1938 crews used the 106 and the locomotive crane to complete the structure.

This crossing over the highway, known as the "Overhead," became a familiar landmark to motorists. (Betty Blumenthal collection)

of large timber operators, including Oregon-American, the scene took on political overtones. Oregon-American's objections to the Wolf Creek route were several. For one thing, it would expose company timber to the public and greatly increase the risk of fire. Equally important, however, the proposed Wolf Creek route encroached on watercourses that O-A itself would depend on for its future railroad. That route also promised to divide the operation so that O-A would be forced to construct parallel spur tracks on either side of the highway.

Keith and Greenman, never wallflowers when it came to requesting help from their political allies, did not hesitate to call on friends in high places when making their route preferences known. Greenman pressed his contacts in Salem through 1931 while Keith pursued his in Washington, D.C. Nevertheless, despite their efforts, and those of Aubrey Watzek following his appointment as Oregon-American's receiver, the State Highway Commission finally chose the Wolf Creek route. In announcing the news to Keith, Watzek wrote on August 27, 1932, *I regret very much that this route has been chosen, as we are now faced with not only the unpleasant task of endeavoring to arrive at what is a proper value of damage for the right-of-way which will be taken, but also the permanent nuisance which the construction of this main highway through the Company's property will create.* The state wasted no time getting started on the survey, and Watzek and Greenman, wanting to make the best of the situation, arranged to rent various buildings at Camp McGregor and provide transportation services for the survey crews in November 1932.

Oregon-American's planned route to reach its timber in the Southwest Unit, on what was to become known as Spur 26, was to cross the proposed highway right-of-way in the SW 1/4 of Section 29, Twp. 4 North, Range 6 West. Purchase of this quarter section from a Pennsylvania resident

Once moved over the right-of-way for the highway the center span was lowered into position.

Completion of the Overhead preceded the movement of O-A's logging operations to its Southwest Timber Unit by nearly two years and the span went unused during that time. (John T. Labbe collection)

named Bowman was negotiated by the "old" Oregon-American, primarily for its control features in that it was the only parcel needed to connect the Southwest Unit and the Inman-Poulsen lands over which O-A had right-of-way easements.

Regardless whether the Wolf Creek Highway was built or not, O-A needed two trestles to traverse low spots near the crossing point. The northern trestle would have been 210 feet in length with an average height of 16 feet. The southern trestle would have been 225 feet long, having an average height of 21 feet. To provide clearance so the highway could pass beneath the northern trestle, O-A had to raise it an additional 8 feet. To accomplish that, the company also had to lengthen the trestle to 500 feet and add a steel clear-span. O-A also had to raise the southern trestle to an average height of 22.5 feet and lengthen it to 300 feet. The company had to raise the approaches to both trestles accordingly which required more than 1,000 yards of additional fill. It also created a 4 percent grade on the north approach of the northern trestle. Although that grade was favorable for Vernonia-bound log movements, it was still an inconvenience.

In addition, the state also had to reimburse Oregon-American for nearly 4.5 million feet of timber on the highway's right-of-way, most of which was old-growth yellow fir. Negotiations were finally completed on October 1, 1937, with the state agreeing to reimburse O-A more than $19,000. That figure did not include added costs the state paid O-A for modifications to the two trestles. Oregon-American began construction of the Overhead Crossing in November 1937. The steel deck girders were delivered in February 1938 and O-A installed them that spring.

Oregon-American's concerns over the Wolf Creek Highway's isolating timber had been greatly diminished by the time actual road construction began. By then, Ruth Realty had sold its timber

Opposite page: When Oregon-American rebuilt Camp McGregor in 1936, the company only provided bunkhouses for single men. O-A granted families ground leases, however, and enough had constructed houses by 1939 that the school, visible in the lower left, was rebuilt. (Dawn Lee collection)

burned in 1932 and 1933 to independent operators. As most of this timber lay in the north and west extremes of the Southwest Unit, its sale eliminated the need for additional rail crossings over the highway. Likewise, what holdings Oregon-American owned along the highway right-of-way had been largely disposed of when the company completed an exchange of lands with the Rupp-Blodgett interests. This left the company with just a little timber south of the highway in Sections 11 and 14, Twp. 4 North, Range 7 West. For a while, O-A gave some thought to removing this timber via motor trucks. However, when it became apparent that the highway would not be completed in time to do that, an alternative plan was drawn involving construction of Spur 1 off Spur 25-12 and logging these parcels using a skyline over the highway right-of-way. The Highway Commission approved this plan in November 1937, and the company used a three-donkey skyline haul spanning more than one-half mile to remove the isolated timber. O-A completed this operation by September 1938. After that, Spur 26 over the Wolf Creek Highway was the only access the company needed to remove logs from its Southwest Unit. O-A completed the Wolf Creek Highway trestle, officially designated by the company as Bridge Number 26-2 (later to become known simply as the "Overhead") by June 1938, well ahead of the shift of logging operations into the Southwest Unit.

Oregon-American's concerns over the increased fire hazard created by opening the Wolf Creek Highway corridor were not groundless. While these fears focused on the hazard created by opening the route to the public, construction of the highway itself proved to be the problem. State Highway Commission and WPA forces working on the highway were directly responsible for the cause of two fires. The first, on the highway right-of-way near the NWNW corner of Section 13, Twp. 4 North, Range 7 West, occurred on November 1, 1937, when a debris fire was set during unfavorable weather conditions. Within an hour, winds carried burning refuse onto O-A cutover lands, burning 14 acres and destroying approximately one-third of a million board feet of cold-decked logs.

The second incident occurred on November 27, 1938. It also was a right-of-way debris fire started near the northwest side of NWSE corner of Section 11, Twp. 4 North, Range 7 West. The weather was dry that day too and winds carried sparks onto O-A's cutover lands. It burned 100 acres and damaged two donkey engines, guylines, a skyline, other rigging, and logs.

Greenman, writing to R. H. Baldock, Oregon State Highway Commission engineer, to inform him of the fire said:

> Our fears about fire originating directly or indirectly through the construction and use of this highway where built through a logging operation, which fears were frequently and freely expressed, to the Commission while rights-of-way easements were being negotiated, were apparently well grounded. We will be very happy when our operations in the vicinity of your road builders are completed and the repeated instances of carelessness and bad judgment displayed by your WPA forces as evidenced by these two fires and other occurrences will not affect us.

The Automobile Comes to Camp McGregor

In 1934 the Oregon State Board of Forestry negotiated an agreement with Oregon-American to

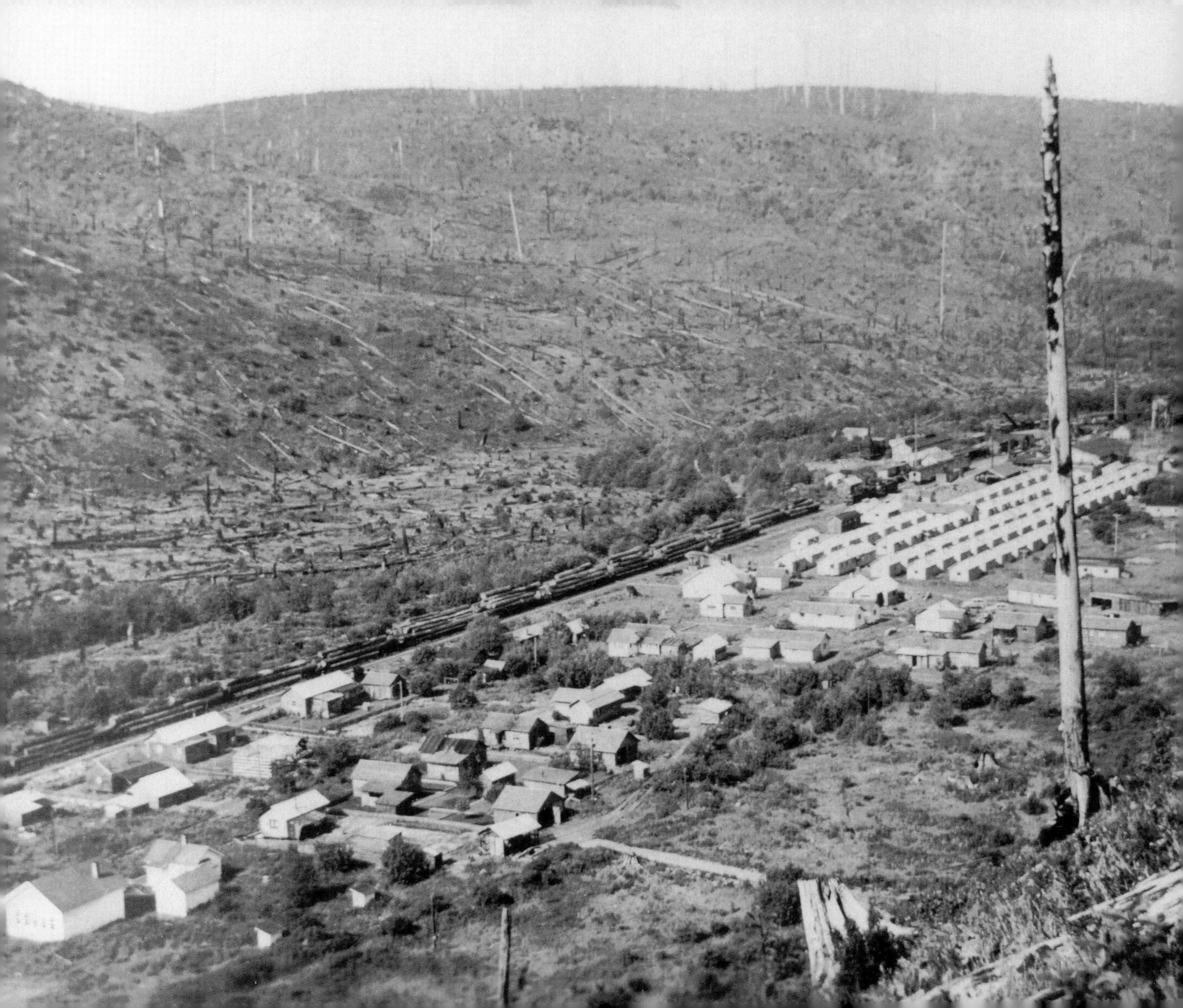

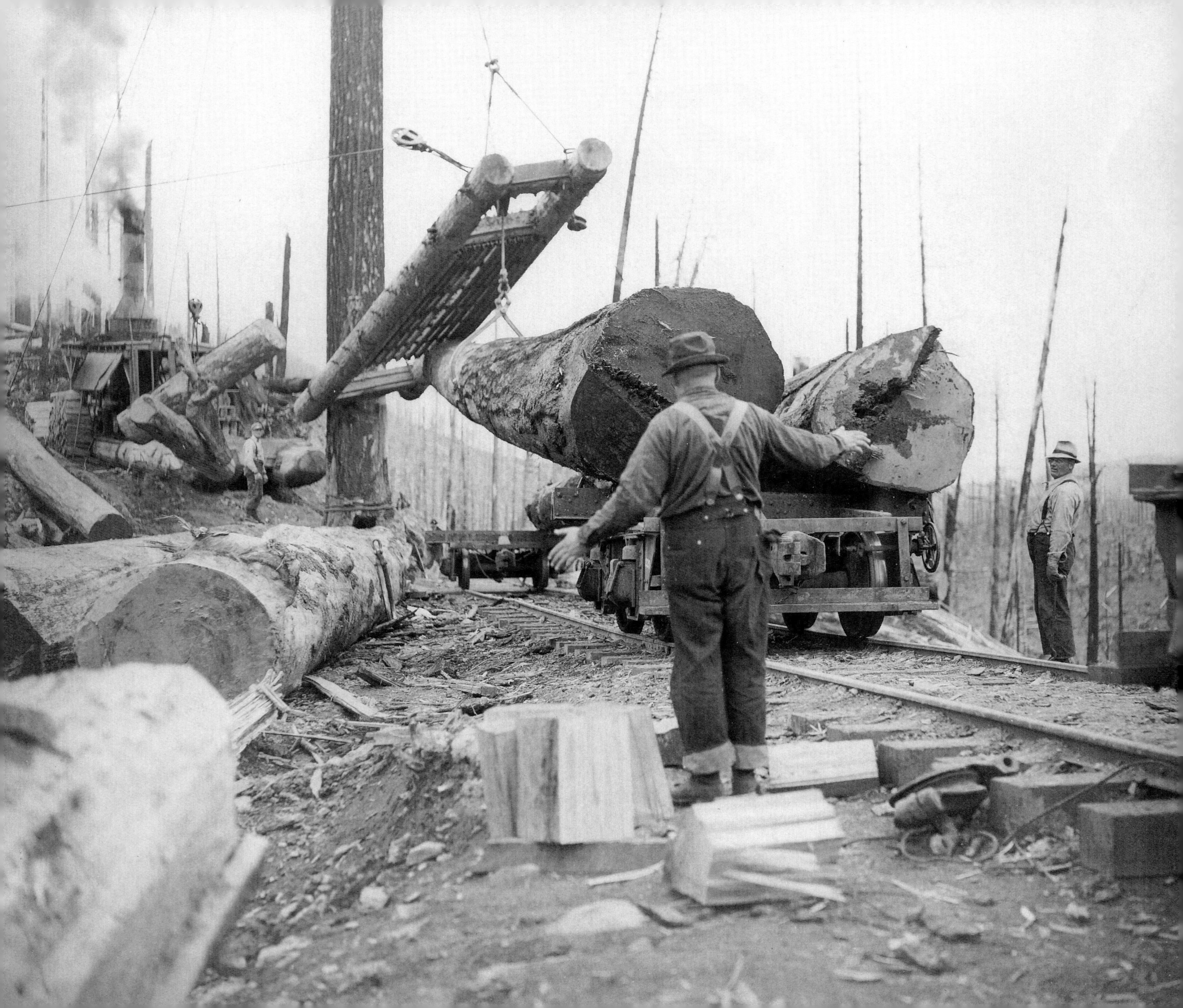

construct a vehicle road over the former Spur 5 Switchback and Spur 5 to the point where it joined the railroad mainline west of Camp McGregor. From there, the easement continued over O-A lands to the southern terminus of the abandoned Spur 17 West and beyond. The road was intended to provide fire-protection access. From the end of the old Spur 5 Switchback, CCC crews built an additional road connecting the route to the outside. When the Wolf Creek Highway, later renamed the Sunset Highway, was completed, it provided the first vehicular link to Camp McGregor and provided a new dimension to the lives of its residents. O-A applied to have this road taken over by Clatsop County in November 1938. With access to the outside world, Camp McGregor and its twenty resident families took steps to rebuild the school there. That task was completed in time to begin the winter term in 1939.

Convenient access to the outside encouraged further development of Camp McGregor so that by 1941, Oregon-American employed 300 people there. Accommodations included eighty-five bunkhouses occupied by 226 men (the bunkhouses could have housed 340 men), and thirty family houses, two of which the company owned.

TECHNOLOGY ADVANCES AND OTHER IMPROVEMENTS

Despite O-A's limited finances, the company made many improvements to the Vernonia mill between 1936 and the beginning of WWII. In some cases, these improvements were simply technological advances that paid for themselves. Market demands for improved product quality drove others. Still others had their origins in the need to extract value from otherwise worthless by-products from the sawmilling operation.

When Oregon-American began cutting lumber in Vernonia in 1924, the company facilitated movement of the product in the mill by 100 or so hand-operated lumber buggies. Horse-drawn wagons moved heavier loads. As early as 1927, O-A began replacing lumber buggies with Gerlinger and Willamette-manufactured motor-driven lumber carriers.

Beginning in 1937, O-A began replacing the older mechanized carriers with newer Gerlinger models that were lighter and powered by Ford V-8 motors. Other operators, having made the conversion to mechanical carriers around the same time, did not need Oregon-American's used hand buggies, and the company was left with most of them, the remnants of which were still in evidence years later. The last of the company's old horses, Shorty and Bob, were put to rest in November 1939, years after the mechanized carriers had replaced them.

O-A added mechanized cant turners to both sawmill carriages in the summer of 1939. This eliminated the need to use hooks and resulted in substantial improvements in grade recovery, particularly where production of clear boards was concerned.

Labor disturbances and work stoppages created problems maintaining continual operation of the mill boilers. To maintain electrical service during such times, or when the regular supply of hog fuel was unavailable, O-A installed a standby boiler and reserve oil tank system in the powerhouse. Although inefficient to operate, it allowed the company to maintain boiler pressure. Installation was completed early in 1940.

With increasing population in the Nehalem Valley, Oregon Gas & Electric's demand for supplemental power from Oregon-American's electrical

Opposite page: Up to 1938 O-A's donkeys were, for the most part, wood-fired. The cost of employing wood-cutting contractors, use of otherwise merchantable timber, and time lost yarding the fuel supply led the company to make the conversion to oil.

Here, a track-side landing is in full swing on Spur 25 just before conversion. This was a salvage show working in timber killed in the 1933 Wolf Creek burn. (H. Brown photograph; Jim Blain collection)

Camp McGregor in 1939

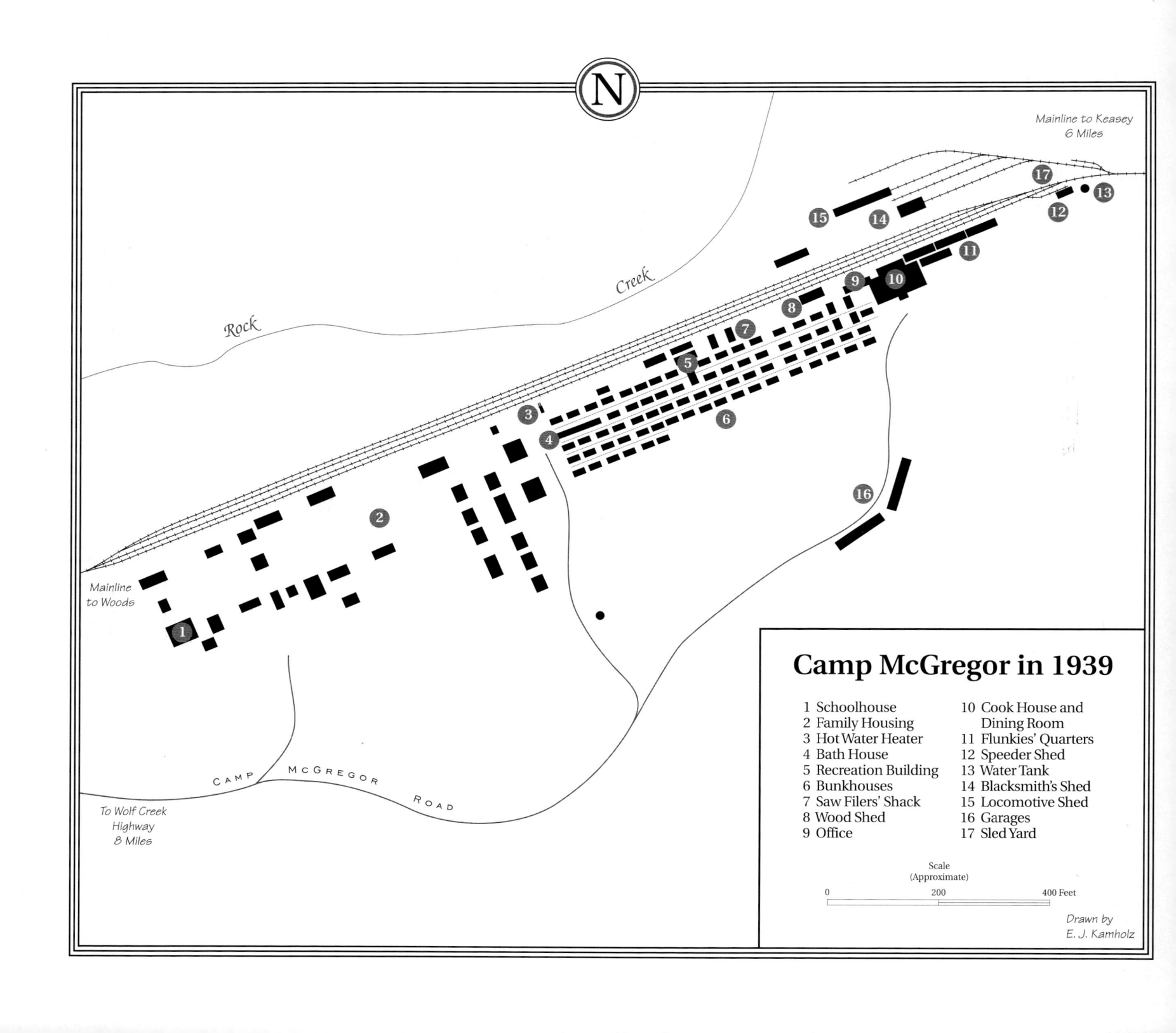

1 Schoolhouse
2 Family Housing
3 Hot Water Heater
4 Bath House
5 Recreation Building
6 Bunkhouses
7 Saw Filers' Shack
8 Wood Shed
9 Office
10 Cook House and Dining Room
11 Flunkies' Quarters
12 Speeder Shed
13 Water Tank
14 Blacksmith's Shed
15 Locomotive Shed
16 Garages
17 Sled Yard

Scale (Approximate)
0   200   400 Feet

Drawn by E. J. Kamholz

Mainline to Keasey 6 Miles

Rock Creek

Mainline to Woods

To Wolf Creek Highway 8 Miles

CAMP McGREGOR ROAD

generating plant grew accordingly to the point that by the early 1940s, it threatened an overload. That forced O-A to place a moratorium on new demands until the company could install power-factoring capacitors. Even so, increasing load demand from OG&E put O-A in the position of having to restrict new demands or else limit production. As a result, electrical service to outlying areas of the Nehalem Valley had to be limited and the utility had to restrict some existing customers, including the City of Vernonia's water-pumping plant, to operate only during off-peak hours.

Stepped-up production, brought on by the addition of a second shift in 1940, called for other improvements. These included the upgrade of planers and the associated modification to the blowpiping system needed to handle the new equipment. Also that year, the company built a log-washing device on the log slip. It used high-pressure streams of water to remove dirt, rocks, and debris from the exterior surfaces of logs as they moved up the log slip, thus saving wear and tear on head-rig saw blades. Reflecting greater demand for kiln-dried rough stock, the company expanded the rough loading dock in the spring of 1939.

Objections to wetness of planing mill wood and how much sawdust it had mixed in with it prompted the company in September 1940 to add considerable blowpiping in the planing mill to better segregate the two by-products. The following month O-A replaced the water-lubricated chain conveyor used to transport the wood scraps with a belted system to eliminate moisture problems.

The pride in and the manner of care taken of the mill was evidenced in an insurance company plant inspection report of October 1941 that stated:

> The plant is very clean and orderly in all departments, as well as around the exterior of the buildings. Several workmen were busy in each unit blowing down dust or sweeping floors. This is a daily occurrence and the plant shows evidence of constant cleaning.

See that trestle here? In my day we'd just slapped a fill in there, right in short-order. We had two of these right by the North Fork above Camp McGregor. Trestles. They were long but they were shallow. One Fourth of July vacation we were shut down so they decided to rebuild them. 'Course all the guys went to town except the bridge crew, the track gang and I. I always got stuck like that.

They put in the shortest one with the pile driver and it took the whole crew. Andy [Olson] said, Ve're never gonna make it in two weeks, Ve're never gonna make it.

I said, Andy, you want to shorten it?

Vell, he says, Ya.

I said, OK. We'll just bulldoze right out in the bushes there and get back up on the hillside, run some big borrow pits and shove the dirt down there, heap it up and level' er off.

I was ready for 'em to lay steel on mine before the others got the first one done. Jeez, that put him a week ahead of schedule. Oh, he was happy. Andy no doubt got a bonus for that come Christmas time but I didn't. Heh, heh.

George Lee, construction

> A program is underway now of re-whitewashing the interior framework of the buildings.... This improves an already well-maintained plant and the insured is to be highly commended for their excellent housekeeping and general maintenance.

A NEW WORLD

O-A constructed the engine shed shown in the foreground in 1937. About the same time, the company brought its car-repair operations from camp to the spur running alongside the machine shop. The timber dock is at the far right. (K. Schmelzer photograph; Jim Blain collection)

And, once O-A installed a dust-collection system for the grinding machines in the sawmill filing room, Greenman commented, *I think ours is about the only institution of similar type in the State of Oregon which now has a complete and fully adequate dust-collecting system attached to its sawmill grinding room machine.*

Other Improvements

Oregon-American made other improvements and additions to the Vernonia mill and camp, including, between 1937 and 1938, the addition of a car-repair shed alongside the mill machine shop after that operation was moved from Camp McGregor, a permanent dining room at the camp, locomotive sheds both at the mill and camp, and a conveyor to transfer sawdust from the sawmill to open-top cars.

To meet the needs of the expanded workforce at the mill, a 24 × 30-foot combined lunch room and time-clock station was added immediately west of the timber dock crane-way in 1941.

The mill and camp were not the only beneficiaries of modernization. Apart from East Side, Oregon-American was, in 1930, the last operator in the region not to have converted its donkey engines to burn oil instead of wood. Prior to the Depression, O-A did convert one engine as an experiment to decide whether the cost was justified, but the dire financial conditions that followed doomed the program before it ever started.

Improving business conditions and anticipated annual savings of more than $16,000 against a $7,500 cost of conversion proved a compelling argument. So, beginning in April 1938, O-A brought the conversion program to life. At first, the company equipped newly converted engines with gasoline-fueled flash boilers to speed up the morning chore of raising steam. Later, those were

The Camp McGregor dining room. It replaced several former Inman-Poulsen camp cars purchased in 1936 for use as temporary dining quarters until the permanent dining room was completed in 1938. (Arlie Sliffe collection)

replaced by Moxley flash boilers that used compressed industrial gas. The program was completed in June 1939.

The oil-burning conversion program also eliminated the need for the donkey engines to spend part of their productive working day hauling fuel for themselves. It also did away with private contractors who supplemented supplies with wood brought from cutover lands using horse-drawn sleds. The loggers transported fuel oil to remote engines using special tanks called "torpedoes" that were moved back and forth with the rigging between the spar trees.

Beyond modernizing existing donkeys the company also made the major step of purchasing its first diesel donkey in May 1939. Learning of a nearly new Skagit Model BU-154 that had just been repossessed, Greenman successfully argued that O-A could recapture its cost of $14,000 in only two and a half years. Many factors led to that conclusion. As the machine would yard, and therefore operate at the most remote points from the track side, significant savings accrued by not having to supply it with water. Loggers also generally believed that a diesel-powered machine was less likely to start fires. This was big plus since the machine would operate in the midst of newly created slashings. More important though, it eliminated the need for a fireman. That alone came to a saving of more than $6,000 per year. Offsetting the advantages, however, the diesel could not yard as long a distance, nor did it have the power of a steam donkey.

Arrangements to buy the single-engined, 250-horsepower Skagit diesel were made through Western Loggers Machinery Company of Portland. Western Loggers delivered the machine on May 15, 1939. The Skagit diesel yarder met every expectation, and then some. By December 1941, Oregon-

A NEW WORLD

When O-A resumed operations in 1936 Connie Anderson was appointed mill superintendent. (Kenneth Anderson collection)

American was ready to buy another one. While it too was a "Skagit," its lineage was storied. Originally manufactured by Washington Iron Works in 1929, it was one of thirty-five "Estep" diesel yarders made by that company. Washington itself manufactured the diesel engine under the Estep brand, hence the name. As manufactured, the engine was enormously outsized considering its horsepower. After its original owner, the Coos Bay Lumber Company, let the machine go, it was picked up by Skagit and refitted with twin, 175-horsepower Waukesha diesel motors operating through torque converters. Skagit remarketed the yarder under its own name as a Model BX-350-TC. Oregon-American acquired the machine through Interstate Tractor and Equipment Company of Portland.[2] (See Appendix A for performance comparisons.)

Although slower, both diesel donkeys held their own against the Willamette steamers. They did, however, cost much more to maintain as Greenman pointed out:

> During the first ten months of 1941, we paid...$1,269 for repair parts for the sixteen steam donkeys which we have in use in the woods.
>
> During the same period we paid... $546 for repair parts for the one Diesel donkey which we have in use.
>
> Had all seventeen of our donkeys been Diesel donkeys and had the cost for repair parts been the same for all seventeen that it was for the one machine we have, the repair part cost for the year through October would have been $9,172, instead of $1,815.
>
> Of course a substantial part of this difference, amounting to $7,357, would undoubtedly have been recaptured and possibly more too in the difference in fuel cost on the steam and Diesel machines.
>
> However, let us permit no slicker salesman to talk us into the notion that the operation of Diesel donkeys is all beer and skittles.
>
> I imagine it takes at least one dollar in labor to put a dollar's worth of repair parts on any donkey engine.
>
> If this assumption is correct, I will leave it to you to determine the difference in repair costs on steam donkeys and Diesel donkeys at the rate outlined above. The figure becomes so astronomical that I just simply don't have the time to ascertain it.

Addressing the problem to Interstate Tractor's vice president, Jim Lakin, that "slicker salesman" he regarded as one of the best in the region, Greenman added the following tongue-in-cheek comments:

> As further evidence of the fact that there are some clouds in the otherwise sunny diesel donkey motor sky…I only need to (point) out that this one bill from Cummins for overhauling the motor on the Skagit yarder we now have amounts to $60 more than we have spent altogether for parts for the 17 steam donkeys we have had in service during the first ten months of 1941.
>
> No doubt your answer to this one will be that the Waukesha motors with which the new donkey is equipped will never need to be overhauled.
>
> Well, I don't believe that one either.

Technological improvements began to find their way into railroad operations too although more so about right-of-way construction than with the railroad equipment and operations themselves. While the introduction of crawler tractors, or bulldozers, might normally be considered a breakthrough in logging, Oregon-American purchased its first such machine, a Cletrac, in 1936 solely for its ability to build railroad rights-of-way faster and cheaper. Faced with the need to build the rail crossing over the Wolf Creek Highway, the company had to undertake two years' worth of railroad construction in the summer of 1937. Accordingly, O-A bought a second Cletrac that year, along with a new 1 ¼ cubic-yard capacity P&H model 555 diesel-powered shovel.

Together these machines contributed largely to the 20 percent reduction in per-mile spur construction costs O-A realized between 1936 and 1941. The initial benefits the bulldozer brought to railroad construction eventually spilled over into the logging end of the business too. Because bulldozers reduced spur construction costs, it meant the railroad could be moved closer to the stump. As a result, O-A required fewer multiple-donkey hauls and had to keep fewer donkeys in service. Wire rope consumption also went down accordingly.

Logging with the Cletracs did not receive serious consideration until June 1939. Even so, neither machine did much in the way of logging until the company bought a cruiser arch in January 1941.

LOGGING OPERATIONS

On November 1, 1937, Andrew "Andy" Olson succeeded E. R. Estey as superintendent of logging operations following Estey's death the month before. A native of Sweden, Olson went to work for

Andrew "Andy" Olson posed on a load of logs at Camp McGregor shortly after his appointment to logging superintendent in 1937. A native of Sweden, Olson supervised logging operations for the company until his death in 1955. (H. Brown photograph; Rose Valpiani collection)

A NEW WORLD

Oregon-American in 1928 and had worked his way up through the ranks as hook-tender, camp foreman, and general foreman.

---

*Y*ou *know the old East Side camp? It was handy, you know, from the end of the road at Keasey. Boy, there's many a door and window frame that were packed out of there on people's backs into McGregor. And a lot of the old bunkhouses were pulled into Keasey and loaded on a flatcar or set of disconnects and ended up as a house at McGregor. About a third of the houses up there were old converted bunkhouses.*

George Lee, construction

Olson's appointment marked the beginning of a nineteen-year period in which Greenman and his top two managers, Connie Anderson as mill superintendent and Olson as superintendent of logging, respectively shaped and executed every Oregon-American operating policy. A major facet of that policy was clearly set forth in a general logging plan prepared in 1939. Besides mapping out the progression of O-A's logging, it also provided many interesting details.

> The Oregon-American Lumber Corporation General Logging Plan
>
> Our fee timber is divided roughly into four separate logging units:
> Weed Creek Unit
> Northwest Unit
> Southwest Unit
> Keasey Unit

The Weed Creek Unit (served by the Spur 17 System), consisting of a small patch of timber left in Sections 9 and 16 4/6, will be cleaned up during 1939. There is less than 10 million feet of timber left on this unit and its removal should be accomplished as promptly as possible for several reasons, among which are the facts that we will need the rail now tied up on Weed Creek and that we should burn the Weed Creek cutover lands as promptly as possible to minimize our liability arising from unburned slash.

The Northwest Unit of our timber (served by the Spur 25 System), from which the major supply of our logs is now coming will last through all of 1939 and pretty much through 1940.

About one-third of the timber yet to come from the Northwest Unit has been fire-killed, but our development is now in such shape that we will seldom be forced to cut exclusively burned logs for we should have one side logging in green timber in this unit at practically all times hereafter.

In winding up our logging on Northwest Unit lands in 1940, or whenever such wind-up occurs, we would doubtless keep one side logging in that unit after the other side has been transferred to the Southwest Unit. Such procedures will permit a more orderly clean-up and should enable us to make our rail available for development in the Southwest Unit to better advantage than if operations were carried on in the Northwest until the timber was all exhausted and then a wholesale move was undertaken.

The Southwest Unit. In order to avoid conflict of our operations with traffic over the Wolf Creek Highway, we built Spur 26 into the SW 1/4 of Section 29 4/6 during last year, erecting a bridge across the Wolf Creek Highway near the forty [acre] corner on the west side of this quarter. During 1939 we will actively carry on the development of this spur until it has been completed into the timber in Sections 31 and 32 4/6 and Section 36 4/7. Thus by 1940 the Southwest Unit will have been developed to the point where we can transfer some of our operations into it as it becomes necessary or desirable.

In the Southwest Unit there is approximately 368 million feet of our own timber and about 450 million feet of Ruth Realty Timber. In addition to these two holdings, lands belonging to the DuBois interests aggregating about 2,000 acres and carrying, as we understand it, around 150 million feet of very good timber. These are the remains of the property at which Ed Kingsley and Coleman Wheeler nibbled during the past ten years and, while their operations have done nothing to improve the character of the property as an operating unit, I believe there still remains enough timber to warrant our serious and careful consideration whenever we are in position to take on additional standing timber. This DuBois stuff is largely at elevations which would make it very difficult and expensive to take out to the Southern Pacific on the south but, by the same token, it is at elevations which are readily susceptible of development from our railroad.

Of the fee timber in the Southwest Unit, approximately 75 million feet or 20% was killed in the fires of 1932 and 1933. The remainder is all green and the quality of the unit on the whole, as disclosed by the cruise reports, is as good, if not better, than anything we have ever logged. I refer now to the fee timber only.

Ruth Realty Company Timber in the Southwest Unit. The original block of Ruth Realty Company timber, which was assembled by Mr. Kerry and was known as the "Yerreck" tract, comprised 10,577 acres and, according to Thomas & Meservey's cruise of 1924, the lands bore about 722 million feet of timber. To the original Yerreck block was added in 1930 some 55 million feet purchased by us from the Turrish and other interests and taken over by the Ruth Company after blocking up by us. The 1930 purchases brought the total Ruth ownership in our country, prior to the 1933 fire, to about 12,000 acres, carrying approximately 777 million feet.

I used to raise trees with a cat. If they needed a spar tree, you're lookin' at a 4-foot in-the-butt tree here. Some were bigger. And they were 160 to 170 feet to the top. If they needed a tree where there was none, they'd yard one out for me. I'd bulldoze up a pile of dirt and shove an old windfall up on it for the spar tree to slide on. Then I'd bulldoze the tree around and shove it up so it was lyin' at an angle. If you didn't, you'd put a cable around it and you'd just slide it along behind you. Then they'd put a cable around the butt and tie it down to a stump somewhere so it wouldn't slide. Then we'd get a block on it and I'd get behind another stump with the cat and raise it. They'd put all the guylines on the top beforehand. There'd be three or four men on each end of the guyline and when I'd pull it up, the hooker would watch it until it was straight up and down and he'd say, **Spike** *her!*

So, they'd spike the guylines and then I'd pull it a little to make it tight.

George Lee, construction

The 1932 and 1933 fires burned over about 5,000 acres of the Ruth lands, these fire attacks having been confined to timber along the north and west edges of the Ruth holdings.

As a result of these fires both the Ruth Company and we felt it would be desirable, from the standpoint of all concerned, for them to work off the bulk of their fire-killed timber to the best advantage possible. After consulting us and obtaining our consent, they sold it to Joe Flora, George Van Vleet and to others, and abandoned [some] to the Counties.

The remaining Ruth timber from the original Yerreck tract, aggregating some 6,000 acres, exclusive of Sections 17 and 18 4/7, is very largely unburned and blocks up perfectly with our own holdings in this area. The timber of which they have disposed was by far the least desirable part of the original Yerreck tract from our standpoint both as to quality and accessibility. Old burns running back a generation or two had attacked the timber on Cronin Creek and Spruce Run in Sections 29, 31 and 32 4/7 and in Section 5 of 3/7, so that the remaining stand was scattering and defective. Assuming we will eventually log the Ruth timber, I think the sale of what has been sold and of the timber on Sections 17 and 18 4/7, will be of advantage to us even though this timber had not burned over in 1932 and 1933.

The only manner in which the Ruth timber is inferior to our own is because it contains a much larger percentage of Hemlock. The quality of the Fir and the Hemlock on the Ruth lands is just as good, if the cruise reports may be believed, and from my own personal observation, as is the quality of these species on our own land.

However, the difference in the percentage of Hemlock in the Ruth timber and in our own is so great that we may find the Ruth timber less profitable for conversion than our own when we get around to logging it. This difference will be disclosed in the following statement of cruises of timber on lands remaining in the hands of the Ruth Realty Company in our territory as of this date:

Total Acres of Timbered Land	7,219.32 Acres
Total Douglas Fir	311,926,000 Feet
Total Cedar	6,182,000 Feet
Total Hemlock	183,475,000 Feet
Total of All Species	501,583,000 Feet

From the above it will be apparent that 37% of the total Ruth stand in all units where Ruth timber is found is Hemlock; whereas only 9% of our fee timber in the Southwest Unit is of this species.

About the best we can hope for in this situation is that Hemlock will be a more desirable wood by the time we are ready to log the Ruth lands than it is at present.

Keasey Unit. Logging of the Keasey Unit should, in my opinion, be deferred for the wind-up of our operations. This unit, in which there is an aggregate of about 125 million feet is comprised of about equal amounts of our own and Ruth timber with some intermingled outside ownerships. My idea would be to leave the Keasey timber until all the balance of our own, the Ruth and any other available timber beyond Camp McGregor is logged and then sustain our milling operations with logs coming from the Keasey Unit while the railroad and equipment are being removed from beyond Keasey.

All of the timber in the Keasey Unit is green; it is practically all young, thrifty timber in which growth is doubtless exceeding decay; it is generally at elevations considerably lower than any of our other timber and it is almost exclusively Fir with but a sprinkling of Hemlock. It would, I think, lend itself admirably to winding up our operations and unless some unforeseen necessity arises for developing it in the meantime, I believe its development should be deferred to the very last.

Purchases of Noncompany Logs

As confidence in Oregon-American's ability to pay off its debts grew, there also grew the realization that, at current lumber prices, the company would exhaust the remaining supply of company-owned timber in the process. By 1939 the industry itself showed enough signs of recovery that management began recognizing long-term profit potential in extending O-A's operating life. Cautiously, the company began looking for ways to supplement its timber reserves.

Orville Miller of Koster Products presented O-A with the first such opportunity in March 1939. As Koster operations near Vernonia were running out of timber, Miller undertook a salvage logging operation on the Detroit Trust Company lands that had previously been under contract to East Side Logging Company.

Miller needed a method of removing an estimated 50 million board feet left behind by East Side. Greenman assured Miller O-A could absorb the 100,000-board-foot-per-day output Miller anticipated his operator, Clay Dooley, would produce. Greenman proposed taking delivery of the logs from Dooley's motor trucks at points along mainline Spur 26 and reloading them on O-A disconnected trucks.

Agreeing to a price of $10 per 1,000 board feet delivered, and noting the logs so delivered would probably compare favorably, although smaller to those from O-A's lands, Greenman wrote, *It does appear that there are strong probabilities that the bulk of this Detroit Trust Company timber will be offered to us.* Thus began a long-term arrangement, beginning with Dooley and later with the Shields family who later took over Dooley's operations. Initially this program of taking delivery of logs from the former East Side operating area started on Spur 26-1, or the "Dooley Spur," lying just to the north of the Wolf Creek Highway. Later that operation moved to O-A's Spur 26-2 just across the highway to the south.

Lunchtime for the construction crew. From left to right: George Lee, Jack Taylor, and Ole Olson (standing). (Margaret Taylor collection)

To serve that operation and to provide a makeup yard once its own logging moved to the Southwest Unit, O-A built a switch yard at the junction of mainline Spur 26 and Spur 26-1 that became known as "Shields." O-A's loggers frequently called the Shields's operation the "Peckerwood Side," undoubtedly because of the smaller-sized logs the Shields delivered to that site.

Coinciding with the start of logging in the Southwest Unit in 1940 and driven by the need to increase log production to supply a second shift at the mill, O-A commenced rehabilitating the Willamette tree-rigged skidder that had been out of service since 1930. Having suffered a scorched boiler shortly before it was shut down, the overhaul provided an opportunity to give it additional steaming capacity by lengthening the boiler some 18 inches. During the overhaul, O-A removed the loading engine and drum set from the front of the unit. That provided even more steam for the skidding engine. The company returned the skidder to service in October 1940. After that, a separate donkey accompanied it to each setting to load logs onto the disconnects. By Thanksgiving 1940, O-A had finished logging the Northwest Unit and all operations were on Spur 26 and heading into the Southwest Unit. Three sides and a rig-up crew were working.

In December 1940, Oregon-American reached an agreement with the Shields operation calling for it to remove burned timber from the SW 1/4 of Section 29, Twp. 4 North, Range 6 West. This represented the first large-scale use by Oregon-American of a contract, or "gyppo," logger to load company logs directly on O-A rail cars. For the sake of accuracy, the Shields were not the first independent logging contractors used by O-A. George Van Vleet had cleared the site for Camp Number 1 on Spur 17 West during the winter of 1928 and Yunkers & Wiecks had logged the NW 1/4 of Section 30, Twp. 4 North, Range 7 West, a parcel of fire-killed timber not tributary to the O-A railroad, in 1937. Neither of these arrangements was more than a short-term expediency, however. The arrangement with the Shields extended over a number of years.

A New Landmark

When Inman-Poulsen began winding down its operations in 1929, it left some hard-to-reach timber along the southernmost extremities of its tract. This timber lay atop a ridge and abutted the northern edge of Oregon-American's Southwest Unit. As the cost of building a railroad spur to reach it was greater than the value of the timber, I-P instead opted to sell it and completed the transaction with Ruth Realty.

Somehow, Inman-Poulsen overlooked a 40-acre parcel in the SW 1/4 of the NW 1/4 of Section 31, Twp. 4 North, Range 6 West until after the sale had closed. By the time I-P discovered the mistake, Ruth Realty no longer was in the market for additional timber. The parcel remained untouched until Oregon-American's logging operations reached the site in 1941, at which time O-A cut the timber on a removal basis. As befitting the incident, Oregon-American dubbed this parcel the "Lost 40" and the site became a familiar geographical reference point for O-A's operations in the Southwest Unit.

MARKETING

The distribution of the company's lumber shipments in 1937 illustrates the enduring brilliance of Oregon-American's strategy to ship its output to distant markets. Of the total West Coast lumber produced that year, only 46 percent traveled via rail or truck; producers transported the balance over water. Of the lumber shipped via ground from the West Coast, 70 percent made it no farther east than the Rocky Mountains. Only 17 percent of the balance of all ground-transported lumber originating from the West Coast made it to the larger lumber-consuming markets of the Midwest, the Ohio River valley, or to the northeastern states.

By contrast, Oregon-American shipped 100 percent of its products by rail or truck (more than 95 percent by rail) and the vast majority of that went to the Midwest, the Ohio River valley, and the northeastern markets. In brief, having overcome the transportation cost problem of reaching these markets through the underweight phenomenon, Oregon-American sold its products with relatively little competition from other West Coast operators.

Even so, the effects of the Depression-era drought that so severely plagued the Midwest farm belt clearly carried over and the percentage of sales of lumber to those states slipped dramatically. This, combined with pressure from the voting trustees to increase output, forced the company to find new products and markets.

While salvage of the timber killed in the Wolf Creek Fire helped O-A produce a greater than normal percentage of high-grade clear lumber, once the company's logging operations returned to green standing timber, the perplexing problem of hemlock utilization again arose. Fortunately, by then, many Willamette and Columbia River paper mills had created a burgeoning market for pulpwood and hemlock had proven an ideal raw material. Thus, as Oregon-American's logging progressed into the unburned timber lying in the northern reaches of the Northwest Unit, it commenced a regular program to log hemlock and ship it via United Railways to Rafton and other points.

O-A made its first shipment of Hemlock to Rafton on October 13, 1939, using its own disconnected trucks. The hemlock-for-pulp program continued almost continuously throughout the operation's remaining life. In finding a method to dispose of hemlock, O-A was not only able to maintain a consistently higher rate of high-grade fir lumber production but was also able to add to its sales volume through sales to the pulp mills.

The successful hemlock-for-pulp program aside, pressure to improve revenues was relentless. Despite many attempts by Greenman to prove that sawing the highest-grade fir logs in the Vernonia mill could gain better realization, George Birkelund successfully swayed the voting trustees to supplement O-A lumber and pulp log sales by selling high-grade fir "peeler blocks" to one of the lumber industry's major competitors—the plywood industry. Peelers were typically sawn from the most desirable parts of the tree from which clear lumber grades were made, thus depriving the company a prime source of raw material. Although never approaching the importance of pulp log sales, this practice, which began in the spring of 1937, continued intermittently for the life of the operation.

The fact that a peeler log sold to the plywood mills only yielded 70 percent of the value of the lumber it could have produced prompted Greenman to conclude to Olin on February 6, 1939,

> My only point in mentioning my views on veneer log prices is to emphasize my conviction that the *sawmill* man who sells veneer logs at any price which permits the veneer manufacturer to beat his lumber prices down with a cheap veneer product, is merely doing one of the things which tends to

A NEW WORLD

O-A's diesel speeder Number 11 in all its glory following delivery from Skagit in November 1938. It is pictured at Keasey on the daily mail run from Camp McGregor.

O-A purchased the big diesel with the proceeds from the company's sale of Alco 102. The operator sat in the high-rise cupola. (Arlie Sliffe collection)

confirm the general belief that sawmill men are all either children or fools.

This internal controversy was a source of ongoing contention between Greenman and his superiors, even after Long-Bell bought the company in 1953.

Beyond the sale of peelers and hemlock logs on the open market, Oregon-American found a considerable market for short-length slab wood and sawdust in Portland. So, beginning in late 1937, the company constructed wood crate superstructures on a fleet of flatcars supplied by the SP&S for service to this market.

Shortly after Oregon-American restarted the Vernonia mill in 1936, the Johnston & McGraw shingle mill burned. Although O-A hoped that Johnston & McGraw would rebuild, the mill remained abandoned. Left without a means to convert its cedar logs, the company resorted to selling them out of the Vernonia pond to independent mill operators, a practice that continued until the mill finally shut down for good in 1957. Until O-A built log-loading facilities on the south side of the millpond, it shipped cedar logs by using the locomotive crane to load them on common-carrier cars. Periodically, O-A carried a consignment stock of finished shingles, from these operators.

For a time, O-A also sold cedar poles on the stump to Johnston, Davis and Company of Houlton, Oregon, beginning in April 1940. The buyers removed the cedar from various parcels in the Southwest Unit where they logged, hauled, and loaded the poles on common-carrier cars brought to landing sites by O-A. Despite these efforts, Oregon-American remained concerned that its selling program was weakening, particularly because of the overall decline in lumber purchases by Midwest farmers.

Accordingly, various programs were initiated to improve sales. The company reinstated the trade-marking program used by the old company on August 1, 1940, to further differentiate Oregon-American's product from its competition. This time, however, the lumber was marked with the O-A brand and not the CC&CC mark. In response to an increasingly discerning trade desiring double-end trimmed lumber, O-A installed three smooth-end trim saws in the dry assorter building.

The hemlock-for-pulp program, having proved successful to date, was stepped-up in April 1940 through another plan promoted by Orville Miller that enabled him to fulfill an obligation he had made to supply Crown Willamette Paper Company with 2.5 million board feet of hemlock. Under that arrangement, Miller supplied Oregon-American a like amount of McPherson lands' fir in

A pre–WWII view of Keasey looking east. By then, East Side and Inman-Poulsen had departed, greatly diminishing Keasey's importance to the United Railways.

The photographer caught speeder 11 on a siding waiting for train 105 Eastbound to Vernonia. (Arlie Sliffe collection)

return for Oregon-American's hemlock delivered to Crown Willamette.

With the improving financial status of the company, O-A rejoined the West Coast Lumbermen's Association, the industry's primary trade association, in mid-1938. The significance of this not only served as a measure of the company's resurgence, but also it gave Oregon-American access to the many services provided by the WCLA, including the right to stamp its product with association grade-marks, an increasingly important feature in selling lumber to governmental agencies, the armed forces, and to the railroads.

Apart from the obvious advantages accruing from WCLA membership, a moral element was involved. When Oregon-American went into receivership, 95 percent of its unsecured debt had been in dues owed the WCLA and the National Lumber Manufacturer's Association. The two associations waived those claims when O-A reorganized, which greatly helped the new company's ability to restart its operations. The associations' actions, done at the personal urging of Keith and Greenman, was in no small way premised on the hope and understanding that the new Oregon-American, when financially able to do so, would rejoin.

Having fulfilled the company's obligation to rejoin the WCLA, Greenman involved himself in many association programs and served in numerous leadership capacities throughout the remainder of his career. In no small way, his contributions helped establish his influence in the Douglas fir industry. Moreover, considerable esteem accrued to Oregon-American because of work he did for the industry-at-large.

Among the company's contributions, Oregon-

183

A NEW WORLD

Top: O-A's second Pacific Car and Foundry Company all-steel donkey moving flat car. The company purchased this used sixteen-wheeler in June 1937, trading in the original eight-wheel donkey moving car in the deal. (John Henderson photograph; Jim Blain collection)

§

Bottom: The company bought all its tank cars used in the 1920s. Some were old to begin with as evidenced by the wood chassis on this one.

Logging in dry weather was always hazardous. O-A stationed water cars in case loggers needed them for fire fighting. The pipeline running down the center of the tracks in the foreground supplied water to donkey engines. (Ken Schmelzer photograph; Jim Blain collection)

American played a pivotal role in establishing standards for the preparation of Douglas fir lumber. O-A loaned Archie Knauss, O-A's dry kiln foreman and a leading authority on the process, to the Oregon State Agricultural College's (now Oregon State University) School of Forestry to help in the development of that institution's dry kiln instruction school in 1930.

By 1941, Knauss's replacement, Fred Tousley, had become very active in the WCLA-sponsored Dry Kiln Club in which member manufacturers having dry-kilning facilities were encouraged to meet at regular intervals to discuss methods, share information, and generally strive to improve the state of that art.

These programs, combined with the surge in business immediately preceding WWII, saw the company's order file grow to 10 million board feet by Thanksgiving 1940. With the increase of hostilities in Europe, U.S. defense activities began representing a steadily growing part of the business.

RAILROAD OPERATIONS

Oregon-American placed its locomotive 102 for sale in May 1937. O-A had retired it from road service in 1928 and, apart from its stint supplying steam to power to the mill powerhouse during receivership, it had remained mostly idle. Alberni Pacific Lumber Company of Vancouver Island, British Columbia, offered $10,000. O-A accepted the offer and the engine left Vernonia Saturday, August 20, 1938. Following its departure, Oregon-American renumbered the 2-spot Lima shay as Road Number 102.

O-A applied proceeds from the Alco's sale to the purchase of a new Skagit Model 6-70, 10-ton, diesel-powered rail car. As Oregon-American's large gasoline-engined speeder, Skagit Model M.A.C. 4-40, Road Number 10, had accumulated some 300,000 miles in its thirteen years and was beginning to show its age, the company needed a reliable replacement. Moreover, because the company also planned to use the diesel speeder to transport loggers to work, it promised substantial operating cost savings since it would replace a steam locomotive used for the same task. The new speeder came to O-A on November 29, 1938, resplendent in its orange body and black trim. Assigned Road Number 11, it cost $8,900.

Until a February 1938 Interstate Commerce Commission ruling that prohibited use of arch-bar truck equipped rail cars on common-carrier rails, Oregon-American used its own fleet of tank cars to transport fuel oil from Portland. During the interim before O-A could build a fuel oil storage tank near its Overhead Crossing in November 1939, the company brought its woods' oil supplies to Camp McGregor in common-carrier tank cars. There the company pumped it to its own tank cars. Not long after the new Wolf Creek Highway opened, O-A began resupplying its new oil tank at the Overhead Crossing using local bulk oil merchants who trucked the oil directly from their plants in Vernonia. The convenience of highway deliveries became so apparent that the company also built a receiving depot and warehouse at the Overhead in 1941.

When Oregon-American began shipping hemlock logs via its disconnects to Rafton in October 1939, bad-order reports from SP&S car inspectors came in a barrage. Reluctant to invest the money needed to bring the cars into compliance, the company modified the program in April 1940. After that, instead of dedicating carloads at the landings, O-A intermingled hemlock logs with fir, brought all the logs to Vernonia in regular log trains, then segregated the hemlock in the millpond for reloading on common-carrier cars spotted on the south levee of the pond. To accomplish this, the company extended the so-called Yukon spur that circled the back of the mill and ended on the south levee of the millpond by four car-lengths. O-A used its locomotive crane to handle the transloading of logs from the pond to cars bound to other commercial destinations. Still, this proved effective only for loading the small hemlock as the crane was not able to handle larger peeler logs. So, for a brief period in 1940 the company brought one of its loading donkeys down from the woods for this task. O-A ran a steam line to it from the mill's boilers. Later, the loading engine that had been removed from the tree-rigged skidder took over those duties.

Mr. Alexander: I wish you would arrange to have locomotive 105 kept cleaner than it has been of late. This locomotive is a piece of equipment of which we want to be proud at all times, and I have frequently in the past had compliments from other loggers and other railroad men on its neat appearance. I do not believe such compliments would be warranted at this time and I hate to think we are running a goodly locomotive like this up and down the tracks and could not be properly complimented at any time by any one who notices equipment of this sort.

Judd Greenman

Addition of a second shift at the mill in September 1940 again made it mandatory to cold-deck logs to carry the mill during winter shutdowns in the woods. In December 1940, an additional 600 feet were added to the Yukon Spur. Stringer logs were placed along both sides of the tracks, and O-A used the locomotive crane to deck logs over and at a

Disconnected trucks proved ideal for some tasks other than hauling logs. O-A equipped this one with an oil tank to fuel the tree-rigged skidder. (Ivan Ergish photograph; John Henderson collection)

right-angle to the tracks. This program allowed the company to stockpile between 2 and 3 million feet of logs needed to keep the mill running during that winter. Eventually, O-A extended the track on the north side of the pond beyond the train-unloading dump site the rest of the way around the pond to connect with the Yukon Spur. This allowed the log train's entire twenty-six loads to be accommodated at the pond during those times when its arrival coincided with the SP&S's switching of the mill.

Oregon-American took great pride in its railroad. Greenman wrote the Oregon State Industrial Accident Commission in December 1938:

> All [our] railroad is laid with 62 pound or heavier rail. Every foot of it is well ballasted with good rock the average ballast depth being in excess of 18 inches.

We believe the construction of our logging railroad to be the equal of any in the State and much superior to the average Oregon railroad over which logging trains are operated.

Despite the rail line's fine condition, train operations on the Camp McGregor to Vernonia run had their share of eventful moments. Unfenced pastures below the county line led to many unhappy run-ins with free-roaming livestock. In one of the messier incidents with those "damnable goats that infested the Keasey area," O-A Extra 105 East, trailing a full set of loads, came around the curve onto the high SP&S trestle immediately above Keasey only to find a herd of thirteen goats in the middle. Before the engineer could stop the train, it ran down eleven of the unfortunate creatures.

CHANGES TO THE OREGON-AMERICAN / NORTHERN LINES' STRATEGIC PARTNERSHIP

The fact Oregon-American's lumber production was only half its pre-Depression level, combined with the decline in overall log shipments as other operators ran out of timber, doomed any prospects for the carriers to operate the Vernonia branch line at a profit. Oregon-American's refusal to commit itself to the Ruth Realty timber only darkened the outlook. Not surprisingly, therefore, the carriers also adopted a pay-as-you-go operating philosophy for the United Railways.

Faced with these unwelcome prospects, the Northern Lines also began reevaluating their overall relationship with Oregon-American. By April 1939, Ruth Realty had completed the disposal of its burned timber from the Southwest Unit reducing its aggregate cruise from 535 to 500 million board feet.

While the Northern Lines were undoubtedly pleased with O-A's assistance in helping them dispose of the burned Ruth timber, and took some comfort from O-A's verbal assurances that it fully intended to acquire the balance of Ruth's green standing timber, Oregon-American decidedly displeased them when it requested the SP&S establish a tariff for movement of hemlock to Rafton.

The 1927 agreement for maintenance of the railroad tracks at the Vernonia mill became another sore spot in the O-A and SP&S relationship. Under that arrangement, O-A track crews handled the maintenance and billed the costs to the railway company. Periodic repairs, coupled with the costs of extending the Yukon spur to facilitate the hemlock reloading operation, prompted the SP&S to complain that per-mile maintenance costs on its tracks on the mill property were approaching those for the entire main line. Matters were smoothed over by O-A's agreement in February 1941 to pay half the costs incurred to maintain the mill tracks.

Still, the ink had barely dried on that agreement before the SP&S realized the larger locomotives it had recently assigned to the Vernonia line were too heavy, which forced them to replace the mill tracks and almost 3,000 feet of rail connecting it to the mainline. Seeking to avoid the job, the SP&S suggested paying O-A to switch the mill yard with one of its own locomotives, a notion Greenman flatly rejected because of O-A's own lack of motive power and a concern that if O-A took over switching its own mill, the SP&S's train crews' unions might strike and demand to haul O-A's logs from the county line to Vernonia in exchange. Other points of dissatisfaction also arose, largely over O-A's complaints about inadequate train service to Vernonia. Collectively, these issues became a thorn in the carriers' side, one they could only remove when O-A was ready to log the bulk of Ruth Realty's timber.

The company built a small caboose on this disconnect. (Jack Holst photograph; John T. Labbe collection)

TIMBER PURCHASES AND TRADES

Despite Oregon-American's limited financial resources and the prevailing attitude not to buy additional timber holdings, the company's property boundaries underwent many changes between 1934 and 1942. While in receivership, Watzek had reduced the company's property tax liability by abandoning selected cut or burned-over parcels totaling nearly 6,000 acres. And, once reorganized, O-A had to face the challenge of blocking out the rest of its tract, a task that had been only partially completed when the company went into receivership. Two factors substantially complicated that task, damages from the 1933 Wolf Creek Fire and construction of the Wolf Creek Highway that isolated part of the company's timber holdings.

Table 7.2

Oregon-American Property Transactions 1934–1942

	Transaction Type	Acres	Cruise	Date
Columbia County	Abandonment	423	Cutover	1934
Clatsop County	Abandonment	5,385	Cutover	1934
Rupp-Blodgett	Exchange to O-A	429	5,448,000'	1936
O-A	Exchange to Rupp-Blodgett	601	17,233,000'	1936
Ruth Realty	Stumpage purchase	160	4,000,000' est	1937
A. Churchill	Stumpage purchase	240	6,000,000' est	1937
Yunkers & Wieckes	Stumpage sale	160	unk	1937
von Platen/ Clatsop County	Land purchase	173	unk	1937
Levy	Stumpage purchase	40	unk	1937
State of Oregon Highway Dept.	Sale of right-of-way for Wolf Creek Highway	403	logged	1939
Detroit Trust Co.	Land purchase	308	17,000,000' est	1940
Salmonberry Timber Co.	Land purchase	2,481	76,345,000' est	1941
McPherson	Land purchase	40	unk	1941
Grand Lodge Knights of Pythias of Oregon	Stumpage purchase	40	unk	1941
W. D. Music	Stumpage purchase	40	250,000'	1942

Oregon-American's land and timber transactions during this period appear in Table 7.2.

Two acquisitions during this period bear further mention. The 1940 purchase from the Detroit Trust Company, though small, was notable because that land mingled with Oregon-American and Ruth Realty holdings in the Keasey Unit. Had George McPherson, who managed the property, successfully obtained a right-of-way easement from Ruth Realty, its logging would have presented a distinct fire hazard to remaining timber in the vicinity.

On learning of the right-of-way application in

June 1936, Greenman protested loudly, not only because of the fire hazard issue but because McPherson planned to have the Detroit Trust parcel logged by L&M Logging Company. As L&M was a partnership of Antone Lausmann and Frank Miller, principals of the former East Side Logging Company, Greenman, in a letter to A. J. Witchel, an assistant superintendent of the SP&S, bluntly explained why Ruth should deny the easement request:

> Timber belonging to the Ruth Realty Company and to us has been very seriously damaged on two different occasions, in 1932 and 1933 by fires which originated in slashings left on lands on which Mr. Lausmann's company had done the logging.
>
> With this experience record, there is no reason in the world to assume that this operation is to be conducted, by this same company on lands controlled by Mr. McPherson in Section 6, Twp. 4 North, Range 5 West, with any more regard for the rights of the adjoining owner than was exhibited by Lausmann and his associates in the past....
>
> I am very hopeful that you will find it possible to block this proposed operation by one means or another.

Ruth took Greenman's points to heart and refused the application.

However, the tables turned in 1940 when McPherson contracted to have the parcel logged by Orville Miller. By contrast, Miller had a rock-solid relationship with Oregon-American and the railway company. His Koster Products Company had long been a supplier of log traffic to the SP&S and when it appeared likely the carrier would grant the easement, O-A had to face the prospect either to

Over the years, O-A acquired a number of ballast cars for railroad construction. A side-dump model is shown here. (John Henderson photograph; Jim Blain collection)

log the Keasey tract early or offer to buy the tract from the Detroit Trust Company.

Logging the Keasey Tract in advance was an unpalatable alternative that would have left Oregon-American in the conventional position of dismantling more than 30 miles of railroad after it had cut all its remaining timber.

The diplomatic Miller was equally reluctant to impair his personal and professional relationship with Greenman. Seeking an alternative, he secured an offer from McPherson to sell Detroit's Keasey timber for $35,000.

Oregon-American jumped at the offer and paid for the purchase out of its own slim cash reserves. The tract, largely consisting of red fir, contained about 56,000 board feet to the acre based on a 1928 cruise that was considered conservative.

The second notable acquisition was for the 2,841-acre Salmonberry Timber Company tract. It was located immediately south of O-A's Southwest Unit and Ruth Realty's holdings in that area. This parcel was a remnant of the original DuBois tract Oregon-American did not purchase in 1917 because it had a clouded title. In the intervening years, the West Oregon Lumber Company had developed and logged parts of the southernmost piece of the tract until the 1932 Cochran fire burned that operation. Henry Chaney, chairman of the Oregon-American board of directors, also happened to be president of the Salmonberry Timber Company and, while liquidating the property, provided O-A the first opportunity to obtain the tract in 1938.

By then the economic outlook for the lumber industry as a whole had taken a decided upturn. The fact that supplies of old-growth Douglas fir were rapidly depleting was, in part, a contributing factor. An aura of speculation developed as operators vied for what remaining stands came on the market. Although perhaps lacking the intensity of the days when Charles Keith took control of Oregon-American, a body of opinion began to reemerge that the price for standing timber had no where to go but up.

Though mindful of the risks inherent in land speculation, Chaney, Olin, and Greenman agreed the Salmonberry Timber Company tract represented the last available large body of timber tributary to Oregon-American's operations and recommended its purchase to the O-A board.

The $180,000 asking price for the tract put the outright acquisition far beyond Oregon-American's financial reach. Given the mandate to pay off existing debts, financing the acquisition was out of the question too. By virtue of Central Coal & Coke's need to have the O-A debt paid off and because Central's future interest would emerge only after Oregon-American had accomplished that, other members of the O-A board of directors laid the decision to buy the STC tract at Sigmund Stern's doorstep. It stayed there, unattended, until the spring of 1941 when Chaney, anxious to dispose of the property, offered it to the Long-Bell Lumber Company and others who had operations in the vicinity.

Stern and Central Coal & Coke's board, predisposed against buying the tract for Oregon-American, suggested O-A approach the Northern Lines to learn whether the carriers had any interest. The Northern Lines' response was emphatically negative, even if it meant a loss of the future rail traffic the timber represented.

In a last-ditch effort to keep the deal alive, Greenman wrote to Stern on March 15, 1941.

> While I can appreciate their desire to liquidate without further speculation it is a definite disappointment to me that the Central people decided not to buy the Salmonberry tract. I believe the time is now here when good timber, advantageously located, as this is, can be converted at a profit.
>
> The fifteen years which elapsed since Fir industry productive capacity was sharply expanded by operators from other regions have taken their toll in timber to the point where good trees, adjacent to milling operations, are extremely scarce and difficult to obtain.
>
> There is more activity in and more turn-over of timber lands in the Northwest today than there has been since 1923 or 1924. Every sort of a tract of timber which offers any operating possibilities at all is being gobbled up. In the course of this activity in timber turn-over the position of many of the substantial operators is being materially strengthened.... Consequently, it seems perfectly logical for us to give very careful consideration to any likely possibility of increasing our timber holdings, since they are not large enough to provide that certainty

of complete liquidation which all of us who have the welfare of the Company at heart feel desirable.

The Central board, and Stern, finally realizing the opportunity's significance and that it was about to be lost, relented.

Terms for the purchase of the Salmonberry Timber tract, which cruised more than 75 million board feet, were made for $165,000 cash. The sale also called for payment of an additional $15,000, carried at 4 percent interest, accountable for after O-A had recovered 55 million feet, at a rate of $3 per 1,000 board feet.

THE COW CREEK FIRE OF AUGUST 1, 1939

Subscribers to the theory that history repeats itself would find strong support in events that followed the 1933 Tillamook Burn. Major fires revisited that troubled territory in 1939, 1945, and again in 1951, leading to a widespread notion the region was under the spell of a six-year jinx. Parallels between the 1933 and 1939 Tillamook Burns and the Wolf Creek and Cow Creek Fires of 1933 and 1939 lent particular credence to that theory.

On August 1, 1939, fire broke out in a logging show near Glenwood, Oregon, not far from the point of origin of the 1933 Tillamook Burn. It marked the beginning of the second fire to bear that infamous name. That same day another fire broke out, some 18 miles to the northwest, in an area previously burned over by the 1933 Wolf Creek Fire. This second fire originated in a logging show on Oregon-American lands located deep in the Cow Creek canyon.

The Portland daily papers gave brief attention to the O-A fire because it forced closure of the newly dedicated Wolf Creek Highway. The papers dubbed O-A's fire the "Elsie" fire, owing to its proximity to that nearby wayside on the highway. Within days, however, news coverage had shifted primarily to the larger Tillamook fire and the Elsie fire faded from public attention.[3]

Both fires raged for weeks and ultimately spread over most of the areas consumed by their respective predecessors of 1933. And, like in 1933, despite their burning in relative close proximity, both fires remained completely separate and never joined.

Whether due to bad record keeping, public apathy, or simply because the sheer size of both fires made the distinction meaningless to the public at large, the identity of the 1939 Elsie, or Cow Creek Fire, like that of the Wolf Creek Fire that burned before it, was lost within a brief time after its last embers had cooled. Finally, like in 1933, recorded history mistakenly attributed much of the damage created by the Elsie/Cow Creek Fire to the Tillamook Burn of 1939.

Oregon-American never determined the cause of the Cow Creek Fire. Hot summer weather had limited logging to a single cold-decking operation for several weeks beforehand. O-A crews were working the "hoot-owl" shift from 5 A.M. to 1:30 P.M. to take advantage of what little humidity carried over from the night before and to avoid working in the hot afternoons when fire was most likely to start. No steam donkeys had been used since the end of June. The new Skagit diesel donkey was the only machine used for yarding work after that.

August 1 found the diesel donkey yarding far down the northern slope of the Cow Creek canyon, below Spur 25-6. A short distance away, the

A NEW WORLD

The Cow Creek Fire (called the "Elsie Fire" in the Portland newspapers) started on August 1, 1939, in the big canyon below Spur 25-6. At the time, O-A was salvaging timber killed in the 1933 Wolf Creek Fire. Fueled by tinder-dry snags and refuse, the fire was the hottest the company ever experienced and eventually covered some 40,000 acres, much of which had burned previously in 1933.

Despite the fact history recorded the 1933 Wolf Creek and 1939 Cow Creek Fires as part of the Tillamook Burns of the same years, neither joined their larger and more famous counterparts to the south.

Opposite page: The Cow Creek Fire caused extensive damage to many of O-A's donkey engines. On Spur 25-8, a crew dismantled the Willamette 12 × 14 two-speed yarder Number 2334.

§

This page: The fire burned yarder 2504, a Willamette 13 × 14 two-speed, on Spur 25-7. O-A had the 2504 and 2334 overhauled in Portland. Both returned to service. The company converted 2504 to diesel power after WWII. (Dusenberry photographs; Martin E. Hansen collection) construction crew was at work extending Spur 25-6 through Sections 1 and 2 of Twp. 4 North, Range 7 West. Shortly after quitting time, speeder Number 11 and the loggers left for Camp McGregor. Locomotive 106 followed, hauling the track workers. Just after the 106 passed Spur 25-4, one of the crew spotted smoke across the canyon close to where the cold-decking show was. Trainmen immediately stopped the locomotive and began backing up to the telephone at the Spur 25-4 junction to notify Camp McGregor of the fire. En route, the locomotive almost ran into superintendent Olson who was following everyone back to camp in his speeder.

Olson raced back to the Spur 25-4 telephone to sound the alarm. Locomotive 106 and crew returned to the fire where a dozen or so Japanese track workers ran down the canyon to make trails around the fire. All told, approximately forty-five minutes had elapsed before anyone could return to the scene. The fire itself began burning in heavy logging debris at the bottom of the canyon, more than 700 feet below the diesel yarder, in Section 1, Twp. 4 North, Range 7 West.

Once word arrived at Camp McGregor, speeder Number 10 was loaded with fire-fighting equipment and men. When speeder Number 11, carrying the logging crew, arrived at camp, speeder 10 left for the fire followed immediately by speeder 11. By 4 P.M. the fire had spread and covered between 20 and 30 acres and had burned into a thick stand of hemlock killed in the 1933 Wolf Creek Fire. The fire ran up these snags and burning bark, mosses, and limbs started blowing in all directions away from the snags, scattering the fire widely. Still, however, the fire remained largely on the ground until that night when strong northeast

The big fire in '39 was kind of a repetition of the '33 burn. It didn't have as much fuel but had a lot of dried snags. That fire jumped us and cut us off. We were busy unrigging with a Cletrac and once we got all the lines hooked up to a locomotive they took off down the railroad with it to keep it from burning. Then we split up and I led the way with the Cletrac and guided the CCC kids from the place where the fire broke over from the Cow Creek canyon into the North Fork, cross-country down to a swamp I knew about.

By the time the train crew got down to where Spur 25 came closest to the Wolf Creek Highway, both trestles just above there were already on fire. They stopped the train, looked the fire over and finally decided there was only "surface burning" on the structures, so they made a run for it. Well, they made it all right but everyone needed to change their pants by the time they got to the other side. But then the only reason they tried it at all was because

winds kicked up and began scattering spot fires to the southwest.

O-A crews worked fire lines through the next night. CCC crews joined them and began building trails from Spur 25-6 south toward the Wolf Creek Highway. A bulldozer was deployed to build a trail from Spur 25-10 toward spur 25-12 to cut the fire off on the south side of the canyon. By 5 P.M on August 2, Olson and Greenman realized efforts to contain the fire in the canyon were futile. As this area had been entirely fire-killed in the 1933 Wolf *they were too scared to stay on the other side because the fire was right behind them.*

I just skimmed the ground with those guys right behind me. When I got to the swamp it was full of water so I dug out a big hole in the middle of it and we stayed right out in the middle with the Cletrac. Stayed there all night. The fire went over our heads.

When the rest of the crew made it back to Camp McGregor that night they were certain we had no way to get out. They thought we were dead. That was even in the paper in Portland.

Those fire association [CCC] boys were mostly from New Joisey. Dead-end kids. They weren't very old, fifteen, sixteen, seventeen, but boy were they tough. And they weren't afraid to work either. Until they got into the bee logs, the honey logs. And then they didn't make it out the next day.

George Lee, construction

Creek Fire, not only was there much accumulated slashing where salvage logging had been completed, dry snags covered the entire area and only made the fire burn more intensely. They redeployed the entire logging crew to unrig spar trees, save equipment and rigging, and build trails around the many donkey engines that were in the area. The Japanese track workers tried vainly to hold fire lines but the flames drove them back.

In the early hours of August 3 the fire drove crews out of the logging area completely. It crossed the saddle separating the Cow Creek and the North Fork of Rock Creek canyons near the junction of mainline Spur 25 and its junction with Spur 25-6. The railroad crew retreated, taking all the rolling stock that could be picked up along the way. Three trestles on the mainline below former Camp Number 1 were already burning by the time they crossed.

The firefighters, once efforts to prevent the fire from crossing mainline Spur 25 below Camp Number 1 proved hopeless, returned to Camp Number 1. Escape by railroad was now impossible, at least until the fire passed. Realizing their predicament, Olson ordered a bulldozer and operator to blaze a trail east and lead the CCC men to safety.

George Lee, who was the company's primary road construction equipment operator, used one of the Cletracs to make a crude trail for the twenty-six men in his charge. He led them to the bottom of the North Fork of Rock Creek canyon. The fire was in hot pursuit, having crowned in the snags. By the time the group reached the bottom of the canyon, Lee had just enough time to dig out a clearing in a swamp so everyone could hunker down and let the fire burn over them.

The fire trapped the remaining twenty-three men from 3 P.M. until 8 P.M. on the hill above at Camp Number 1. They had to endure the heat as the fire burned its way past. By nightfall the fire had cooled sufficiently so they could walk down the mainline to Spur 25-12. From there they made a cross-country trek westward to the Wolf Creek Highway. Passing motorists then transported the men to Spur 25-14 where a speeder returned them to Camp McGregor late on the night of August 3. By the time Olson and crew returned to Camp McGregor, Lee and the CCC crew had still not shown up, and

A NEW WORLD

for a while, everyone presumed the fire had burned them.

The fire raged on and, though now fueled only by slashing that had burned four times before, it threatened to burn Camp McGregor on August 3 and 4. Firefighters did not bring the fire under a semblance of control until August 12 after they had built many miles of bulldozer and hand trails. Those tactics proved completely ineffective in areas where slashing from the 1933 burn had not been cleared and it was only after the fire moved beyond the active logging areas that it was brought under control.

The Cow Creek Fire was an expensive proposition for Oregon-American. Beyond direct fire-fighting labor expenditures, it destroyed $30,000 of felled and bucked timber, and either destroyed or damaged equipment valued at $125,000.

Among the casualties were four Willamette yarders, Numbers 2400, 2363, 2504, and 2334. O-A never returned Number 2334 to service. The fire also damaged five loading engines, Numbers 2167, 2336, 2358, 2062, and 2061, the first three severely. The company eventually restored its depleted yarder roster by exchanging two obsolete Willamette Humboldt yarders that had lain idle since 1929 for a used Willamette 12 × 14 Two-speed yarder, Number 2476. O-A made the exchange through Western Loggers Machinery Company of Portland in May 1940. The company immediately converted Number 2476 to an oil-burner using surplus parts bought from Clark and Wilson Lumber Company. The fire burned three railroad trestles on Spur 25 so badly O-A had to replace them. It also burned two more trestles the company bypassed with fills when rebuilding Spur 25.

It was expensive for other operators too as the fire paid no attention to property boundaries and spread extensively. Greenman provided additional details about the fire to insurance company adjusters on November 18, 1939:

> The fire of August 1, 1939 was the hottest woods fire with which I ever had any experience. I have heard the same thing said by many experienced forest fire fighters who participated in efforts to suppress the fire.
>
> The reason for the severity of this fire probably lay in the fact that it burned to a large extent in a snag area created by a previous fire that burned over much of the same ground in 1933 and at that time killed practically all of the timber on lands that reburned in 1939.
>
> The fire burned out of control for about three weeks. By this I mean that during the period of three weeks, between August 1 and August 21, there were frequent out-breaks of the fire at different locations which sent it completely out of control of the forces working on it.
>
> For about thirty days approximately 1,000 men were used in the effort to cut off and control this fire. About half of these men were CCC enrollees and the other half were employees of the logging and lumbering concerns whose property was being damaged by the fire.
>
> Our own efforts at suppression resulted in expenditures in excess of $25,000 compared with an insurance recovery of $8,370. I think the total cost of suppression efforts on the fire if CCC enrollees were paid prevailing wage rates would run substantially more than $100,000. And the damage done by the fire to standing timber, logs, equip-

ment, etc. I am satisfied aggregated one-half million dollars.

The fire burned over a total of somewhere from 40,000 to 50,000 acres. Of this total acreage, about one-half was cut over land and the remainder was standing timber, most of which had been previously fire-killed.

THE STRUGGLE FOR UNION DOMINANCE

Problematical as day-to-day dealings with organized labor might have been to Oregon-American and its fellow operators overall, no single labor issue created more havoc in the industry during the 1930's than the rivalry between the CIO and the A F of L and the jurisdictional disputes that arose as each tried to dominate the other.

The A F of L and its affiliate organization, the Sawmill & Timber Workers Union, enjoyed rapid success organizing West Coast camps and mills during the early days of recovery following the Great Depression. However, internal strife between the A F of L and the Carpenters and Sawmill & Timber Workers Union developed and eventually caused many members of the STWU to sever their affiliation with the Federation in 1937 and join the John L. Lewis-led Committee for Industrial Organization. The CIO-affiliated International Woodworkers of America, or IWA, was thus born and came to enjoy great success convincing labor forces in the woods and mills to denounce the A F of L and join the new union.[4]

Matters became complicated if an operator's logging workforce voted to sign up with the CIO but mill workers chose to retain their A F of L affiliation. Sometimes where this occurred, sawmill workers refused to handle logs cut by the CIO crews.

Despite efforts to the contrary, logging and sawmill employers were unable to escape the consequences of the battle, whether in their own organizations or elsewhere. For example, in the aftermath of a change in affiliation at a mill from A F of L to CIO, the A F of L trade unions, which were dominant at most job sites, often declared lumber originating from a CIO mill as "unfair" and boycotted use of the product.

Inman-Poulsen's dam was built between two ridges that narrowed down to Rock Creek. They had great borrow pits on the north side across the creek across from the railroad. They rigged a big Fresno scraper like a logging tree and skinned the scraper up along the ridge and then hauled it back and dumped the dirt over a log cribbing they made across the creek, eventually burying it.

The logs were still covered by dirt so they didn't burn out in the '33 fire. Later, the dirt eroded and left the ends of the logs exposed. They got old and dry and when the '39 fire came through it ignited them and burned them out. That dropped the dirt down some more and the water eventually washed everything away. That emptied the pond.

George Lee, construction

The Western Operators Association Bulletin of July 10, 1937, described the situation in the industry as of that date:

> Latest developments indicate that the fight between the A F of L and the CIO on the west coast appears heading for an early showdown, with the battleground principally within the ranks of the waterfront employees and the lumber workers. Oddly enough, each of these groups is headed by a mili-

tant foreigner, Bridges of the Maritime Federation of the Pacific and Pritchett of the Woodworking Federation. Both are high in the esteem of J. L. Lewis, chairman of the CIO and each is making a phenomenal success in building up opposition to the A F of L.

In the lumber industry, the results of all this movement will soon become known, as voting on the issue of withdrawing from the A F of L is now in progress… the employer will, unless careful, be drawn in by indirection or otherwise, and asked to declare himself.

Now among lumber workers many observers take this view: That the unmistakable drift away from the A F of L is not so much an espousal of the CIO as it is a protest against the present union, or for that matter any organization. These workmen, particularly in the logging branches, are individualists, trained in direct action, and they smart under regimentation. Most of them are union members, for the one reason that it is pushed on them and they know little and care less about what is going on….

For the employers, the chances to write a decent ticket for the industry are the brightest if they declare a policy of hands-off. This does not mean, however, that they should not encourage their workmen to do some constructive thinking and in the meantime give some thought to the Roman strategy "Divide and Rule."

Oregon-American's election took place on August 19, 1937. Both mill and woods employees voted overwhelmingly in favor of changing affiliation to the CIO's International Woodworkers of America, Local 5-37.

The mere fact that most of O-A's labor force voted to change affiliation did not, however, result in a complete and unanimous change in membership. Nearly 100 of O-A's mill crews voted to remain in A F of L Local 2557. The election only meant the IWA had earned the right to represent most of the workers both in the woods and in the mill.

Since the O-A labor agreement was open-shop, the minority union was free to continue representing those who elected not to change affiliations. The resulting dual-union situation presented a ready-made opportunity for a showdown between the A F of L and CIO parent organizations. The threat of a showdown for complete dominance, in effect a demand for a closed-shop agreement, posed Oregon-American with a particularly acute dilemma, for the employees who elected to remain with the A F of L were all mill employees and, for the most part, the highly skilled employees at that. Their ranks included sawyers, millwrights, electricians, edgermen, and foremen, the latter group comprising those whom the company had rehired on an hourly wage versus salaried basis when it resumed operations in 1936. In short, Local 2557's membership represented both the employees who had the longest tenure and the ones the company relied on most to keep the mill running. The loss of these employees over a union jurisdictional fight would have drastically reduced production.

Expressing a sense of impending doom, Greenman observed:

> I don't know what the outcome of various sundry difficulties with labor here in the northwest is going to be except that it is reasonably certain that unless some sort of permanent peace can be estab-

lished the industry is going to be ruined. Portland and northwest Oregon has become the battle ground for every difference that has come up between the operators and the men so far, and of course these battles have all left their scars. I believe the labor leaders themselves recognize this and would like to transfer their scraps to some other section of the northwest if they could. However, in the very nature of things there have been attracted to the camps and mills of this district the most radical group of men in the industry and regardless of the desires of the operators or the labor leaders these men continue to put on a show every time any excuse arises.

When negotiations for a new contract opened in the spring of 1938, O-A reached agreement with the bargaining committee on all points except the ratification clause.

Caught in the tug-of-war between the dominant CIO and the minority A F of L unions, Greenman outlined the company's precarious situation:

I believe that execution of the agreement by the Company at this time and its acceptance by the Union [Local 5-37] will simply be signing the death warrant of our operations. We are merely getting by in our business and in the process of getting by we are doing a considerable volume of business which will be denied to us if we are placed on the unfair list by the A F of L.... We are not now on the unfair list simply because of the fact we do have a considerable number of A F of L men in our crew and an active and aggressive Local which the A F of L wants to foster and encourage. If this agreement is signed, I am confident they will withdraw their fostering and encouragement from this Local and will place our name on their unfair list with all the damaging consequences that follow such action.

O-A managed to sidestep that issue by eliminating the ratification clause completely before forwarding the unsigned agreement to Local 5-37. The local's leaders obtained membership approval after Oregon-American, in a separate letter, promised to live up to the agreement's provisions.

While the general nature of labor conflicts characterizing the industry may have been fewer and less serious in 1938 and most of 1939 than they had been in 1937, Oregon-American found such peace illusory. On September 14, 1939, IWA Local 5-37 took a strike vote demanding every man working in that jurisdiction be a member in good standing of the CIO local within ten days. The measure passed by a four-to-one margin.

IWA Local 5-37's ultimatum to A F of L employees was merely a thinly disguised effort to force Oregon-American into a closed-shop agreement under which membership in Local 5-37 became a prerequisite to employment. Due to its large size and relative geographical isolation, higher-ups in the CIO infrastructure purposely selected Vernonia as a battleground and clearly orchestrated the strike vote from a distance. The local merely went along.

As it turned out, the CIO could hardly have made a poorer choice. By the time the issue was settled, any mental association of Vernonia and Oregon-American with "backwater" had undoubtedly changed to one of association with the word "backbone." Having avoided all but minor localized boycotts of its products by the A F of L–affiliated unions, only to be threatened by shutdown if O-A did not meet the CIO-affiliated International Woodworkers of America's demand for a closed-shop, the company made a direct appeal to all employees and residents in an open letter to the *Vernonia Eagle* only days before the September 25, 1939, strike deadline. It emphasized that to agree to the IWA's demand requiring every employee to belong to any union was illegal under the Wagner Act. It also questioned the motives behind putting people out of work and deplored the "wall of bad feeling" that was building between employees and the company over a question the company was legally forbidden to address. Apart from outlining its position to the community-at-large, Oregon-American's appeal failed to sway the Local and on September 25, 1939, the strike commenced.

Although IWA Local 5-37 represented both Oregon-American's mill and woods employees, each group represented separate bargaining units. The woods crew remained on the job even though the mill crew was out on strike. Following the Cow Creek Fire, Oregon-American had plenty of work to rehabilitate its logging and railroad equipment so could keep its loggers occupied, even after the millworkers struck. That situation remained unchanged until October 13 when the company moved its first trainload of hemlock for subsequent shipment to Rafton.

That evening, the business agent for the CIO mill sublocal called a special meeting with the Camp McGregor sublocal and convinced the loggers that if they kept working and allowed the company to continue shipping logs, such action effectively was support of a company effort to break the strike. Accordingly, the loggers walked off the job on Monday, October 16, 1939.

The paralyzing effect of the Oregon-American strike quickly spread beyond the Nehalem Valley, and by October 19, 1939, Governor Charles A. Sprague had called representatives from both the IWA Local 5-37 and the Sawmill & Timber Workers Local 2557 to his offices in Salem to reach some sort of settlement. Under the scrutiny of the governor and the public-at-large, and without representation from union higher-ups, the eight delegates, four each from the two locals, came to a proposed settlement. It called for each member of Local 2557 to contribute fifty cents per month to Local 5-37 but allowed their affiliation to the A F of L to remain unchanged. Settlement was made contingent on the approval of each local's membership. IWA 5-37 members approved the proposal by a vote of 299 to 1. Members of Local 2557 flatly rejected it, claiming *the assessment would, in effect, have amounted to their joining the CIO.*

Greenman advised Governor Sprague on October 21, 1939:

> The position of the CIO leaders has been greatly improved by this experience for they are not in the position of having carried out their part of the bargain while the A F of L is in the position of having turned down a possibility to end the strike. This has naturally made the CIO leaders more certain of themselves and somewhat more difficult to deal with.
>
> The CIO leaders asked me last night, immediately after the results of the voting at both of the meetings were known, to open negotiations immediately on a closed shop clause in our working agreement....
>
> This matter is apparently so effectively stale-

mated again that I am wondering if you will not use your good offices in an effort to bring about some sort of a settlement which will be acceptable to both unions.

Writing Calvin Fentress of Baker, Fentress & Company following a public rally called in Vernonia on November 7, 1939, Greenman provided additional background:

Nor is it [news] that Harold Pritchett, president of the IWA with whom we have to deal in our labor relations at Vernonia and pretty much over the northwest, is a Communist. I met Pritchett soon after he was elected to the presidency of the IWA and was immediately impressed with his fanaticism and his desire to make over the capitalistic system, so I have long known that we were dealing with people who were directed by enemies of the American Way.

Mr. Pritchett was here at Vernonia last night, attending a meeting of the Local Union and as an exhibition of the irresponsibility of the leaders of the CIO, I will tell you that yesterday morning the newly-appointed State Director of the CIO, William Dalrymple, whom [John L.] Lewis sent here following the San Francisco convention to take charge of CIO affairs in Oregon, definitely promised the manager of one of the employers' associations, to which we belong, that he and Pritchett were coming to Vernonia last night to advise the Vernonia Local in their opinion the Oregon-American contract had been broken and to instruct them to get together with the Oregon-American management and arrange for a return to work as promptly as possible.

Instead of instructing the Vernonia Local to restore their contract to good standing and make arrangements to return to work, I am told Dalrymple and Pritchett at last night's meeting advised the boys to *hang tough and continue their strike for they would eventually win the closed shop.*

I believe that a closed shop contract made with the IWA at this time would result in such chaotic conditions so far as managerial control is concerned, that satisfactory operating results would be impossible to obtain.... I am satisfied there is deep significance in the fact that the IWA does not have one single closed shop contract in the northwest lumber manufacturing industry. The significance is that no management as yet has felt itself sufficiently strong or sufficiently rash to get completely in bed with these fellows and put themselves entirely at their mercy.

I am certain you understand that the sole and only purpose of the strike at Vernonia is to force the closed shop onto this institution. A great many other excuses have been made for this strike at one time or another but when these superficial reasons are answered one by one, as they have been repeatedly, and the real motive back of the strike is exposed, it is invariably exposed as being an effort to obtain at least one closed shop agreement in the Fir lumber manufacturing industry. This fact was proven no longer ago than yesterday by the Executive Committee of Columbia Basin Sawmills in some negotiations they carried on with representatives of the Union in an effort to settle our matter. After four hours of discussion the Union representative frankly admitted they were attempting to force a closed shop on the Oregon-American and would be satisfied with nothing less.

I think this is an opportune time to say that, unless we are prepared to yield on this question of a closed shop, to which I am unalterably opposed, we may as well reconcile ourselves to a long shut down for I believe the IWA feels that it *must* have a closed shop contract somewhere in the industry to match similar contracts which have been made by the A F of L and it will probably pay a terrific price in the effort to get such a contract.

I dislike to take this discouraging attitude about the future of our labor difficulty but the further it goes the more apparent it becomes that the strike is being directed and engineered by executives of the Union occupying high positions who could have only one motive in concerning themselves with such a strike as this, that being the motive of establishing a condition here at Vernonia at any cost, which they have been unable so far to establish elsewhere.

As the strike continued into November 1939, the CIO's new state director, William Dalrymple, called a meeting of top managers of the CIO and various employer representatives, ostensibly to settle the strike. The meeting lasted only as long as it took for Greenman to question Dalrymple's "impartiality." Dalrymple's response was to walk out of the meeting.

Dalrymple's hasty exit put the negotiations back into the hands of Local 5-37 and the District Council. Greenman again appealed to Governor Sprague, requesting intervention by the State Board of Labor Conciliation. Governor Sprague called representatives of Local 5-37 to his office on November 27, 1939. Under pressure, the local's leaders obtained a resolution from the membership on December 5, 1939, to have the dispute submitted to an arbitration board.

Three representatives were named to the arbitration board, one each from Local 5-37 and Oregon-American, and the Reverend Raymond Walker, chairman of the State Board of Labor Conciliation. Walker's determination sided with Oregon-American. The company willingly gave the union a face-saver and agreed to let the question of whether or not its labor agreement was a closed-shop go to arbitration. As O-A had sought countless legal opinions over that issue, it was a foregone conclusion that an arbitrator would rule Oregon-American's agreement an open shop.

Once the arbitration board made its ruling in favor of the company, the union called off the strike. Work resumed on December 6, 1939. In the aftermath of the nearly two-and-half-month-long strike, Greenman wrote to Reverend Walker on December 21, 1939:

> We are well satisfied with the outcome of the arbitration, particularly since the recommendations made by the Board are all recommendations which we ourselves made to the Union after they had taken a strike vote and before they called our employees out.
> I believe I can say confidently that no more mistaken and misguided strike was ever undertaken by any group of men of whom I have any knowledge.

The strike was costly. Seventy-two days without work amounted to some $200,000 in lost payrolls. Although IWA Local 5-37 repeated its demand for sole representation rights in subsequent contract negotiations, the lessons of the ill-fated 1939 strike had so effectively sunk in that the issue was never again pressed with vigor. The dual-union arrangement at the Vernonia mill continued for the remainder of the company's operating life. As for Harold Pritchett, passage of the 1947 Taft-Hartley Act and its requirement that union members avow any ties to the Communist Party, led to his eventual deportation.[5]

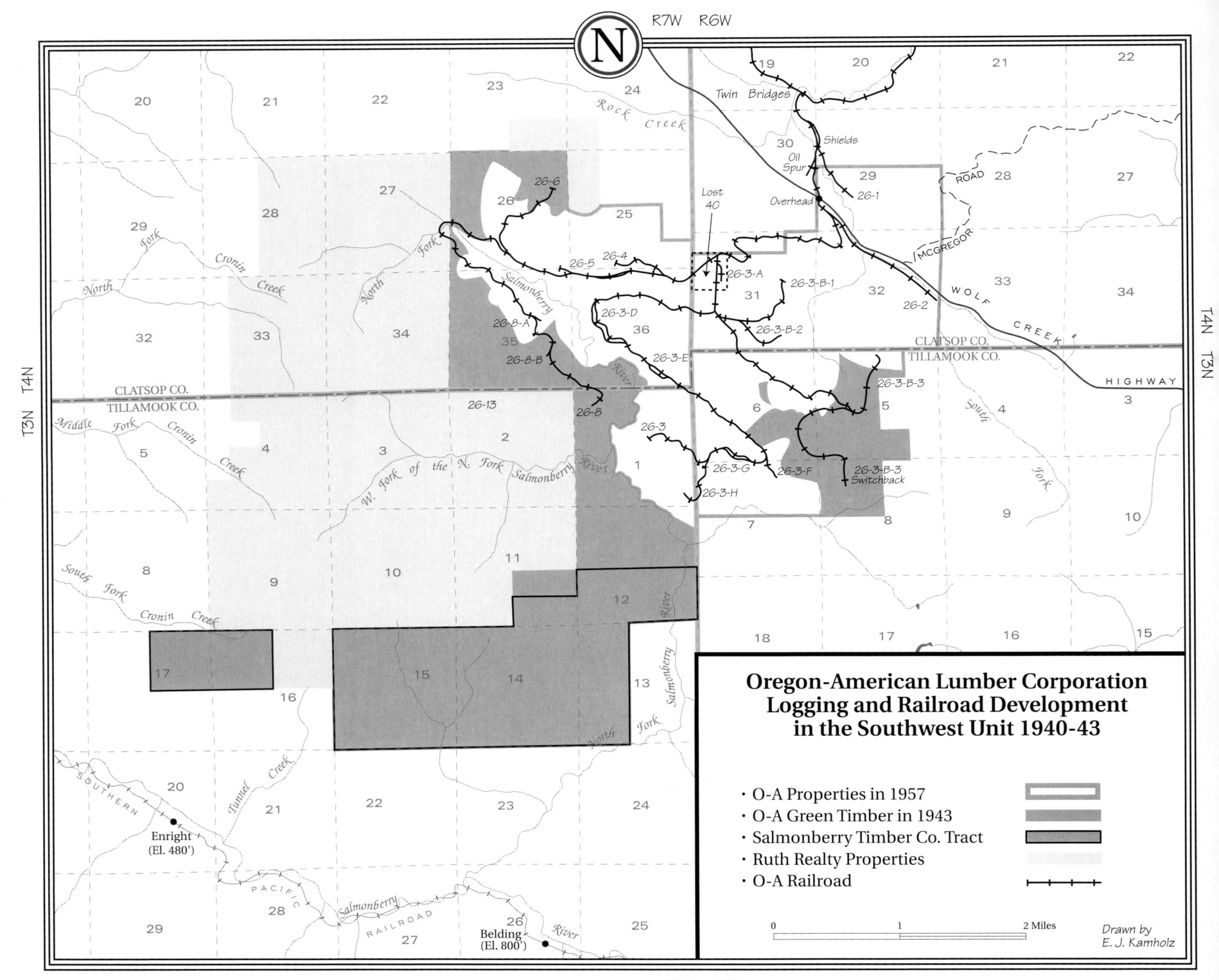

Oregon-American Lumber Corporation Logging and Railroad Development in the Southwest Unit 1940-43

- O-A Properties in 1957
- O-A Green Timber in 1943
- Salmonberry Timber Co. Tract
- Ruth Realty Properties
- O-A Railroad

0 — 1 — 2 Miles

Drawn by E. J. Kamholz

LUMBER GOES TO WAR

Historically, successful warfare has had as much to do with how well the victors could supply themselves with rations and equipment as it concerned the battles themselves. Probably no better example exists than WWII as the combatants waged full-out campaigns that spanned the globe. Ultimately, the allied forces' superior marshaling of resources maintained the forward push, ultimately tipping the balance in their favor.

Achieving victory on the WWII supply front called for extraordinary measures. Once underway, the mobilization effort touched virtually every aspect of day-to-day living as government decrees overruled free-market forces of supply and demand. Industries that once converted raw materials or supplied finished goods destined for industrial and domestic consumption instead found themselves supplying government orders for armed-forces housing, weaponry, foodstuffs, transportation equipment, and the like. Priorities, rationing, and the loss of labor into the armed forces became daily facts of business life. Unprecedented demand for production, limited resources, and a proliferation of new government rules and regulations severely challenged the industries of the country. But produce they did.

Nor was business alone in facing the challenge. The citizenry universally shared diminished living standards resulting from shortages of everything from food to motor fuel to automobile tires and so on. Despite the inefficiencies and sacrifices of the WWII era, it represented a remarkable concentration of national effort toward a common goal.

MILL OPERATIONS

The demand for lumber had strengthened sufficiently by 1940 that O-A felt confident it could afford to expand its operations. Accordingly, on September 16, 1940, the company began operating a second shift at the mill, the first one in more than ten years. Since it entailed operating only the longside band mill, however, it was really just a shift-and-a-half operation. Even so, production increased by 175,000 board feet daily. The program eventually caused O-A to add some 200 men to the mill crew, initially beginning with expanded employment in the sawmill and stacker buildings, and later involving additions to the planing mill staff to handle the added output.

In January 1941 the shift-and-a-half operation produced 11,430,378 feet, or 95 percent, of the average double-shift production made by the mill when it ran both head rigs on a full, two-shift basis between 1925 and 1929. While the sawmill operated on a shift-and-a-half basis, Herman Dickson, assistant engineer, conducted several time studies of head-rig operations. His analysis sheds light on the daily sawmill routine and appears in Table 8.1.

A November 1942 productivity analysis appearing in Table 8.2 also shows how efficiency had improved since 1938.

Opposite page: By late 1940 all logging operations had moved south of the Wolf Creek Highway. Soon, Oregon-American began harvesting the large Ruth Realty Company holdings along with its own.

Table 8.1

Vernonia Mill Head Rig Operations

<u>4/17/42 Day Shift</u>

	Downtime in Minutes
6 saw changes on both rigs total	29
Mechanical Failures	7½
Unavoidable Causes (e.g. blockages)	0
Voidable Causes	14
Total	50½

Cut: Gang on 1" Fir Logs
    Log Scale = 322,910' B.M.
    Stacker plus Timber Dock Tally = 349,150' B.M.

<u>4/20/42 Night Shift (Long-Side Only)</u>

	Downtime in Minutes
3 saw changes	13
Mechanical Failures	0
Unavoidable Causes	2½
Voidable Causes	5
Total	21

Cut: Gang on 2" Fir Logs
    Log Scale = 199,280' B.M
    Stacker plus Timber Dock Tally = 218,926' B.M.

THE WARTIME LUMBER MARKET

Given the war machine's critical and immediate need for steel, lumber was quickly pressed into service as a replacement material at construction projects. The resulting surge in demand for structural timbers enabled the fir industry to achieve nearly an ideal utilization of its logs for the first time since the 1920s. In Oregon-American's case, the manufacturing practice reverted to much like it had been when the company was making "Jap Squares," or large, square timbers that sawmills produced and sold for additional milling elsewhere. This change in cutting practice used more of the logs and reduced waste created by added sawing. As a result, sawmill overrun, or the actual yield beyond the log's scale and a critical factor in profitability, was much higher than normal.

Table 8.2

Productivity per Man Hour
(Board Feet per Employee)

	Woods	Mill
1938	157	93
1939	121	94
1940*	177	97
1941**	232	115
1942	231	113
		(Jan.-Oct.)

*(The year the mill went to 1½ shifts and when O-A returned the skidder to service in the woods.)

**(The first full year of 1½-shift mill operations and of skidder operations.)

One of many bureaucracies created to manage industrial output, the War Production Board claimed that movement of just one man overseas required 300 board feet of lumber. The rapid expansion of the armed forces fueled demand for barracks, bunkers, bridges, docks, wharves, hangars, pontoons, ship decking, boats, and a seemingly infinite number of other construction projects for which lumber was a natural fit. So varied were lumber's uses, rumors wafted back to the home front that when transport ships arrived at their destinations, military personnel took every foot of lumber

O-A found that fire-killed trees salvaged from the Wolf Creek Fire accumulated much more dirt, rock, and other debris when logged. Because this embedded material dulled the head rig saws faster, the company installed a log washer on the slip in 1939. (H. Brown photograph; Jim Blain collection)

used for storing the cargo ashore for further use. In extreme instances, they stripped wooden fittings from ships as well.

A commonly used WCLA yardstick, the ratio of unfilled orders expressed as a percent of total lumber stocks, provided a convenient way to gauge the rising demand for lumber during the war. A ratio of 50 percent was generally considered a benchmark of strong demand. In August 1940, the ratio stood at 57 percent and orders began exceeding production. Olin, reporting to the board, wrote:

> The whole market situation is in a frenzy with no one knowing just what the market is nor how much they can ask for certain items and still be able to get the business. There seems to be no rhyme nor reason for some of the high prices at which some of the government orders are being placed except that politics may have its place in the situation.
>
> The big question is "How long can it last?"

By the end of November 1940, government orders for lumber used in national defense programs was on a continuing upswing. Also, however, signs appeared that consumption in the private sector had begun to weaken as uncertainty about the future increased.

In March 1941, defense orders had grown so much that producers began giving them preference over civilian orders, forcing the industry to turn down many new orders from the private sector. By August 1941, 70 percent of lumber production was dedicated directly or indirectly to the defense program and prices had begun to rise sharply.

In a step to prevent runaway inflation, another new bureaucracy, the Office of Price Administration, or OPA, issued its first list of so-called ceiling prices on October 1, 1941, thus setting maximum prices that producers could charge for lumber. Greenman served as chairman of the Fir Lumber Advisory Committee to the OPA when it adopted the first price ceilings.

The pulp and peeler log-loading station on the south levee of the millpond. When O-A initially began selling pulp and peeler logs, the locomotive crane was used to load the cars. A loading donkey performed the chore for a brief period in 1940. Later, the loading engine the company removed from the tree-rigged skidder replaced it. Steam piped from the mill boilers powered the engines. (H. Brown photograph; Jim Blain collection)

By July 1942, unfilled orders for the industry as a whole stood at nearly 132 percent of gross stocks. In O-A's case, the ratio had climbed to 250 percent. By April 1943, Oregon-American's order file had bulged to 30 million board feet. Some of its orders were more than a year old. WCLA mills reported orders at 200 percent of gross stocks. Reflecting the need to fill orders and the widespread nature of shortages in workers, the government mandated a forty-eight-hour workweek.

By September 1943, stocks at retail yards throughout the country were just about depleted. Civilian buyers were willing to accept just about anything that they could nail up. At one government auction in Portland that month, so much more business was available than mills were willing to accept, auctioneers resorted to drawing numbers out of a hat to assign orders.

By September 1944, WCLA mills reported that the unfilled orders-to-gross-stocks-ratio had climbed to 242 percent. Lumber shipments to the civilian market had fallen to such insignificant levels that when the WCLA requested Oregon-American to participate at a retailer's convention, Sales Manager Walter Vaughan's reply no doubt reflected the frustration every lumber sales department must have felt when anyone raised the subject of civilian orders:

> Somehow I just can't get enthused about this method of promoting dealer relationships....
> I doubt if the average dealer cares a hell of a lot about our troubles in the meantime. He must be

A ground-level view of the pond full of logs looking west toward the sawmill. The smokestacks were 128-feet tall and 102 inches in diameter. (Jim Blain photograph)

sick of alibi after alibi without hearing a rehash. I know I'm pretty sick of passing them out so they must be sick of hearing them.

What the dealer wants is lumber—not why he can't have it—and I'd rather stay away from them until there is a prospect of giving them some.

Life Under Government Control

While during the early part of the war, government orders directly and indirectly accounted for most of the business on the industry's books, there remained significant amounts of nondefense business, largely destined for residential construction. Since much of the government business was for timbers and other structural grades of lumber, the civilian business played an important role because it absorbed the "side" lumber, or boards, siding, flooring, studding, and so forth that producers made from the 30 to 40 percent of the log that was unsuitable for timbers.

The steep ramp-up of government business was anything but smooth. Heavy-handed orders passed down by the many wartime bureaucracies sometimes created the exact opposite effect than intended. In October 1941, for example, the Supply Priorities and Allocation Board, or SPAB, issued an edict strongly inferring that civilian lumber orders were not in the best interests of the war effort.

Given the general spirit of patriotism that had developed nationwide, the private sector responded quickly and civilian orders dropped sharply. The effect on the lumber industry was to dry up that

LUMBER GOES TO WAR

The sawmill crew posing on the long-side carriage.

1–Louis Laramore, button saw; 4–Charles Dubendorf, saw filer; 6–Charles Wall, foreman; 10–Kenneth G. Anderson, long-side setter; 13–Forest Blount, short-side sawyer; 14–Albert Blount; 19–John Moore; 20–Thurman East, resaw edger; 23–John Small; 24–Louis Taylor, trimmer loader; 25–Bill Bailey, short-side edger tailer; 27–Jim Smith; 31–Fred Roediger, resawyer; 32–Albert Hunteman, resawyer helper; 33–Leslie Fitzloff; 34–Fred Mangat, trimmer loader; 35–Claude Gibson, millwright/emergency sawyer; 36–Glen Gibson, gang sawyer; 37–Ben Hall, millwright; 38–George Laird, order chaser; 39–Andy Brimmer; 40–Earnest East, long-side sawyer. (Fred Roediger collection)

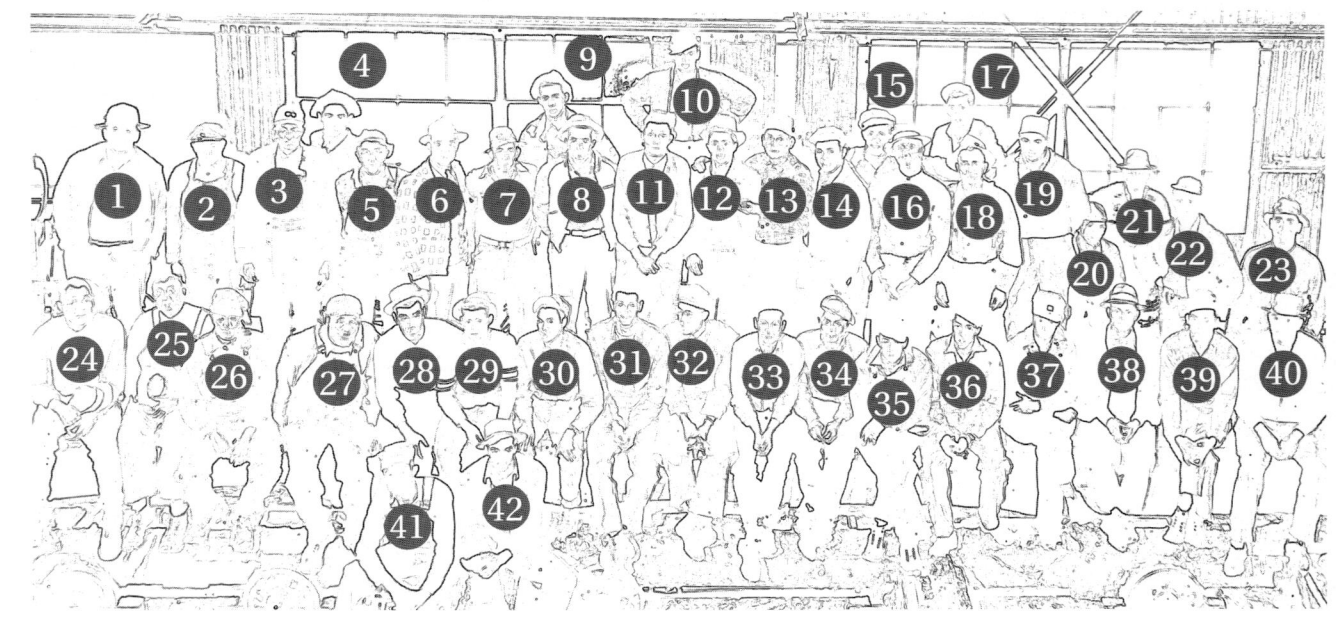

210

Periodically, O-A brought the locomotive crane down from the woods to remove bark and debris that accumulated in front of the log dump brows. To obtain sufficient reach, crews had to use the longer lattice boom. (Vernon Goe photograph; John T. Labbe collection)

part of the market that had been so effectively able to absorb all the side lumber left over after filling timber orders for the government. The arbitrary SPAB order set off a furor of protest from the lumber producers and Oregon's political representatives. Greenman, voicing his outrage to Oregon's Senator McNary in Washington, D.C. on October 27, 1941, wrote:

> My quarrel is with the fact that the SPAB announcement, which has killed off the demand for lumber for private building uses…could have been accomplished without completely upsetting a private building program that was contributing to the defense program and to economic and social betterment.
>
> This concern, at the urgent insistence of representatives of several governmental agencies, has for a year been producing lumber to its maximum capacity. We are working between eight and nine hundred men, about 40% of whom are employed on or in connection with a night shift which we instituted in September 1940 to make the lumber that governmental administrative officials were telling us was sorely needed to carry on the defense program.
>
> We never have and cannot now come anywhere near supporting that night shift with business which we can count on as being available *directly* for the defense program.
>
> As a consequence, we are already considering plans to lay off between three and four hundred men who have been employed at good wages and under good working conditions in making lumber which has been going into private building construction and which is not now wanted because the

This old wagon survived the demise of horse teams. Towed by an old Fordson tractor, O-A used it to haul refuse between the log dump and an open fire near the burner. (Vernon Goe photograph; John T. Labbe collection)

average private builder has been made by SPAB to feel that his government will think him unpatriotic if he goes ahead with the construction of a house.

In the same vein, Oregon Governor Sprague observed, *It is my judgment that neither SPAB nor OPM is fully aware of the implications of this policy or its ultimate effect upon the 60,000 workers engaged in the lumber industry in Oregon.* For all the protest, the SPAB order stood and demonstrated not only the new bureaucracy's power but also the chilling effect such measures could have on free-market forces.

Operators, unwilling to pave their own path to financial ruin, limited production of side lumber, which as predicted, led to layoffs. In Oregon-American's case, thirty or so employees in the planing mill and shipping department were let go in November 1941.

The effects undoubtedly would have become worse but, with the December 7, 1941 attack on Pearl Harbor by Japanese forces, government demand for all kinds of lumber surged yet again, which more than offset the negative effects of the SPAB order.

Another seemingly ill-timed move took place just when government orders began to overwhelm the industry. Then, the Justice Department threatened to sue the WCLA and sixty-six of its member companies and four other industry associations for alleged restraint of trade. Arising largely out of industry pricing practices and the general sharing of competitive information about association activities, the WCLA's legal counsel encouraged the named offending companies, including Oregon-American, to enter a consent decree involving promises to alter business practices. In addition, the Justice Department levied small fines.

Anxious to maintain the focus on producing lumber for the war effort and hoping to avoid a lengthy and expensive trial, and potentially stiffer fines if found guilty, the named parties quickly agreed to the consent decree despite their general feeling that no antitrust laws had been broken.[1]

DOING WITHOUT

The industry's ability to keep pace with the burgeoning demand steadily eroded as competition for materials and labor increased. Greenman, outlining his prognosis for the industry, wrote to Calvin Fentress of Baker, Fentress & Company on March 27, 1942:

> Our logging camps and sawmills are being rapidly stripped of men who are drifting into the war industries next door to our operations where wages are based on cost plus contracts rather than on business principles.

The loss of labor to shipyards, airplane factories and other war plants cannot go on forever without seriously interfering with production in the camps and mills.

Our own situation, which I think is fairly typical of most of the large lumbering operations in Oregon and Washington, is fast reaching the critical point. We do not have enough men now to operate our logging camp at the capacity sufficient to produce enough logs to keep the mill going at its present operating capacity.

By then, labor shortages had already caused industry output to fall 5 percent behind that of 1940 when it needed to be 15 percent greater just to supply the needs of the government.

Priorities and Rationing

By winter 1941 it was a given that the government would establish rigid priorities to ensure availability of war materials. Oregon-American and others in the industry began placing advance orders for motors, wire rope, saw blades, and a host of other items needed to maintain production.

When the bureaucracies implemented priorities, the lumber industry was given a relatively low priority ranking of "A-10." With nine other industries standing ahead of lumber as for preference, obtaining scarce materials and equipment needed to keep the sawmills running became more difficult.

For example, by May 1941, saw manufacturers began notifying civilian customers that they could not deliver stock orders in less than six months. Other suppliers advised their customers that the Office of Production Management had ruled they could not ship steel plate unless they were provided with priority numbers, preference ratings, or some affidavit connecting the order to a specific defense order. Similar restrictions were placed on other scarce materials.

O-A had a particularly difficult time obtaining delivery of a D-8 Caterpillar tractor ordered in Feb-

Top: The long-side edger shown here squared the lumber. The gang edger on the left handled lumber cut by the gang saw. Timbers went through the bull edger on the right. Visible in the foreground are long, steel "anti-kickback" fingers invented by Oregon-American. These devices prevented many injuries, and the company provided the design to the industry at no charge.

§

Bottom: This side view of a timber going through the bull edger clearly shows how the anti-kickback fingers worked. (H. Brown photographs; Columbia County Historical Museum)

213

ruary 1941. With the lumber industry's low preference rating of A-10, the Caterpillar Company was obliged to fill orders based on assigned priority ratings and, consequently, kept delaying delivery of O-A's machine. The company ran into similar obstacles on orders for a replacement lumber carrier, electric motors, alloy steels, and so on.

Table 8.3

Skidder Production October 1940–April 1941

Location	Feet
Logged to tree No. 7	14,164,580
Logged to tree No. 8	10,706,580
Total Logged	24,871,430
Total Days Worked	123
Average Production per Day	202,068 Feet

Even after the OPM upgraded O-A's Caterpillar tractor order with an A-5 preference rating, the Caterpillar Company delayed scheduled delivery another month, prompting Greenman to comment, *I am sort of in hopes that OPM does not give us an A-1-A rating because if they did I think they would move the scheduled delivery back to 1943 and we really are going to need the tractor before that time.* Caterpillar finally shipped the bulldozer from Peoria on December 18, 1941. Oregon-American's order for its Gerlinger lumber carrier had a similar history.

Out-and-out rationing of other critical materials also went into effect for such items as automobile and truck tires and tubes. By the end of April 1942, foodstuff rationing commenced, and one of the first such restrictions were placed on sugar. Advisories to Andy Olson from Greenman and F. M. "Merle" Ruhl, O-A's office manager, clearly outlined the effect on the Camp McGregor cookhouse:

> The cookhouse quota for sugar for the months of May and June combined amount to 1,873 pounds.... Because [this] is approximately 60% of your normal requirements for a like period, some planning and economy must be put into effect immediately.
>
> We have been using about 2½ pounds of sugar per man per week in our cooking and on the table in the dining room. After May 1 our total consumption of sugar must not exceed 1 pound per man per week.

By March 1943, the government cut per-capita consumption of point-rationed commodities, including canned goods, to 80 percent of December 1942 levels. Civilians were encouraged to plant "Victory Gardens" and O-A volunteered land and prepared plots for all interested employees. O-A considered raising hogs at Camp McGregor to supplement anticipated fresh meat shortages. However, due to OPA regulations requiring the company to surrender the same number of meat points as though buying the meat from a packing house, O-A dropped that plan.

By August 1943, rationing of meats and fats had become so severe that keeping the loggers fed reached a state of emergency. Loggers simply needed more food than clerks and only after the industry forcefully reported this to the Food Distribution Administration were per-capita allotments increased.

The government set up similar restrictions for rain gear and gloves, both essential items in the production of logs and lumber. Tire and gasoline shortages led to extensive use of car-pooling for twenty-five or so woods employees living outside Camp McGregor. Their situation became so difficult that by November 1943, Local 5-37 demanded the company provide some alternative form of transportation. O-A applied to government authorities for a truck chassis and bus body. Once approved, Wentworth & Irwin, Inc., of Portland handled the bus assembly. The bus itself was a cobbled-up affair, consisting of a 1942 Ford truck chassis and cowl fitted with a GMC cab and body.

Bus service commenced just after New Year's Day 1944. The round-trip began at Keasey, where O-A stored the machine in the rented warehouse part of the Keasey railroad station. The bus traveled to Vernonia, and then to the Wolf Creek Highway Overhead Crossing, a one-hour-and-thirty-minute trip. The company charged riders between twenty-five and fifty cents per day depending on the distance traveled.

Workers

The defection of workers to airplane factories and shipyards, coupled with the loss of able-bodied men to the armed forces, had a profound and lasting effect on the lumber industry's ability to produce for the war.

For all the confusion that immediately followed the attack on Pearl Harbor, it only took a week for the government to freeze the assets of Japanese nationals. The Federal Reserve also prohibited banks from handling checks paid to or written by Japanese nationals, among other restrictions. That prevented O-A from paying its thirty or so Japanese employees. Within weeks the relocation programs commenced and Oregon-American's railroad section crew and other Japanese employees in Vernonia were rounded up and sent to internment camps.

The biggest log I recall coming into the mill measured 11 feet, 11 inches in diameter. It went to the short-side, which could handle logs up to 10 feet thick. They had to chop large notches out of the log by hand so it could clear the carriage's knees. It took them two hours to get the log moved back far enough to get it past the saw and remove the first slab. After that, it took only eight more minutes to finish sawing it.

Fred Roediger, resaw

By March 1942, the labor turnover rate had reached 23 percent in the woods and 11 percent at Vernonia. Net labor loss amounted to 15 percent of Oregon-American's loggers and 5 percent of the mill crew. The War Production Board finally took stock of matters in June 1942 and, working through various agencies, initiated a broad program to address the lumber industry's workforce shortages. The WPB instructed union employees to accept cash instead of vacations. The agency permitted employers to claim "critical occupations" for which they could obtain temporary draft deferments. It began programs to give lumber producers priority assistance for parts and supplies and appointed a West Coast Lumber Administrator to carry out programs in the region.

The government lifted restrictions so employers could hire high school boys for mill work during summer vacations. The WPB ordered the mills to hire women, a step operators took with reluctance. At Vernonia, O-A put women between the ages of twenty-one and forty-five to work in August 1942.

The blacksmith's shop at Camp McGregor. (Vernon Goe photograph; John T. Labbe collection)

Reflecting operators' dislike of the idea, the company paid women the minimum wage of eighty-two and a half cents per hour, based on their "relative skills and strength." By the end of the war Oregon-American had twenty-nine women working in direct production positions, including one woman who tagged logs at Camp McGregor.

However, none of these programs addressed the most critical shortage of all, the loggers themselves. Losses to the armed forces and defections to better-paying jobs in the airplane factories and shipyards so depleted the ranks of Oregon-American's loggers that it could no longer keep the mill supplied. So, on September 30, 1942, O-A scaled the mill operation back to a single shift.

By the next month the average age of all men employed in the woods had risen to forty-nine years. Only seventy-six single men remained in Camp. Of them, only sixteen were between the ages of seventeen and forty-six. In less than a year, logging had become an "old man's game."

On October 16, 1942, the War Manpower Commission announced it would use the United States Employment Service, or USES, to help industry manage. With 3,000 full- and part-time offices, USES helped recruit labor from distant regions of the country once employers exhausted local labor supplies. O-A immediately applied to fill sixty-one woods positions with the hope seasonal loggers from California's Sierra Nevada region could fill them. However, employee shortages were not a problem confined to the woods of Oregon and Washington, so by the end of that year, O-A had hired only thirty-three men. Even after eliminating the second shift at the mill, getting enough logs to keep the day shift going proved difficult. Accordingly, O-A began bussing surplus able-bodied mill employees to the woods each day to work at logging.

In 1938, following the sale of engine 102, the company renumbered shay Number 2 the 102. It came from the factory equipped with a steam brake. One of its earlier owners installed an air pump and automatic brake equipment. O-A later removed it. (Albert Farrow photograph)

When these programs failed to provide enough woods labor, a Lumber Advisory Committee of the WPB announced a more drastic program that called for the return of men who had left the logging camps for other work, primarily in the shipyards. The Lumber Advisory Committee also instructed local draft boards that anyone employed in "essential activities in the forestry, logging and lumber industry" not be classified 1-A for induction into military service.

The long hours and isolation of working in the woods led to ancillary problems as well. Commenting about giving loggers some much-needed time off, Greenman wrote on May 8, 1943:

> I am convinced our lay-off at Camp on the Saturdays following pay day, which was originally designed to give the fellows who live in Camp a chance to get out once a month and thereby *avoid* absenteeism during the working week has become a device which *contributes* to absenteeism by reason of the fact that the fellows get away with too much fire water while they are out of Camp and then are unable to return to work on the Monday following that lay-off.

By year-end 1943, 153 former Oregon-American employees were in the armed forces. The company's total employment in the woods and in the mill had dwindled to only 454.

The quality of workers recruited through USES for logging also consistently fell short of the need and, on August 18, 1944, Olin commented:

> The facts are that the men who want to work and will work are working and the others who are drifting from one place to another just won't work any place longer than two or three days. We now

Top: Train 105 eastbound has just come off the Keasey grade. After knocking down the brakes the crew could relax until arriving at Vernonia. (John T. Labbe photograph)

§

Bottom: After clearing the mill spur switch, Train 105 stopped on the SP&S line south of Vernonia before backing the log train into the mill.

The company's wood car and a flatcar were in the consist the day this scene was captured. Oregon-American enjoyed an extremely favorable trackage rate over the 11-mile stretch of common-carrier track west of Vernonia and took advantage of it to haul firewood and equipment between the mill and the camps. (Jim Blain photograph)

Top: On the trip from the woods to the mill, the 105's hardest task was backing the loads uphill onto the mill lead. (Jim Blain photograph)

§

Bottom: Caboose 367 passing through the Vernonia yard as the log train backs into the mill lead. M. F. Brady built the caboose on a wood frame. A cargo door was added so the company could use the caboose to transport supplies to Camp. O-A shortened the chassis when it rebuilt the caboose in 1943. (John T. Labbe photograph)

Log unloading was an exercise in art, science, and adventure. First, the loads had to be visibly spotted so the center of gravity was in front of the crane. The conductor relayed signals to the engineer by remote control using an electric horn and light system. The tracks were sloped toward the pond to let gravity do part of the work. Next, a brakeman used a long rod to grab the brow log cable and drag it across the rails and connect it to the unloader. The crane operator then drew the cable up against the load to keep the logs from rolling the wrong way. Once ready to slide the logs off into the pond, the train crew used sledges to release the cheese blocks holding the logs on the bunks. Finally, the crane operator simultaneously applied power to the electric motor and pressure to the brake frictions. Tension on the cable rolled the logs off the cars. The shifting weight of the loads often caused the disconnects' wheels to lift off the rails. Rerailing was a common chore in the sequence. (Blain and Kamholz photographs)

have had 15 men sent to us by the USES and only two are still on the job. One of these men is in his late sixties and probably won't last long. The other man got hurt the first day he worked, was laid off on compensation for several days, and has just returned to work. The average time worked by all of the men was 23 hours. Another discouraging fact is that every few days one of our old men quits, having found some job that looks better. This means that we have just lost a man, with no replacement in sight.

Safety Awareness

Scarcity of labor resulted in at least one direct improvement in the lumber industry—safety awareness. Through cooperative efforts by the government, industry, and organized labor, many improvements made the woods and mills less hazardous places to work. By February 1942 Oregon-American began work on an educational safety campaign for its loggers and by July of that year had invited representatives of the National Committee for the Conservation of Manpower to prepare a report suggesting improvements in the physical plant and operating practices at the mill.

Among the dangerous logging practices that came to light in the O-A Camp during this period included sending high-climbers up landing trees to conduct maintenance while donkey engines continued operating and the failure of fallers and buckers to observe reasonable safety rules, which in one instance cost a bucker his life when he failed to take cover after others had called the warning of a falling tree. Increased vigilance by Oregon-American resulted in a marked decrease in accidents. By year-end 1943, those rates had fallen by 33 percent in the woods and 44 percent in the mill.

The company obtained the support of IWA Local 5-37 and, working together through the Plant Safety Committee, made considerable progress sharpening employees' safety consciousness. Creation of the safety committee proved highly productive, both because of the recommendations made by the group, and for the fact that it improved labor relations by putting both sides to work solving common problems. Many changes and improvements to the physical plant at the mill were direct outgrowths of the Plant Safety Committee's work. These included installation of a blowpiping system in the planing mill filing room and the movement of high-voltage power lines away from monorail lines and other potential conductors of electricity.

This latter improvement arose, interestingly, out of

Top: The ground crew of train 105 posing on a large load at the millpond. From left to right were William "Bus" Byers, Jack Heenan, conductor, and Vincent "Shorty" Monaco. Byers was a big man but is dwarfed by the top log.

Tree fallers used 7½-foot-long crosscut saws. When a tree was too big like this one, they made multiple undercuts to gain working room. (Vivian Laird Reynolds collection)

§

Bottom: En route to Shields with a string of loads, locomotive 104 spots an empty tank car at the oil spur. Before completion of the Wolf Creek Highway, O-A took delivery of fuel oil for the railroad and logging equipment in company-owned tank cars shuttled between Willbridge, Vernonia, and the woods.

O-A built a receiving station near the Overhead crossing and had oil delivered there in trucks. (Bob and Fred Wenzel photograph) concern that the Nehalem Valley was, following the removal of all timber from its surrounding hillsides, more likely to experience the direct effects of high winds. This was not an idle fear. Pioneers could recall when wind was unknown in the valley but more than once after loggers had cut the protective barrier of trees, Vernonia suffered considerable damage from heavy windstorms.

Old hard runnin' Cletracs. The two big newer ones were a pretty good machine but they were not the tractor the Caterpillar was. They were an arm and back breaker and nobody liked to run them. You couldn't turn 'em on a dime, y'know? They had a differential instead of throwout clutches like a Cat has. A Cat you throw one side out and tramp the brake and the other side will spin it around. In it's own place. The Cletracs had a differential so you just slowed one side down.

So, if you were running one you had to figure all your maneuvering before picking up your load for once you picked it up against the blade, you could not turn it. You had to do all your maneuvering while you were backing up. When you stopped rollin', you had to have it aimed right where you wanted to push your load. I could do just as much work with a Cletrac as I could with the Caterpillar but your mind had to be w-a-a-a-y ahead of your work. If you wanted to end with a big load of dirt someplace you had to figure out where you were going to end up with that blade full of dirt long before you got to it because you couldn't get right to it and kick it around like a Cat. Couldn't do it. Most operators didn't seem to realize that. You had to think all your work out ahead.

George Lee, construction

LOGGING OPERATIONS

Reactivation of the Willamette tree-rigged skidder in October 1940 proved timely, for with the increased appetite for logs created by the second-shift operation at the Vernonia mill, the company's logging operations were hard-pressed to keep pace. Between October 1940 and April 1941, the skidder operated in only two locations and amply demonstrated its log-getting abilities as shown in Table 8.3.

Congratulating Olson on the crew's performance, Greenman wrote, *It seems to me this is a remarkably good average for any piece of logging equipment in any kind of show at any time and if you can do so without getting their heads swelled, I hope you will tell the boys who are working on the skidder that we think they have done a mighty good job so far.* By year-end 1941 the skidder operation had logged a total of 56,830,000 feet, averaging 198,012 feet per day. Greenman commented further to Olson, *It is very apparent that your skidder is getting by far the cheapest logs you are producing. Had we been able to produce logs on the high lead side as cheaply as we did on the skidder in 1941, our total expenditures for labor would have been more than $40,000 less than they actually were. And this ain't hay in anybody's logging camp.* No small contribution to this performance related to the skidder's reliability. Out of a total of $4,029 spent on donkey repairs during the first six months of 1942, only $281 were spent on the skidder.

Despite the skidder's impressive output, keeping the mill supplied with logs became more difficult, and as early as 1941, the company began searching for ways to supplement its supply. In the spring of that year, O-A paid to add enough rail on the United Railways' Eastmann Spur to accommodate an additional five or six cars. The Cedarwood Products Company was logging to Eastmann Spur, located just east of the Columbia/Clatsop County line, and through this arrangement O-A was able to buy an additional 1.5 million board feet of fir logs.

Because of continuing problems with employee turnover, simply adding more machinery was not a solution to log production problems. And, as the war dragged on, organized labor began chafing over government-implemented restrictions on work rules and so forth. Workers displayed an increasingly short fuse when it came to settling their disputes with management, which only worsened the problem. Olin, advising the board of directors of the deteriorating situation, wrote on April 1, 1944:

> Our log output was materially below average [last week] and the possibility of being obliged to revise our mill operating schedule downward has become more in the category of a probability. This has been brought about by the skidder crew demanding more wages and being refused, two-thirds of the crew quit and shut the machine down. The reason advanced for a wage increase was based on the contention that the ground was too rough and steep at the landing to which the skidder has just been moved but a raise in wages on that account is just out of the question. The facts are that this crew—a good share of them at least—has been shirking the work for some time and if we are successful in building up a new crew, the net result may prove to be a benefit. Several of the key men are still with us but not in sufficient numbers to operate the skidder and as that machine is the principal log producer the output of logs without it will not be sufficient to keep both rigs in the mill cutting lumber.

The fallout from shutting down the skidder included the elimination of one woods train crew and more layoffs in the sawmill since the log supply could only keep one head rig in operation.

Gyppo Loggers

Within two weeks following the March 1944 walkout by O-A's skidder crew, the company began contracting with independent logging operators to supplement log production. O-A first contracted with the partnership of Joe Wornstaff and Ezra Barker to fall, buck, yard, and load O-A timber in the W1/2 of the NW1/4 of Section 25 and in the NE1/4 of Section 25, Twp. 4 North, Range 7 West, at the end of spur 26-6.

Wornstaff had been Oregon-American's power shovel operator (shovel-runner was the official job

Top: Donkey engines pulling themselves out to distant landings took a toll on sleds. Sled building was an art accomplished largely with hand tools. The company used independent contractors that specialized in this work. (Columbia County Historical Museum)

§

Bottom: Close-up view of the fall block and chokers in a North Bend-rigged yarder setting. The main line, usually a 1½-inch-diameter wire rope, is visible to the left. When pulled by the yarder, the line raised the fall block toward the carriage overhead (not shown), lifting the log with it thus reducing hang-ups along the skid road. The ⅞-inch haulback line returned the setup to the choker setters for another turn. It is visible connected to the right of the fall block. The carriage ran back and forth on a 2-inch-diameter tight skyline. (H. Brown photo; Kamholz collection)

We even worked Saturdays and Sundays for awhile there for government orders. It was very essential that they had that lumber. And it was really choice lumber. They really kept me humpin'. Besides that, every spare minute I was fixin' up some of the equipment. I always maintained my own. Always.

We had food rationing. We had food stamps, meat stamps, butter and gasoline stamps and we'd have to stretch them out. We'd have a stamp for a bottle of booze now and then. And, if we were going to have a big Fourth of July shindig or something, we'd hoard them.

But we always got by with meat. There was a lot of fish in the creek and meat in the hills. Who suffered? Spuds weren't rationed.

But then I don't know why Greenman was bellyachin' about exceeding rations. They had all the meat they could use for the cookhouse. He was probably thinkin' about what how it coulda' been.

George Lee, construction

title) on the right-of-way construction crew from the mid-1920s until receivership. After reorganization Wornstaff's nephew, George Lee, doubled in brass serving as shovel-runner and bulldozer operator. As a practical matter, Lee was O-A's entire construction crew during the war. Wornstaff and Lee constructed miles of vehicle roads and spurs that today crisscross the company's former operating territory.

On July 23, 1944, a second contractor, Doyle and Rogers, was added to log 100 acres carrying approximately 10 million board feet of timber on various parcels on spurs 26-6 and 26-7.

To no one's surprise, O-A's use of gyppo loggers met its share of objections from Local 5-37. However, apart from the union's demands that independent crews build their roads to acceptable standards and employ a full compliment of workers, the company made good use of this new source of labor.

Diesel Donkey Conversions

Although costing more to maintain, Oregon-American found its two diesel donkeys to be a decided improvement over their steam counterparts. The diesels consumed less fuel, required fewer men to operate, and were considered far less likely to cause fires. They also eliminated the need to pipe boiler water from remote sources. Consequently, O-A used the diesel machines extensively to yard logs in areas most remote from the trackside. The company's roster of steam pots, enough to equip four sides, represented a sunk investment, even if an obsolete one, so complete conversion to diesel remained beyond financial reach.

The destruction of O-A's original Skagit diesel donkey in the Music Fire had a direct bearing on the company's decision to convert some of its steam units to diesel, a program that commenced in September 1943. When O-A received the insurance proceeds for the burned donkey, it placed an order with Loggers & Contractors Machinery Company in Portland to equip one of O-A's existing steam-powered 12 × 14 Willamette 2-speed units with twin diesel engines.

Loggers & Contractors built the power conversion unit for just less than $15,000. Oregon-American installed the new power train on Willamette donkey engine Number 2476 at the Vernonia machine shop between March and June 1945. The steam-to-diesel conversion worked out entirely to O-A's expectations and set the course for more conversions following the war.

Power Saws

The company had far less success getting its cutting crews to mechanize, however. In February 1943, O-A purchased a Reed-Prentice gasoline-powered saw and Greenman encouraged Olson to pick out a pair of fallers who might be interested in learning how to use it with the hope of overcoming union resistance to mechanization. By that time, power saws were becoming almost universal in the Northwest.

Nevertheless, Oregon-American found it very difficult to convince its cutting crews to adopt use of power saws in their work. Not only was the union against the conversion, but also the machines themselves were extremely heavy and unwieldy to operate. Ultimately, O-A's cutting crews traded in their hand tools for power saws but not until the operation was in its twilight years.

LETTERS TO THE BOYS AT WAR (AND TO THOSE INTERNED)

Despite near-superhuman efforts to keep production going at Vernonia, concern for the well-being of those in the armed forces ran high. The company maintained addresses of former employees in the service and, commencing in October 1942, Greenman wrote periodic form letters, reproduced by Vernonia High School typing classes, advising the military personnel of events at the company and in the community. Additionally, the company arranged to have the *Vernonia Eagle* sent to former workers in the service.

Judging by the replies, the recipients appreciated the program. A small sample of replies read:

> I received your letter and I can't explain how a guy feels when he receives something like that. This is what one could call morale building. Not many of the fellows get deals like that.

And,

Powder Bill Marchuk was shootin' out a swing road one day. Rainin' to beat the band. Had his tin outfit on, his ol' hat's pulled down and he's sittin' on a powder box with an open side and he's makin' up primers. When he'd finish one he'd toss it in the box until he had enough to shoot all the stumps. He was all hunched over that box, protecting it from the rain with his body.

Bill always smoked a pipe and since it was rainin', he had it turned upside down to keep it dry. A spark fell out of it into the caps and blew up the entire box of them. The copper from those jackets perforated the back of his legs and butt like buckshot. He waddled off that old swing road all bow-legged 'til he found a telephone and called a speeder to take him back to camp.

Burt Hawkins, the timekeeper and first-aid man—he was great big ol' gruff guy, an old army captain, and looked the part too—gets in the room with Bill and says, **get your pants down and climb up on that table.** *By this time the whole office crew and the speeder monkey are standing around watching. There's ol' Hawkins with his alcohol swab. Every time he'd touch ol' Powder Bill, Bill would go about this high off the table and Hawkins would have to stop to laugh. He laughed until the tears ran. Then he'd adjust his glasses and get his tweezers and start pickin' out little pieces of copper jacket. That was real entertainment. Powder Bill. Only thing they never had was a moving picture of it.*

George Lee, construction

> I received with pleasure your letter of October 14th and wish to thank you for your kind offer to have the paper sent to me.
>
> I would certainly like to be sawing wood again for you. I never held a real job except with you and I have always had a feeling that I worked for a fine company and now I am sure of it.

Greenman and others were also concerned for the well-being of Japanese nationals that the government had interned following the bombing of Pearl Harbor. He had been personally acquainted with many of them dating from his Union Mills days. The injustices heaped on them weighed heavily. For example, a former member of the section gang wrote:

> I do hope you are OK and doing all you can for the good old Uncle Sam every day.
>
> It sure was one nightmare to leave dear old Oregon and dear friends to evacuate to this new city of Mindioka.
>
> We hear and read a great deal of the prejudice against the Japanese on the coast. Well we can't very well blame them at this time as there exist too many propaganda. Still we are happy to say we have a big obligation to pay to this country for the happy years we have enjoyed in the past. I am sure there will be good will among every one when the war ends and I am very happy indeed to have good many real friends on the coast who really trust and remember us. Our gang from Keasey, Oregon are all in very good spirits and hoping for the day that we can go back to the coast.

At the bottom of the letter, Greenman wrote, *One of the section men from camp. Have known him 31 years.*

THE YERRECK TRACT

As Oregon-American's logging moved westerly into the Southwest Timber Unit, it brought the company's operations ever closer to the main block of Ruth Realty timber, the Yerreck tract.

While O-A had logged a scattering of burned Ruth Realty timber in Sections 18 and 29 of Twp. 4 North, Range 6 West, its operations did not reach any of Ruth's green timber until 1941. Negotiations for timber lying in Sections 24 and 25 of 4/7, a 360-acre parcel acquired from Inman-Poulsen, were concluded in March of that year. O-A gave Ruth a 15-percent down payment on the modest price of $2 per 1,000 board feet for Douglas fir. Total cost of the transaction amounted to about $43,000.

Olin observed, *I think we are fortunate in making this first purchase of Ruth Realty timber in the Southwest Tract at such reasonable prices and I hope it may be an indication of what we may expect in further purchases.* Indeed, the terms were so reasonable that Ruth permitted Oregon-American to begin logging before the contract had even been signed.

The stand of timber on those Ruth parcels cruised more than 100,000 board feet to the acre. The density and lay of the land that allowed log-gathering in full circles was a large contributor to the high skidder productivity during the early part of WWII.

By fall 1942, Oregon-American had logged its way up to the western edge of the Yerreck tract and began negotiating with Ruth for enough timber to continue operations for another year or two. In April 1943, an agreement was reached for Section 27 and the NE1/4 of the NE1/4 of Section 34, Twp. 4 North, Range 7 West. Terms were similar to those for the Ruth timber acquired two years before with O-A paying $3.50 per 1,000 for Douglas fir and $1.12 for all other species as removed. This time O-A made a 25-percent down payment, and the total cost of the transaction came in around $50,000. O-A and Ruth finalized that contract in June 1943.

Buoyed by the easy terms, Chaney, Olin, and Greenman began laying the groundwork to acquire yet another nibble from the Yerreck tract later that year. This time, however, the reception from the SP&S's Portland office was very different. First, M. C. LaBertew, vice president and general manager of the SP&S, expressed the opinion that, to date, Ruth had sold O-A timber much too cheaply. He added that he had personally been embarrassed in front of his superiors when a potential buyer for the remainder of the Yerreck tract appeared and offered more than O-A had been paying just for small parcels of the timber.

LaBertew added that it was time the carriers ceased acting as O-A's banker. He also made it clear that if Oregon-American expected to acquire the remaining Yerreck tract timber, it would have to negotiate for the entire tract, pay prevailing market rates, assume the taxes, risk of fire loss and carrying costs, and make a substantial down-payment in the process. The Northern Lines' abrupt change in policy was, of course, directly related to a decade's worth of deteriorating prospects from their Oregon-American business arrangement, made worse by the overall traffic decline on the Vernonia branch line.

First, the collapse of the lumber market during the Depression greatly reduced the market value of the Ruth holdings. The 1932 and 1933 fires further diminished their value. The Oregon-American Lumber Corporation's refusal to obligate itself to acquire the Ruth timber following reorganization made the outlook for recovery even less assured. Viewed in light of the fact that Oregon-American was only producing half the pre-Depression rail traffic and that other sources of traffic on the Vernonia branch line had all but dried up, the carriers felt amply justified in demanding O-A make up for the losses.

Looking more deeply into the economics of the situation, had the original terms of the Ruth timber purchases remained in effect, the contract price would have capitalized to $9.00 per 1,000 board feet for the Yerreck tract and $7.50 for the Keasey timber. With prevailing stumpage prices for Douglas fir only running from $6 to $7 per 1,000 board feet, the carriers were understandably concerned they might never recoup the $4 million already sunk into the timber they had bought for Oregon-American's use. And, despite the anticipated 400 million board feet of lumber traffic the Ruth timber represented, the carriers' estimated maintenance costs of $645,000 for the Vernonia branch line for the six years needed to convert the timber, further dampened the profit outlook.

A station is 100 feet. At any given spur they began staking where the switch took off. Every 50 feet. Number one, one-fifty, two, two-fifty. For grade stakes, they'd offset one on the bank after you had roughed it out. Now gradin' with the shovel, they put it up ahead as a "T" cross. Had it marked on there how much to cut out. Say you hold your stick up here, take your "T" gun sight, and the stake said you had a 5-foot cut up there. You had a 5-foot marker on your stick here and you'd line it with your handle on that cross up ahead to see if you were on grade here. Then you'd go ahead and dig.

I got so I'd go 3, 4, 500 feet without checkin' it. Be right on it. Within a couple of inches. The ballast would pick that up. Truck roads though, you can go up or down. You didn't have to grade.

I didn't hire out for cat skinner. I hired out for shovel operator. During the war, I was the whole construction crew. I had three cats and two shovels, all to myself.

George Lee, construction

The Northern Lines recognized they had Oregon-American cornered on the issue because, apart from timber acquired from the Salmonberry Timber Company, O-A had cut most of its remaining trees in the Southwest Unit. Moreover, the fact that O-A's STC tract timber was inaccessible without trespassing the Yerreck tract only strengthened the carriers' position. The cost of and time required for O-A to extend its logging railroad through the

Ruth-owned timber to reach isolated tracts of company timber were prohibitive. As a practical matter, railroad development could not be justified beyond what timber O-A could bring out over it within a year or two.

Furthermore, the topography of the Southwest Unit was extremely rugged. Removal of O-A's timber was going to require two separate railroad approaches constructed at elevations nearly 1,000 feet apart. The grade down the North Fork of the Salmonberry River canyon in Sections 2 and 3 of Twp. 3 North, Range 7 West was particularly difficult. Contours dictated routing the line in and out of the West Fork of the North Fork of the Salmonberry River canyon, a detour of more than 2 miles just to gain a half-mile's worth of progress closer to Oregon-American's timber to the south. That route also required O-A to build three long, tall trestles only promising to add to the expense. All told, the costs to build all that nonrevenue-producing railroad just to reach outlying timber was not worth the undertaking. Nevertheless, since O-A had no alternative source of timber to keep the mill supplied while it was building access spurs, failure to acquire the Yerreck tract timber would have resulted in a lengthy shutdown, an unacceptable alternative.

The Northern Lines, fully cognizant of these matters, chose the perfect time to square their account with Oregon-American. Hoping the carriers' stance might soften after they transferred LaBertew to a job with the Great Northern in October 1943, O-A resumed talks with J. C. Daries, the SP&S's right-of-way and tax agent, who had previously been the chief negotiator for the Ruth interests.

As an austerity measure taken during the Depression, the SP&S had not had a full-time president since 1932. Instead, the Great Northern and Northern Pacific, equal owners of the SP&S, alternated executive control over that company. From that time forward, the presidents of the two Northern Lines alternated as president of the SP&S, the GN president one year, the NP president the next year, and so on. The Northern Pacific's turn at the SP&S's management helm began in 1944. The NP enjoyed the dubious distinction of being a penny-pinching outfit and that philosophy carried over to the SP&S each year the NP was in control.

Matters drifted along until mid-March 1944 when Daries, accompanied by W. E. Holt, Western Land Agent of the North Western Improvement Company, the land management subsidiary of the Northern Pacific, visited Olin and Greenman in Vernonia. At this meeting, Holt commented that Mr. Denny, president of the Northern Pacific, had personally requested Holt to look into Ruth's holdings near Vernonia and determine how best to make the sale. He added the Northern Lines had it in mind to dispose of the entire Ruth tract and they wanted O-A to buy it. Olin, reporting the meeting to Stern on March 17, 1944, wrote, *Mr. Greenman and I gathered from [Holt's] remarks that while we expect that they will endeavor to get what the timber is worth they are not going to ask for the last cent but will present some proposition that will be mutually attractive. We do not believe that they have any thought of disposal of this timber to any one but our company.* Olin's optimism proved badly misplaced. First, Holt decided not to rely on adjusted Thomas & Meservey estimates and had the Ruth timber recruised. The new cruise showed much more timber than O-A had been estimating, which raised the ante. Holt also proved almost unmoveable in his conviction that the Ruth timber was worth more than reflected in past sales to Oregon-American. Finally, with the negotiations removed from the more friendly confines of the SP&S and placed at a higher level in the Northern Lines' bureaucracy, a diminished sense of urgency by the carriers set in, much to O-A's frustration. So much so that on December 30, 1944, nearly nine months after Holt took over as the Northern Lines' negotiator, Greenman reported:

> The Ruth Realty Company's proposal of December 20, 1944 [on Yerreck tract timber] rejects the several alternative methods of selling this timber to us which we have proposed… and apparently undertakes to foreclose further consideration of such methods.…
>
> By no means do I feel we should accept Mr. Holt's dictum in this matter as being the final word on the subject but I must confess that, after having marshaled and fired at him every argument in my arsenal of facts for a deal which would require them to share the risk of profit in this timber with us, I am getting discouraged about the possibilities in that direction and am reaching the conclusion that, if we make a deal with them at all, it will be based on prices and terms not much different from those set out in Holt's letter of December 20.
>
> The negotiations for this timber were opened by us just a little over a year ago… and, during all of the ensuing period, they have proceeded with as much vigor as the somewhat dilatory tactics employed by the representatives of the Ruth Company would permit. I have used all of the ingenuity I possess in an effort to persuade Mr. Holt and his superiors that any proposal they made to us for their timber should give ample recognition to the quasi-partnership status of our past relations and to the traffic potential inherent in this business.…
>
> When one recalls the almost endless flow of words that we have used in an effort to develop a better proposition than we now have before us, I think he is amply justified in concluding that, if we buy this timber, it will be at prices and terms not greatly different from those set out in Holt's letter.
>
> The agreement to recommend reservation of the Keasey tract for sale to us at some future date is a concession for, at the outset, Holt was firm in his position that the carriers intended to dispose of all of this timber as promptly as possible to relieve themselves of the liabilities of ownership.

At this point in the negotiations, the Northern Lines were demanding a price of $6.65 for Douglas fir that was 58 percent of the stand, and from $2.29 to $5.54 on other species, for an average price of $5.50 overall. Aggregate cost of the transaction would have totaled nearly $1.7 million. Terms called for a 10 percent down-payment with twenty semi-annual installments of about $76,000 each. Oregon-American was to assume all risks of ownership.

Recognizing that shutting off the log supply to Vernonia was to no one's best interests, the carriers relented slightly on their demand that O-A acquire the entire balance of the Yerreck tract and sold Oregon-American the timber on the E1/2 of Section 28 4/7 in December 1944. The terms, however, were much stiffer than anything O-A had paid to date and amounted to $6.60 for Douglas fir, $4.01 for cedar, and $2.65 for hemlock and white fir, the latter species accounting for about 84 percent of the stand. The aggregate price of this transaction totaled $56,000.

Another dimension to the negotiations arose when the Clark & Wilson Lumber Company announced plans to liquidate its operations in December 1944, leaving uncut a substantial parcel of timber in its Pebble Creek tract. Given the proximity of this timber to Vernonia, Oregon-American immediately sought to buy it. Clark & Wilson had, over time, fully developed its own railroad system for hauling its logs eastbound from the Nehalem Valley, over St. Helens Mountain and to its own dumping facilities on the Columbia River. The Northern Lines had only partially capitalized on the traffic potential it presented once the logs had been milled at Clark & Wilson's Portland and Prescott mills. Greenman advised Holt of this development on February 7, 1945, and, in making the case that should O-A buy the remaining Clark & Wilson timber O-A would ship all the resulting lumber via the Northern Lines, he also pointed out the complications the acquisition would present:

> Because it would take too much money, we could not buy the Clark-Wilson timber and at the same time complete a contract for the purchase of the Yerreck tract with its requirements of a relatively large sum of cash in the form of down payment.
>
> The question we want to put to you is whether or not, in the event we find it desirable to buy the Clark-Wilson timber, you will permit us to defer the purchase of the entire Yerreck tract for two or three years, and at the same time sell us in piecemeal lots, of not less than a full section, such Ruth timber as we may need to maintain our production in the Clatsop-Tillamook area.

With the prospect of this potential windfall in mind, Holt promised to take the proposal to his executive officers. He also suggested that if O-A bought the Clark & Wilson timber, he would recommend the carriers give O-A the right to defer the purchase of the remaining Yerreck tract timber.

On March 9, word reached Greenman and Olin that Holt had died. In a note to Olin, Greenman commented:

> This is a shocking thing and is somewhat disturbing to me because, tough as we felt that Mr. Holt was, I believe we were making progress with him and all of the ground we have plowed with Holt will have to be worked over again with the successor regardless of who he may be.
>
> I would assume that someone from St. Paul or elsewhere on the Northern Pacific System would be put in Holt's place. If that is done it will of course practically mean starting [all over] again unless it should happen that this matter was turned back to the S P & S people for handling. Let's hope the latter will happen.

On March 21, 1945, Olin wrote Stern:

> We now have a letter from [the Northern Pacific] informing us that our counter proposal was not acceptable.... Now that Mr. Holt is out of the picture, we are trying to have this matter sent back to the Portland office of the S P & S where it was in the first place and in this the S P & S vice-president and General Manager, Dixon, is cooperating as he was not pleased when it was sent to the Seattle office.

Later he added:

> As to the end of the European war having any softening effect on the officials of the Northern Roads,

my reaction is that the cessation of hostilities in that area will not be considered one way or another; in fact I feel confident that if they went out cold-blooded to sell that timber for all they could get, we would have to pay considerably more than we are now figuring on, if we were to be the final purchasers. In other words, I feel, and I know Judd does, that they have given the freight possibilities a lot of consideration.

Pressing to avoid further delays, Chaney, Olin, and Greenman traveled to Seattle on March 27, 1945, to meet with the respective executive vice presidents of the Northern Pacific and Great Northern, MacFarlane and Balmer. O-A stated its unwillingness to accept Holt's offer of December 20, 1944, and Macfarlane countered with an offer to sell parts of the Yerreck tract piecemeal. He, however, would not commit to reserve the balance for Oregon-American.

Once the negotiations reached the Northern Lines' executive offices, O-A lost any further avenues of appeal. Faced with losing the balance of the Yerreck tract to a competitor, Chaney, Olin, and Greenman finally made an offer for the entire balance of the timber. Oregon-American offered a down-payment of $400,000, the balance carried at an interest rate of 3 percent, paid on stumpage rates of $5.50 for Douglas and noble fir, $2.50 for hemlock, cedar, and white fir, and $4.00 for Sitka spruce. Oregon-American also agreed to assume full risk and liability for the timber. The total price for the tract worked out to $1.4 million. Consistent with the snail's pace that had thus far characterized the negotiations, the Northern Lines did not finally agree to O-A's offer until November 1945.

A sense of lingering bitterness over the carriers' handling of the Yerreck negotiations was evident in Greenman's letter to SP&S's T. F. Dixon on December 20, 1945:

> We have always assumed the [Ruth] Keasey timber would be reserved for us, barring some unforeseeable major change in our relations. I believe your people recognize us as the logical purchasers of that timber, a recognition well reflected in the last sentence of a letter written to us by Mr. W. E. Holt under date of December 20, 1944, in which sentence Mr. Holt said "I will recommend that the Keasey block be reserved for you as per our discussion and I believe that there should be little difficulty in working out a satisfactory agreement to cover the matter."
>
> Because of the fleeting nature of man's existence on this precarious planet, I think it would be a healthy precaution for us to have some sort of a written commitment from your people at this time that the Keasey timber will be reserved for us. As proof of the desirability of a commitment I submit that the man I quoted above, who intended to recommend such a reservation, is dead and I don't know that he ever carried out the intent he outlined in his letter of a year ago.

Dixon was only marginally responsive in his reply of January 28, 1946: *Please be advised that the Ruth Realty Company agrees to give the Oregon-American Lumber Corporation a preferential right for five years to purchase at the Realty Company's price and terms if and when the Realty Company desire to sell the timber on the Keasey Block—1,049.06 Acres.*

Liquidation of the Clark & Wilson Lumber Company Timber

Once Clark & Wilson decided to liquidate, one of its first tasks was to scrap its railroad. To keep the company operating until a buyer could be found for its Pebble Creek tract, Clark & Wilson immediately agreed to sell logs from the tract to Oregon-American and employed gyppos to log the timber and haul it on motor trucks to the Vernonia pond. During the period between December 1944 and March 1945, Oregon-American took delivery of nearly 12 million board feet of logs from Pebble Creek.

The War Production Board, in an attempt to maintain overall lumber production, interposed itself in the sale of the Clark & Wilson properties. On January 24, 1945, the WPB issued an opinion in which it literally threatened to confiscate the Clark & Wilson timber to ensure its availability to log-buying mills, presumably those on the Columbia River. The conditions the WPB placed on the sale of the Clark & Wilson timber and to allocate the logs produced from it to distant mills, quickly cooled Oregon-American's interest in purchasing the Pebble Creek tract.

Greenman, challenged Fred Brundage, the WPB's Western Log & Lumber Administrator on January 25, 1944:

> Having eliminated us as prospective purchasers of the timber, let's take a look at what you have left.
>
> I think it is fair to ask you how much interest you think you can develop in getting this Pebble Creek unit of C-W timber put in the river for the purpose of "protecting the supply of logs available to log-buying mills" at the [cost of logging it to the Columbia River].
>
> I think your letter completely overlooks the fact that the C-W timber never has been available to those "log-buying mills" about whom you are so solicitous.
>
> It also overlooks the fact there will be vastly greater use of critical tires and gasoline if these logs are trucked 35–40 miles over the Coast Range to the River than if they move five miles downhill to the Vernonia pond.

Crown Zellerbach ultimately purchased the Clark & Wilson properties in 1945, including the Pebble Creek tract.

The timber's isolation was not lost on the new owners. Crown was heavily committed to the business of manufacturing pulp and paper and the Pebble Creek stand was comprised largely of Douglas fir that was most suitably used in the production of lumber. Because of the timber's isolation and the attendant expense of getting it to market, Crown Zellerbach realized it represented more value as trading stock for additional supplies of pulp-species logs than anything else.

Greenman and Crown Zellerbach's E. P. Stamm considered many ways to use the Pebble Creek timber to their respective companies' advantage. Eventually, Stamm agreed to a Greenman proposal that called for Crown to deliver all its Pebble Creek timber, including pulp species, to the Vernonia pond. In return, Oregon-American agreed to segregate and buy the saw logs, then transload the pulp species on cars for shipment to Crown's mills. In addition, Oregon-American agreed to provide Crown Zellerbach one-half as much hemlock and other pulp species as Crown Zellerbach provided fir to Oregon-American. Other details of this April 1945 arrangement involved Oregon-American's agreement to handle the loading of the pulp logs on cars with Crown Zellerbach absorbing the loading costs.

Describing the arrangement to Chaney on April 20, 1945, Greenman wrote:

> This is not as good a deal as outright purchase of all the logs from the Pebble Creek unit would have been but it was the best we could do and should result in bringing 30–35 million feet of net increased log footage over and above the pulp species which we make in return. This figure of 30–35 million includes approximately 12 million already delivered by Clark & Wilson.

As it turned out, Pebble Creek held much more timber than anyone suspected, and between November 1944 and year-end 1952, Oregon-American took delivery of more than 70 million board feet of logs from the arrangement. It thus gave the company a ready outlet for the abundance of low-grade hemlock and thin-barked fir species found on the Yerreck tract and, in the process, provided an additional half-year's supply of Douglas fir logs to the Vernonia mill.

JAPANESE ATTACKS ON THE PACIFIC COAST: OREGON-AMERICAN FOREST FIRES AND A BIG WHAT IF?

If West Coast residents harbored any sense of distance from the hostilities of WWII, the Japanese quickly dispelled such thoughts with their December 7, 1941 attack on Pearl Harbor. Underscoring the vulnerability of the region, enemy submarines began attacking Allied shipping in the Pacific Ocean within hours following the Pearl Harbor debacle.[2] By Christmas Day 1941 the Japanese had torpedoed an American oil tanker off Crescent City, California. Similar incidents ranged up and down the coast through 1944.

The Japanese were keenly aware that attacks along North American shores could reap both physical damage and psychological mayhem. So, to the extent they could make resources available, the enemy broadened the scope of its attacks on coastal targets to include direct bombardment. On February 23, 1942, Japanese submarines began sporadically shelling land targets, first in California followed by more attacks up and down the coast. These attacks brought the specter of hostilities particularly close to residents of northwestern Oregon when, on June 21, 1942, a Japanese submarine shelled Fort Stevens, Oregon, at the mouth of the Columbia River, only 44 miles from Vernonia.

Then, on September 9, 1942, the Japanese launched a small airplane from a submarine that dropped incendiary bombs in the rugged forest area some 8 miles inland from Brookings, Oregon. Although the bombs misfired and only caused a minor blaze, the daring attack led to concerns that expanded direct aerial bombing missions were likely. While distant, the Japanese's 1942 seizures of Attu and Kiska Islands in Alaska's Aleutian chain added yet another fear, the possibility of a ground invasion.

By 1944, however, the tide of the war in the Pacific had clearly shifted in favor of the Allies. As a result, the number of hostile incidents along the West Coast dropped off noticeably. However, the pause was illusory. In 1944 the Japanese began a potentially far more threatening phase of the campaign. It came in the form of bomb-laden balloons launched from Japan's home shores bound for the North American mainland.³

Between November 1944 and August 1945, the enemy launched more than 6,000 balloon bombs from various parts of Japan. Most were equipped with a single, 15-kilogram, high-explosive, antipersonnel bomb and four thermite incendiary bombs, each weighing 5 kilograms. The balloons were designed to release each bomb at intervals determined by changes in atmospheric pressure. The Japanese constructed the balloons of paper and filled them with hydrogen. They were large enough to lift their payload to a peak altitude of 30,000 feet. At that height, the balloons caught prevailing upper air currents commonly known today as the jet stream, that fast-flowing air current that prevails from east to west across the Pacific Ocean. On average, the balloons' journey lasted three days. Once they had released their deadly cargo, a device triggered a fuse that burned the balloon and its remaining hydrogen, thus destroying final traces of evidence.⁴

While the self-destructing design often erased evidence of the balloons themselves, hardware used to carry the explosives, and sometimes the explosives themselves, survived intact. Accordingly, authorities recovered remains of nearly 300 balloon bombs before the war's end, spanning an area from Alaska to Mexico and from Hawaii to Michigan. In Oregon alone, parts of forty-five different devices were discovered, exceeded only by another fifty-seven discovered in British Columbia. One such device accounted for the only Japanese-caused WWII casualties suffered on the United States mainland when a party of picnickers accidentally triggered an unexploded antipersonnel bomb near Bly, Oregon, on May 5, 1945. It killed six innocent people.⁵

I was shovin' out debris around the landing on Spur 26-2 and a lot of it was burning. Pretty soon I found a box and looked a little closer and realized I'd run over a powder monkey's dynamite cache. He had about three boxes of dynamite there. Y'know, those primers for the choker holes? There they were, covered up with slabs of bark and the fire burnin' all around them. And there's me almost runnin' the dozer right over the top of them.

I spent the coldest night of my life up here on this hill (alongside Spur 26-3). It was in February. I was on the dozer about sixteen hours and here comes Hageman.

George. Can you stay over and run the pumps for me?

I'm worn out, *I said.* I'd been workin' my butt off all day. It was hot during the day, even in February. All I had on was a sweatshirt. Nothin' to eat for hours.

Fred said, *I'll leave somebody out here to carry gas from the railroad tracks to you.* It was about a third of a mile. He left ol' Ole Olson, Andy's brother.

Well, when it got dark, Ole just knew with all that fire going that there had to be cougars all over the place and he wouldn't go up to the railroad tracks to get that gas unless I went with him. Cougars.

You know it froze that night? There was a leak in the pipeline and it sprayed water up on a clump of brush and before long it was a solid mass of icicles clear to the ground. We pulled a bunch of burning poles and stuff out of the fire and started one of our own. Stood by that fire. You'd have to stand there and turn around and around like a chicken on a rotisserie. To keep warm. Y'know, I got so I couldn't hardly stand on my feet I was so tired. And if you laid down or somethin' you'd freeze to death.

Finally my brain cut in. Some guys it takes awhile. I built two fires just a couple of feet apart. I lay right down in there in the bushes. Went sound to sleep. That kept me real nice and warm. I told Ole, Now, you stay awake here, you keep them fires goin' just right. I'm gonna sleep. *So, I slept like a log.*

I don't know, hour and a half or so, I started gettin' cold on one side so I woke up and there's Ole, sound asleep. So I built the fire up good again. Kicked him awake. I said, Now I gotta get some sleep! *So Ole, he'd watch awhile and finally I got my batteries charged up again and I was all right. That was a cold night.*

George Lee, construction

Ship sinkings, shellings, and the Bly tragedy aside, Japanese attacks to land targets along the lower forty-eight states' caused little or no physical damage. Despite military and FBI attempts to suppress publicity about them, word did leak and newspapers around the country carried the stories.[6] The enemy clearly took the psychological advantage, for it sharply increased public awareness of the enemy's reach and resulted in the expenditure of no insignificant amount of effort to guard against the possibility of more and larger assaults.[7]

Word of inland forest bombing attempts was particularly portentous news to lumber industry, forestry, and government officials. Yet besides shutting down logging operations altogether, an unacceptable alternative during the war, about the only tangible step operators could take was to prepare for this eventuality.

Defensive Measures

Immediately following Pearl Harbor, government, industry, and citizens took steps to mobilize against attacks. In Vernonia, special mill whistle signals were established to announce impending air raids. The City of Vernonia used its local fire siren to announce daily blackout signals. O-A applied blackout paint to mill powerhouse windows. The city and a first-aid section of civilian defense authorities created emergency facilities at the local IOOF hall, using surplus beds brought down from Camp McGregor. Fire-fighting brigades, always a feature of the Vernonia mill's operation, began holding regular drills. Sand and shovels were strategically placed along the mill's monorail tracks so operators could easily transport them in case of fire.

Opposite page: A pre-WWII view looking east over Vernonia with the sawmill in the background. The "Yukon Spur" ran around the back of the mill to the pulp log reload. The SP&S mainline to Keasey ran right-to-left in the foreground. (Delano Photographics and Northern Light Studios/Brubaker collection, Portland, Oregon)

On January 14, 1942, Greenman advised all supervisory personnel, *It is entirely conceivable to me the Japanese might, during the dry days of next summer, undertake at least a token bombing of industrial plants in the northwest and certainly nothing would be more vulnerable to incendiary bombing than our sawmills and our tinder dry forest would.* Given a logging operation's liberal use of blasting powder to eliminate stumps from rights-of-way, blow choker holes, and so on, having tons of explosives on hand was common. Concerned over its vulnerability to attack, the company built an underground powder magazine large enough to accommodate two boxcar loads of the stuff in a rock bluff near Twin Bridges.

In the summer of 1942 O-A, having large areas of unburned slashings, blasted holes in the beds of small streams to accumulate water supplies.

Oregon-American Forest Fires During WWII

With one notable exception, Oregon-American's forest fires during WWII were the result of slashing fires gone awry. The first began on the morning of February 26, 1943, when a slashing fire was set near a logging camp operated by W. D. Music in the southeastern corner of Section 33, Twp. 4 North, Range 6 West. The fire started on lands under management of the McPhersons and got out of control in the face of strong easterly winds that arose after the fire had been burning for a while. Burning debris was blown across the Wolf Creek Highway and ignited a snag-infested area on Oregon-American property. Once the fire established itself in the snags, the wind spread it widely.

On March 1 the fire burned O-A's 250-horsepower Skagit diesel donkey, destroying it in the process. Eventually the fire covered an area of 3,000 acres, of which 75 percent had been cutover. Nearly 100,000 board feet of felled and bucked timber on the Spur 26-3 system in Sections 5, 31, and 32 of Twp. 4 North, Range 6 West was destroyed.

Burning slashings in midwinter was unusual. However, a twenty-eight-day period had passed without rainfall and it provided an opportune situation. Since snow blanketed the higher elevations, no one was too concerned over the fire's spreading when it was initially set. By contrast, the dry conditions made the fire difficult to suppress and firefighters did not bring it under control until March 11, 1943. Often the fire burned right up to the snow line.

The second major Oregon-American fire started as a normal fall slashing fire set on October 2, 1944. Rains on October 4 and 5 prevented the fire from accomplishing its objective, and on October 9, the Northwest Oregon Forest Protective Association urged O-A to set more fires and put additional men on the burning, concentrating on an area near the Spur 26-3 Switchback. O-A agreed to take these measures starting on the morning of October 10 but the night before a southeast wind arose. The company delayed setting the fires because of the potential threat to a large volume of felled timber located across the North Fork of the Salmonberry River canyon close to O-A's Spur 26-8.

Nevertheless, a representative of the association sent to help in the burning disregarded the windy conditions and set fires along Spur 26-3 in Section 1, Twp. 3 North, Range 7 West. Later in the day, the prevailing southeast breeze turned into gale-force winds and pushed the fire line into 160 acres of the downed timber lying across the canyon in Sections 35 and 36, Twp. 4 North, Range 7 West and Sections

41083
Brubaker Aerial Sur

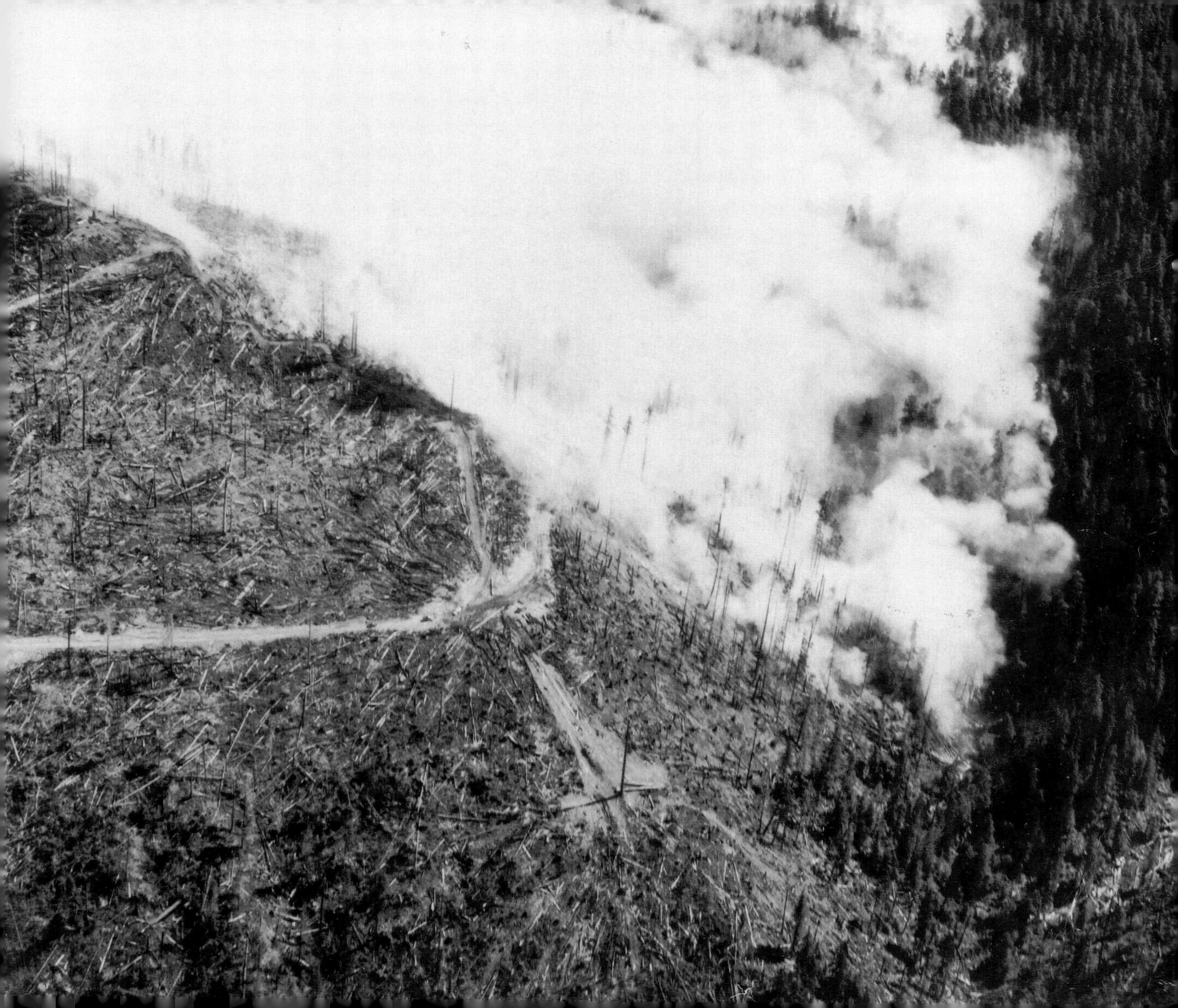

1 and 2 of Twp. 3 North, Range 7 West, where it caused considerable damage. In addition, the fire severely burned two yarders and one loading engine. Matters might have deteriorated further had the wind not changed direction on October 11. Rain began falling the following day and extinguished the fire. The fire consumed more than 3 million feet of felled and bucked timber.

The third Oregon-American fire of the era was the most significant, both due to its size and mysterious origin. This fire, which broke out on July 9, 1945, started on O-A cutover lands in the northwestern corner of Section 1, Twp. 3 North, Range 7 West in the steep North Fork of the Salmonberry River canyon between spurs 26-3 and 26-8.[8] That same day yet another forest fire broke out along the Wilson River in the general vicinity where the 1933 and 1939 Tillamook Burns had originated.[9]

By July 13, the fire on Oregon-American property, by then called the Salmonberry Fire, had spread over several thousand acres, all on cutover or previously burned-over lands. By July 18 it had grown to more than 5,000 acres but, in comparison to the Wilson River Fire, some 15 miles to the south, it remained relatively small. By July 28, the Salmonberry fire had spread sufficiently to surround O-A and Ruth Realty green standing timber in the Southwest Unit on three sides to the east, south, and west. The Wilson River Fire had, by then, grown to around 100,000 acres. Soon the two fires joined to become one and from that point on became known as the Tillamook Burn of 1945. The fires continued to burn until firefighters finally brought them under control late in August. The combined area burned over in the 1945 Tillamook Burn was more than 180,000 acres.[10]

While fire losses to the O-A and Ruth green timber were negligible, the fire caused extensive damage after it left O-A property. One distant operator sued Oregon-American and intervening property owners.[11] The lawsuit proceedings stretched out for years until ultimately found in favor of the defendants.[12]

Like so many forest fires, officials never determined the cause of the 1945 Salmonberry Fire. Greenman, however, had a definite suspicion as to the fire's cause. *It was our firm opinion, concurred by the State Forester*, that this particular fire started from something dropped from above, possibly a fragment of one of the bombs the Japanese were sending over via balloons during the war.* Greenman made that statement in connection with the lawsuit claiming Oregon-American was negligent for allowing the fire to escape its property boundaries. The trial also reflected his conclusion, but only as one of two theories of cause. The other theory stated the fire originated from forest refuse ignited by light rays magnified through a discarded soft-drink bottle. As liability after the fire spread, rather than the actual cause of the fire, was the central issue of the lawsuit, court proceedings did not dwell on the fire's actual cause.[13]

These tantalizing tidbits and a corroborating statement from counsel for one defendant do not, in and of themselves, prove anything about the actual cause. Company records mentioned no physical evidence of a balloon bomb, nor was the Oregon Department of Forestry able to substantiate Rogers's thoughts on the matter. On the contrary, none of the foregoing does anything to *dis*prove the notion an incendiary device dropped from above caused the 1945 Salmonberry Fire. As the military and the FBI were well aware of the threat, and went to great lengths to suppress publicity surrounding the discovery of balloon bombs or their remnants,

*Nelson Rogers

Opposite page: If, in fact, it was the result of a balloon-borne incendiary device as Judd Greenman and State Forester Nels Rogers surmised it might have been, the forest fire that began mysteriously on Oregon-American's property on July 9, 1945 could have been a tremendous morale booster for the Japanese. A Navy pilot took this photo shortly after the fire began.

The Salmonberry Fire traveled widely and eventually joined with the Wilson River Fire that started on the same day some 10 miles to the southeast. Together, they covered 180,000 acres in what was to become the Tillamook Burn of 1945. Oregon-American suffered little damage to its stand.

This view is looking southeast over the North Fork of the Salmonberry River. The abandoned right-of-way is near the end of Spur 26-3. (U.S. Navy photograph; Clarence and Walter Bradford collection)

Oregon-American's first diesel donkey was a Skagit Model BU-154 purchased in 1939. Shortly after it was pressed into service that summer, it barely escaped burning in the Cow Creek Fire. Its luck ran out when the Music Fire of February 1943 destroyed it.

The company was pleased with its performance. So much so that following WWII, O-A converted a number of its steam donkeys to diesel power. (Oregon-American Lumber Company, Special Collections and University Archives, University of Oregon)

ruling out a possible connection between the fire and a balloon-borne incendiary is premature without further investigation.[14]

Over time, people have discovered balloon bomb wreckage as near as Neah-Kah-Nie Mountain on the Pacific Ocean coastline. That is only 22 miles west of the Salmonberry Fire's originating point. Others have found wreckage near the town of Clatskanie, some 27 miles to the northeast. If, and the authors hasten to state it is a *big* if, the explosion of a Japanese balloon-borne incendiary bomb ignited the Salmonberry Fire, then the event would have represented a spectacular success for the Japanese, both as for the actual damage it created and for the extensive diversion of labor required to combat the fire. Further, if that indeed was the cause of the fire, either the lack of connection made at the time or suppression of the facts surrounding the fire's cause effectively denied the Japanese an enormous psychological victory, despite the fact that American bombers had already driven the balloon-bombing campaign out of existence.[15] (See Appendix C for additional discussion.)

FINANCE

Hardships created by the war did not carry over to Oregon-American's financial situation. Government-imposed ceiling prices provided generous sales margins and, despite lower production, the company was consistently able to report profits.

Second mortgage bonds traded in the mid-50s following repayment of the first mortgage RFC loan in 1940 and enabled the company to continue paying back its original debts at a substantial discount. However, following the O-A's first sizeable interest payment on the second mortgage bonds made on September 1, 1941, values soared. By December of that year, bonds were trading at 93 percent of their face value. By then it was evident that steeply discounted redemptions were history for Central Coal & Coke, Baker, Fentress & Company, along with a few others owning large blocks of the securities, were not ready to accept anything but full payment.

By September 17, 1942, only $1,462,200 of the second mortgage bonds remained unpaid and the redemption price had reached 100 percent of face value. In July 1943, Oregon-American's capital stock tax return declared a value of $11 million, the equivalent of nearly $25 per share. Considering the fact that when O-A reorganized in 1935, there had been no stockholder equity to speak of, only a mountain of debt; this marked a substantial improvement.

Signifying the Oregon-American Lumber Corporation's resurgence, the company declared its first stock dividend of $2 per share in 1943. At their November 1944 meeting, the board of directors authorized an additional payment of just over $200,000 to reduce second mortgage bonds to only a half million dollars. On January 1, 1945, the voting trust provisions of Oregon-American's reorganization plan expired and holders of the stock trust certificates were issued the company's common stock. At the April 9, 1945 meeting, the board of directors amended the corporation's bylaws to enlarge the board from five to six members. George Birkelund's sage counsel to Oregon-American during his tenure as the chairman of the voting trustees earned him the new position.

PULLING THE PLUG ON OREGON GAS & ELECTRIC

Because of growing demand for electrical service in the Nehalem Valley, Oregon Gas & Electric Company found itself increasingly dependent on surplus electricity produced by the Vernonia mill powerhouse—a situation that became intolerable for Oregon-American because it often meant shutting down its own equipment just to keep the utility supplied. Accordingly, on April 23, 1943, O-A put OG&E on notice of its desire to cancel the standby power supply agreement.

While the company continued the arrangement until the utility could find a new source of power, O-A mandated the utility expand no further until other supplies were found. By 1945, OG&E had changed hands to became the West Oregon Electric Cooperative, a Rural Electrical Administration-financed utility that arranged for electricity supplied by the Bonneville power system, a process completed in 1946. At that time O-A stopped supplying power.

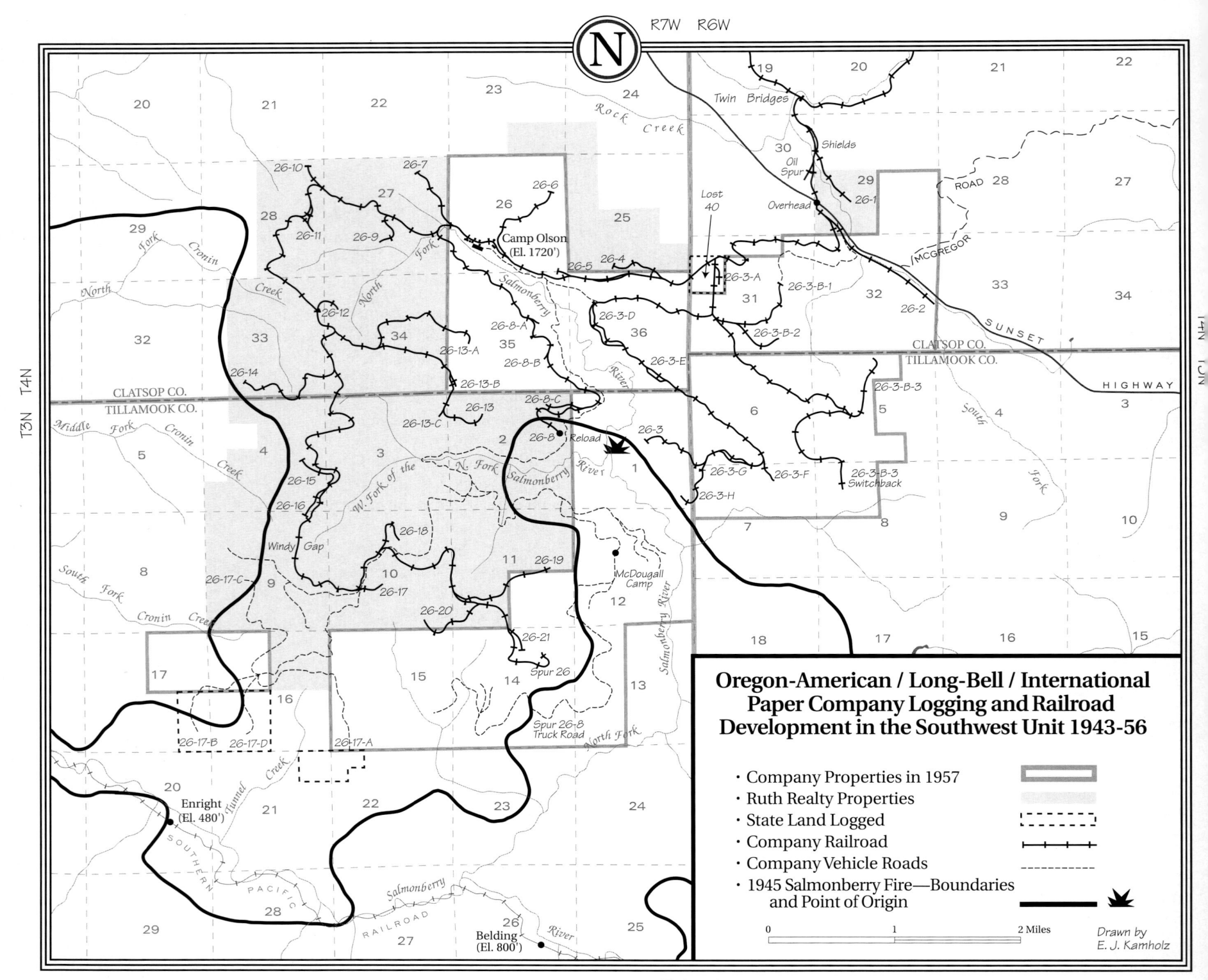

Oregon-American / Long-Bell / International Paper Company Logging and Railroad Development in the Southwest Unit 1943-56

- Company Properties in 1957
- Ruth Realty Properties
- State Land Logged
- Company Railroad
- Company Vehicle Roads
- 1945 Salmonberry Fire—Boundaries and Point of Origin

0   1   2 Miles

Drawn by E. J. Kamholz

THE GLORY YEARS

Douglas fir lumber operators' road to the future came to a pronounced fork in the immediate aftermath of World War II. The road a producer took was determined not so much by choice as it was by the amount of timber he owned or had under contract. Equally important was whether he had acquired that timber before the scarcity of supply drove up its value.

If an operator was blessed with a captive supply of timber secured before the price of undeveloped stands skyrocketed, then his road was paved smooth by a civilian housing market that displayed an insatiable demand for lumber—at virtually any price. Profit margins of such operators swelled for as long as the market held up, or their timber supplies lasted. By contrast, if an operator had no such cheap timber inventory available, his road was far more likely to be a bumpy one. While he might have found it possible to maintain production by working hand-to-mouth from timber purchased at the open-market rate, he could continue serving the burgeoning market only to the extent demand kept lumber prices rising faster than the cost of his timber and the labor he needed to produce something from it. As a result his profits were much harder to come by, often forcing him to operate on the brink of closure.

To illustrate just how much the price of timber rose after WWII, in 1951 Oregon-American paid more money for the timber on 210 acres of state lands adjoining the land it acquired from the Salmonberry Timber Company than the company paid for the entire 2,481 acres in that tract in 1940, a more than *tenfold* increase.

By virtue of having Ruth Realty's timber along with its own, the Oregon-American Lumber Corporation was clearly poised to travel the better road. In doing so, it was finally able to realize the long-awaited payoff Charles Keith had envisioned when he set up operations in the west nearly thirty years earlier. Between 1947 and 1951, Oregon-American enjoyed a brief, but spectacular, period of financial success. This period, like no other in the company's history, was Oregon-American's "Glory Years."

In the broader picture, however, the outstanding financial showing O-A and other long-established operators reported during this time merely represented the last gasp at life by an industry destined for change. For despite the fact that their road was smooth, it also had an abrupt end, coinciding exactly with the moment each operator brought in his last, cheaply acquired, old-growth log.

For the industry as a whole, once privately held old-growth timber supplies were eventually consumed, the "cut-out-and-get-out" era of logging ended forever. No longer could operators pursue that long-held philosophy and survive. Producers who envisioned any future in the wood-products business were forced to face the wasteful past of their forbearers and take steps to ensure a continued existence.

Oregon-American, holding steadfast to the old philosophy and bolstered by its remaining timber,

Opposite page: The 1945 Salmonberry Fire threatened O-A's timber stand but eventually moved south to become part of the Tillamook Burn of that year.

Oregon-American opened Camp Olson in 1947 and it remained the hub of company logging operations until 1955.

O-A's big Skagit Model 6-70 diesel speeder's distinctive cupola cab was the victim of this March 26, 1946, derailment on the first trestle west of Camp McGregor. Although a broken wheel center was the "official" cause of the mishap, the operator's son told the authors his father had been speeding. (Arlie Sliffe collection)

lasted longer than most cut-and-run outfits. Nevertheless, even during those peak years, the knowledge that business-as-usual was the shortest path to inevitable demise tempered what pride the company might have had for its accomplishments.

MARKETING IN THE POSTWAR ERA

The federal bureaucracy created to mobilize war production dismantled itself very slowly and resupply of normal distribution channels lagged as a result. The federal government's creation of home-loan financing programs for returning veterans kept lumber demand high. By spring 1946 the unfilled orders to gross stocks ratio for 133 reporting WCLA mills stood at 176 percent and, while not as high as the 240-percent ratio reported at war's end, it was very substantial, nevertheless.

Wholesalers and retailers, desperate for anything to sell and regardless what selling arrangements they had before the war, besieged producers directly for lumber. Greenman, characterizing the situation, replied to one such unsolicited appeal on May 7, 1946:

> There is not a chance in the world that we will be able to let you have any lumber.... Obviously, if we could increase shipments into your good state at all, the increase should go to those people who have long depended on us for lumber....
>
> We would like to be able to send lumber to each one of our good friends scattered over the nation and you would be surprised at the number of good friends we have developed since lumber became so scarce.

Despite the fact that little remained in the way of the labor shortages that had plagued the industry during the war, a severe shortage of housing in the Vernonia area, coupled with a nagging shortage of logs, made it impossible to expand production.

While construction of bunkhouse-style accommodations for an expanded mill force was briefly considered, O-A never carried out that plan. Not only was there a concern that setting up such a camp would attract a lower-caliber-type mill hand, it failed to address the bigger problem of how to increase the supply of logs.

The origins of the log supply shortage were several. First, the carryover effects from the wartime woods labor shortage kept the company behind schedule in its own logging program. More important, however, nearly a year's worth of railroad construction time was lost during the protracted negotiations for the Yerreck tract. That made it impossible to speed up logging. Fir logs supplied by Crown Zellerbach provided some measure of relief. Yet since Oregon-American was obligated to supply Crown with half as much footage in pulp species, most of which was to come from Ruth's Yerreck tract, this arrangement offered only partial relief.

Coupled with the return of the forty-hour workweek, the mill cut dropped from 83 million board feet in 1945 to only 70 million board feet in 1946. When the government finally dropped controls on lumber prices and distribution in late 1946, Oregon-American's annual report described the resulting frenzy:

> With the ending of price and distribution controls in November, the huge, pent-up, war-restricted demand for lumber surged over the industry in an uncontrollable flood. As a consequence, prices late in 1946 became chaotic; long-established industry practices were thrown overboard and general confusion resulted. Builders with partially completed houses needing upper grade lumber for finishing, stormed the mills with fantastic offers of price and specifications to cover their needs. Industrial lumber users denied raw materials for making their products by price or priorities, clamored for their share of the available supply. Lumber hungry foreign nations importuned their American agents to get some lumber to them at any price.

Nationwide, builders erected some 860,000 new structures in 1947, largely as government-financed civilian housing. With more than one million buildings constructed in 1948, the lumber industry entered a period of unparalleled prosperity. Despite the robust market, however, Oregon-American's log shortage problems persisted and the mill could only produce 72 million board feet in 1947.

The Economics of Inflation—Lumber is Called to Washington

Once the government lifted the war-era ceiling price controls, runaway demand caused lumber prices to soar. Wage increases granted during and immediately following the war also drove costs higher. Lumber manufacturers were quick to pass those added costs to their customers. Lumber, at the time, was paying an average hourly wage of $1.60, one of the highest of all the mass-producing industries. Between 1938 and 1948, labor costs for the industry had increased by 128 percent. To the extent

Top: By the end of WWII most of O-A's remaining timber was more than 25 miles southwest of Vernonia and more than 9 miles from Camp McGregor. Travel time to and from work became a big issue with the unions so the company built a new camp closer to the center of logging operations in 1947. Oregon-American named it after logging superintendent Andy Olson. (Margaret Taylor collection)

§

Bottom: Moving crews used the Number 4 Cletrac to drag bunkhouses from their Camp McGregor resting place to the assembly point where the locomotive crane loaded them on disconnects. The process was reversed at the other end. The new camp opened for business when loggers returned from the July Fourth vacation shutdown. (Margaret Taylor collection)

THE GLORY YEARS

The mill foremen at their weekly luncheon. The photo was taken around 1948.

Front row, left to right: C. L. "Connie" Anderson, vice president, general manager; R. A. Simmons, chief engineer; Walter Linn, timber dock foreman; Fritz Hausler, dressed shed and loading dock foreman; and A. J. "Paddy" Hughes, chief electrician. Second row, left to right: Hamp Roberson, sawmill foreman (hidden behind Linn); Dave Marshall, master mechanic; Herman Dickson, assistant chief engineer; Mike Ludwig, rough dock and monorail foreman; and George Laird, order chaser. Third row, left to right: Art Davis, assorter and stacker foreman; Ralph Aldrich Jr., head grader; Holly Holcomb, planing mill foreman; Charles Wall, plant superintendent; and Fred Tousley, dry kiln foreman. (Wick Miller Men-at-Work Pictures. Kamholz collection)

Oregon-American's prices were any reflection of the lumber industry trend, its average price increased by 290 percent during the same period.

Increasingly, the lumber industry found itself under federal government scrutiny to account for why lumber prices were rising so much faster than prices for other building materials. Matters reached a head when a Joint Committee on Housing convened hearings in mid-January 1948. Representatives ordered leaders from all corners of the lumber industry to Washington, where they urged companies to make voluntary price reductions.

Greenman represented Oregon-American before the Congressional Committee on January 12, 1948. Never hesitant to make his opinions known, Greenman's moment in the spotlight was controversial and his message was anything but conciliatory. It was also in stark contrast to the contrite testimony of his fellow lumbermen:

My company made about 1 percent of the total amount of Douglas fir and hemlock lumber produced in the region.

As all good American citizens must be, I am deeply sympathetic with the desire of the Congress to make available more and cheaper housing for Americans. I think that I differ somewhat with some of my colleagues, and possibly with the Joint Subcommittee on the most practicable means of accomplishing this desirable end.

I do not concede that profits in the lumber industry as a whole today are greater than are needed if this industry is to replenish its timber and amortize its plants at current costs and values....

The profits of the industry are, of course, derived by selling its products at a price in excess of the cost of production.

Costs of production of lumber vary greatly between mills. Many factors affect this; quality of timber, location of mill, cost of standing timber, type of equipment, efficiency of labor.... Today many mills can operate at a profit, but others are still marginal; will close at the first turn of the market. Late last spring the market eased, prices dropped, and many small mills closed....

Full industry production can only be secured when all mills are profitable....

The increase in Douglas fir production in 1947, as compared with 1946, which was the greatest for any softwood region within the industry, was brought about solely by relatively high prices, which made it possible to start new operations based on high-cost timber, high-cost plants, and direct operating charges substantially above the average for the older and more firmly established operations.

In my opinion, this committee, desiring as it does to expand and cheapen available housing, will be well advised if it lets Douglas fir lumber prices alone.... After more than forty years of experience with them, I am thoroughly confident that these prices will take care of themselves; they will not long remain out of relationship with prices of competitive building materials, if they now are out of such relationship....

Later, when describing the hearings to the Oregon-American board of directors, he added:

> I think all the lumber men there [there were about sixty from all over the nation representing all divisions of the industry including wholesalers and retailers] were sympathetic with the position in which the Congress finds itself, but if any lumberman there felt he had any answer to the dilemma, he kept his thoughts to himself.
>
> The Weyerhaeuser position, based entirely on

Some Vernonia office staff posed for the camera in 1951. From left to right, back row: Isabel Kaspar; Delores Bergstrom; J. Walter Vaughan, sales manager; unidentified female employee, F. Merle Ruhl, office manager; Mary Weise; and Connie Anderson, vice-president and general manager. Middle row: Larry Weise; Vera Finnell; Katherine Hoffman Skuzi; Julie Kanzler; Rose Valpiani, secretary to the president; and vice president, Wesley Pace. Front: Dick Fletcher.

Anderson began with O-A as shipping clerk in 1924. He rose to mill superintendent when the mill reopened in 1936. O-A promoted him to vice president and general manager in 1947, and he continued in that capacity until the mill's dismantling was completed in 1961.

Ruhl was the company's longest-term employee, serving continuously between 1924 and 1958.

Mrs. Valpiani played a key role arranging the donation of the company's records to the University of Oregon. (School Memory Pictures, Wick Miller photograph; Rose Valpiani collection) their fear of being crucified as a monopoly, is well set out in Mr. Bell's statement....

I believe I can say with confidence that the position of the rest of the industry is set out in my statement....

I see all this construction going on today, it catches my eye. I was in it for forty-eight years. They've got all these little machines today and they work and work but accomplish very little. I just stand there and shake my head.

I punched that road from the Sunset Highway into Camp Olson, graded and finished and everything in five days. That's five miles. I didn't even have a helper on that. Didn't have no stakes or nothin'.

Andy said, Just make me a road in there. Do what you want. *He always let me do what I wanted. I did it anyway.*

George Lee, construction

Despite the posturing, the Congressional hearings proved little more than window dressing and the government did not impose controls.

Weyerhaeuser Timber Corporation, by far the nation's largest lumber producer, bowed to Congressional wishes and reduced its prices immediately following the hearings. However, by April 1948 Weyerhaeuser made an about-face and increased them again after recognizing that its symbolic gesture had produced no effect on the overall high price of lumber.

Governmental pressures aside, the strong demand for lumber to meet the postwar building programs continued to drive prices in a relentlessly upward spiral. In September 1948, Oregon-American's shipment of 7 million board feet sold at a record average price of just more than $100 per thousand.

New Destinations for Oregon-American Lumber

The boom in residential construction markets also fueled a change in the final destination for Oregon-American's lumber production, a trend that had begun during WWII. Until the war's outbreak, the Midwest farm belt represented O-A's primary market. Consistent with that phenomenon, shipments to Iowa served as a bellwether indicator of market conditions. In 1940, for example, 13 percent of O-A's lumber shipments went to that state. By 1942, however, defense-related business caused O-A to ship the bulk of its lumber to western destinations and only 3 percent of the company's shipments went to Iowa. While O-A lumber shipments to Iowa rose again to around 8 percent in 1947 and 1948, they tapered off to only 3 to 4 percent after that. During the war years, shipments to Oregon, California, and Washington consistently rose and became the main shipping destinations for O-A's lumber. Meanwhile, however, the effectiveness of the company's wholesale distribution network had improved to the point that O-A was shipping lumber to nearly every state in the country.

Important changes in the end-use of lumber occurred after the postwar period too. Reflecting the shift from agricultural-related sales to the rapidly expanding and government-financed housing market, 84 percent of O-A's sales in October 1949 went for residential construction. Much of that demand was directly or indirectly underwritten by FHA mortgage guarantees, a form of price support. As such, the industry widely recognized the construction boom would last only as long as the administration continued underwriting it.

Nor were market changes confined to end-user destinations. As owners and builders built existing and new homes with oil- and gas-burning heating and cooking appliances, the demand for fuel wood dropped so sharply that by the end of 1946, Oregon-American found it more difficult to dispose of its waste wood and sawdust. As a result, the company was forced to release most of the twenty-two SP&S wood service cars it had equipped with racks for handling this business until only a few were left, their primary use confined to hauling wood scraps to the logging camp.

A similar situation developed in the market for lath. The O-A lath mill, which the company had leased to various independent contractors since 1925, was finally shut down for good in 1950 and replaced by a waste-chipping unit in June 1951. The decline in the market for lath aside, another justification for investing in the chipper arose from the opportunity to recover greater proportions of the waste from hemlock and other thin-barked wood species, the volume of which increased markedly because of the relatively higher proportion of the stuff found on Ruth Realty's Yerreck tract. O-A sold its chips to kraft paper mills for use in making pulp.

In 1950 the United States built 1.3 million new dwelling units, an all-time record. Although still unable to obtain sufficient logs to fully capitalize on the opportunity, O-A shipped nearly 76 million board feet of lumber at an average realization of $83.

The housing boom's inevitable demise came in 1952. Faced with increasing labor costs, government belt-tightening limited home mortgage financing guarantees to only 650,000 new units that year.

O-A's Industrial Works 40-ton wrecking crane used different booms depending on the task at hand. Here, the heel-boom was used to load a donkey boiler at Camp Olson. (Jack Holst photograph; Jim Blain collection)

Combined with mounting public opinion that the lumber industry had been making too much money, the market finally softened. By mid-year 1952, the industry saw new orders drop by more than 9 percent and inventories rise by 11 percent. Prices began slumping and the boom was over.

Lumber Purchases from Small Sawmills and Sales of Cedar

Unable to increase its own production following the war, Oregon-American actively sought to purchase lumber from small independent mill operators in and around the Nehalem Valley. For a time during 1947, O-A took nearly 100,000 board feet monthly from these sources for resale. These purchases supplemented O-A's own output and enabled it to offer those items demanded by its customers that might not have been possible to produce from company-owned timber.

Although the proportion of cedar diminished as O-A logged the remainder of its timber, sale of cedar logs from the Vernonia pond continued to provide an important source of revenue. Establishment of the Cedarwood Timber Company shingle mill on Vernonia's west side provided a steady outlet for O-A cedar and when Cedarwood constructed its own log pond located alongside the short SP&S spur serving the shingle mill in 1948, O-A began reloading cedar on common-carrier cars for the short trip to the shingle mill spur.

That old donkey had a Ford V-8 engine in it. Piece of crap. Constantly breaking down. I was out there in a snow storm repairing the clutch they'd ripped out of it. Just as fast as I'd lay the nuts and bolts down, the snow'd cover 'em. Finally, I just left everything like it was and gave up and got out of there.

When it finally quit snowin', ol' Hageman was hot about gettin' that donkey fixed.

I took a can of gasoline out there and slopped it around the snow and lit it. You didn't dare scrape it, you'd lose everything. I melted it down and exposed all them parts. Then I put it together.

George Lee, construction

NEW LEADERSHIP

The dawning of 1947 found Olin contemplating his retirement and Greenman approaching his sixty-second birthday. The long-term issue of management succession became a dominant issue for Oregon-American's board of directors. By spring a new course was set.

On May 1, 1947, Olin stepped aside and Greenman replaced him as president. The board appointed Connie Anderson general manager replacing Greenman and promoted Charles Wall to mill superintendent taking over for Anderson. In April 1948, the board made Anderson an executive officer of the corporation, elected him to the board of directors, and gave him the title of vice president.

Reflecting a desire to further spread the workload, more changes followed so that by the end of 1951, the company's executive staff members were Chaney, chairman of the board; Greenman, president; Anderson, vice president; F. M. Ruhl, treasurer; R. B. Fletcher, assistant secretary; Omar C. Spencer, secretary; and David L. Davies, assistant secretary. Ruhl and Fletcher were full-time office employees. O-A's board of directors also reduced its size and after that consisted of Chaney, Sigmund Stern, George Birkelund, Greenman, and Anderson.

LOGGING OPERATIONS

Oregon-American's logging operations underwent many changes in the postwar years. Use of independent contractors expanded greatly, first by hiring many gyppo loggers to increase log production. Later, independent contractors were secured to hasten construction of right-of-way extensions. New methods of transporting logs also emerged and the company extensively modernized its roster of logging equipment.

Gyppos

The ranks of gyppo loggers swelled rapidly throughout the industry beginning in 1946. The government helped this trend by lifting controls on equipment purchases and the cheap sale of war-surplus heavy equipment, primarily trucks. This greatly lowered the economic threshold to go into the logging business. Coupled with higher prices and demand for lumber, operators found it increasingly worthwhile to have gyppos salvage lower grades of

The McDougall Camp on Spur 26-8. Natt McDougall Company crews used this temporary affair while they constructed O-A's truck roads during 1947–48. (H. Brown photograph; Rose Valpiani collection)

logs that had previously been left on the ground during times when logging them to the mills was economically unfeasible.

Oregon-American began using gyppos when independents like Wornstaff and Barker, and Doyle and Rogers were pressed into service to fill the critical void in log production caused by the 1944 skidder crew's walkout. Joe Doyle, a former Oregon-American woods locomotive engineer before starting anew as a gyppo, was a pioneer in O-A's endeavor to recover marketable logs from the leave-behinds. Since Doyle had developed a reputation as an enterprising type, Greenman encouraged him to expand his operation into sawmilling in 1946. With some assistance from the company, Doyle purchased and set up a 10,000-board-foot-per-day portable sawmill on Spur 26-6 where he cut railroad ties and rough lumber from logs salvaged from O-A property. Doyle shipped the output from his mill to Vernonia where O-A sold it as company-produced lumber. Hendrickson Lumber Company established a similar operation in March 1949 when it set up shop on Spur 26-14. Oregon-American also helped finance the partnership of Vern Dusenberry and Verle DeVaney, who operated a small sawmill producing lumber from logs that came from the former Oregon Gas & Electric Company lands near Keasey. Although the sawmilling by independents on O-A lands experiment was short-lived, largely because 80 percent of the salvageable timber available was hemlock and generally failed to meet grade standards required to mix with O-A's regular lumber, salvage logging operations continued for years.

To the extent possible, purchases from independent suppliers offset O-A's overall log shortage problem. This program alone accounted for up to 40

THE GLORY YEARS

A Natt McDougall Company earth-mover climbing out of the big hairpin curve that crossed the West Fork of the North Fork of the Salmonberry River canyon. O-A hired McDougall and the Williams Construction Company to build both truck roads and the railroad rights-of-way during 1947–48 as the company sought to expand logging following WWII. (H. Brown photograph; Stephen Waite collection)

percent of total logs cut in the Vernonia sawmill in years during and after WWII and, while failing to provide anything near the ability of the mill to produce to capacity, it extended the life of the operation by several more years as these logs came from stands other than O-A's. Acquisition of logs from independent sources became such an important part of O-A's log supply that it hired a full-time log-buyer in April 1951.

Truck Logging

While securing the balance of the Ruth Realty timber in the Yerreck tract enabled Oregon-American to log the balance of the Southwest Unit timber in the most desirable order, the stiff challenge of extending railroad Spur 26-8 southward down the North Fork of the Salmonberry River canyon remained. Through the end of WWII, every indication pointed toward an extension of the railroad.

In fact, O-A began scouring the used locomotive market for additional motive power needed to shuttle logs between the southern fringes of the company's property and mainline Spur 26 as early as 1941.

Uncertainties surrounding O-A's acquisition of the remaining Ruth timber prevented the company from actively developing the extension of Spur 26-8 until after the war. Once hostilities ceased, the economics of logging changed almost overnight. For example, not only did it usher in an era of cheap war-surplus equipment, it also signaled the return of heavy equipment manufacturers to the commercial marketplace. Combined with the availability of improved roads, these forces quickly established an industry trend toward transporting logs by truck rather than by rail. Wholesale replacement of its sunk investment into existing railroad equipment and facilities made conversion to truck logging economically unfeasible for Oregon-American. However, transporting logs from distant places via trucks to a central collection point presented the company with a ready-made solution to the troublesome extension of railroad Spur 26-8.

Several key factors influenced the Company's attitude toward truck logging. First, extending Spur 26-8 as a truck road eliminated the need to build three, tall railroad trestles aggregating nearly 1,000 feet in length to ford parts of the canyon. O-A estimated the construction costs for the trestles alone at $180,000, an amount for which they could build miles of truck roads. Rough terrain and the inability to get the railroad close enough to the stump also meant an increase in the number of three-donkey hauls needed to get the logs to the railhead. The company estimated that the added cost was another $135,000.

Although the economics clearly favored extending Spur 26-8 as a truck road instead of a rail line, the real impetus lay in the fact that truck roads could reach areas containing higher quality fir logs a full year earlier than it would have taken to build the railroad. Given the overall log shortage situation and the lesser amount of high-quality fir in the Yerreck tract, the benefits of truck logging were impossible to ignore.

By July 1947 company officials had finally concluded to break with the all-railroad tradition and began laying the groundwork for a reloading station at the terminus of existing railroad Spur 26-8, in the SENE of Section 2, Twp. 3 North, Range 7 West, and commence with a truck logging program from that point south. Once fully developed, the trucking program would grow to account for one-half the company's total log production.

As for extending the railroad mainline Spur 26 and its off-spurs, the delay in securing the balance of the Yerreck tract effectively stymied any opportunity for progress until May 1946. O-A hastened the railroad's extension by hiring Wornstaff and Barker to clear, grub, and grade the mainline and laterals 26-13, 26-13-A, B and C, and 26-14. Wornstaff and Barker lacked the resources needed to complete the task as fast as O-A desired, however. So, by April 1947, O-A hired the Williams Construction Company of Tigard and the Natt McDougall Company of Portland to extend the truck road on Spur 26-8 and the mainline railroad

O-A's first truck logging side. The company used its newest Cletrac fitted with Carcomatic triple drums to yard. One of the company's diesel conversion units handled the loading. The trucking contractor, C. N. Day Company of Salem, Oregon, hauled logs to the reload station at the end of the railroad Spur 26-8. (H. Brown photograph; Jim Blain collection)

THE GLORY YEARS

Top: A pair of C. N. Day Logging Company trucks heading toward the reload station on the Spur 26-8 truck road. Note the oversized log bunks. The terrain along the North Fork of the Salmonberry River canyon is rugged, and Oregon-American found it cheaper to move logs from the southernmost reaches of its property by truck rather than by railroad. Truck logging operations accounted for about half the company-produced logs between 1948 and 1956. (H. Brown photograph; Rose Valpiani collection)

§

Bottom: The reload residence. Immediately above the cabin is the vehicle road to Camp Olson. Above that is railroad Spur 26-8. (H. Brown photograph; Rose Valpiani collection).

Spur 26. The Natt McDougall Company was headed by the same Natt McDougall who had completed the PA&P, along with O-A's mainline to Camp McGregor and its Spur 5 system. After he left the A. Guthrie & Company, McDougall had formed his own operation in 1932.

Instead of building just enough rights-of-way to reach the next year's worth of logging, O-A chartered Williams and McDougall to complete nearly 10 miles, essentially the balance needed to complete logging not only the rest of the Yerreck tract, but O-A's Salmonberry Timber Company tract as well. The contractors completed these tasks by the end of the 1948 building season at a cost of $288,000. When completed, the combination of newly built vehicle roads, combined with abandoned railroad rights-of-way that Oregon-American had converted to vehicle roads on its property, totaled more than 78 miles.

Once the company had built enough truck roads to commence logging, Oregon-American contracted with Clarence N. Day of Salem, Oregon, to truck logs to the reload. Operations began on July 29, 1948. Besides providing the trucks and trailers to haul logs, the C. N. Day Company also supplied the labor at the unloading site. Oregon-American crews and equipment handled the logging and loading of the trucks. O-A completed support facilities for the reload operation by November 1948. They included a garage for two log trucks, a fuel storage tank, a water tank, sleeping quarters for two men, and a small family house for one of Day's employees. O-A also bought a newer road-grader for road maintenance purposes.

Truck logging offered O-A distinct advantages in removing logs from the Salmonberry River canyons, largely because trucks could negotiate

Two C. N. Day Company trucks at the Spur 26-8 reload. Here O-A dumped the loads and reloaded the logs on disconnected trucks for their final movement to Vernonia. Oregon-American crews handled the logging and Day's trucks hauled the logs to the reload. At the left is one of O-A's three-drum Willamette loading engines shortly after the company converted it from steam to diesel power. (H. Brown photograph; Stephen Waite collection)

much steeper grades and tighter turns. In some instances Day's trucks had to climb unfavorable ruling grades well more than 7 percent and descend favorable ruling grades of up to 20 percent. Moving loads sometimes demanded the use of "snap trucks," essentially the double-heading of a single load of logs with two tractor trucks. During favorable weather conditions Day's trucks delivered an average of twenty loads per day to the reload.

Diesel Technology Comes of Age in the Oregon-American Woods

Equipping the company's oldest Cletrac tractor with a triple-drum Carco hoist added yet another dimension to the log-getting process. When originally outfitted with the triple-drum hoist in October 1945, O-A put the so-called drum-cat to work chunking-out rights-of-way and cold-decking logs. Soon it proved its worth yarding small hemlock. The machine and a crew of eight loaded out a record 79,000 board feet per day on Spur 26-10 and was so successful that by February 1946, the company bought an internal-combustion-engined loader to complement the cat logging operation.

By the time WWII ended O-A's experience with diesel donkeys had whetted the company's appetite for more. The machines' performance had been stellar and set the stage for replacing as many of the aging Willamette steam donkeys as possible. Recognizing the superior design of the triple drum set on its Willamette steam loaders, O-A placed orders to have two of them converted to diesel power by Loggers & Contractors Machinery Company in early 1946. Loggers & Contractors' conversion units used

THE GLORY YEARS

Top: The reload in full swing during the early days of its life. On the right, a converted diesel loading engine relieved a C. N. Day truck of its load while the steam pot behind the tree on the left moved a log from the pile to an awaiting pair of disconnects.

To save labor, O-A soon replaced the steam donkey with a diesel. The company also abandoned the crotch-line loading rig-up shown here in favor of a heel-boom. (H. Brown photograph; Rose Valpiani collection)

§

Middle and bottom: A crew transloading one of O-A's diesel conversion yarders from the donkey moving car to a C. N. Day truck for transport to a new landing out on the truck road. Those oversized bunks on the truck and trailer came in handy. The yarder itself weighed about 75 tons. (Betty Blumenthal collection)

single, rebuilt Cummins model HB1, diesel power plants, each having 150 horsepower. L&C matched the engines with four-speed Fuller transmissions and mounted them on L-beam frames equipped with radiators, fans, batteries, starters, sprockets, chain drives, and air controls. Costing $4,500 each, O-A installed the power units on donkey engines 2358 and 2061 in the Vernonia machine shop after the boilers and steam engines were removed. The conversion projects commenced in April 1946.

Attention then focused on converting a yarding engine to diesel, and on November 15, 1946, O-A ordered a Loggers & Contractors conversion unit for engine 2504. The conversion unit for this yarder had two new Hercules model DFXH, 240-horsepower diesels equipped with Twin Disc hydraulic couplings. L&C installed the power units, sprockets, chains, and air supply on heavier, I-beam chassis and delivered them to Vernonia where the conversion was completed. The conversion of loader Number 2062 followed this in 1947. L&C

equipped it with a 200-horsepower diesel power plant. In 1948, the converted Number 2062 had a brake flange added to its main drum that enabled it to operate as a small yarder.

The company's decision to truck log gave added impetus to the diesel conversion program. Without a nearby railroad to help justify the bother of supplying water, O-A completely ruled out the use of steam yarders remote from the truck landings. The company required, all told, three yarding engines and a loader for the truck logging program. Two of the yarders moved logs while the loggers used the third one for rigging ahead.

The yarder conversion program was limited to surplus Willamette, air-controlled units O-A had on its roster and, finding themselves short on that account in early November 1947, the company was left to decide whether to make their next conversion yarder a gear-shifted machine in contrast to one equipped with a torque-converter or another type of hydraulic coupling. Wanting some operating experience before making a final decision, O-A decided to use its BX-350-TC Skagit yarder when truck logging commenced, so this machine served to round out the initial complement of yarding machines for the truck operation. By April 1948 the company had gained sufficient experience with the second conversion yarder to make it clear that engine 2504's friction drive coupling system left much to be desired, so O-A returned the machine to Vernonia and Loggers & Contractors replaced the original system with air clutches and torque converters.

The company also deployed its drum-cat to the truck road operation and at times it accounted for up to fifteen carloads per day. Based on the satisfactory results gained from the original system, a triple-drum setup was added to another bulldozer in mid-August 1948.

They logged a lot of odd corners with the triple-drum Cletrac. Some were pretty good sized settings. It could reach out 1,200 feet, 2,400 feet if you logged in a circle. That's where some of the hanky-panky came in because all of that got reported as skidder production.

The tower skidder was Andy Olson's pet and all that bragging about its production was politics. That skidder wasn't as hot as they let on that it was.

George Lee, construction

Given the excellent profits of 1948 and 1949, the company's desire for additional internal combustion yarding engines prompted O-A to purchase new machines instead of converting more of its old steam units. The first of the new machines, a Berger Engineering Works, Inc. Model BD-250, arrived from Seattle in early June 1949. (See Appendix A for performance comparisons.) The Berger yarder exceeded expectations, and on February 10, 1950, O-A purchased a second Berger. Oregon-American traded its Skagit diesel conversion unit, the Model BX-350-TC in the deal. Testimony to O-A's complete satisfaction with the new machines was evident in Greenman's letter to Berger on January 11, 1951, *We have had two of your splendid Berger donkeys in service quite awhile now.... We don't need to be sold with the good qualities of the Berger donkey. We think we have two of the best donkeys that ever were built in the northwest in these two Berger machines. We are very proud of them.* O-A also extended the diesel conversion program

Opposite page: The Lidgerwood tower skidder at work on the Spur 26 mainline north of the junction of Spur 26-15 on October 1, 1948. Note the carriage that ran along a tight skyline. The tower and tree-rigged skidders both provided superior lift and reach in rugged terrain. However, the Lidgerwood could only handle logs up to 64 feet in length compared with the 80-foot length that O-A's other equipment could handle. The company had to increase its bucking pay rates to compensate for the shorter lengths.

The Lidgerwood moved on special trucks. Note the extensive cribbing beneath the skidder. Once positioned, internal jacks raised and leveled the machine. If needed, crews could raise it high enough to allow empty disconnects to pass underneath, thus allowing the spur it resided on to also serve as a tail track. (H. Brown photograph; Jim Blain collection)

to some railroad construction equipment as well. By 1950, the company removed the boiler from its piledriver and replaced it with a diesel engine.

The final addition to Oregon-American's diesel yarding complement came on December 10, 1951, with the purchase of a Skagit Mobile Logger Model SJ8-W. O-A used this portable outfit primarily to log short corners.

The Lidgerwood Tower Skidder

The terrain over which railroad Spur 26, soon to become known as the "High Line," crossed, featured many steep drop-offs, sometimes to both sides of the tracks. As such, finding enough room to build off-spurs was difficult. Sometimes, loggers had no choice but to create logging sides in a leapfrog manner, one after the other along the single right-of-way.

The Ruth stand, through which the High Line traveled, ran heavily to hemlock, and to smaller trees at that. Not only did this make for more difficult logging shows, but also it made it more difficult to gain on the log shortage problem. To illustrate, the company logged stands carrying more than 100,000 board feet to the acre in 1940 and 1941. Timber in the Yerreck stand, however, yielded an average of only 60,000 board feet to the acre. When O-A returned the tree-rigged skidder to service in the spring of 1946, the poor logging chance caused its output to decrease to only 160,000 board feet per day, down from 200,000 feet per day in 1941.

Still, with its tight skyline, longer reach, and ability to bring logs directly to track side without relying on a remote donkey to yard its logs, the skidder was the most suitable machine for logging those situations. As it became apparent the company's log shipments were going to become increasingly dependent on that single machine, and that its production was unlikely to improve because of the poor stand, O-A began to search for a second skidder.

After passing on machines offered by Eastern and Western Lumber Company and Long-Bell, attention finally centered on a Lidgerwood tower skidder at Crown Zellerbach's Cathlamet Washington, operation. Crown Zellerbach had modified this unit extensively in 1940 by replacing the skidding engine's original piston valves and cylinders with 12½ × 14 models manufactured by Washington Iron Works. Extending its flues from their original 7-foot, 6-inch length to 10 feet also had improved the unit's steaming capacity.

The Lidgerwood tower skidder was a self-contained unit complete with its own loading boom and a massive steel spar that crews could raise and lower whenever they moved the machine. These integral loading boom and spar features offered some distinct advantages because when conditions prevented yarding in full circles, crews could move and rig-up the unit at new landings more quickly. The Lidgerwood was not without its drawbacks, however. While the Willamette tree-rigged skidder could yard and load logs up to 80 feet in length, the tower skidder could only handle logs up to 64 feet. Nonetheless, Oregon-American bought the Lidgerwood machine and took delivery via the SP&S at Keasey on Friday, December 13, 1946. After reoutfitting, O-A put the unit to work on Spur 26-13 in February 1947. By the time O-A put the machine to work it cost the company more than $32,000, nearly half of which was for wire rope alone.

A REVITALIZED LABOR MOVEMENT

The same war-mobilization effort that had so radically rechanneled the country's industrial output also brought to heel the militant attitude that char-

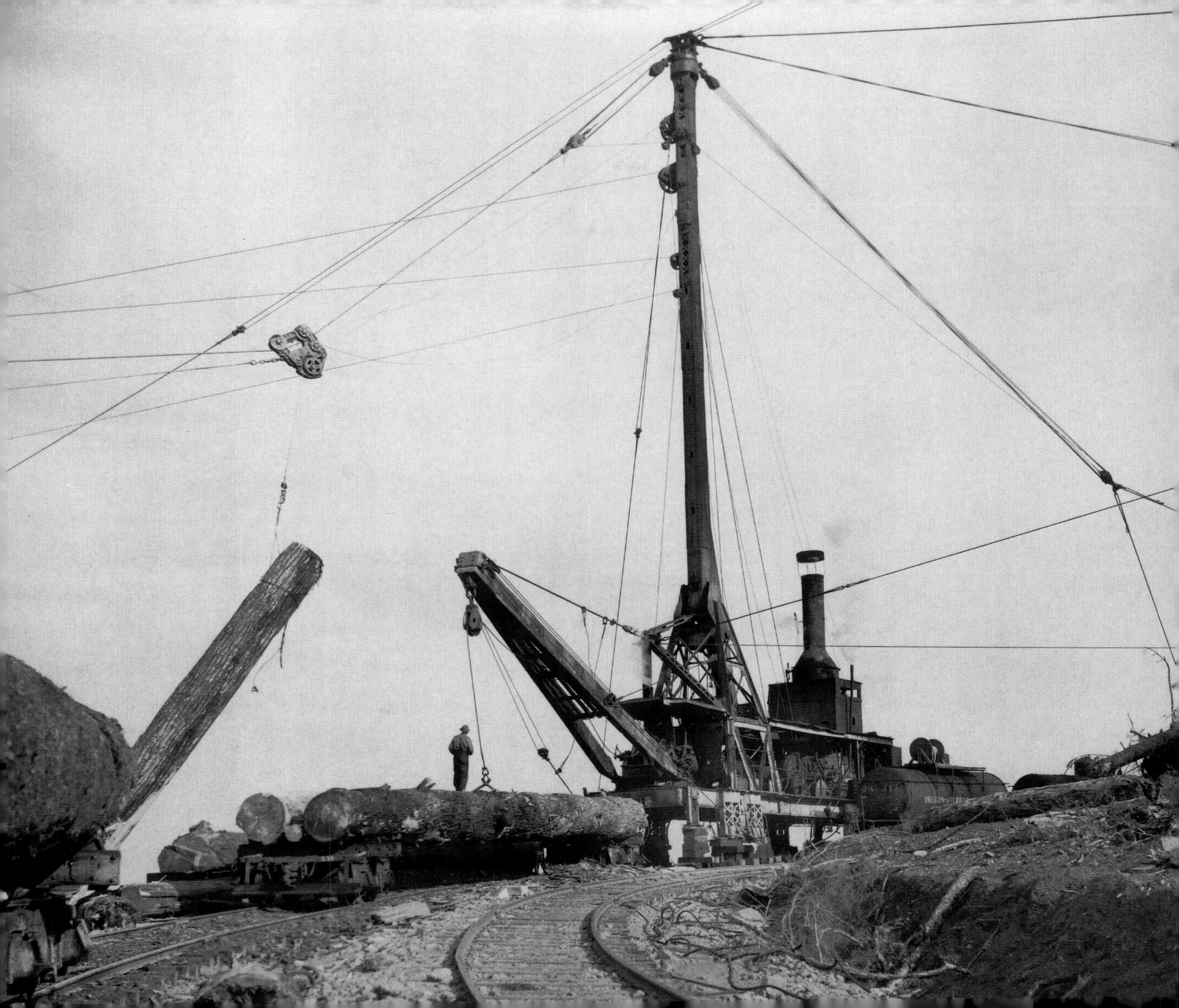

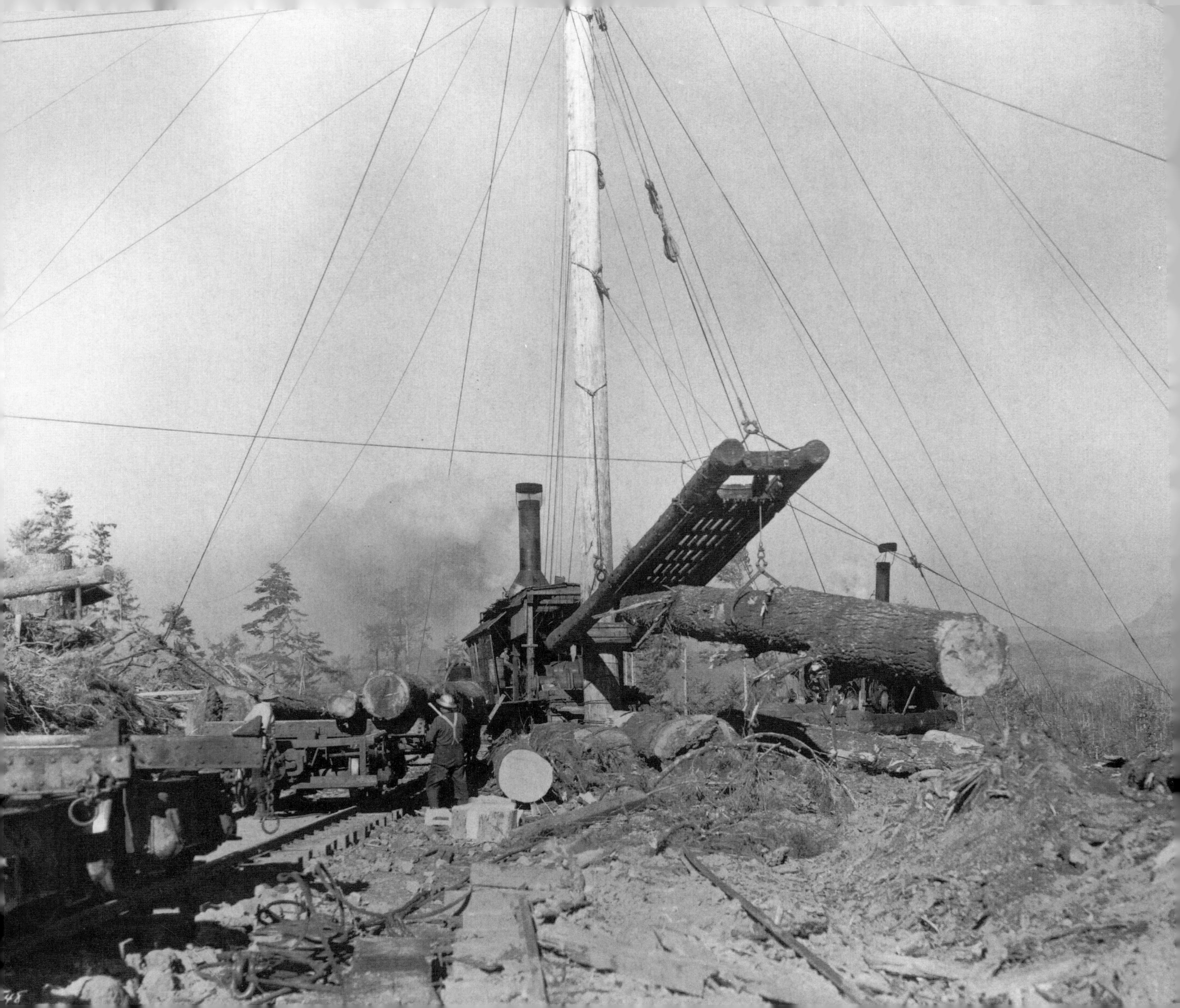

acterized the post-Depression labor movement. During that period, organized labor's disputes with employers came under the jurisdiction of the War Labor Board. The WLB used a carrot-and-stick approach by granting higher wages in return for the forty-eight-hour workweek, pay instead of vacations, and other concessions. It also convinced unions to cede to a "no-strike" policy and successfully averted major labor disturbances of the type that so typified the movement in the late 1930s.

Yet while the war years might have given the outward appearance of labor peace, government-mandated restrictions did nothing to quell organized labor's desire for a larger slice of the economic pie. Thus it was no surprise that once the War Labor Board passed out of the picture, organized labor quickly began to reassert itself. This was especially true in the lumber industry where postwar profits exceeded the norm and made it an inviting target. The itch to make up for lost time developed quickly in the rank and file and the incidence of "quickie" strikes increased dramatically in the months immediately following Japan's surrender. Contract negotiations took on a similarly hard line as well.

Against this backdrop, unions representing loggers discovered a potential windfall in a highly controversial federal Wage and Hour Administration interpretation of the 1938 Fair Labor Standards Act governing time-and-a-half pay for overtime work. That interpretation claimed the western logging industry had failed to pay overtime rates to loggers as they traveled to and from work on company-provided transportation. The fact that the administration's findings were based on a study made in 1940 but were not made public until after the war, presented a particularly vexing problem to employers. Since the industry had routinely not paid for travel time before, during, or after the 1940 study, the exposure for unpaid time would have been astronomical if the courts ultimately upheld the administration's interpretation.

On learning of the Wage and Hour Administration's finding, CIO unions representing loggers lost no time orchestrating a strategy to capitalize on the opportunity. Coordinated by the Portland law firm of Greene and Landye, various local unions sued a select group of employers for those presumably underpaid. By virtue of the fact Oregon-American conveyed its logging crews to and from work solely by logging train and statistics were therefore easy to compile, the company was again singled out by the CIO, this time as a travel time test case. IWA Local 5-37 sued Oregon-American for 143 current and former employees, claiming time spent riding the log train to work and back constituted work under the Wage and Hour Administration's interpretation. The suit claimed back pay damages amounting to nearly $1.5 million, dating from 1939.

The Oregon-American case, and a similar one brought against the St. Paul & Tacoma Lumber Company, galvanized industry management to action. Faced with an exposure estimated to be as high as $120 million, employers quickly mobilized a lobbying effort at Washington, D.C. to have the Wage and Hour Administration's ruling overruled. Neither court actions nor lobbying efforts did much to settle the matter, however, and only after the federal government passed the so-called portal-to-portal bill in May 1947 did any clear sense of direction develop. That bill established guidelines for travel time pay that effectively undermined the entire basis of the union claims for back pay, and by August of that year, the courts dismissed the case against Oregon-American.

Opposite page: In view of Saddle Mountain to the right, the Willamette tree-rigged skidder and a steam loader labored on Spur 26-13-A. The stand here was small, consisting largely of Western hemlock. O-A sent most of its hemlock to Crown Zellerbach as pulp logs. In return, Crown provided Oregon-American fir logs from its Pebble Creek tract.

Due to the lack of large trees in the area, loggers had to bring the spar tree from somewhere else and raise it. (H. Brown photograph; Rose Valpiani collection)

THE GLORY YEARS

Scenes of the Lidgerwood tower skidder at work on Spur 26-19 in 1952. (Ralph Swan photographs)

A New Camp

When Oregon-American reopened in 1936, financial burdens facing the company made it impossible to rebuild the moveable logging camps. By 1940, therefore, the company's loggers often had to travel up to 10 miles between Camp McGregor and work. Although the company's financial picture had improved by then, war-related material shortages coupled with uncertainties surrounding the acquisition of the Yerreck tract timber from Ruth Realty derailed any plans the company had to move its camp closer to the woods. In a development related to the improvement of vehicle roads and the abandonment of civilian rationing programs that immediately followed the end of the war, loggers also found it increasingly convenient to abandon life at remote camps and commute from their homes. As these changes took hold, operators soon quit moving their camp sites as logging grew ever more remote from the mills. In fact, since more than half the industry's woods workers were commuting to work from their own homes, logging camps were simply beginning to disappear altogether.

The pending travel time lawsuit and the company's desire to limit potential future liability led Oregon-American to buck that trend and break ground for a new camp shortly after the 1947 winter shutdown. Located in Section 26, Twp. 4 North, Range 7 West, along mainline Spur 26 some 7 miles southwest of Camp McGregor, Camp Olson, named after logging superintendent Andrew Olson, was opened following the July 1947 vacation shutdown.

Bunkhouses for single men were loaded on disconnected trucks at Camp McGregor and moved up the hill. The company built a new dining room and blacksmith's shop on the site. Railcar-mounted support facilities, including offices and housing for

The cut on the horseshoe curve below the Lost 40 slid during the winter of 1949. George Lee was clearing the mess using a small shovel mounted on a flatcar when the hillside really let go. He narrowly escaped getting buried alive. He returned with the big shovel to right the equipment and then reopened the line. (Emily Peterson collection)

the cooks and dining room staff from Camp McGregor, were also moved to the new camp. O-A completed construction of Camp Olson by the end of September 1947. Camp McGregor remained an active community, however. Families and the grade school were far too entrenched to uproot, so daily train transportation service continued between there and the woods.

RAILROAD OPERATIONS

Completion of the Wolf Creek Highway and a willingness by Oregon-American's suppliers to make direct truck deliveries to the company's warehouse, cold-storage plant, and fuel-oil depot near the Overhead Crossing accelerated the demise of inbound rail traffic to Vernonia and beyond. Except for a water tank and two storage tracks, the SP&S had all but abandoned its facilities at Keasey by the end of WWII. Since the only remaining traffic west of Vernonia was the Oregon-American log train, the railway company had a strong incentive to increase the train-mile rate that had been in effect since 1924. SP&S offset what reluctance O-A might have had to the fifty cents per car rate increase by agreeing to buy 1,000 ties annually for maintenance on that part of the line. When it agreed to the new

THE GLORY YEARS

Right: Train 105 eastbound negotiating the horseshoe curves on mainline Spur 26 just below the Lost 40. (H. Brown photographs; Stephen Waite collection)

§

Opposite page: Camp Olson viewed from Spur 26-13-A. Mainline Spur 26 ran through camp from right to left. Joe Doyle's portable sawmill on Spur 26-6 was above and to the right of camp.

Doyle, a former company locomotive engineer, began salvaging logs Oregon-American had left behind when marginal grades of lumber could not find a market. As good logs became more scarce, Doyle and others recovered the former rejects adding to O-A's overall log supply. With backing from the company, it was a natural adjunct to Doyle's business for him to saw the stuff. He sent his output to Vernonia where O-A intermingled and marketed it as company lumber. (H. Brown photograph; Jim Blain collection)

terms on July 1, 1946, Oregon-American also assumed complete responsibility for upkeep and maintenance of the telephone and telegraph wires between Vernonia and Keasey.

When the railway company converted to diesel power in 1952, O-A had to assume responsibility for the Keasey water tower. As the end of all operations on the line began to loom on the horizon, provisions were also set in place to renegotiate the trackage rate for O-A log trains after 1954. Despite these steps to put the Vernonia line's finances on a paying basis, the SP&S continued to minimize its maintenance outlay on the route. Consequently, O-A found it necessary to do

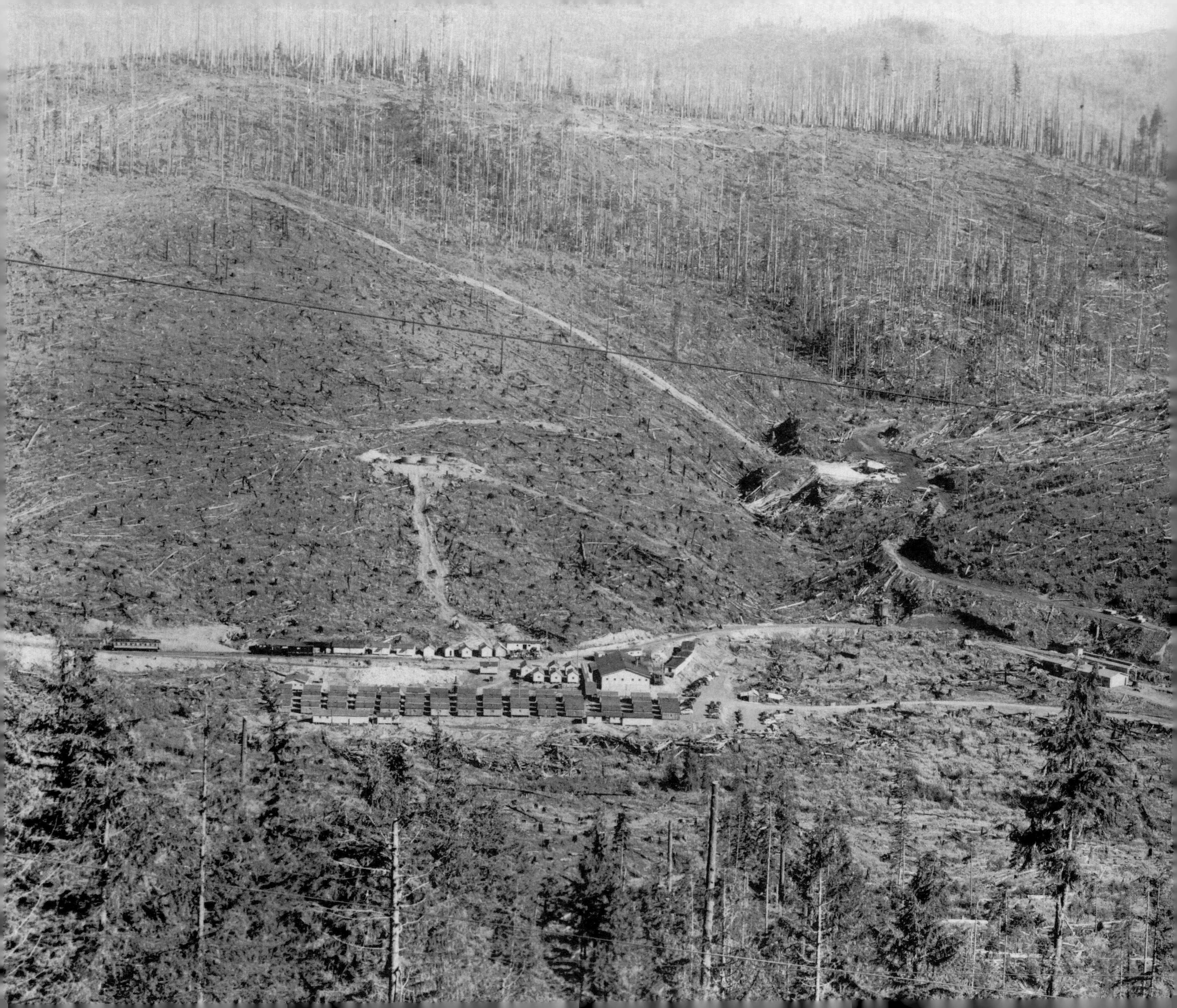

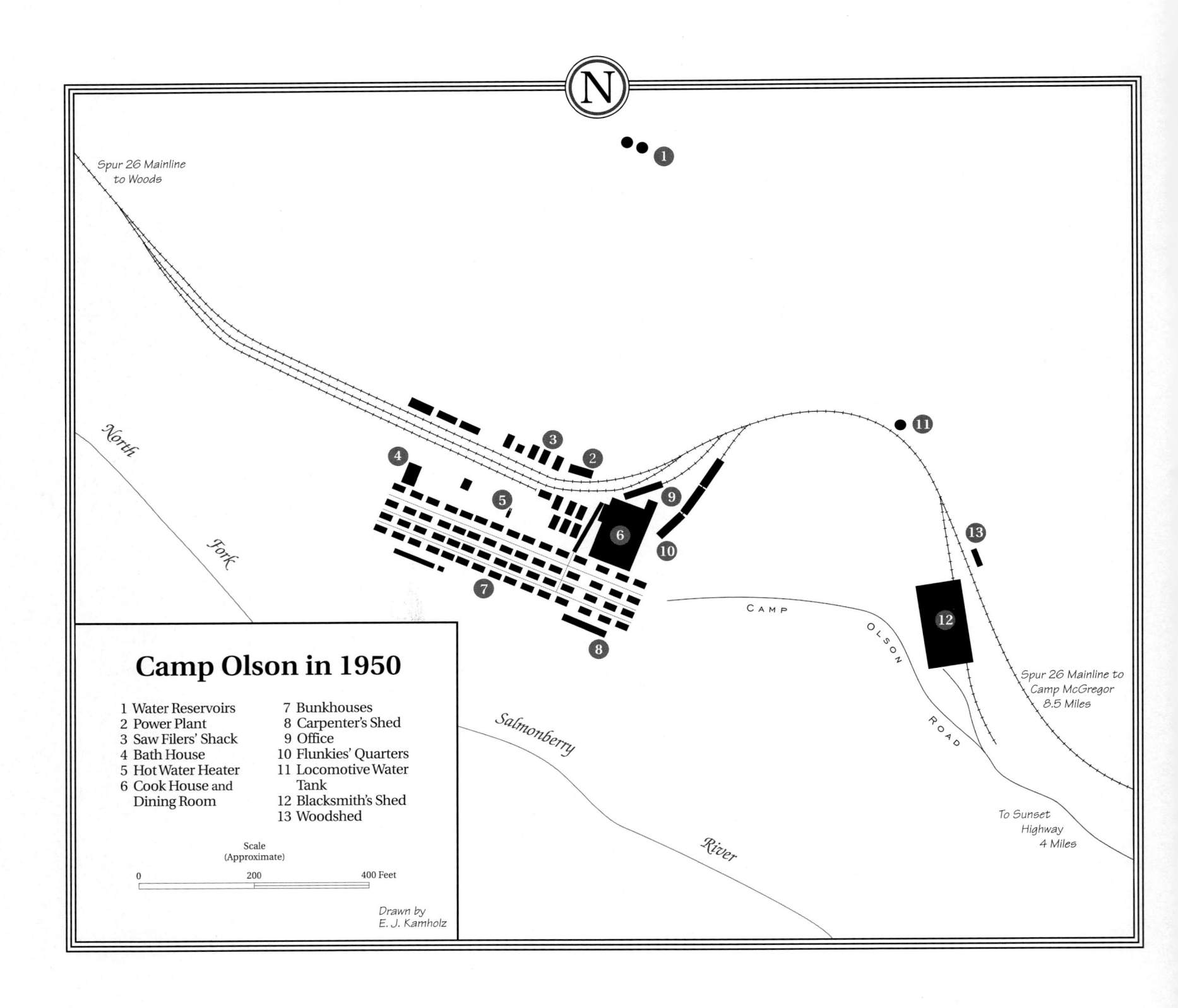

Camp Olson in 1950

1. Water Reservoirs
2. Power Plant
3. Saw Filers' Shack
4. Bath House
5. Hot Water Heater
6. Cook House and Dining Room
7. Bunkhouses
8. Carpenter's Shed
9. Office
10. Flunkies' Quarters
11. Locomotive Water Tank
12. Blacksmith's Shed
13. Woodshed

Scale (Approximate): 0 — 200 — 400 Feet

Drawn by E. J. Kamholz

Spur 26 Mainline to Woods

North Fork

Salmonberry River

Camp Olson Road

Spur 26 Mainline to Camp McGregor 8.5 Miles

To Sunset Highway 4 Miles

The blacksmith's shop at Camp Olson. (Vernon Goe photograph; John T. Labbe collection)

periodic, unauthorized work on the mill yard tracks to overcome the railway company's neglect.

Direct Shipment of Pulp Logs from Woods to Rafton

Once operations in the Yerreck tract began in earnest, O-A found it was logging almost pure stands of hemlock and white fir. To avoid the bother of segregating saw logs in the Vernonia pond, the company, for a brief period, carried out a program of loading pulp species logs directly on common-carrier cars in the woods. The added expense of bucking logs to 40 feet in the woods, coupled with meeting SP&S's more stringent loading requirements, limited this program to about 1 million board feet of logs, however. The drum-cat handled all the yarding and loading.

The Motive Power Crisis

Accelerating the right-of-way construction program began paying log production dividends by year-end 1947. However, as more logging sides began operating, keeping enough locomotives in working condition to move the increased log production proved problematical. By then Oregon-

Once up there at Camp Olson, all the guys got a case of the runs. So, they had a union meeting about it. Then they went to Andy. That water is contaminated. We want a purification system. Andy talked it over with Greenman and pretty soon here comes a chlorinator.

The carpenters built a little concrete base and a doghouse over it and I assembled the equipment in my spare time.

Well, one night after supper there's a big inspection committee come out there to look it over and everything. I had it all set up except I hadn't turned on the juice yet. They never noticed it wasn't runnin.' Right away, everyone started feelin' better.

Oh, they'd talk about it on the job how much better they were feelin' since that chlorinator was put in. I didn't activate it for another two weeks. Andy and I had a lot of big laughs over that one.

George Lee, construction

American had put off renewing the tubes on locomotives 103 and 106 for so long that the company's insurers were pressing to have the work completed. The 105 was due for an overhaul too, only adding to the problem.

THE GLORY YEARS

Top: This could almost pass as a builder's photograph but was taken in June 1953 when the 105 was more than 28 years old. It graphically illustrates the pride Oregon-American took in the appearance of its equipment. A. C. "Chet" Alexander was the engineer and Howard Colvin the fireman. Alexander operated the main line haul between the woods and Vernonia the entire life of the operation. (Jim Blain photograph)

§

Bottom: Early in 1948 O-A had to overhaul many of its locomotives. By then, logging operations were more than 25 miles from Vernonia. Because of a shortage of motive power, the company had to lease an SP&S 0-6-0 switch engine.

The Number 5, lacking an engine truck and trailing truck, derailed more often than O-A's engines. Because of this, loggers called it the "mole." (Oregon Historical Society, DHR SP&S 5A)

O-A brought shay 103 to the Vernonia machine shop first, and by February 20, 1948, work on it had been completed. The company shopped locomotive 105, the irreplaceable workhorse that moved the logs from the woods to Vernonia, next in anticipation of the heavy hauling season ahead. By then, the main-line haul often began the run to Vernonia at Shields where woods locomotives brought loads from the woods for the hand-off. Shields was 20 miles from Vernonia, so the side-tanker 104, the only other Interstate Commerce Commission-certified locomotive on O-A's roster, could not make this run without stopping for water. So, when O-A shopped the 105 in March, Oregon-American leased a tender-equipped switch engine from the SP&S to handle the mainline haul until work on it and the 106 could be completed. The company figured both jobs would be finished around July 1, 1948.

The SP&S Number 5, a 75-ton 0-6-0, had a driving wheelbase slightly longer than O-A's rod engines. However, once it had successfully negotiated the curve at Twin Bridges, the sharpest on the mainline, confidence the switcher could operate anywhere on the system grew. As a precaution, however, O-A restricted its movement beyond the vicinity of Shields except for emergencies. After several weeks on duty, the switcher proved satisfactory and the company made plans to keep it for the time it took to complete rehabilitation on the 105 and 106. Even so, the SP&S Number 5, lacking an engine truck and trailing truck, had a pronounced tendency to derail. While in O-A service it thus earned the dubious title of the "mole" owing to how much time it spent on the ground.

The 105 was out-shopped and broken in for a week on the Vernonia-to-Shields run beginning on May 3, 1948. The 5-Spot was tied-up during that week. On May 10, O-A put the 105 on the swing run from Camp Olson to Shields and returned the switcher to work between Shields and Vernonia. O-A brought the 106 to Vernonia for repairs on May 7, 1948. Although perhaps less than ideal, that arrangement at least maintained a supply of logs to Vernonia.

The Wreck of the 104

At 8:30 A.M. on Thursday, June 3, 1948, its motive power stretched to the limit, Oregon-American suffered the worst calamity of its operating history. A compilation of Greenman's reports to the board and others describe the events of the day:

> After operating for 25 years and hauling about 2 billion feet of logs without a serious railroad accident, we had one yesterday which more than made up for all of our previous good experience.
>
> Our train Number 104, comprised of a rod locomotive, an empty oil car and thirteen big cars of logs, was stopped on a fairly steep grade about one mile west of Camp Olson by the section foreman while he completed some repairs to the track. That the train was in perfect mechanical condition is evidenced by the fact that all witnesses agree it was stopped without the slightest difficulty.
>
> When the train started again, it almost immediately gained excessive speed; quickly getting out of control and reaching such speed that after a half-mile run down the grade the locomotive, because of its great speed, jumped the track on a curve and overturned, instantly killing the fireman and timekeeper who was riding on the locomotive and so seriously scalding and shocking the engineer that he died within an hour on the way to the hospital.
>
> The damage to the train, while extensive, is partially insured, the locomotive and the oil car being covered against damage resulting from collision or derailment. The thirteen sets of logging trucks are not insured but those things are so constructed that extensive damage is almost impossible.
>
> I now estimate the total damage to the equipment and track at $15,000, of which probably $10,000 will be covered by insurance.
>
> After careful investigation, I am confident we will never completely understand the cause of this catastrophe because of the conflicting statements about it. To illustrate, before he died the engineer said the train ran away because the brakemen had not set up enough brakes. On the other hand, the brakemen contend the train ran away because the engineer started out too fast.
>
> Regardless of the cause, the incident is a shocking one and extremely regrettable because of the fine character of the men who were killed and the upsetting consequences within the organization of such an occurrence.
>
> Incidentally, to support the statement that it was not a lack of training or experience which caused the wreck, I added up the aggregate years of logging railroad experience put in by the five men

THE GLORY YEARS

Thursday, June 3, 1948, locomotive 104, tank car OALX 107 and thirteen big loads of logs were backing down mainline Spur 26 toward Camp Olson when a section gang stopped the train on the 6 percent grade. When allowed to continue, the train got away. The brakemen jumped but the engineer, the fireman, and a timekeeper rode it out in the cab. All three were killed when the entire train derailed at the junction of Spur 26-8, more than a half-mile down the hill.

§

This page, top: What might have been lacking in clarity was more than made up for in drama when Arlie Sliffe took this photograph from the cab roof of the 105 only moments after the wreck. Steam was still escaping from the 104's broken pipes as help climbed up to the wrecked locomotive's cab. The tank car on its side to the left had been in the lead and leveled an unoccupied scalers' shack. (Arlie Sliffe photographs; John T. Labbe collection)

Opposite page, bottom continued: Logs surrounded the 104. The impact drove one completely through the smokebox door.

Members of 105's train crew were waiting for the 104 at Camp Olson and claimed they heard 104 working steam before it wrecked. Apparently the engineer made a desperate attempt to slow the train by reversing the locomotive. The valve gear is in the forward position and corroborates their story. (Herb Erickson collection)

§

This page, top: The 104's sand dome cap lying next to the track in front of the disconnect in the foreground suggests this was where it left the rails. In the background, the 103 has inched down to the scene. (Arlie Sliffe photograph; Jim Blain collection)

§

This page, bottom: After the debris was removed the extent of the 104's damages became more apparent. (A. Sliffe photograph; Jim Blain collection)

271

operating this train and they come to more than 120 years, the minimum experience of any of them according to our records, having been nineteen years, while the engineer had worked in train service for almost forty years.

The men killed in this wreck were Jeff McGregor, Jerry Manning, and Frank Wills. The locomotive turned over at the curve on Spur 26 where Spur 26-8 leaves the main spur. Logs from the cars plowed through the bunkhouse stationed near the Spur 26-8 switch. The wreck was pretty well cleaned up last night so the track can be repaired and we will be able to resume operations Monday morning, June 7th, probably maintaining adequate train service by running the 103 at night, with a night shift, having her work empties up the hill.

Dave [Marshall, machine shop foreman] thinks he can get 106 out of the shop by Saturday, June 12th. We can't tell yet how much of a job we will have on the 104, but surprisingly the engine seems to me to be damaged less than one would think after this experience.

Greenman also wrote the Clatsop County Deputy County Coroner that day:

As I promised you I would, I talked with two of the three brakemen involved in the train wreck... about the cause of the wreck. I did not get signed statements from them because both of them were badly upset and I did not want to press them for information while they were as nervous as they were. The third brakeman did not appear for questioning at my request so I got no statement from him.

The statements of Bob Woods, head brakeman, and William Huber, rear brakeman, coincide in general and were to the effect that the train was

Arlie Sliffe took those pictures? Well, no wonder. When it happened I was building the road into Camp Olson. Here came Andy. He was very upset. Yorge. We had a big accident. 104 tipped over up there. We need the crane. We need the bulldozer. Come on with me.

There was another cat close to camp. I loaded it on the flatcar, fired up the crane and rolled it right down around the bend to the Spur 8 junction. Those pictures had already been taken before I got there. See all that mess? I unstacked all those logs and threw them out to one side and then unloaded the cat.

Them three guys were still in there yet. I had to put the cat line around the 104's oil tank to pull it away from the boiler to get 'em out. Then my helper and I packed 'em out and laid 'em in a row there. They were still in that locomotive when those pictures were taken.

The engineer wasn't alive when I got there. He got half-way out the cab window and that's as far as he made it. He was cooked. You don't get two hundred pounds of live steam goin' on you and survive. The timekeeper, ol' Frank Wills, he was just squashed right between the boiler and the tank. The other guys, they weren't squashed, they were just cooked.

I inherited that job, packing them guys out of that. Didn't like it either.

Then I bulldozed all that track that got mangled up right out into the brush. Graded it down flat. The track gang came in with a carload of new ties and placed them all down and spiked the rails on 'em and made a skeleton track. They had their big track lining bars and ol' Andy, he's back there lookin' it over and then he'd motion to 'em, three, four, or five of them guys with the bars. They pry that whole track, ties and all, until it finally suited him. Then they took the 106, hung a block on a stump and ran a line from it and got a hold around the dome. I got on the other side of the 104 with the cat and snubbed it. They pulled it up with the 106. We tipped it up and when it went over it clicked right on the rails. Ol' Andy, he knew his stuff.

With thirteen loads behind you, that's a lot of weight pushin'. The hotter the brakeshoes get, the more they swell up, the tighter they get. You stop for ten minutes and they cool off and then they all loosen up at the same time, they release. So then if you're on a steep grade and it takes off, you know, like nothing to sixty in so many seconds.

Anyway, that train took off and the brakemen could not reset the brakes. The train picked up too much speed and they couldn't do it. They really tried though.

George Lee, construction

signaled to a stop by the section foreman about in the middle of a mile-long grade where the track-repair men were working. The train came to a full stop without any difficulty whatsoever; stood for about five minutes while the track repairs were completed, and then started out down the remainder of the grade which at that point and on down the hill ranged from five to six percent, being six percent on the straight-of-ways and five percent on the curves where it is compensated.

The statements of both brakeman is that the train started out too fast after its stop and within a few hundred feet was traveling so fast they could not set up sufficient brakes to hold it.

I carefully examined the ground yesterday and was able to find physical evidence that the brakemen had been setting up brakes, but obviously they did not set up enough of them to hold the train or there would have been no run-a-way.

Opposed to the statement of the brakemen is the one made by the engineer before he died to the man who was accompanying him in the ambulance, in which statement Mr. McGregor said in effect that the train ran away because the brakemen did not set up enough brakes.

The tragedy shook everyone in the company from top to bottom. Just how much so was evident in several safety awareness incidents that arose in the days following the wreck. For example, on June 14, 1948, conductor Jack Heenan of train Number 105 reported overgrown grass on the mainline between the county line, and Shields and Greenman promptly ordered logging superintendent Olson to have the section crew tend to the problem because *we don't want any run-a-ways occurring because of grass on the track.* And at its June 15, 1948, meeting, the

THE GLORY YEARS

Top: Track crews had to restore the line before righting the engine. Railroad operations resumed by the following Monday. (Arlie Sliffe photograph; John T. Labbe collection)

§

Bottom: A squabble over insurance coverage delayed the 104's rehabilitation. O-A eventually gave the task to the SP&S's Vancouver, Washington, locomotive shop. The company loaded the engine on a heavy-duty flatcar and sent it to Vancouver on August 5, 1948. It returned to Vernonia under its own power on August 24, 1948, sporting a new smokebox, cab, deck, and paint job, among other items. (Fort Vancouver Historical Society)

Camp Olson Safety Committee announced availability of narcotics for the benefit of any man seriously injured or otherwise in great pain.

Repairing the 104

Restoration of the 104 required repair or replacement of many parts including a smokebox, front truck, cab and deck, turbo generator, headlight, injectors, five superheater units, and other incidental parts. Given its age and the fact that steam locomotives were rapidly becoming obsolete, the Baldwin Locomotive Works advised it would be unable to provide parts in less than four months. Nevertheless, enough steam locomotives were still in operation throughout the Pacific Northwest to warrant major repair facilities, so O-A sought bids from two in the Portland area, the SP&S and the Willamette Iron & Steel Works.

Finding a place to repair the 104 proved the least of O-A's troubles, however. Instead, the insurance company adjuster delayed the SP&S repair bid until he could determine when the damage from the wreck as opposed to damage that occurred beforehand. As the policy only covered damages arising from the derailment itself, not the flat spots the engineer had created on the driving wheels when

Former Union Pacific Railroad Number 61 at work at the Spur 26-8 reload. O-A purchased it for little more than scrap value in 1948. Renumbered 107, the big shay was kept busy until the Southwest Timber Unit played out in 1955. Engineer Oscar Farlin was at the controls this day while Eric Anderson fired. (Jim Blain photograph)

he had locked the brakes attempting to stop the train, the adjuster might have been justified for some delay. However, more than a month after the wreck the question remained unresolved. Greenman finally delivered an ultimatum to the adjuster on July 21, 1948:

> We are getting much disturbed over the fact that forty-eight days after locomotive 104 was wrecked it still stands here in our machine shop with no determination made of the manner in which it shall be repaired.
>
> Now, we like the S P & S Railroad. In fact, we probably like them much better than you do because our very life depends on them. On the other hand, we don't like them well enough to let them be the cause of interminable delay in making repairs to our damaged locomotive.
>
> If we do not have a specific proposal from the S P & S by Monday morning, July 26, we will load this locomotive and ship it to the Willamette Iron & Steel Company, of Portland, with instructions to them to repair it and return it to us as quickly as possible....
>
> We think our position in this respect is well justified by the fact we are spending $1,500 per month for locomotive rental while our damaged locomotive is out of service. We realize that this expenditure is no concern of yours or the insurer, but it very definitely is a concern of ours. We intend to cut this expenditure off just as quickly as possible.

The adjuster finally cleared the SP&S to respond to O-A's bid request on July 26.

The 104 was loaded on a 50-foot, 120,000-pound capacity flat car and shipped to the railway company's Vancouver, Washington, locomotive shop on

The 107 was distinctive because of its straight boiler. At some point before arriving in Vernonia, the UP had equipped it with an unusual application of power reverse gear. The engineer operated the controls. A rod traversing the backhead controlled the air cylinder on the fireman's side of the cab. (Jim Blain photograph)

August 5, 1948. Once shopped, the SP&S wasted no time making the repairs. On August 24, 1948, less than three weeks after being shipped out, the SP&S moved the 104 from Vancouver to Portland after which the locomotive proceeded to Vernonia under its own power. Oregon-American finally returned the SP&S switcher Number 5 to its owners in the local freight run of August 31, 1948. The SP&S repair bill for the 104 amounted to $8,608.98. In the end, only $225 of that bill were occasioned by the engineer's effort to prevent the locomotive from running away in the first place.

The Union Pacific Number 61

The 104 mishap and O-A's temporary shortage of motive power prompted Greenman to consider adding another engine to the company's locomotive roster. On June 8, 1948, the M. F. Brady Equipment Company of Portland alerted him that two Union Pacific shay locomotives, Road Numbers 59 and 61, were for sale. The heavier of the two, the Number 61, was, at the time, located at Tintic, Utah. By July 23, however, the flow of logs to Vernonia had resumed sufficiently that Greenman replied to Brady:

> We have come to the conclusion that we will not buy another locomotive.
> I have no doubt that the larger one of these two locomotives would be adapted to our service without great difficulty, but $9,500 is a relatively large sum to put into a piece of equipment which in just a few years will, in our opinion, have nothing more than a junk value. Shay locomotives are

In September 1950, the Tophill tunnel on the SP&S line to Vernonia caved in. That halted all traffic on the line for more than a week. The Natt McDougall Company, assisted by an O-A bulldozer and crew, worked around the clock to daylight the tunnel. (Kamholz collection)

hard to find, but they are even harder to sell.

However, Brady successfully persuaded Greenman to reconsider and O-A made a bid for $3,500.

> I realize this sounds like a ridiculous price, Jim, but I believe it does represent more than the scrap value of the engine and I am being perfectly frank and honest when I say that we have no need for the engine at this time at all. If we bought it, we would shove it off on a side track and use it solely as a standby machine, calling on it only when we had trouble with one of our other locomotives.

The Union Pacific made a counteroffer of $4,500 that Greenman accepted on August 19, 1948. Oregon-American took delivery of the locomotive at Vernonia on September 22, 1948, assigned the big shay Road Number 107 and put it in woods service about a month later.

The 107, a three-truck, Class C model, was built by Lima in 1907 and when delivered to Portland, weighed slightly more than 100 tons. The UP had operated the engine in common-carrier service and when delivered to Vernonia, it was still Interstate Commerce Commission-qualified, a feature Oregon-American soon let lapse.

Mechanically, the 107 was distinctive for several reasons. First, Lima built it with a straight-top boiler in contrast to the wagon-top style boilers that characterized most shay locomotives. Also, when the engine arrived in Vernonia, it sported a power reverse that, uncommon for a shay, was even more unusual as UP had mounted the cylinder activating

On August 23, 1952, O-A displayed Willamette locomotive Number 106 at the Vernonia depot to greet a National Model Railroaders' Association excursion special from Portland. Hard as it might be to believe, this was a twenty-five-year-old logging engine. Company President Judd Greenman instructed his foremen to shine the engine until it looked like the Union Pacific's "City of Portland." They didn't disappoint the boss. (Kamholz collection)

the power reverse mechanism on the fireman's side of the cab, although the driving engines and gear it reversed were on the engineer's side. A rod between the engineer's reverse lever and the activating cylinder traversed the locomotive's backhead.

Collapse of the SP&S's Tophill Tunnel

The Tophill tunnel was an ongoing headache to the railway company from the day it opened in 1922. Bored through the crest of foothills lying east of the main backbone of the Coast Range, the earth surrounding the tunnel constantly shifted, necessitating frequent repairs. It finally caved in on September 1950 and cut off service to Vernonia for several weeks. Given its troubled past and the likelihood of continuing problems if rebuilt, the SP&S elected to daylight the tunnel.

Denied a means to get cars in and out of Vernonia, O-A was forced to shut down the planing mill and shipping departments on September 18 and the sawmill and allied departments the following day. O-A operated the sawmill an extra day simply to produce enough fuel to keep the power house supplied.

The "Pride of the Woods" Goes on Display

If Oregon-American had a single moment in its history that captured the pride the company took in the appearance of its equipment, it was when the SP&S operated a special excursion train to Vernonia for the National Model Railroaders' Association that held its convention in Portland in August 1952. Announcing the event to key employees, Greenman wrote:

> The sponsors of the trip would like to have these delegates see a shay locomotive while they are at Vernonia. These people are the kind of folks who

build model railroads in their basements, sometimes investing many thousands of dollars in them, and they are interested in all kinds of railroad equipment. Many of them have never seen a geared locomotive and that is the reason for their desire to see one while here.

I have agreed…that we will bring down and park a Shay locomotive on one of the S P & S tracks in Vernonia.… This locomotive to be examined by these railroad enthusiasts while they are here.

Right off the bat…I want to make the following suggestions [that] any locomotive we bring down here for this purpose wants to be cleaned up and shined until it looks like the Union Pacific's "City of Portland" because the people examining it will be superb critics.

I think this opportunity to display a shay locomotive to several hundred people from the east provides us with a good chance to do some advertising and I want to capitalize on it to the fullest extent.

That employees embraced Greenman's suggestions was evident. Oregon-American displayed the

Top: On February 8, 1950, locomotives 104 and 105 double-headed a snowplow to clear Spur 26 west of Camp McGregor. (George Lee collection)

§

Middle and bottom: The train was getting a run at the 4 percent grade approach to the Overhead crossing when, at the upper end of Shields siding, the 104 ran over an ice-filled switch. It left the track and veered 65 feet before running head-on into the end of a log. Only that kept the locomotive from ending up in Rock Creek.

A crew of fifteen worked three days to get 104 back on the tracks. (Arlie Sliffe photographs; John T. Labbe collection)

newly painted and lettered Willamette locomotive 106 with a load of logs on August 23, 1952, and finding a twenty-five-year-old woods engine more presentable would have been a tall order.

In November 1947 we left Camp McGregor with the woods crew from the family camp on a dark and foggy morning. I was firing the 104 at the time and as we reached the upper end of the yards I was checking the steam and water. All of a sudden I heard the engine hitting something and when I looked out I realized that we were on the wood spur and were hitting wood that was too close to the track. I hollered at the engineer to stop but the rails were rusty so when he applied the brakes, the wheels just slid and we went over the end of the stub and ended up with the wheels axle-deep in the soft dirt.

I thought the superintendent would be mad, but when he arrived, he just laughed and said, **Well, if you'd had balloon rubber tires, you could have gone right up the county road.** *The road was just about 30 feet beyond the end of the stub.*

The superintendent was a very good rigging man and he knew just how to place the rigging so when the 105 arrived, they used it to pull the 104 back onto the rails with very little effort. The only damage was to the sandpipes.

Arlie Sliff, engineer

WINTER, AND MORE WINTER

Although Oregon's north coast belt might not technically qualify as a rain forest, onshore weather flows drench this region with an average of 80 or more inches of "liquid sunshine" annually, enough by far to create significant weather conditions as moisture-laden winter storms encounter the first obstacle to their inland journey, the Pacific Coast Mountain Range.[1] This unbroken line of rugged peaks, ranging from between 2,000 and 4,000 feet in elevation and lying parallel and only 20 or so miles inland from the coastline, represent the first place in the flight path of winter storms where conditions to form snow and ice routinely arise. Beginning as early as November, winter can linger until as late as May. Still, owing to the general warming effect of the Pacific Ocean, these conditions typically do not persist and, except in the most unusual years, prevailing inflows of warm ocean air keep the snow and ice from accumulating for extended periods.

Until the late 1940s Oregon-American was spared lengthy, weather-related work delays in the woods, in large part because its operations lay at lower elevations or on the margins of the heaviest snow zone. However, once O-A removed its timber from the lower elevations in the Southwest Unit and there was no where else to go but up, so to speak, weather delays took on new meaning. Adding to that mix of severe weather potential, Mother Nature created some of the worst winter weather conditions ever recorded in the Pacific Northwest during the winters of 1949–51. The effects on Oregon-American operations were severe.

In his January 15, 1949 weekly report to the board of directors, Greenman wrote:

> The longest cold spell in the memory of the oldest inhabitants in the Northwest has stopped our operations with the exception of planing and shipping lumber, but it now appears to be moderating and we hope to get going again on Monday, January 17th. We had below-zero weather here at Vernonia on two different days during this spell of cold weather and ever since New Year's the temperature has seldom risen above the freezing point. We had to suspend logging operations on January 1 and were forced to shut the mill down on the 11th because ice in the log pond reached such thickness we could not move the logs.

By February 10 weather conditions had limited logging to only parts of four days, during which only a half million board feet of logs were loaded. The Vernonia log pond had a foot of ice in it, preventing the movement of logs, and sawmill operations ground to a halt for more than a week. More than 2 feet of snow lay on the ground in Vernonia, elevation 620 feet. At the maximum, between 3 and 4 feet of snow lay on the truck road and nearly 7 feet covered the railroad near the 3,000-foot elevation.

Through the first of March loggers were only able to venture to work on eight days and then only to selected areas along the lower elevation truck road. The railroad was finally opened enough to get one skidder back in operation by the middle of the month. Fortunately, the mill reopened earlier than that but only because of logs bought from independent suppliers.

Unprepared for the 1949 winter, Oregon-American took steps to maintain its log supply for the

Left: During the winters of 1949 through 1951, some of the worst snowfalls ever recorded blanketed the Pacific Northwest. Along the crest of the Coast Range snowdrifts sometimes exceeded 20 feet.

§

Right and bottom: Digging out an ice-filled cut was sometimes more than a mere shay and a snowplow could accomplish so crews had to use more drastic methods. Here, a crew loaded the P&H diesel shovel on a flatcar ahead of the locomotive to dig out the right-of-way. (Arlie Sliffe collection)

THE GLORY YEARS

One of Camp McGregor's water tanks during the winter of 1949–50. (George Lee collection)

next year. First, the company went on a buying spree that spring and acquired unprecedented quantities of logs from independent operators. By late summer that year, O-A filled the Vernonia pond completely and commenced a log-decking program. Previous log-decking campaigns had limited effectiveness because of shortcomings in decking equipment, so in the fall of 1949 O-A brought the Willamette tree-rigged skidder to Vernonia. That enabled the company to lay up a reserve of decent-sized fir logs for the coming winter.

Those preparations for the 1949–50 snow season proved timely indeed. That winter, the heaviest snowfalls ever recorded visited the Pacific Northwest. By December 15, 1949, more than 18 inches of snow lay on the ground at the 3,000-foot level and Camp Olson was closed early.

By February 1, 1950, Vernonia had received nearly 11 feet of snow, the severest storm dropping 42 inches alone. Yet because it had gone into the winter with a full log pond and a good-sized log deck, the mill only lost three working days in January, all due to frozen pond conditions. The stockpiling strategy worked so well, in fact, that the mill produced at a rate faster than the SP&S could shuttle cars in and out of Vernonia. As late as February 1950, the railway company still was using two locomotives and a snowplow on the regular Vernonia turn.

In the woods, crews made every effort to keep the truck road and railroad plowed in anticipation of any warming trend that might have allowed loggers back into the woods. At times they bucked drifts on the railroad so deep that the snow level was higher than locomotive stacks. When unable to clear ice-filled cuts with a plow, they loaded the P&H shovel on a flatcar and nudged it up to the drifts ahead of a shay so the shovel could dig its way through.

The winter of 1950–51, although not as severe as the preceding two years, was noteworthy in its own right, because while it snowed less, what did fall lingered and plowing continued into the month of May. As the company again found itself short of logs, O-A did not build cold decks at Vernonia for the next three years. Winter production at the mill suffered as a result. In January 1952, for example, the mill was only able to operate for three days and only sixteen in February. March storms also forced a period of shutdown.

A MILESTONE THE SIZE OF A CITY

When Charles Keith made the calculated gamble to place his Oregon-American mill at Vernonia in 1921, his decision ran counter to the prevailing trend of Pacific Northwest sawmill siting practice. Then most large operators consciously strove to put their mills near major watercourses, which allowed them to capitalize both on open-market log supplies and water shipment of their finished products. However, despite his reliance on a single railroad carrier, distant markets that soon collapsed in the wake of the Great Depression, crippling fires, and the creditor's noose, the brilliance of Keith's rail mill strategy never dimmed.

Perhaps no greater quantitative measure of its success ever occurred than Wednesday, March 24, 1948, when at 3:30 P.M., the Vernonia mill sawed its one-billionth board foot of lumber since restarting in 1936. Counting lumber produced between 1924 and 1932 when operating under the banner of the Oregon-American Lumber Company, the mill had produced nearly 1 billion, 900,000 board feet in total.

To put this accomplishment in a visual perspective, the average single-family home in those days typically required 15,000 board feet of lumber to build. Vernonia's billion board-foot output between 1936 and 1948 therefore represented enough lumber to build homes for nearly 70,000 families. Counting total production dating back to 1924, it amounted to enough lumber to build 125,000 homes.

Announcing this milestone to employees, Greenman noted, *This is truly a lot of lumber and we believe, with the exception of one single mill in Washington, no other Fir country mill, dependent on rail transportation, has ever cut as much lumber as we have.* The other rail mill Greenman referred to was that of the Snoqualmie Falls Lumber Company that, by then, had produced nearly 3 billion board feet of lumber.[2]

---

*O*ne afternoon there was a blizzard and the waterlines froze up on the 103 while it was plowing snow between Spurs 26-10 and 26-11. So, they drained the water and abandoned it. It sat all night through a big storm.

Andy came to me and said, Yorge, we gotta get that locomotive down outta there.

I plowed with the Cat all the way up to where the 103 was. The snow was clear over the 103 and all I could see was a tiny black speck next to the bank. That was the smokestack. I plowed out all around the front, back, and one side and got it exposed.

Right after that here came the 105 and its caboose. Y'know ol' Heenan, Byers, and Monaco? They were sittin' in the caboose drinkin' coffee and keepin' warm by the stove while I was out there about paralyzed. They just hooked up and away they went down the hill and left me up there all alone. I was about froze and they had a hot coffee pot in there.

Boy o' boy did the air burn.

George Lee, construction

GINGER CREEK

The Keasey, or Ginger Creek Operating Unit, named for the small stream that drained the tract's western slopes into the Rock Creek basin, contained the balance of Oregon-American's timber. The Ginger Creek tract, like the Southwest Unit, was a patchwork of intermingled Oregon-American and Ruth Realty properties. At its core was some original DuBois tract timber to which bits and pieces had been added over the years, some of it belonging to Ruth, other subparcels to O-A. As Oregon-American had blocked the tract up under the assumption the company would log it as a contiguous entity, regardless of who, O-A or Ruth, owned individual parts, the company had given no thought to logging the properties strictly along ownership lines. That is, until Ruth Realty took steps to force O-A's hand in purchasing its Ginger Creek timber well before the company planned to log it.

We had drifts of snow 35-feet deep up on the high ridge at Windy Gap. It'd come up over those ridges and build up like a comb on a wave. All the big cuts in the railroad would just be level, full of snow, maybe fifteen-twenty feet deep. I'd inherit plowin' it all out. And they wanted it plowed right while it was snowin'. Andy was a thorough believer not to wait until the weather changed to start plowin'. He wanted to be ready to jump right on the logging. I've plowed up there with a blizzard goin' so I couldn't see the blade on the front end of the cat. All day long.... You ain't supposed to be out like that by yourself, one man. Supposed to be two.... I used to be out sixteen miles from camp, all by myself in the blizzard. Day after day after day.

So, I was underpaid. Nowadays I'm smarter, see. They had to pad it some or I wouldn't do it.

George Lee, Construction

The sharp postwar run up in timber prices, coupled with buyers' aggressive efforts to secure what timber was left, presented the carriers with an irresistible opportunity. So, less than a year after granting O-A preferential rights to its Ginger Creek timber, Ruth notified Oregon-American on January 24, 1947 that it was planning to accept an offer for its remaining timber unless O-A matched it within three weeks.

Oregon-American's board of directors had mixed reactions to the ultimatum. George Birkelund, normally a voice of moderation, was all for suing Ruth. Greenman, by contrast, agreed Ruth's demands were excessive but was skeptical that anyone could make profitable lumber at that asking price. Accordingly, he believed it best not to respond at all. Moreover, he argued that O-A would be extremely vulnerable if it sued the carriers for breach of the contract since the company's very existence depended on trackage rights for logs, cars for lumber shipments, and timber from the Yerreck tract, the control of which all rested with the Northern Lines.

As a practical matter, the intermingling of both companies' holdings in Ginger Creek made removal of Ruth's timber problematical unless it came out over the Oregon-American railroad when O-A removed its own timber. Moreover, if O-A removed only its timber, Ruth's holdings became more vulnerable to fire. Coupled with O-A's reluctance to bid and behind-the-scenes effort by Charles Hart and Omar Spencer of the Hart, Spencer, McCulloch and Rockwood law firm that represented both Oregon-American and the SP&S, Ruth ultimately decided not to sell.

Besides some casual inquiries into Oregon-American's ultimate intentions to acquire the Ruth Ginger Creek timber by officials from the Northern Pacific and the SP&S, nothing further developed through the end of 1950. Then on February 16, 1951, apparently tiring of O-A's wait-and-see approach, the carriers switched tactics and announced that instead of selling their Ginger Creek timber to O-A they had decided to hold it for their own future lumber needs.

Good sawlogs became increasingly scarce after WWII. O-A was caught short during the winter of 1948–49 and after that tried to stockpile logs, even though the mill was only operating a single-shift. Because the mill's electric log-decking engine was too small, the company used the tree-rigged skidder to build cold decks in the later years of operation.

O-A built its 1949–50 cold deck, shown here, between August 30 and November 25, 1949. It contained 4,798 logs scaling 6,498,598 board feet. The mill consumed the entire deck in only seventeen days between January 23 and February 14, 1950. (The Oregon-American Lumber Company, Special Collections and University Archives, University of Oregon)

THE GLORY YEARS

In 1950 we had 8 or 9 feet of snow on the ground at Shields. Andy and a bunch of us were snowed in at Camp Olson. Andy and I were trying to keep the railroad open with the 106. We had it in pretty good shape. I was the engineer and fireman, and Andy was the whole braking crew.

We went to bed one night and woke up to about 4 feet of brand new snow. Cold too. All the switches were frozen and you couldn't get to them. We tried the steam hose but they'd freeze back almost as fast as you could thaw them out. Couldn't hack it so we gave it up.

So that's when I went down to the carpenter's shack and built me some homemade skis. Oh that was funny, me making those skis. I bent plywood up and reinforced it with a piece of 1×4 flooring and some wire. Ol' Andy, he had a fit. I finished them and put 'em on a hot kitchen range. Then I filled a gallon can full of candles and melted them and made a swab. I heated the skis on that stove and swabbed on that hot wax and boy it soaked right in there. I gave 'em three or four coats. Then I put them on and went up on the cookhouse roof and skied off. Ol' Andy was rollin' in the snow, it was so funny. But you know, two hours later, about midnight, he was down there makin' himself a pair.

We all took off the next morning. Andy chickened out. He only went as far as the Sunset Highway then caught a ride to Portland. The rest of us went all the way to Camp McGregor.

George Lee, construction

For its part, O-A accepted the news at face value, going so far as to reduce its timber account by the amount of Ruth's Ginger Creek holdings and modifying its depreciation and amortization schedules accordingly. Having resigned itself to logging only company timber, O-A revised its logging plan. To that end Oregon-American applied for and received easements in those cases where the logging railroad had to cross Ruth lands. Once Ruth granted the easements, Oregon-American had the SP&S install a turnout for the Ginger Creek spur in early 1952. Official designation of the new line was Spur 27.

The company again contracted with the Natt McDougall Company to build 4.5 miles of railroad grade. Track-laying began in June 1952, setting the stage for the final phase of Oregon-American's operating life. In anticipation of the eventual transfer of its logging operations, O-A had contracted with Frank Berglund of Wauna, Oregon, to remove timber from the NWNE and NENW of Section 31, Twp. 5 North, Range 5 West in April 1950. This area was not readily accessible with the railroad.

Table 9.1
Oregon-American Profitability 1947–1952

	Sales	Net Profits	Net Profits as a Percent of Sales
1947	$5,356,416	$1,232,320	22.9
1948	6,490,580	1,624,721	25.0
1949	5,347,983	825,526	15.4
1950	6,296,669	1,204,971	19.1
1951	6,766,537	1,192,762	17.6
1952	5,226,459	639,614[3]	12.2

The Ginger Creek stand contained a sizable quantity of large cedar that was more valuable as piling than for shingles. O-A undertook a program to remove it ahead of full-scale logging between April and December 1952. The company hired Harold Bergerson, a gyppo logger from Vernonia, for this task. Bergerson also logged small hemlock along with the piling and loaded the logs on company disconnected trucks once O-A developed its railroad.

Snow blanketed the mill office on January 10, 1950. That winter half the company's logging operations were at an elevation of nearly 3,000 feet. Drifts on the railroad were so deep that work did not return to normal until May.

Northwest Oregon's winter of 1949–50 was the worst in recorded history. By February 1, 1950, Vernonia, elevation 620 feet, had seen 128.8 inches of snow fall with the worst storm dumping 42 inches alone. (The Oregon-American Lumber Company, Special Collections and University Archives, University of Oregon)

FINANCES AND A BITTERSWEET ENDING

On July 1, 1946, Oregon-American retired the remaining half million dollars of its outstanding income mortgage bonds. This milestone marked repayment of the last of all the bonded indebtedness created in connection with the Vernonia operation by Central Coal & Coke, Delta Land & Timber, and the Oregon-American Lumber Company dating back to 1924. Once the company finished paying off its debts, it could apply all its available earnings to dividends. The effect on the company's profitability between 1947 and 1951 was a major reason Oregon-American could to lay claim to this period as its "Glory Years."

Combined with the federal government's home mortgage guarantee programs that fueled a strong demand for lumber, a brief rundown of O-A's sales and profits during this period clearly illustrates how good these years really were (see Table 9.1).

In 1948, Oregon-American's net profit was the equivalent of $41.48 per share and by mid-May 1949, Oregon-American's stock value had risen to $93 per share—a long way from July 1936 when it

THE GLORY YEARS

Top: Shay 103 at Camp Olson on July 21, 1949. (Albert Farrow photograph; Jim Blain collection)

§

Bottom: O-A's Willamette locomotive 106 at rest at Camp Olson. (Jim Blain collection)

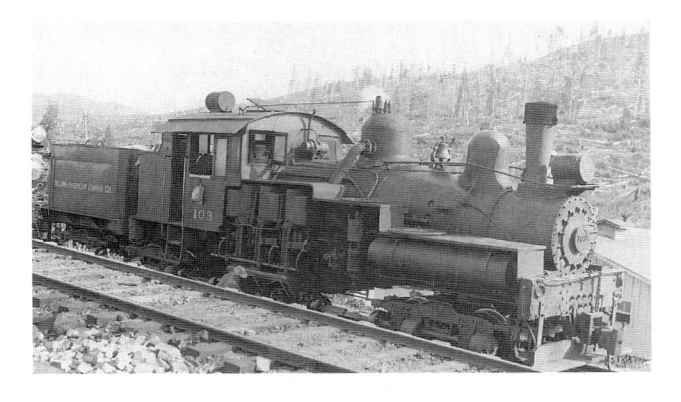

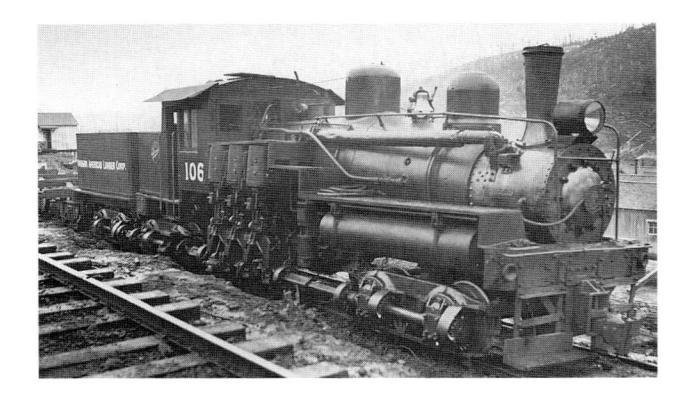

had been virtually worthless. Greenman advised the board on January 15, 1949:

> Of one thing I am reasonably certain. No future year of our life is likely to afford a market opportunity which will enable us to convert as many dollars from our trees as we did in 1948. And, we should all constantly remember that these moneys we call "profits" are principally "conversions" which, if applied to replenishing raw material supply and restoring plants at current costs would leave but little which could truly be labeled "profits."

While a few other old-line companies were similarly enjoying banner years, Oregon-American's financial performance was truly outstanding. Well-deserved kudos came from near and far.

C. H. "Harlan" Watzek, a relative of O-A's former receiver, Aubrey Watzek, wrote from the Roaring River Logging Company in Portland on December 8, 1947:

> Dear Judd:
>
> Answering 12/5, your pencil comparison with Long-Bell is returned. After I checked it carefully I patted you on the back in no gentle manner. There are many orchids for you in it.
>
> Aubrey and I both enjoyed above.
>
> Your hard work, ability and good judgment has brought O-A a long way since those days and the way has steadily been rosier, thanks to you!

Sigmund Stern, never one to express himself in superlatives, made an exception when he commented on first-quarter 1948 performance:

> Dear Judd:
>
> [This] statement is outstandingly good. How long this situation can last no one can foretell. That these fantastically high prices must break sooner or later seems to be beyond doubt, and it is anybody's guess; and I don't think anyone is a better judge than yourself.

L. C. Stith, secretary and treasurer of the Long-Bell Lumber Company, wrote Greenman from Kansas City, Missouri, on April 19, 1948, *I always thought of you as "big time." At least you have always been carried in my own thoughts as one of the outstanding lumber operators in the country.* Although profits were only half that of 1948, O-A's performance in 1949 still shone in comparison with its competitors, prompting even more complements, including one from Corydon Wagner, vice president of the St. Paul & Tacoma Lumber Company: *I noted in the February 24th issue of the Mississippi Valley Lumberman a news item on the net income of the Oregon-American in 1949. I am so impressed with this excellent showing that I feel impelled to write you my congratulations. I knew you were good, but did not know that anyone could be as good as these results indicate.* Greenman, ever the realist, replied:

> We are not kidding ourselves at all. We know very well that if we had to replace our trees and our plant (and, of course, it would be impossible to replace our trees with others of like quality) we probably would not be able to show any profit at all. This is one of those "sugaring-off" operations of which there have been many in other regions, but not very many out here as yet.

Nor were industry leaders the only ones who recognized the achievement. Lucille Keith, Charles Keith's widow, wrote Greenman,

> I own only 10 [Oregon-American] shares and one bond which my brother left me—all that Mr. Keith and I owned was put for collateral at the banks which, of course, vanished.... The company did so well last year... I know my dear husband would be gratified with the performance.

The major reason O-A posted such profitable years between 1947 and 1951 was that it could write off its stumpage and depreciation at rates far below their replacement value. To illustrate, every time O-A dumped a carload of logs in the Vernonia millpond, those logs netted the company $125 in pretax profit before they even went up the log slip. Cutting those logs into lumber only added to the company's profits. Little wonder the value of O-A's stock had risen to $116 by the end of 1951.

Yet just as much as the company's financial success between 1947 and 1951 was the result of conditions not directly under its control, so were the events that in 1952 brought the run to an end. A significant reduction in government financing of new dwelling units led to sharp declines in the overall demand for building materials, including lumber. However, even more telling was the loss of operating time in the woods caused by extreme weather conditions that forced operations to close. Unable to secure enough logs to build a reserve at Vernonia, twenty-five mill operating days were lost in the winter because of heavy snows and another twenty-two more were lost in the summer and fall to low humidity conditions. Added lost time totaling sixteen and a half days were also lost during a labor strike that spring. Lost operating time alone accounted for nearly $1 million in lost profits. For the year, O-A shipped only 59 million board feet.[4] Facing a future of considerably dimmed business prospects and the end of its road in sight, the time had arrived to develop a strategy for Oregon-American's final days.

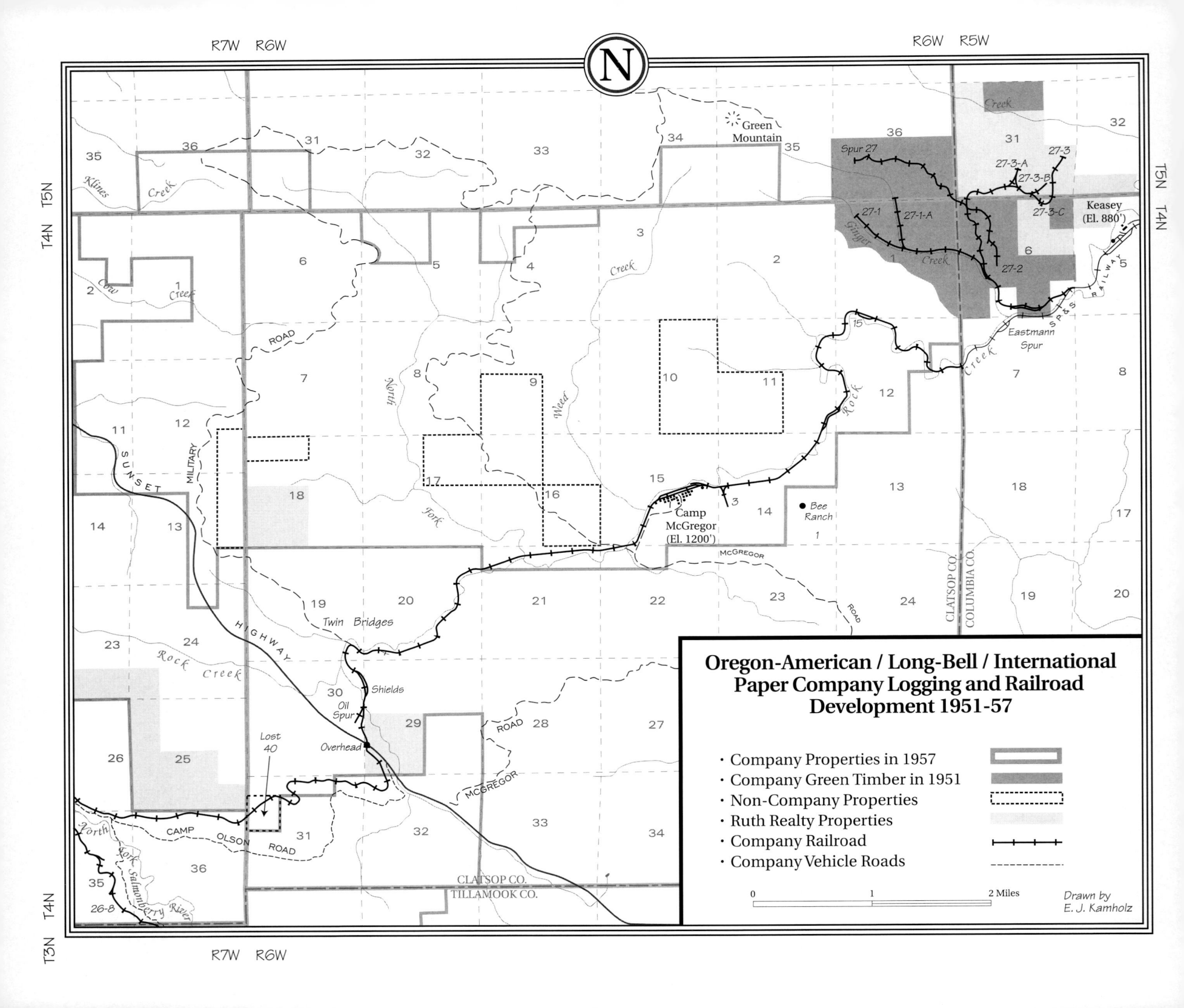

Oregon-American / Long-Bell / International Paper Company Logging and Railroad Development 1951-57

Legend:
- Company Properties in 1957
- Company Green Timber in 1951
- Non-Company Properties
- Ruth Realty Properties
- Company Railroad
- Company Vehicle Roads

Drawn by E. J. Kamholz

THE LAST STAND

During the lumber industry's migration west, many believed the timber supply there was infinite. That myth gradually faded, but the industry was slow to take heed and slower still to react. Gone were the days when survival meant simply cutting one stand of timber only to move to the next. When the remaining supply had diminished to the point where no "next" stand remained, hard reality dictated that "next" stand would have to be grown. Not unlike the farmer who, centuries before, had learned that survival depended on reserving part of each crop for the seeds to plant the next, operators began to embrace the practice of tree-farming as their only salvation. By 1950, that fundamental shift in operating philosophy had finally begun to take hold.

With change from the extraction to conservation state of mind came the realization that improved utilization had to be the cornerstone of tree-farming practice. Before that, sawmills, pulp factories, and plywood makers had competed against one another, sometimes for the same sales dollar but more often for the common raw material each required for its own products. The ultimate outcome of this mind-set was waste, for the scraps created making lumber or plywood were every bit as likely consumed in a refuse burner as sold to a competitor that could make paper, particle board, or another product from it.

So, instead of narrowly defining themselves as sawmillers, pulp manufacturers, or plywood manufacturers, specialized operators slowly began taking a shared approach to the same, limited raw material. This yielded better results because it used every scrap of every tree cut. The more that realization became a governing standard, the more operators began diversifying their operations into the very businesses once considered direct competitors. With the emergence of this holistic approach to the business came the dawn of the integrated "wood-products" industry.[1]

When faced with gut-wrenching changes like these, industries often consolidate. So it was in the fledgling wood-products industry. Larger, better-heeled concerns began to prey on their smaller competitors, both to clear the way for their own strategic ends and to obtain operating economies of scale. Motivating that consolidation was the need to compress the time it took to grow a new supply of raw material. By itself that *was* the economy of scale issue, for survival depended on the sheer volume of wood fiber that could be grown in the shortest period. That accomplishment, however, required land, and a lot of it. It also required the kind of land that would grow trees. Although cutover lands were of little value to the dying breed of cut-out-and-get-out operators, they were essential to operators that planned for a future. Thus, as the wood-products industry began to configure itself in the post–WWII era, it also began to buy cutover lands at such a pace as to drive up their value.

Opposite page: Oregon-American delayed logging the Ginger Creek Unit until last because timber there was the Company's least mature. That proved to be a wise strategy, for between 1921 and 1952 the volume of standing timber doubled.

THE LAST STAND

Top: Train 105 crossing the Overhead as it began the descent to Shields siding. The fragile, wood chassis of caboose 367 was a concern and out of fear the heavy weight of the loads might buckle it, train crews had to handle the caboose carefully. (Bob and Fred Wenzel photograph)

§

Bottom: Shay 103 switching empties at Shields. The siding here served as a principle makeup track from 1939 to 1956 and was named after a "gyppo," or independent contract logger, that supplied logs to O-A for many years. O-A stored the donkey moving car on the stub track at the far right. The track was formerly the take-off point for Spur 26-1 or the "Dooley Spur," so named for the gyppo outfit that used it. (Bob and Fred Wenzel photograph)

Preparing for a Future

Unsure which way the industry redefinition ball was going to roll, Oregon-American remained true to its original, self-liquidating course. However, once the rest of the industry set a course, the company had to take stock of its position. O-A needed a better measure of its remaining timber regardless of whether to simply determine how much time it had left or to chart a new course of its own. When Oregon-American reorganized in the 1930s, the company could not afford to replace the flawed Thomas & Meservey timber cruise of 1921. Besides, the predecessor company had gained sufficient experience to know T&M had overstated that cruise about 20 percent.

However, by the end of WWII, new markets emerged for hemlock and other thin-barked evergreen species. This not only altered log recovery practice, but also it greatly improved overall utilization to the extent that cruises premised on old recovery methods were no longer representative. Nor had O-A's other green standing timber remained static. The cruise of the Salmonberry Timber Company tract was more than a decade old. The Ginger Creek cruise was three times as old and, like compound interest, the volume of recoverable wood in both tracts had steadily increased. With that in mind, Oregon-American commissioned a recruise of all its remaining timber. When it was completed in June 1952, the company found that nearly 286 million board feet remained, exactly double that reflected on its books.[2]

Another development became apparent too. Once they had logged an area, many operators sought to rid themselves of the long-term burden of property taxes and fire patrol assessments. The typical method of doing this was to burn the slashings, obtain State Forestry releases, and then simply stop paying the property taxes. Eventually, this led to foreclosure and the lands reverted to the state or counties. Despite pressure to economize, once Oregon-American resumed operations in 1936, the company resisted following that widely accepted practice. So, except for some 6,000 acres abandoned in 1934 while the company had been in receivership, and 400 acres that O-A deeded to the state for the Wolf Creek Highway right-of-way, there remained in Oregon-American's possession more than 20,000 acres of land, fully developed with roads and railroad rights-of-way.

After finishing most of its logging in the Southwest Unit O-A needed its logging camp closer to Ginger Creek. The company disbanded Camp Olson during the Thanksgiving 1955 holiday weekend and returned the structures to Camp McGregor. (Betty Blumenthal collection)

293

Looking west over the Middle Fork of Cronin Creek canyon. The Lidgerwood tower skidder's last setting was here on Spur 26-15. At an elevation of nearly 3,000 feet above sea level, it was only 5 miles from here to Cronin Creek's confluence with the Nehalem River, elevation 400 feet. Most of that drop occurred in the first half-mile. Logging this kind of terrain was slow and hazardous, and the company often had to pay differential falling and bucking rates to keep crews on the job. (Kamholz collection)

The notion of selling cutover lands had briefly arisen in the 1940s. O-A had offered large blocks for as little as $2.50 an acre. Finding buyers had proven elusive, however, since most of the prospects were small livestock ranchers looking for rangeland. Most of them were unable to pay even that low a price. Meanwhile, Central Coal & Coke had found extensive oil deposits in its cutover acreage in Louisiana and Texas. So, when oil companies began exploratory drilling in northwestern Oregon in 1945, hope of duplicating that experience provided a real impetus to keep O-A's holdings intact. Although that prospect never developed, cutover land values, driven by the demand for tree farm land, began to increase. So, the silver lining to O-A's disappointing 1952 operating results was the discovery that its remaining timber was double that on its books and that it was holding an increasingly valuable resource in its cutover lands. How the company could best act on that knowledge was another matter, however.

Oregon-American's capital stock, 39,166 shares, was closely held by only 493 holders of record. By virtue that Central Coal & Coke owned 25,000 of those shares made it clear that any decision governing O-A's future would be made in Kansas City. When the Sigmund Stern-led Central Coal & Coke Corporation assumed control of Oregon-American, it ran O-A on a hand-to-mouth basis, only investing in the lumber company when it would clearly yield a handsome payoff. By 1950, Central had become so solidly entrenched surviving on the annuity-like proceeds generated by its southern oil royalties and Oregon-American profits that investing in a new future for O-A would have been entirely out of character. And the investment would have been large. Machinery was old and outdated. People who had devoted their working careers to nurture the company through good times and bad were at, or beyond, retirement age. Replacing both and underwriting the cost of buying more timber and cutover lands needed to perpetuate the operation would have required an investment far beyond Central's financial reach. Lacking both desire and resources needed to transform it as a participant in the emerging wood-products industry, Central decided to rid itself of Oregon-American while O-A's value was at its highest.

An Old Friend

While Central Coal & Coke deliberated Oregon-American's future, similar discussions had already taken place elsewhere in Kansas City. The Long-Bell Lumber Company itself was running out of old-growth timber.[3] However, in contrast to Central, Long-Bell was laying the groundwork for its future.

Established in 1875, Long-Bell's history had closely paralleled Central Coal & Coke's.[4] Both companies operated from Kansas City, Missouri. R. A. Long and Charles Keith had resided in the same neighborhood. That neighborly relationship extended to their respective holdings in the southern pine region too where some of the two companies' properties were in the same locale.[5] And, as Long-Bell and Central depleted their respective reserves of southern pine timber, both companies set down new roots in the Pacific Northwest at the same time.[6]

Being the larger of the two, Long-Bell's appetite for new operating territory demanded it invest in more timber. Once it secured a suitable tract in southwestern Washington, Long-Bell constructed a sawmill complex suited perfectly for a deep-water port on the Columbia River, just 30 miles north of Vernonia. In keeping with its greater means, Long-Bell created an entire city to support its mill. The city, named Longview in honor of R. A. Long, was unique for its time because it was company planned from the ground up. Consistent with Long-Bell's and Central's shared history, the firm of Hare & Hare planned both the Vernonia mill housing tract and the city of Longview.

The Lidgerwood tower skidder's last show on Spur 26-15 with Windy Gap in the background. Here it operated a 3,000-foot skyline angled downward at a 45-degree angle into the rugged Middle Fork of Cronin Creek canyon. The view from here was spectacular. On a clear day, those working track side could see ships 20 miles out in the Pacific Ocean. Looking east provided a panoramic view of peaks along the Oregon and Washington Cascade Mountain range.

When these scenes were captured on October 12, 1956, the day's work had been completed. The following month loggers brought out the last logs. The company scrapped the machine in place. (Kamholz collection)

295

THE LAST STAND

Top: Engineer Ralph "Boomer" Reynolds and the 103 backing one of the last trains of logs to come out of the Southwest Unit across the Overhead crossing on October 12, 1956. The shay has just begun its descent into Shields, a half-mile away.

More than 1 billion board feet of logs crossed this landmark after logging commenced on the south side of the Wolf Creek Highway in 1940. (Kamholz collection)

§

Bottom: Fred Hageman was O-A's last logging superintendent. The "Dutchman" was a longtime employee and succeeded Andy Olson in 1956.

International Paper Company converted the Vernonia operation's cutover lands into a tree farm after logging was completed, and Hageman oversaw the property for a number of years before he retired. (Betty Blumenthal collection)

When Long-Bell's West mill at Longview began operations only days after the O-A mill in Vernonia opened in 1924, it was one of the largest ever built. Long-Bell's comparably sized and adjacent East mill went on line in May 1926. By the time Long-Bell exhausted its timber supply for the two mills in 1960, their combined output had reached more than 8.5 billion board feet, enough lumber to build nearly 600,000 single-family homes.[7]

Although technically competitors, the long-standing close corporate relationship between Long-Bell and Central extended beyond Kansas City. Warm personal and professional relations developed between Judd Greenman and the top managers at Longview. This was particularly the case in Greenman's friendship with John Tennant, who, as a Long-Bell vice president, had been in charge of his company's Northwest developments since the early

Aerial view looking west of the Thanksgiving weekend 1956 Salmonberry Fire that covered much of the Southwest Unit after logging had been completed. The South and Middle Forks refer to two branches of Cronin Creek. The North Fork of the Salmonberry River flowed from right-to-left down the steep canyon in the foreground. The big canyon at the right facing the camera is the West Fork of the North Fork of the Salmonberry River.

The weather was bitterly cold and winds were strong. The fire was difficult to control. (*Astoria Budget* photograph; Oregon Department of Forestry collection)

1920s. Both men were thoroughly engaged in trade and other industry groups and dealt together on a breadth of issues ranging from WCLA programs to industrial relations with organized labor.

The extent and nature of ties between Longview and Vernonia only deepened with time. Greenman often made professional and personal visits to Longview as did Long-Bell people to Vernonia. Personnel from O-A were also privy to the inner sanctums at Longview, often to inspect equipment and procedures that O-A might adapt at Vernonia. So close were the relationships that each company freely traded operating statistics and wage rates with the other.

Long-Bell's operating philosophy had been, in many ways, even more expansive than Charles Keith's. This was particularly true in marketing its lumber, because Long-Bell had developed a sizable chain of retail outlets that allowed it to control its products all the way to the consumer.[8] Long-Bell had also grown much larger after starting operations in the Northwest. By 1952 it boasted annual sales of $92 million and employed nearly 7,000 people.

In its quest to develop a future business foundation, the Long-Bell Lumber Company had already begun finding other businesses and additional properties. In Oregon alone it had taken over existing operations at Vaughn and Gardiner. Long-Bell had also built its own plywood plant in Longview.[9] Because Oregon-American had some timber left and a built-up tract of cutover land suitable for conversion into a tree farm, it fell squarely within Long-Bell's strategic parameters for acquisition. So, not unlike asking an old friend for help during troubled times, Central Coal & Coke's strategy for exiting the lumber business led it to Long-Bell's door.

297

THE LAST STAND

Top and middle: O-A's crummies were of mixed heritage. In the 1920s the company used old boxcars to move logging crews. In 1938, O-A bought two former Union Pacific passenger coaches for the task. Later, a former Oregon Electric mail coach was picked up, as was a former section car from the SP&S. All served one purpose, keeping loggers out of the rain while transporting them between the camps and work.

§

Bottom: These former Inman-Poulsen camp cars were picked up shortly after Oregon-American reorganized and served as the first kitchen and dining cars when the new company rebuilt Camp McGregor in 1936. When Camp McGregor's permanent cookhouse was dedicated in 1938, O-A converted them to living quarters for kitchen crews and storage. From 1947 to 1956 they were part of the Camp Olson complex. Here they awaited their fate at Camp McGregor in 1957. (John T. Labbe photographs)

THE LONG-BELL ERA

Negotiations began in March 1953. When the sale was closed on May 29, 1953, Central surrendered its 25,000 shares of Oregon-American stock to Long-Bell for $4,961,116.47, the equivalent of more than $198 per share.[10] Long-Bell also bought the remaining minority interests at that time.[11] Thus came the end of the Oregon-American Lumber Corporation and the beginning of that proud organization's final days.

The only time that I actually got scared was when I was firing the 107. After breaking over the hill at the Lost 40, the track leveled off about 300 yards above the Overhead. The brakemen wouldn't knock off the brakes there, and the engineer would pull the train across this stretch with an almost wide-open throttle until he crossed the Overhead where the grade started down again.

This time when we reached the Overhead we were over half-way across before he realized that he hadn't closed the throttle. We were picking up speed pretty fast and the brakemen who had come into the cab had worried looks on their faces.

Like any other seasoned lumbering concern, the Long-Bell Lumber Company had a very strong financial orientation to the varied aspects of its business. Also, however, Long-Bell displayed an enduring sensitivity to the heritage of its departments and a decidedly familial outlook toward its employees.

These qualities and the close relationships enjoyed by many of their respective employees enabled Long-Bell to assimilate the Oregon-American's operations with ease. Consistent with that approach, Long-Bell appointed Judd Greenman general manager of the Vernonia operation. The company also named Connie Anderson assistant general manager. Long-Bell made few other personnel changes in the Vernonia operation, however.[12]

The head brakeman said we'd better jump and he did.

Shields siding was another 300 yards from the Overhead, and the track leveled off there. The 106 was in the siding waiting for us and its brakemen were standing at the switch. When they saw us coming with the engine and loads rocking as if they were going to tip over, they hit for the brush.

I was worried that we might split the switch as we had done that a few days before. If that would have happened, we would have really piled up. As it was, we got across the switch points O.K. and once the loads got off the grade it was no trouble to stop.

Arlie Sliffe, engineer

While giving its new operation the officious title of the Long-Bell Lumber Company, Vernonia Division, Long-Bell allowed the Vernonia Division to operate largely the same as it had all along.[13] In many ways the change of ownership was practically cosmetic. Apart from applying the Long-Bell name

Top: The speeder shed and turntable at Camp McGregor.

§

Middle: The venerable Skagit M.A.C. model 4-40 gas speeder Number 10. It was kept in continuous service on the O-A line from beginning to end, including daily mail runs between Camp McGregor and Keasey during the company's Depression-era receivership. When the original Buda engine wore out during WWII it had already turned more than 350,000 miles. Equipped with a brand new Waukesha power plant, it kept right on going until the end.

§

Bottom: Logging and improvising go hand-in-hand. This is one of the trucks belonging to the Lidgerwood tower skidder. Loggers also made it serve as a snowplow car. (John T. Labbe photographs)

Top: In 1953 Central Coal & Coke sold its majority interest in Oregon-American to the Long-Bell Lumber Company. In 1956 Long-Bell merged with International Paper Company. In the waning days of Vernonia operations locomotive maintenance was less important than it had been to the former owners. (Jim Blain collection)

§

Middle: Crossing the high SP&S trestle west of Keasey in July 1957, 104 backed a load of logs down from Ginger Creek to the makeup yard. (Ron Harr photograph; Ken Schmelzer collection)

§

Bottom: Train 104 and crew waited on the Spur 27 mainline at Telephone 1 while 106 and crew backed down. Once the 106 was in the clear on Spur 27-1, the 104 continued up the mainline to the Spur 27-2 junction for another clearance from the Camp McGregor dispatcher. (John T. Labbe photograph)

in place of Oregon-American's, little else changed. Still, in the hearts and minds of employees and others who had long associated with Oregon-American, the Vernonia operation was, and continued to be, "The O-A."

The Capstone of an Illustrious Career

By the time Long-Bell absorbed Oregon-American, the Vernonia operation was merely finishing out the final act of a play that had been scripted for years. The next major hurdle, conversion of the property to a tree farm, would not commence until the last load had been brought to the mill and the railroad converted into vehicle roads. Absent new issues, management of Oregon-American took on the nature of a caretaker's job.

Beginning in 1947, Connie Anderson had assumed ever more of the operating responsibilities at Vernonia. So, with handling the long-range strategic issues removed to Longview and Kansas City, Greenman was able to devote more of his energies to industry activities. Throughout his career, Judd Greenman maintained a high profile in political circles. That carried over into the social responsibilities arising from that status. During the depths of the Depression, for example, Governor Charles Martin appointed him chairman of the State of Oregon Welfare Committee. Later, he was a director in the Northwest Oregon Forest Protection Association.

Other than his presence at Vernonia, Greenman made his biggest mark serving the industry at large. He had been a member of the West Coast Bureau of Lumber Grades and Inspection for nearly thirty years. He was a trustee for the Columbia Basin Loggers, Columbia Basin Sawmills, and the Lumbermen's Industrial Relations

Committee, organizations that grew alongside organized labor to formulate industry positions.

It was Greenman's involvement in the workings of the West Coast Lumbermen's Association that eclipsed his other contributions, however. An ardent supporter and active member, he served tirelessly in many capacities and was vice president for Oregon between 1946 and 1953. Still, while his contributions were many, the press of business at Vernonia had prevented him from accepting higher elective office. That changed when Long-Bell acquired Oregon-American. Freed from many of the duties that had consumed his energies while at Oregon-American's helm, Greenman took an even more active role in industry affairs. On November 11, 1954, his fellow lumbermen elected him to the presidency of the National Lumber Manufacturer's Association for 1955. His ascendancy marked the final jewel in the crown of a true giant of the industry. As he neared the end of his term of NLMA presidency, Greenman announced his retirement from Long-Bell, effective November 1, 1955. Connie Anderson assumed his duties and title.[14] With Greenman's last day at the mill office, the Vernonia operation passed a symbolical torch.

Logging

By 1953 the center of logging activity had shifted to the Ginger Creek tract. Finishing the remaining odd lots of timber in the Southwest Unit commanded fewer and fewer resources. Again the operation saw its camp-resident loggers traveling long distances to their daily work.

Thanksgiving weekend 1955 marked the official closing of Camp Olson. Over the holiday period, a crew of thirty men braved 16-degree temperatures, a thaw, and then rainstorms to get sixty-five

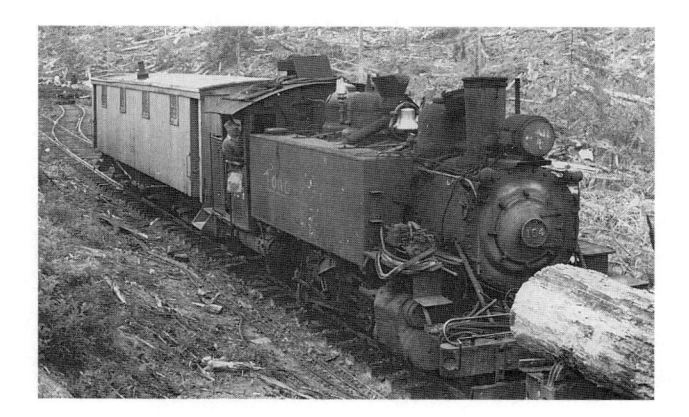

Top: 104 has just eased some loads down Spur 27 to Telephone 1. While waiting for clearance, the brakies got off to recheck the loads for the rest of the trip down to Keasey. To the left are Spur 27-1 and the water tank.

§

Middle: Locomotive 104 working empties to the skidder side on Spur 27-1.

§

Bottom: The 104 on Spur 27-1 heading toward Telephone 1. (John T. Labbe photographs)

THE LAST STAND

Top: The line car was a homespun device used to move spar tree guylines from one landing to another. O-A built the machine in 1938 from old parts and an incline donkey drum. The locomotive supplied steam for the engine. If the new landing was nearby, loggers often simply dragged guylines from the old one using one of the company's bulldozers or locomotives. (John T. Labbe photograph)

§

Middle: O-A often put the locomotive crane to work loading logs along the right-of-way. (Ken Schmelzer collection)

§

Bottom: The 105's water pump was mounted on the tender. It used the locomotive's steam for power. Pumps like this performed many tasks ranging from fighting fires to moving fuel oil between tanks. (Jack Holst photograph; Jim Blain collection.)

bunkhouses skidded to the track, loaded on disconnected trucks, and returned to Camp McGregor. They even took up the wooden sidewalks and put them back down at McGregor so that by the Monday following the holiday weekend, Camp Olson was but a memory.[15]

That Christmas Eve, news arrived that the camp's namesake, Andy Olson had succumbed to a heart attack, driving the finality of Camp Olson's closure home. Born in Sweden in 1886, Olson immigrated to the United States in 1906. He eventually found his way to Oregon-American by 1928 and there he put his roots down for good. Olson had been a strong leader and was popular with his men. The "aching void" created in his passing was heartfelt and widespread.[16] Fred Hageman, Olson's longtime "side-rod," or assistant logging superintendent, assumed Olson's position, and Glenn Johnson moved up to take the vacancy created by Hageman's promotion.[17]

A Return to Our Roots

Decidedly against prevailing trends in the logging industry, the truck logging and reload phases of the operation were closed down after crews brought the last logs out of the Salmonberry Timber Company tract to the Spur 26-8 reload station in August 1956. For the next year, Long-Bell's Vernonia Division was the only outfit left on the West Coast to move its logs entirely by railroad.[18]

For that matter, steam logging itself returned to dominate the scene. Except a diesel donkey side and some remote yarding and a drum-cat operation, movement of logs to the railhead again became the domain of steam equipment and remained so to the end. Moreover, the Lidgerwood tower skidder was still hard at work logging its last setting on Spur

26-15, in Tillamook County at the head of the extremely steep and deep canyon that formed the headwaters of the Middle Fork of Cronin Creek. One of an estimated half-dozen or so Lidgerwoods left in operation anywhere, Long-Bell moved it to this last show on Spur 26 because it carried enough skyline to reach the tail trees some 3,000 feet down in the canyon. The canyon walls were so steep the skyline angled down as much as 45 degrees.[19] *The Log of Long-Bell* correspondent Bill Davis's description of the setting a month or so before it was finished illustrated the scene:

> The most remote logging side of Camp McGregor's is the Lidgerwood tower skidder, now logging in Tillamook County on top of the Coast Range, where leverman Irvin Armstrong can, on a clear day, watch the ships at sea. It was here, last winter, that high winds blew watchman Lee Carrigan's cabin off the mountain.
>
> Foreman Ted Johnson, when he looks down from the landing, sees only the tops of the tin hats worn by the choker setters. Chaser Mike Zaruk and head loader Carl Revis work with only the sky above them. On the other side of the machine, third loader Johan Petersson lets the disconnected trucks down the track and turns to view the tops of Saddle and other mountains rising like islands out of a sea of fog.

Top: The 102 on Spur 27-3 in July 1957. Once the logging crew boarded the crummy, the shay took them back to Camp McGregor. Pipe lying alongside the rails supplied water to the steam donkeys at the end of the spur.

Weeks later the last log was loaded. Except to haul out the equipment and pick up rails, the "duece's" operating days were over. International Paper Company donated the locomotive to the city of Vernonia the following year where it remains on permanent display. (Kamholz collection)

§

Bottom: Keasey enjoyed a resurgence of life once O-A began logging Ginger Creek although little of it involved common carrier traffic. Here, viewed from the 105's cab, engines 104 and 106 have each brought down their loads and are preparing to return to the woods. Before leaving for Vernonia, the 105 switched the loads to get the heaviest ones at the front of the train. (Fred Spurrell photograph; Jim Blain collection)

THE LAST STAND

Top: 104 and train from Ginger Creek approaching the west switch at Keasey. O-A typically kept its woods locomotives pointed uphill to maintain adequate water levels over the firebox crown sheets. (John T. Labbe photograph)

§

Bottom: 106 taking water at Keasey. The 104 has just brought a load of logs down from Ginger Creek and awaits its turn at the tank. While Ginger Creek operations were underway, Keasey served as the makeup yard for Vernonia-bound trains.

When the SP&S converted to diesel power, O-A took over the Keasey water tank. The original one collapsed after operations commenced in the Ginger Creek tract, and the company replaced it with one of its own design. (Fred Spurrell photograph; Jim Blain collection)

Top: O-A logged Ginger Creek last because its stand was immature compared with the rest of O-A's holdings, not that you could tell from the size of this load. The authors recall single-log loads during this era that were even more impressive. (Homer Fairly photograph; Robert Scott collection)

§

Bottom: The diesel side on mainline Spur 27. The sled logs, fairleads, and roof of one of the company's two Berger yarding engines are visible to the left of the tracks. Loading is one of several former Willamette Iron & Steel Works steam donkeys that O-A converted to diesel. The "squirrel," or counterweight used to swing the heel-boom between the cars and the pile of logs in the foreground, is clearly visible suspended to the right of the spar tree. (John T. Labbe photograph)

THE LAST STAND

Top: Due to shortcomings in earlier designs, primarily related to excessive weight, power saws failed to gain acceptance by O-A's cutting crews until the operation's twilight at Ginger Creek. Here a team begins the undercut.

§

Bottom: The undercut, visible at the lower right of the tree, has been completed and, as the saw operator with his back to the camera completed the back cut, his partner began driving the wedges, at first to keep the saw from binding, then to rock the tree over. (Homer Fairly photographs; Robert Scott collection)

Top: *"DOWN THE HILL!"*

§

Bottom: For the most part, operators paid falling and bucking crews on a piecework basis. Immediately after trading in their axes and crosscut saws for chain saws, cutting crews' enjoyed an earnings windfall using the faster machines. That is, until the company adjusted the rates. (Homer Fairly photographs; Robert Scott collection)

Once the skidder had completed logging a half-circle around the spar tree, crews had to turn it facing the opposite side of the tree before completing the rest. Loggers didn't need a fancy wye track to accomplish this task. Instead, they used a couple of locomotives to move the unit to the nearest siding or spur where they put the trucks from one end down one track and the trucks from the other end down another. Then one end was pulled past the other, and the opposite was pushed back toward the switch. Once the ends were swapped, the unit was pushed back out on the track from which it came and returned to the spar tree. Here, locomotives 103 and 104 power the move at the junction of Spurs 27-1 and 27-1-A. (John Henderson photographs; Jim Blain collection)

The only piece of equipment not powered by steam is the pump operated by Irwin Butler, more than a mile down over the mountain and across a canyon. Butler is the only one of the crew who never sees the fine view from the top of the mountain. The choker setters see it twice a day; in the morning on the way down to the logs and again in the evening when, tired from the steep climb after a day's work, they are not too weary to pause on their way to the crummy and dinner 15 miles down the track.[20]

By the end of October 1956, the Lidgerwood crew loaded the last log to come out of the Southwest Unit and Long-Bell scrapped the machine in place. Now the operation concentrated all its logging at Ginger Creek.[21]

Ruth Realty's Keasey Timber

Facing isolation and expensive removal of its Keasey timber unless sold to Long-Bell before it finished logging the Ginger Creek tract, the Ruth Realty Company instead decided to sell its timber there in May 1955. Long-Bell estimated Ruth's holdings at something more than 50 million board feet, most of which was Douglas fir. At the time news of the purchase was made public, Long-Bell also announced plans to ship peeler-grade logs from the Ruth tract to its Longview plywood mill.[22]

INTERNATIONAL PAPER COMPANY

The trend toward industry consolidation continued, and the Long-Bell Lumber Company merged with International Paper Company on November 5, 1956. Yet another of the industry's venerable names ceased to exist.[23]

International Paper Company was founded in

1898 and its subsidiaries owned or held leases on 21 million acres of woodlands in the United States and Canada. At one time, International Paper produced approximately 60 percent of the newsprint consumed in the United States. International Paper operations were in the Provinces of Ontario, Quebec, and New Brunswick in Canada and in Maine, Pennsylvania, New York, South Carolina, Florida, Alabama, Mississippi, Louisiana, and Arkansas.

The Long-Bell merger gave International Paper its first presence on the West Coast and provided it with standing timber and cutover lands in Washington, Oregon, and California. totaling a half-million acres. In addition, another scattering of timber holdings owned by Long-Bell in Arkansas, Louisiana, Mississippi, and Texas were added to the total. Combined sales of the merged firms in 1959 exceeded $1 billion and employed nearly 49,000 people.[24] Still, Vernonia's days were so limited the merger seemed more cosmetic than real.

Top: After loggers turned the skidder they had to move the heel-boom to the opposite side of the spar tree too.

During its 1940 overhaul O-A extended the unit's boiler and removed its loading engine to provide additional steam to the skidding engine. After that, a separate loading engine accompanied it wherever it went. In this case, it was one of the company's converted diesel loaders. (John T. Labbe photograph)

§

Bottom: The leverman's side of the tree-rigged skidder. The pump supplied air to control the drum frictions. The whistle punk, stationed out on the skid road, sent operating signals to the leverman using the electric-powered "Toots-E" whistle visible on the roof toward the front.

O-A replaced the unit's original four-wheel trucks with an eight-wheel truck at the rear and a six-wheel truck on the front to improve weight distribution. (Homer Fairly photograph; Robert Scott collection)

THE LAST STAND

The first significant fall rains of 1956 arrived the third week of November. After the storm passed the skies cleared for a few days and presented authorities with what they thought were ideal conditions

THE LAST STAND

Viewed from a distance it becomes readily apparent just how large the tree-rigged skidder was. (John T. Labbe photograph)

to burn slashings. So advised, the company sent a crew of loggers to set fire to Southwest Unit logging debris Monday, November 19.[25] At the other end of the property, cutting crews at Ginger Creek were about to work themselves out of a job, for the "thirty-four-year search" for the company's last standing tree was about complete.[26]

The rains atop the Coast Range had proved heavier than thought so fire-setters found it nearly impossible to ignite the moisture-laden slashings. Unable to create a burn line the loggers started many spot fires around the property in the hope they might burn and join to achieve the desired result. Try as the loggers might, they could not keep the fires burning without assistance. By Wednesday they deemed the exercise so completely futile the company abandoned the effort and sent its crews home for the Thanksgiving holiday.[27] That same cold, clear day of November 21, 1956, the company's last tree was found, felled, and bucked at Ginger Creek. The event of that day did not pass without controversy. While someone was photographing John Wagberg and Jack Zenger in what they thought was the final act, the Erick Peterson and Knut Klasson crew were at work farther out in the brush and claimed they severed the last tree from its trunk. History will never yield which claim is correct, for no single person witnessed both trees' fall. The participants have taken their claims to the grave, convinced no less than on that day in 1956 the honor of cutting the last tree was theirs alone.[28]

Thanksgiving Day, loggers virtually deserted Camp McGregor; everyone had either left to find new work or was home to enjoy the holiday. During the loggers' absence, Mother Nature again served notice just who was the ultimate steward of the land. First, an east wind arose that quickly evaporated the moisture that had foiled the slash-burning exercise. The wind also revived the remains of the spot fires that had been set and before long the entire area was ablaze. The wind's velocity soon increased, driving the flames to the west. By Sunday the fire had escaped the company's boundaries and was burning out of control, down the Cronin Creek canyons, toward the Nehalem River.

International Paper called every able-bodied logger to return and fight the fire and by Sunday had mobilized the mill crew to join the battle. Once the fire left the company's property, the Oregon Department of Forestry assumed control of the firefighting effort and brought in convict labor to fortify the fighting force. When it became evident they needed more help, the company extended its recruiting to the streets of Portland's Skid Road district where they hastily assembled and hustled a ragtag group of indigents to the scene in two rented passenger busses. The Forestry Department's Larry Fick, who was in charge of the effort, later claimed it was the first time he ever directed firefighters dressed in Oxford shoes.

Extreme contrasts marked the scene. On the ridgetop along the old 26 line, crews suffered winds so fierce that standing up was difficult. Yet a crew that they sent to halt the fire's progress at the bottom of the canyon found a winter wonderland there with everything blanketed in a coating of frost so thick it created a natural fire break of its own. The fire burned some heavy equipment and, for a time, those who remained on the ridge were in danger of being overrun by the flames. A week or so later the fire burned itself out but only after much work by the 300 or so people brought in to contain it.[29]

While the skidder pulled in one turn of logs, choker setters prepared another. Once the skyline carriage returned, the setters removed the empty chokers from the butt rigging and attached the ones slung around the next logs bound for the track side. (Ralph Swan photograph)

THE LAST STAND

Top: A cat side on Spur 27-3. At the lower right is the Number 5 cat, a Cletrac bulldozer equipped with a Carcomatic triple-drum setup. The "drum-cat" was often used to log "short corners" or odd patches of timber not otherwise accessible by a skidder or yarder. This setup could reach out 1,200 feet. One of the diesel loading engines operated the heel-boom. (Homer Fairly photograph; Robert Scott collection)

§

Bottom: Speeder Number 11 took on a more utilitarian appearance after O-A rebuilt it in 1946. Here it approaches the Keasey station on the daily mail run. (John T. Labbe photograph)

This was the last pair of steam donkeys to operate in regular service on the Pacific Slope. The photograph was taken at their final setting on Spur 27-3 in July 1957, a month before they swung and loaded their last logs. Once finished they were left for the scrapper's torch. No one bothered recording their serial numbers.

In 1994, the authors returned to the site. The sled logs, roads, and a few assorted pieces of sheet metal were the only reminders of days past. A fine stand of second-growth Douglas fir trees blanketed the area. Loggers returned and cut them a year later marking the end of a second era of logging in the region. (Kamholz collection)

THE LAST STAND

Another view of the last steam side. The yarder used to swing logs to the trackside landing was on the left and the loading engine was to the right. The disconnects shown to the right of the spar tree were on a graded tail track. Once one load was completed, it was moved down the track to make room for the next. Meanwhile, another set of empty trucks was uncoupled and rolled down the tail track into the loading position under the heel-boom. If the landing's topography didn't provide a suitable grade, cars were pulled into position using the loading engine's auxiliary drum and line. (Kamholz collection)

A pair of prime fir logs arrives at the landing. Oregon-American used the North Bend rigging system shown in this scene extensively. It used a tight skyline and a carriage that ran back and forth between the spar and tail trees. The carriage is visible in the upper middle of the picture. (Kamholz collection)

THE LAST STAND

The first logs have been loaded on a set of disconnects and a loader checked their position before adding more. Once the rest of the logs were on, the loader rolled the completed car downhill and out of the way. (Kamholz collection)

The heel-boom swung on an axis around the spar tree. Once a loader set the tongs on a log from the pile behind the tracks, the engineer engaged the main drum to lift, or "heel," the rear of the log up against the boom. Once he got the log high enough to clear the disconnected trucks, he engaged another drum to swing the boom over the disconnects. Once he had the boom in position, he slowly released the tong line and lowered the log into position. A counterweight, made from a log section called a "squirrel chunk" and connected to the other side of the boom, swung it back over the pile of logs waiting to be loaded. The counterweight itself was suspended from a block that ran up and down one of the spar tree's guylines. (Kamholz collection)

THE LAST STAND

Engine 104 switching one of O-A's Berger diesel yarders aboard the big donkey moving car after the diesel side was finished. (John T. Labbe photograph)

The Last Show

By June 1957, crews had rigged the last spar tree at Ginger Creek and the end was at hand.[30] Whether for reasons of practicality, nostalgia, or simply to make it end as it had begun, loggers rigged a Willamette two-speed steam donkey and companion loader for the trackside swing and for the next month the hillsides overlooking Keasey reverberated to the beat of their exhausts. Oregon-American had finally come full-circle and was ending within sight of where it had begun. While that pair of steampots was symbolic of O-A's thirty-five-year operating life, they also marked the passing of an era in the annals of logging itself, for they were the last two working pair of a steam swing machine and loader to operate on the West Coast.

Many have written about that unique breed of men called the logger. Few captured it any better than Bill Davis, who eulogized the company in the July 1957 issue of *The Log of Long-Bell*:

> *They* sound *like they're logging!* exploded Fred Hageman. Those quotes are dressed up a bit. Logging superintendents express themselves in language seldom seen in print.
>
> Fred was talking about steam logging, a subject he is well able to speak about with the authority of a lifetime of experience. He wasn't speaking of the past. The two steam sides operating under his supervision were two-thirds of the logging operation that put eight million feet of logs in the pond at Vernonia during the month of April 1957.
>
> As superintendent of Camp McGregor, Fred runs what is believed to be the last all-railroad logging operation left on the Pacific Coast. It is also thought to be the only operation still using steam power for most of its work.
>
> It was in 1922 that the crew left the railhead at Keasey and started up Rock Creek cutting right-of-way. That crew used pack horses for supplies and equipment until the rails were laid to the small valley where Camp McGregor was born. The camp was named after W. H. McGregor, who at that time had the title of Manager of Logging and Land.
>
> While the right-of-way crews chopped and sawed their way through the virgin timber the mill

at Vernonia was being built. The Oregon-American Lumber Company had come to northwest Oregon.

The Oregon-American Lumber Company bought Willamette steam donkeys and tree-rigged skidders. They purchased Baldwin rod engines and Lima Shay locomotives. Everything was new. The mill was the biggest and best in the west. The logging equipment had to meet the same standards. Everything was the "last word." Everything was steam powered.

And they logged! One year the mill at Vernonia worked two shifts and cut something like 140 million board feet of lumber. Two steam sides and one steam skidder yarded and loaded all the logs cut by the mill that year. That was logging with steam.

Just over a couple of hills to the north of Camp McGregor were other big logging camps of that time: Green Mountain, Benson, and the camps along the Kerry line. Up in Washington were Ostrander, Ryderwood, and Deep River. And from these camps came the loggers. There were boomers, the short stake artists, and the backbone of the logging world that is hardly ever mentioned—the career loggers.

Bill Milan is a typical career logger. He was 150 feet up the tree when the pass line broke. It was a delicate job getting him picked up. Six years later he crawled from his hospital bed, strapped on his spurs, adjusted his belt and went 200 feet up a tall fir to top it. He has raised a family. He owns his own home in Sherwood, Oregon. When he gets dressed up to go to town he looks like a professor.

It was the boomer and short stake artist that supported the Portland police department and the dens of iniquity of the "roaring twenties." The career loggers built or bought their homes in Portland and other valley towns or rented homes in the family camp where families lived much the same as they would in town. Camp McGregor included a school for the children.

At the other end of Camp McGregor was a bachelor camp where single men and married men who had homes in other communities lived. They slept four men to a bunkhouse, bathed in one of two bath houses, and ate in the dining room. They had to. There wasn't any transportation to get them home every week-end. In fact, they worked most week-ends.

And they logged! With steam—using two and three donkey hauls. They rode on a steam railroad to work and back. They rode to town and from town. The food, fuel, clothes—everything that was needed came in over the rails—behind a steam locomotive.

Camp McGregor was burned out in 1933. The bunkhouses were rebuilt in town and loaded on disconnected trucks and taken to the camp site. The

The company's Skagit SJ-8 mobile yarder logging right-of-way logs on the Ginger Creek Spur. The track had been completed to that point and some disconnects await loading. Looking the opposite direction, the grade ahead has been chunked-out and is ready for steel. (Ralph Swan photograph)

THE LAST STAND

A 1958 aerial view of the Ginger Creek tract after operations had ended and the company had removed all its equipment and rail. The heavy curved lines are former railroad rights-of-way. Note the several types of hub and spoke patterns on the ground. The hubs were donkey landings and the spokes were skid roads created when the ends of the logs dragged along the ground en route to the landings. Yarders dragging logs from their stumps to cold decks created the lighter of those lines. The heavier lines were roads created by trackside yarders as they "swung" logs from the cold decks to the railhead. A bulldozer and arch moved logs in the area at the lower left.

The long straight stretch in the rail line to the far right is the former Keasey yard. (Oregon Department of Forestry)

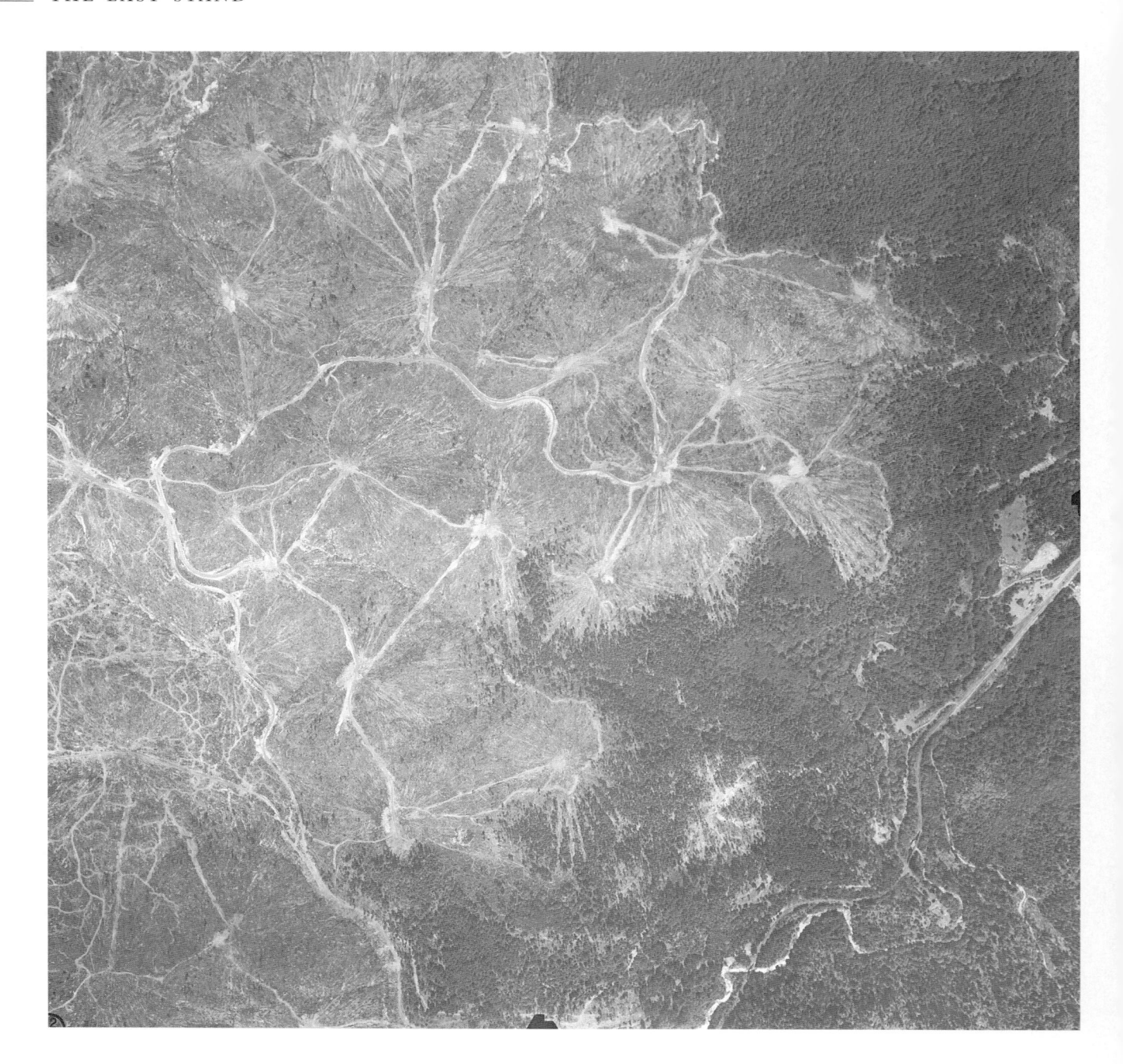

boys went back to logging. There were bridge crews to build and maintain bridges, section crews to keep up the track, right-of-way crews to clear the way for new spurs, steel gangs to pick up the rails from the old spurs and put them down on the new.

Jimmy Elton quit the other day. Jimmy is a brakeman. Brakemen for disconnected trucks are a scarce article these days. The brakes on each truck have to be set by hand. The amount of pressure must be determined by the weight of the load. Fred Hageman heard about his leaving from the dispatcher, "Red" Dunlap. *What does he mean by walking off without saying anything?* (A watered down version of what Fred had to say). For answer, "Red" quietly opened the door and looked out across Rock Creek and up the hill where an old spar tree is still standing. Just as quietly Fred ducked his head and walked away.

That spar tree was being logged more than a generation ago. Fred was pulling rigging there at the time. One morning the hooker showed up with his hair combed. Fred took off down the hill, waded Rock Creek and stormed into the office. *Find my name in that ink bottle and get me some transportation,* he instructed the timekeeper. The timekeeper found his name in the ink bottle all right, but informed Fred that if he stayed between the rails he couldn't get lost. This is the truth as told by "Red" Dunlap. "Red" helped count ties on the way out.

From McGregor the rails were laid up the hill and along the western summit of the coast range. Men working the landings on this spur could look across the Willamette Valley and see Mt. Hood, two more snow caps to the north of Hood and Mt. Jefferson and The Three Sisters to the south. When the logs had been loaded from here, the CCC boys came and made a road, using in part the old railroad bed. That road is still passable from Keasey to Wheeler on the coast. Part of that road is used by men at Camp McGregor to get to the Sunset Highway. Portlanders on their way to Seaside can see where it comes out when they stop at the Sunset Wayside and Spring.

The "25" line was laid west of north of camp and ended near the Quartz Creek bridge on the Sunset Highway. It was along here that the logging crews met the construction crews building the new road to the coast—now known as the Sunset Highway.

The "26" line followed the timber across the highway and into Tillamook County. Over the ridges and across the draws went the railroad, the steam donkeys and the miles of pipe line needed to furnish water for the donkeys and locomotives. Sometimes the pipe line would be a mile long. Sometimes the water could be gravity fed, but most of the time it was not.

The blast of the locomotive whistling for clearance and the donkeys whistling for water could be heard for miles. The syncopated sound of the donkey's piston and turning drums rattled around the hills. Glenn Johnson could tell by the whistles and the noise of the donkeys just about what was going on. From a mile away he could see the steam and smoke and tell what the humidity was and how hard the engine was pulling.

When the standing timber got too far away from Camp McGregor, the camp was loaded on the railroad and taken up the hill, where it was set up again and renamed. Andy Olson was superintendent then and the relocated camp was named after him.

But the forest had to fall before the steam. Spurs were laid, trees were logged, and spurs taken up again. The old railroad beds became fire trails. Down both sides of the canyon, made by the

THE LAST STAND

The final log train was on August 27, 1957. The last logs loaded in the woods are ones being dumped. (Bob and Fred Wenzel photograph)

North Fork of the Salmonberry River, went the loggers. And here, in 1948, the first reload was built and trucks were used. The C. N. Day Company, of Salem, had the contract to haul the logs to the reload. You remember Joe Day from the Rose Bowl game of 1941.

That spur ended when the loggers could look across the canyon and down on Cochran on the Southern Pacific Company's railroad. The next spur went up over the hills to the very top of the coast range. From Windy Gap the whole country looked like a thousand islands rising from the seas of the valley fog. The largest island, of course, was Saddle Mountain. The sun came up, the fog went away, and off the west was the blue Pacific.

This summer of 1957 sometime shortly after the annual vacation period, the last log will be yarded, loaded, and hauled to the mill pond. The steam pots will be cooked, drained and probably sold for junk.

The Shays and the rod engines will be put away by the hostler, George Devine, and the echo of the steam whistle will fade from the hill.

The last old timer will hang up the rigging.[31]

Signs of demise began cropping up all over the property. With the last of the Spur 26 rails picked up, a familiar landmark to travelers on the Sunset Highway gave way to Oregon State Highway Department crews as they removed the Overhead Crossing span on July 23, 1957. More than 1 billion board feet of logs traversed the Overhead during its lifetime.[32]

'THIS IS GOODBYE'

Bill Davis headlined his last article to *The Log of Long-Bell* that way in August 1957: *By twos and threes and bunches, they are going. Where once the dining room had five tables and fed two hundred men, there is one table left, for less than forty men. Seems odd.... Thirty-five wonderful years have come to an end.*[33] On the afternoon of August 27, 1957, locomotive 105 brought the last train of logs to Vernonia. A hastily prepared sign nailed to the last load read "The Oregon-American Lumber Company 1922–1957. Ain't No More."

News that Judd Greenman had passed away that day reached Vernonia as the last load slipped into the mill pond.

After 2.5 billion feet of logs had been run through the sawmill, it cut its last log Wednesday, September 11, 1957 and soon the layoffs began in Vernonia. The planing mill followed suit in December 1957.[34]

Friday noon, December 20, 1957, longtime millwright Maynard Grunden pulled the handle to blow the Vernonia mill whistle for the last time. The fading echo of its mournful blast heralded the end of a way of life. Rose C. Valpiani, *The Log of Long-Bell* correspondent, wrote:

> One never misses the water until the well runs dry and we have discovered that we didn't realize how much we would miss the mill whistle until the day after it blew for the last time.
>
> At noon, on Friday, December 20th, to be exact, those of us who were still working in the office practically stood at attention waiting for the familiar sound with a feeling of sadness. The blast was short and final, but it will echo in our memories for a long, long time.
>
> Our sawmill whistle traveled a long way to Vernonia. R. A. Simmons, former chief engineer of this plant, now deceased, first heard it when a small boy in Texarkana, Texas. Later it was transferred to one of the Delta Land & Timber Company's mills in Conroe, Texas, where Mr. Simmons was employed. When this plant burned down, Charles Keith, then president of Central Coal & Coke Corporation, the parent company, asked Mr. Simmons if there was anything on the plant he would like to have. Mr. Simmons expressed a desire to have the whistle which he brought with him to Vernonia [When the mill was built]. Mr. Simmons installed the whistle which became a part of community life in Vernonia, signaling the beginning and ending of numberless work days, adding its urgent blast to the shriek of sirens when fires broke out, and in a more joyful mood, helping to welcome for more than a third of a century the birth of each succeeding year.
>
> The sound of this whistle had become such a habit and was so much a part of our daily life that at times we would not even hear it, but now that it has been silenced we miss it keenly.[35]

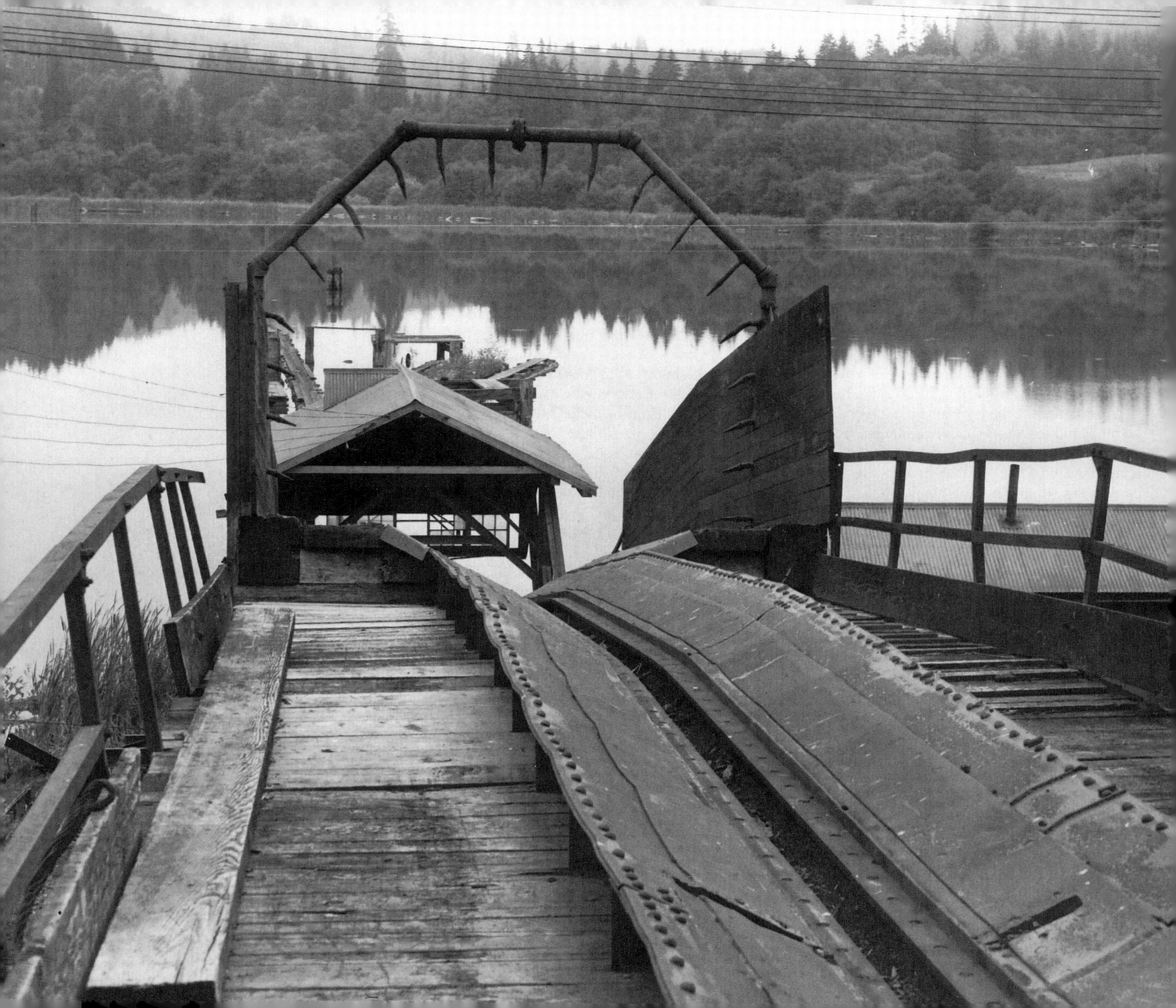

EPILOGUE

Lumbering and other natural-resource industries played a dominant role in the United States's civilization process well into the twentieth century. Commodities extraction not only provided the raw materials needed to house and serve a growing population but also created large-scale employment, which fueled even more demand. On the heels of this process came economic prosperity, and with it social development. Villages, towns, and cities sprang up overnight to serve the needs of employers and workers alike, often turning into booming industrial and commerce centers in their own right.

Being finite, however, natural resources ran out if operators took no steps to regenerate them. Even so, our country's supplies were so bountiful that until recently operators had the luxury to simply leave once they exhausted supplies in one place, only to move somewhere else, along with the jobs.

As glamorous as stories about business growth, prosperity, and social development might be, they remain incomplete, however, unless they account for events in those villages, towns, and cities after the industries that created them went away. So, to the extent Oregon-American's story embodies the life and times of an early twentieth-century lumbering concern, attention now turns to events in Vernonia after the mill closed.

On one level, tracing the destination of equipment and facilities answers questions about "whatever happened to such and such?" In its own way it provides a tidy but impersonal way of completing this story. But, like an obituary, it brings us to closure without capturing the essence of how the survivors coped with the change. The other level, how Vernonia dealt with its future after the mill closed, is equally important and warrants attention too.

Tracking down equipment and facilities is the easier task to relate. Former mill employee Weaver Clark bought locomotives 104, 105, and caboose 367 from International Paper in December 1957. Driven by nostalgia, Clark said he planned to build a permanent display commemorating their service.[1] International Paper Company brought shay 103, Willamette locomotive 106, and the tree-rigged skidder to Vernonia and scrapped them. The company sold some remaining rolling stock to other operators but junked the rest.

Friday, April 18, 1958, a small contingent of workers left on the mill payroll completed loading the last boxcar of lumber to leave the Vernonia mill.[2] International Paper donated shay 102 to the City of Vernonia. It moved under steam to its Bridge Street display site in June 1958.[3] In July 1958 the M. L. Stines Construction Company of Portland began taking up the SP&S rails from Vernonia to the Clatsop/Columbia County line. The contractor returned locomotive 105 to service to help with this task.[4] International Paper deeded sixty-six company houses to the City of Vernonia on October 31, 1958.

Opposite page: The millpond standing empty after the mill cut the last log on September 11, 1957. (Jim Blain collection)

EPILOGUE

Top: The last boxcar of lumber shipped from the Vernonia mill was loaded Friday, April 18, 1958. Pictured are, from left to right: Charles Minger, Rueben Pederson, Ernie Christiansen, Art Nanson, and George Rowland. (Kamholz collection)

§

Bottom: The empty loading dock—a scene that only occurred three times in the mill's life—before it began sawing in 1924, after the Depression-era shutdown in 1933, and finally after shipping the last load of lumber in April 1958. (Jim Blain collection)

The city later annexed the tract, but residents still call it the "O-A Hill."[5] In December 1958 Fred Riley and Milo Burke of Los Angeles began the task of dismantling the sawmill.[6] They sold some equipment at auction and disposed of the usable lumber piecemeal. They scrapped everything else. Also, in December 1958, International Paper seeded 900 acres of cutover lands near Keasey.[7] In a related development, the company also began falling more than sixteen thousand snags on its 26,000-acre Vernonia Tree Farm to reduce the fire hazard.[8]

With only incidental inbound traffic on its line, the SP&S abandoned the Vernonia depot on August 31, 1960. The railway company razed the structure the following winter.[9] As a part of the plan to dispose of all its land holdings in Vernonia proper, International Paper deeded a parcel formerly occupied by the so-called Japanese Colony to the city of Vernonia. It was dedicated as the Conrad L. Anderson Park on August 28, 1960, and today remains a popular gathering spot.[10]

Saturday morning, April 19, 1958, the SP&S local carrying the last load of lumber from the Vernonia mill left for Portland. As the train crossed Highway 47 and passed in front of the Vernonia depot, conductor Dan Mooter stood in the doorway of the caboose accompanied by brakeman Roland Pickard. The engineer that day, Dan Jenkins, was also the SP&S engineer who hauled the first load of lumber from the mill in 1924. (Kamholz collection)

Undoubtedly Vernonia's moment of glory following O-A's closure occurred when Hollywood movie producers Andrew and Virginia Stone filmed segments of the MGM movie *Ring of Fire* there in September 1960. David Janssen, well-known television star, played the lead role. The movie company made quick work of burning the former planing mill building on the afternoon of September 14, 1960, one of the last mill structures remaining at the time. Besides the pyrotechnics and the fact that several hundred townspeople gained a few day's work as extras, little more can be said for the movie. Follow-

EPILOGUE

Top: During the demolition of the Vernonia mill, MGM Studios arranged to film part of the movie *Ring of Fire* there in 1960. In one scene, the film company ran the former Manary Logging Company/C. D. Johnson Lumber Company/Georgia-Pacific Number 9 alongside the burning planing mill. (Jim Blain collection)

§

Bottom: Lead actor David Janssen and others fled the locomotive's cab when the heat became too intense. A movie company employee moved the train to safety. (Rose Valpiani collection)

ing its premier showing at Vernonia's Joy Theater on May 14, 1961, the film quickly sank into obscurity.[11]

By August 31, 1961, Connie Anderson had completed the task of overseeing crews dismantle the mill and retired.[12] After that, only Fred Hageman remained on International Paper Company's Vernonia payroll. Employed as fire warden for the Vernonia Tree Farm, he continued in that role for several years before he too retired.[13]

International Paper also deeded the Vernonia mill office to the city, and in 1963 the building was dedicated as the Columbia County Historical Museum.[14] Since then, it has operated almost continuously in that capacity. Later, International Paper also donated the Vernonia millpond to the city and, after being rededicated as Lake Vernonia, it became a popular fishing spot.

In October 1960, the Vernonia, South Park & Sunset Steam Railroad incorporated to promote steam excursion trains between Vernonia and Banks. The group negotiated the purchase of locomotives 104 and 105, along with former O-A caboose 367. It was 1964 before the group could find coaches, put the 105 in operating condition, and make arrangements to lease the SP&S line. Once accomplished, volunteer fans ran weekend excursion trains every summer until the operation folded on October 19, 1969. The VSP&SS later sold the rolling stock to private parties. By then, freight traffic to Vernonia had diminished to nothing so the SP&S filed to abandon the line. The company's successor, the Burlington Northern, lifted the rails beyond Banks in 1973. Once the right-of-way ownership reverted, the state created a linear park and created a bike trail over the former roadbed.

Consistent with its sale of other properties in the Northwest, International Paper Company disposed of the Vernonia Tree Farm in 1992. Stimson Lumber Company, the new owner, has resumed active logging in the tract.

Now we come to how the mill's closure affected Vernonia and in particular on how the town and its residents handled themselves once the source of its economic lifeblood disappeared. The moment large-scale logging and sawmilling were no longer sustainable, Vernonia was swept into a sustained period of economic and social decline. Despite International Paper Company's creation of the tree farm, and Crown Zellerbach's parallel effort on its former Clark & Wilson holdings, neither were labor-intensive undertakings. Offered no more than the promise of a new crop of trees some thirty years in the future, neither loggers nor anyone else could afford to wait for that future harvest to put their next meal on the table.

While a handful of small, independent sawmills and gyppo logging outfits in the area absorbed a few displaced workers, most who chose to continue in their former occupations had no choice but to do so elsewhere. Treated as social outcasts during their entire history at Vernonia, the African Americans were among the first of those to leave.

History will never yield who felled the company's last tree on November 21, 1956. One felling crew, John Wagberg and Jack Zenger, claimed their tree was the last and had the photographs to prove it. But, farther out in the brush, the crew of Erick Peterson and Knut Klasson were absolutely convinced they cut their final tree after Wagberg and Zenger felled theirs.

We met Erick Peterson in 1993 when he was ninety years old. He wasn't very tall but maintained the powerful physique of a man half his age. For its hardness, his right hand might just as well have been made of iron.

Erick's conviction remained as firm as his grip, for when we introduced ourselves the first words out of his mouth were, I'm Erick Peterson and I cut the last tree.

The Authors

Others in O-A's workforce were well along in years and had reached that stage in life when finding new work was neither vital nor attractive. Many chose to retire in Vernonia. While some former employees of working age found work in new occupations outside the Nehalem Valley, others chose to continue living there and commute to their jobs. In the midst of the larger exodus of wage-earners, both groups provided a valuable measure of population stability.

EPILOGUE

Not surprisingly, the overall loss of jobs took its greatest toll on local businesses. The Chamber of Commerce and local leaders went to some lengths to attract new sources of employment, but apart from a small candle factory and a shale processing plant, Vernonia's geographical isolation, combined with the absence of an alternative and exploitable natural resource deposit, proved insurmountable obstacles to industrial development. As consequences of that fact became clearer, the number of storefronts steadily dwindled.

That was our pasture. In the back was this grove of trees and my brother Larry had a tree house up there...a nice one. There were rows of garages...I suppose they were for when all the single men lived there. They had corrugated tin roofs and somehow we used to get on top of them and walk around. We did a lot of climbing.

I used to walk down to the commissary and get like two quarts of milk. You know, when you got the real kind with the cream on top? I'd have one on each hip walking along.

Carol Lee, a Camp McGregor kid from October 1943 to August 1953 during a visit to her former home on June 21, 1992

Not content to simply give in to the inevitable, Vernonia's civic, spiritual, and business leaders strove to define and promote other features that would make Vernonia a special place to live. The results of that search were twofold. First, and from a purely commercial standpoint, the Nehalem Valley had always offered a bounty of recreational benefits. Sightseeing, golfing, camping, picnicking, rock and fossil hounding, along with fishing and hunting had long attracted outsiders. Until 1957, the area's reputation for these pursuits had largely remained unpublicized. Faced with bleak economic prospects, Vernonia began actively promoting the pursuit of those activities. More than anything else, the resulting inflow of tourism dollars helped offset the economic fallout.

Another feature arose from the close-knit and familial social structure that had evolved during the Oregon-American years. Friendship, the notion of how it developed and the desire to maintain it, solidified a new civic consciousness. Tied to the valley's rich historical past, that notion led to promoting Vernonia as the "Friendship Town."[15] Launched in that spirit, the town celebrated its inaugural Vernonia Friendship Jamboree in 1957. It became an annual event that drew friends, families, guests, and tourists alike.

These efforts further emphasized the Nehalem Valley's recreational potential and the benefits of quiet, country living. Still, these features have not proven a substitute for the lack of local employment. So, for the present, at least, the town's destiny is locked in the hands of residents who prefer living in an isolated rural setting, just close enough to be within easy access of major population centers some 30 miles or so distant. Nevertheless, throughout the years since 1957, Oregon-American remains a common thread that ties Vernonia's past, present, and future.

Many of O-A's former employees and their offspring still reside there. Whether they managed to hang onto jobs like the ones they had in Vernonia by commuting out of the valley, started new careers, or otherwise found ways to get by, there remains today a pioneer spirit about them that sets them apart from others who have since decided to make Vernonia their home. That spirit is easy to find. Undoubtedly, some of it is a carryover from the Nehalem Valley's first settlers, some descendants of whom still live in the area. Over time, that spirit has been supplanted by yet another kind developed by those who have moved to Vernonia. Theirs resembles more of a frontier spirit, born of having forsaken convenience for the benefits of small-town life. And beyond today? Perhaps as urbanization creeps westward from Portland and spills over into the Nehalem Valley, new opportunities will emerge. Certainly that appears to be a more likely outcome than some tree-farm operator's willingness to invest the hundreds of years needed to regenerate a "new" old-growth Douglas fir forest of the type that was central to Vernonia's rise to prominence in the first place. Vernonia seems destined to remain locked between the legacy of its rich past and a future that is yet to unfold.

APPENDIX A – COMPARISON of DONKEY ENGINE OPERATING CHARACTERISTICS and PERFORMANCE

	Willamette Steam 12×14 Two-Speed	Willamette Steam 13×14 Two-Speed	Skagit Diesel Model BX-350-TC Conversion Unit	O-A Diesel 401 Torque Converter Conversion Unit (Former Willamette 12×14 Two-Speed No. 2476)	O-A Diesel 402 Hydraulic Coupling Conversion Unit (Former Willamette 13×14 Two-Speed No. 2504)	Berger Diesel Model BD-250
Mainline Speed (Feet/minute)						
Low	300	397	133	259	231	138
2d	NA	NA	NA	NA	329	NA
3d	NA	NA	NA	NA	492	NA
High	650	851	680	535	700	735
Haulback Line Speed (Feet/minute)						
Low	NA	NA	490	NA	Unk	360
High	1,545	1,775	1,700	1,342	1,200	1,900
Mainline Pull (Pounds)						
Low		126,200	72,000			61,000
High		58,800	14,000			11,500
Haulback Line Pull (Pounds)						
Low		NA	19,500			23,400
High		30,600	5,600			4,450

APPENDIX A — COMPARISON OF DONKEY ENGINE CHARACTERISTICS AND PERFORMANCE

	Willamette Steam 12×14 Two-Speed	Willamette Steam 13×14 Two-Speed	Skagit Diesel Model BX-350-TC Conversion Unit	O-A Diesel 401 Torque Converter Conversion Unit (Former Willamette 12×14 Two-Speed No. 2476)	O-A Diesel 402 Hydraulic Coupling Conversion Unit (Former Willamette 13×14 Two-Speed No. 2504)	Berger Diesel Model BD-250
Line Capacity (Feet and Diameter of Wire Rope)						
Main	2,150 (1 3/8")	2,155 (1 3/8")		2,150 (1 3/8")	1,810 (1 1/2")	1,500
H.B.	4,360 (3/4")	4,000 (7/8")		4,360 (3/4")	4,000 (7/8")	3,740
Strawline	4,200 (7/16")	4,500 (7/16")		4,200 (7/16")	4,500 (7/16")	Unk
Weight (Pounds)						
Engine	73,000	79,400	48,000			42,000
Lines	11,000	11,000	10,000			10,000
Sled	65,000	65,000	50,000			50,000
Total	149,000	155,400	108,000			102,000
Cost in Year of Conversion						
	$15,750 (1925)	$15,750 (1928)	$15,000 (1941)	$17,600 (1944 Conversion Cost)	$17,500 (1947 Conversion Cost)	$25,675 (1949)
Operating Cost (Per Year)						
Labor	2 Men		1 Man			
Fuel	Fuel Oil		Diesel			
Consumption	700 Gal./day		40 Gal./day			
Labor	$3,177 (1941)		$1,892 (1941)			
Fuel	5,390 (1941)		550 (1941)			
Water	880		NA			
Total	$10,797 (1941)		$2,442 (1941)			

APPENDIX B – MILEPOSTS

Milepost numbers on the Portland, Astoria & Pacific, United Railways, and the Spokane, Portland & Seattle changed several times during the history of the roads. When the PA&P was completed in 1922, its milepost numbers started at Wilkesboro. After absorbing the PA&P in 1923, United Railways began its milepost numbers from Linnton. Later, when the United abandoned a small portion of track from its connection to the SP&S's Astoria line in favor of a connection near Sauvie Island, its milepost numbers began from that point, called United Junction. When the SP&S absorbed United Railways, the milepost numbers were changed yet again to reflect the distance from Portland. Locations listed span all years of operation. Not all existed concurrently, however.

	From Linnton	From United Junction*	From Portland
Wilkesboro	0.0	16.4	26.4
Banks	1.2	17.6	27.6
Davies	2.9	19.3	29.3
Vernonia Co./ Thornburg	3.8	20.2	30.2
Carsten	4.7	21.1	31.1
Manning	5.3	21.7	31.7
Buxton	8.1	24.5	34.5
DuBois/Elwood Lumber	8.2	24.6	34.6
Chiltern Spur	9.6	26.0	36.0
Tophill	12.3	28.7	38.7
Tunnel #2	12.6	29.0	39.0
Outfit Spur	12.9	29.3	39.3
Haydite	13.8	30.2	40.2
Schmidlin	15.1	31.5	41.5
Koster	16.0	32.4	42.4
Braun	16.4	32.8	42.8
Koster #2	16.7	33.1	43.1
Beaver Spur/ Connacher	17.7	34.1	44.1
McPherson	20.1	36.3	46.3
Treharne	20.4	36.8	46.8
Vernonia	22.1	38.5	48.5
Poynter	24.2	40.3	50.3
Homewood (formerly Keasey)	26.8	43.3	53.3
Zan	27.6	44.1	54.1
Early	28.4	44.8	54.8
Tara	28.7	45.1	55.1
Lausmann	29.2	45.6	55.6
Logspur	29.4	45.8	55.8
Keasey (formerly Sitts)	30.6	47.0	57.0
Eastmann	32.0	48.5	58.5
Clatsop/ Columbia County Line	32.4	48.9	58.9

*The distance from Linnton to Wilkesboro via the old line, and United Junction to Wilkesboro on the new line is the same.

APPENDIX C – SUPPLEMENTAL NOTES on the POSSIBLE CAUSE of the SALMONBERRY FIRE of JULY 9, 1945

A detailed account of the Japanese balloon-bombing campaign is presented in Bert Webber's *Silent Siege—III, Japanese Attacks on North America in World War II*. The book provides extensive records of balloon-bomb landings.

When asked to comment on Greenman's statement that the Salmonberry Fire of 1945 might have been caused by *a fragment of one of the bombs the Japanese were sending over via balloons,* Mr. Webber replied (in part):

> A search of the balloon bombing incident lists in *Silent Siege—III* for the date of July 9, 1945, does not show any balloon incident on that date. If the fire had been Japanese caused, it would have appeared on the government's list and there would probably have been a recovery team sent to investigate while the fire was in progress....
>
> A fire on your July date could be attributed to latent ignition of a[n]... incendiary bomb dropped early. This is highly plausible. We know that such bombs did explode at later dates, as the kids near Bly, Oregon, as an example, were killed in May 1945 from a bomb dropped much earlier on an unknown date.... While we like to believe all the incidents were reported at the time, postwar research by me has shown numerous balloon incidents that did not get into the official lists. Maybe yours is one of the "missed" incidents. I would keep track of this and not idly pass it by.
>
> By the process of elimination, it would appear that Mr. Judd Greenman's comment that the fire might have been caused by "a fragment of one of the bombs the Japanese were sending over via balloons" would be reasonable. Of course we know now there were no incendiary "fragments" but entire incendiary bombs were dropped. The smallest bomb was only 5kg but that could be very deadly.
>
> As all other sources have been eliminated and the active menace from the Japanese was present until about mid-March 1945—latent afterward—I could conclude there is *plausibility* that your fire was Japanese-bomb-caused.

APPENDIX D – ELEVATIONS at SELECTED POINTS of INTEREST

(Measured at Spur Terminus Unless Otherwise Noted)

PA&P/United Railways/SP&S
- Tophill — 1,000'
- Vernonia — 620'
- Poynter — 660'
- Homewood — 760'
- Lausmann — 800'
- Keasey — 880'
- Col./Clatsop County line — 960'

Oregon-American Mainline to Camp Olson
- Camp McGregor — 1,200'
- Inman-Poulsen HQ Camp — 1,200'
- Twin Bridges — 1,280'
- Shields — 1,360'
- Overhead Crossing — 1,440'
- Lost 40 — 1,760'
- Camp Olson — 1,760'

Spur 5 and Spur 5 Switchback
- Jct. Spur 5 and Switchback — 1,465'
- Spur 5 — 1,440'
- Camp No. 1 — 2,000'
- Spur 5 Switchback — 2,010'

Spur 17 System
- Windy Junction — 1,760'
- Spur 17 North — 2,000'
    - East — 1,600'
    - South — 1,760'
    - Camp No. 1 — 1,760'
    - West — 1,760'

Spur 25 System
- Camp No. 1 — 1,840'
- Spur 25-6 — 1,920'
- Spur 25-6-1 — 2,160'
- –12 — 1,840'
- Spur 25 — 1,850'

Spur 26 System
- Spur 26-3-B-3 Switchback — 2,440'
- –3 — 2,080'
- –8 (Reload) — 1,840'
- –10 — 2,100'
- –13 — 2,480'
- –15 — 2,800'
- –16 — 2,840'
- Windy Gap — 2,720'
- Truck Road Jct. — 2,800'
- –19 — 2,800'
- –21 — 2,960'
- Spur 26 — 2,880'

Spur 26 Truck Roads
- Spur 26-8 — 2,100'
- –17A — 2,560'
- –17B — 2,400'
- –17C — 2,160'
- –17D — 2,240'

Spur 27 System
- Spur 27 — 1,520'
- –1 — 1,280'
- –3 — 1,440'

APPENDIX E – MAJOR TREE SPECIES of the OREGON-AMERICAN LUMBER COMPANY TIMBER TRACT

Common Name	Scientific Name	Characteristics
Douglas Fir	*Pseudotsuga menziessii*	Douglas fir is the most common evergreen tree west of the Cascade Mountain Range. As such it accounts for the largest part of Oregon's wood crop and furnishes more timber products for human use than any other tree. Depending on the color and quality of the wood, Douglas fir is often called "red" or "yellow" fir. Both kinds of wood may be in the same tree, the course-grained center being reddish and the fine-grained outer portions of the stem, yellowish. Yellow fir is considered more desirable than red fir because of its color, fine grain, and easy working qualities. The formation of red fir wood is commonly attributed to rapidity of growth, and since the rate of growth diminishes with age, the trees in old forests are likely to contain a relatively larger proportion of the yellow wood. Consequently, young Douglas Fir forests are frequently called red fir forests and older stands classed as yellow fir forests.
Western Hemlock	*Tsuga Heterophylla*	Western Hemlock typically grows mixed with other tree species. Except for flooring and siding, Hemlock was largely unmarketable until the 1930s. As a result, lumbermen often wasted immense volumes of it. Today, Western Hemlock is commercially prized, for no species excels it in quality and yield for pulp used to manufacture higher grades of news, book, magazine, and tissue papers.

Common Name	Scientific Name	Characteristics
Western Red Cedar	*Thuja plicata*	Growing singly or in clusters, Western Red Cedar is one of the lightest of coniferous woods. It is soft in texture, even and straight grained, highly attractive in natural coloring and pleasant to smell. Since the heartwood defies decay, it is the choice wood for exposed uses. Its important uses include shingles, lumber, poles, posts, piling, fencing, siding, and interior trim. Western Red Cedar was the most important tree to Northwest Native Americans, who used it for dwellings, boats, clothing, ropes, blankets, and baskets.
Grand Fir	*Abies grandis*	The only true fir that grows below about 1,500 feet. It mingles with other conifers and generally does not form true stands.
White Fir	*Abies concolor*	Often confused with Grand fir, White fir is the most important of the so-called true firs and today is widely used for sawed products, plywood, and paper-making. In old-growth tree stands primarily consisting of Douglas fir, Grand and White fir were frequently classed as a "thin-barked" fir species and were generally considered inferior.
Noble Fir	*Abies procera*	Also a true fir, Noble fir also mingles with other species. Noble fir does not account for a large percentage of overall tree stands and is therefore of minor commercial importance, although it produces good-quality material. It is widely cultivated for Christmas trees. Sometimes Noble fir is also called "Larch."

EQUIPMENT ROSTER
ROD LOCOMOTIVES

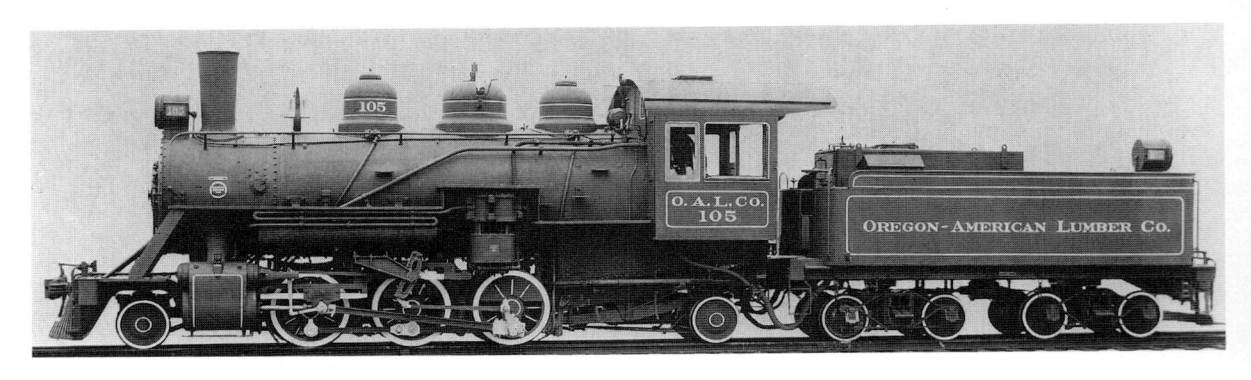

	Road Number					
	100	101	102	104	105	SP&S No. 5
Builder	Alco	Alco	Alco	Baldwin	Baldwin	Alco
Shop Number	61857	61858	61859	56851	58193	44744
Acquired	See below	See below	See below	1923	1925	1907
Class	176	176	176	10-30-1/4D	10-30-1/4D	A
Type	2-8-2	2-8-2	2-8-2	2-6-2T	2-6-2	0-6-0
Driver Size	48"	48"	48"	44"	44"	51"
Cylinder Size	20"D×28"S	20"D×28"S	20"D×28"S	18"D×24"S	18"D×24"S	20"D×26"S
Weight (Working Drivers, Pounds)	136,000	136,000	136,000	117,500	105,430	150,000
Weight (Working Total, Pounds)	176,000	176,000	176,000	149,500	211,000	239,183
Tractive Effort	35,700	35,700	35,700	25,500	25,500	31,200
Boiler Pressure (Pounds)	180	180	180	170	200	180
Fuel Capacity (Gallons)	1,800	1,800	1,800	900	1,500	1,900
Water Capacity (Gallons)	5,000	5,000	5,000	2,000	3,500	4,000
Wheelbase (Drivers)	14' 3"	14' 3"	14' 3"	9' 4"	9' 4"	11' 0"

100. Ordered by PA&P in 1920 and acquired by Oregon-American Lumber Company in 1921. Rented to Spokane, Portland & Seattle Railway Company during November 1922 but rarely used thereafter. Weed Lumber Company (Long-Bell Lumber Company), Weed, California, Road Number 100 by 1926. Yreka-Western, Yreka, California, Road Number 100, 1955. Scrapped 1955.

101. Ordered by PA&P in 1920 and delivered to Vancouver, Washington. Locomotive never accepted (that is, paid for). Minarets and Western Railway Company, Fresno, California, Road Number 101, 1922. Southern Pacific Railroad Company, 1932. Aberdeen & Rockfish Railroad Company, Aberdeen, North Carolina, Road Number 40, 1936. Valley Railroad, Essex, Connecticut, Road Number 40, 1977. Currently in service.

102. Ordered by PA&P in 1920 and acquired by Oregon-American Lumber Company in 1921. Vancouver Equipment Corporation, Vancouver, B.C., 1938. Albierni Pacific, Vancouver Island, B.C., 1938. Canadian Forest Products, Ltd.'s Englewood Railway, Woss, B.C. Road Number 113.

104. Oregon-American Lumber Company, Road Numbers 1/104, 1923. Oregon-American Lumber Corporation, 1935. Long-Bell Lumber Company, 1953. International Paper Company, Long-Bell Division, 1956. Weaver Clark, 1957. Vernonia, South Park & Sunset Steam Railway Company, 1960–69. Fred Kepner.

105. Oregon-American Lumber Company, 1925. Oregon-American Lumber Corporation, 1935. Long-Bell Lumber Company, 1953. International Paper Company, Long-Bell Division, 1956. Weaver Clark, 1957. Vernonia, South Park & Sunset Steam Railway Company, 1960–69. Fred Kepner.

SP&S No. 5. Leased from SP&S between March and August 1948.

EQUIPMENT ROSTER
GEARED LOCOMOTIVES

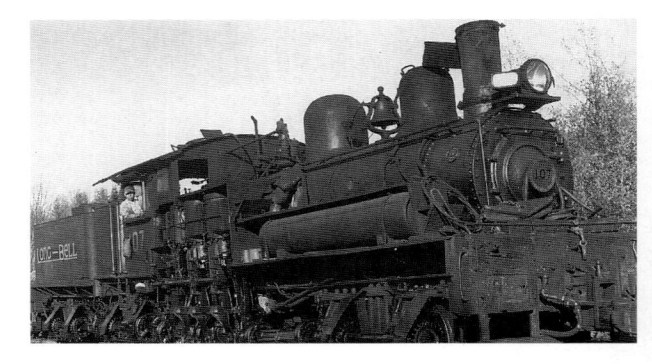

	Road Number				
	2/102	103	106	107	116
Builder	Lima	Lima	Willamette	Lima	Lima
Shop Number	2490	3181	26	1812	2757
Acquired/Built	1928/1912	1922	1927	1948/1907	1914
Class	40-2	70-3	70-3	80-3	70-3
Type	2-Truck Shay	3-Truck Shay	3-Truck Shay	3-Truck Shay	3-Truck Shay
Driver Size	29 1/2"	36"	36"	36"	36"
Cylinders/Size	10"D×12"S	12"D×15"S	12"D×15"S	13 1/2"D×15"S	12"D×15"S
Weight (Working Pounds)	87,964	166,600	174,000	135,550* 200,100**	152,300
Tractive Effort (Pounds)	16,900	30,350	36,000	35,100	30,375
Boiler Pressure (Pounds)	180	200	200	200	200
Fuel Capacity (Gallons)	800	1,200	1,200	6 Tons 1,366***	5 Tons Unk***
Water Capacity (Gallons)	1,560	3,000	3,000	3,500	3,500
Wheelbase	4' 2"	4' 4"	4' 4"	4' 8"	4' 4"

*As Built Dry Weight. **As Delivered to O-A Working Weight. ***Converted to oil by prior owner.

2/102. Acquired by Western Cooperage (Astoria Southern Railway), Astoria, Oregon, Road Number 2. Clark County Timber Company, Yacolt, Washington, 1922. Porter Carstens Logging Company, Estacada, Oregon. Western Loggers Machinery Company, Portland, Oregon. Oregon-American Lumber Company, Road Number 2, 1928. Oregon-American Lumber Corporation, Road Number 2, 1935. Renumbered Road Number 102, 1938. Long-Bell Lumber Company, 1953. International Paper Company, Long-Bell Division, 1956. Placed on display at Vernonia, Oregon, 1958.

103. Oregon-American Lumber Company, 1922. Oregon-American Lumber Corporation, 1935. Long-Bell Lumber Company, 1953. International Paper Company, Long-Bell Division, 1956. Scrapped at Vernonia, Oregon, 1957.

106. Delta Land & Timber Company, 1927. Oregon-American Lumber Corporation, 1935. Long-Bell Lumber Company, 1953. International Paper Company, Long-Bell Division, 1956. Scrapped at Vernonia, Oregon, 1957.

107. Acquired by San Pedro, Los Angeles & Salt Lake Railroad, Tintic, Utah, Road Number 61. Los Angeles & Salt Lake Railroad, Tintic, Utah, 1916. Union Pacific Railroad, Tintic, Utah, 1921. Oregon-American Lumber Corporation, Road Number 107, 1948. Long-Bell Lumber Company, 1953. Scrapped at Portland, Oregon, 1955.

116. Central Coal & Coke Company (Missouri and Louisiana Railroad), Neame, Lousiana, Road Number 116. Delta Land & Timber Company, Conroe, Texas. Delta Land & Timber Company, Vernonia, Oregon, Road Number 116, 1926. Willamette Iron & Steel Works, Portland, Oregon, 1927. Spaulding-Miami Lumber Company, Grand Ronde, Oregon, Road Number 5. Oregon-Coast Range Lumber Company, Grand Ronde, Oregon, Road Number 5. Polk Operating Company, Grand Ronde, Oregon, Road Number 5. Scrapped (date unknown).

ROSTER – DONKEY ENGINES and SKIDDERS

Willamette Iron & Steel Works builders photographs.

Top left: Tree-rigged skidder.

§

Others: 12"×14" compound-geared two-speed donkey engine.

Manufacturer	Description	s/n	Acquired	Disposition
Willamette Iron & Steel Works	12"×14" Humboldt Yarder	1664	1918	Traded for No. 2476, 1940.
		1665		Traded for No. 2476, 1940.
		1985		Traded for credit on No. 2504, 1928.
		1916		Retired 1929.
	11"×13" Loading Engine	2061	1922	Converted to diesel, 1946.
		2062		Converted to diesel, 1947.
	13"×14" Hi-Speed	2164	1923	Converted to yarder, 1948. Retired by 1946.
		2165		Replaced 2166 as Camp McGregor bathhouse hot-water heater by 1946.
	11"×13" Humboldt Yarder	2166	1923	Chunkout engine. Converted to Camp McGregor bathhouse hot-water heater by 1938. Retired 1946.
	11"×13" Loading Engine	2167	1923	Still in service 1949 (last recorded date in Greenman Collection).
	11"×13" Humboldt Yarder	2176	1924	Chunkout engine. Traded for credit on Willamette 12"×14" Two-Speed, in 1925.
	11"×13" Loading Engine	2336	1924	Still in service 1949 (last recorded date in Greenman Collection).
	Tree-Rigged Skidder:			
	12"×14" Skidding Engine	2359	1924	Firebox and boiler extended 1940.
	10"×11" Transfer Engine	2360		Loading engine removed 1940.
	11"×13" Loading Engine	2341		Scrapped Vernonia, Oregon, 1957.
	12"×14" Compound-Geared Two-Speed Yarder	2347	1924	Retired by 1946.
		2363	1925	Burned in 1939 Cow Creek fire. Engine not rehabilitated.
		2365	1925	Retired by 1946.
	11"×13" Loading Engine	2358	1925	Converted to diesel 1946.

EQUIPMENT ROSTER—DONKEY ENGINES AND SKIDDERS

Manufacturer	Description	s/n	Acquired	Disposition
Willamette Iron & Steel Works	Electric Log Decking Engine	2375	1925	Retired 1930.
	12"×14" Compound-Geared Two-Speed Yarder	2386	1925	Still in service 1950 (last recorded date in Greenman Collection).
		2334	1925	Still in service 1949 (last recorded date in Greenman Collection).
Willamette Iron & Steel Works	12"×14" Compound-Geared Two-Speed Yarder	2400	1925	Retired by 1946.
	7 1/4"×10" Three-Drum Hoisting Engine	2436	1926	Pile Driver. Converted to diesel 1950.
	13"×14" Compound-Geared Two-Speed Yarder	2477	1927	Still in service 1949 (last recorded date in Greenman Collection).
		2504	1928	Converted to diesel 1947.
Skagit Steel & Iron Works	BU-154 Diesel Yarder	909	1939 (Used)	Destroyed in February 1943 Music fire.
Willamette Iron & Steel Works	12"×14" Compound-Geared Two-Speed Yarder	2476	1940 (Used)	Acquired in trade for Humboldt yarders 1664 and 1665. Converted to diesel 1945.
Skagit Steel Iron Works Works Estep	BX-350-TC Diesel Conversion Yarder (Former Washington Iron Diesel Yarder No. 4169).	117	1941	Traded for credit on Berger yarder s/n 853.
Lidgerwood Company	Steel Tower Skidder (Extensively modified by former owner, Crown-Zellerbach)	3016	1946 (Used)	Scrapped Spur 26-15, 1956.
Willamette Iron & Steel Works	Gasoline Conversion Loading Engine	1850	1948 (Used)	Unknown.
Berger Engineering Works	BD-250 Diesel Yarder	853	1949	Sold 1957.
		879	1950	Sold 1957.
Skagit Steel & Iron Works	SJ8-W, Type 3G-L-T-N.G. Mobile Logger	SJ8A9	1951	Unknown.

EQUIPMENT ROSTER
BULLDOZERS and GRADERS

	1[1]	2[2]	4[1,2,3]	5[3]	3[3]	—[4]	—[3]	—[3]
Builder:	Cleveland Tractor Company				Caterpillar Tractor Company	Austin Mfg. Company	Galion	Allis-Chalmers
Shop No.	6356	6578	1HA076	10Y546	SR2338	D3105	MD-12072	4195
Type:	FDL	FDL	FDLC	FDE	D-8 Tractor	Austin Western Motor Grader	Motor Grader Model 103	Allis-Chalmers HD 14
Acquired:	1936	1937	1942	1947	1942	1942	1948	1950

1. Cletrac 6356 traded in for credit on Cletrac 1HA076, 1942.
2. Cletrac 6578 traded in for credit on Cletrac 10Y546.
3. Disposition unknown.
4. Replaced by Galion Grader, 1948.

Sold by Pittenger Equipment Company, 1949.

EQUIPMENT ROSTER
LUMBER CARRIERS

	—[1]	1[2]	2[3]	42[4]	47[5]	2[6]	3[7]	1[8]	4[9]
Builder:	A. Streich & Bros., Co.	Dallas Machine & Locomotive-Works	Willamette Iron & Steel Works		Dallas Machine & Locomotive Works, Inc.				
Shop No.	Unkown	264	44	42	HS 228	389	423	501	5572
Type:	Hand-Operated Lumber Buggies Approx. 100 in number.)	Gerlinger Lumber Carrier	Willamette Lumber Carrier		Gerlinger Lumber Carrier				
Model:	Special 25	RPF Mechanical Lift	Mechanical Lift		HS Hydraulic Lift	4-M	4MH, 1-A	4MH	4MH 4560
Acquired:	1924	1930	1927	1927	1930	1937	1938	1940	1942

RESEARCH NOTES

The *The Oregon-American Lumber Company: Ain't No More* is predominately based on documents contained in the Greenman Collection, part of the Division of Special Collections and University Archives, Library System, University of Oregon. The Greenman Collection is comprised largely of the personal correspondence of Judd Greenman, general manager and president of the company from 1925 to 1956. Documents contained in the collection precede Greenman's arrival at Vernonia but end in 1952, the last year the company operated before it was sold to the Long-Bell Lumber Company.

The authors selected nearly 16,000 documents totaling some 23,000 pages from the 84-linear-foot collection, which is thought to contain 65,000 documents overall. Because the collection was not cataloged and therefore lacked any coherent structure conducive to organized research, the authors assigned selected documents unique numbers preceded by a prefix number corresponding to the box number in which each document was stored. Actual document numbers were assigned sequentially in order of each document's appearance in its respective box. Selected materials and their assigned numbers were then microfilmed. The sheer volume of these source materials necessitated the design and development of a searchable database to enable recorded documents to be sorted by document number, date, and topic code. Every entry includes a brief description of each document's contents. The system thus developed, while suited to the authors' needs, neither encompassed the entire collection nor conformed to conventional library cataloging methodology. Still, however, it does provide a means to retrace the authors' research, certainly to the box in which a particular document is stored and even to the general location within each box where the document resides. The microfiche and the database are available at the Division of Special Collections and University Archives.

Voluminous references to the Greenman Collection make it impractical to include them in a commercial work. Citations for secondary works are included, however. Those interested in retracing the authors' research of the Greenman Collection should note that a fully cited manuscript of *The Oregon-American Lumber Company: Ain't No More* is also on record with Special Collections and University Archives.

CONSTRUCTING AMERICA

1. Stanley F. Horn, *This Fascinating Lumber Business* (Indianapolis, Ind.: The Bobbs-Merril Company, 1943), p. 21.
2. Ibid.
3. Nelson Courtland Brown, *Logging, The Principles and Methods of Harvesting Timber in the United States and Canada* (New York: John Wiley & Sons, Inc., 1949), p. 12.
4. Ibid.
5. Ibid.
6. Ibid.
7. Ibid.
8. Ibid.
9. http://douglass speech.nwu.edu/ooah/ooah7.html, p. 3.
10. Ibid.
11. Ibid., p. 5.
12. Ibid., p. 6.
13. Horn, p. 21.
14. Brown, pp. 3–6.
15. Ibid., p. 12.
16. Ibid.
17. Ibid.
18. Horn, p. 181.

RESEARCH NOTES

19. http://mckenna.cses.vt.edu/hist3124/ch6.html, p. 14.
20. Lenore K. Bradley, *Robert Alexander Long, a Lumberman of the Gilded Age* (Durham, N.C.: Forest History Society, 1989), p. 17.
21. Ibid., pp. 17–18.
22. Ibid., p. 26.
23. Ibid., pp. 17–18.
24. Ibid., p. 31.
25. http://mckenna.cses.vt.edu/hist3124/ch6.html, p. 1.
26. Ibid., p. 1.
27. Ibid., p. 5.
28. Brown, p. 13.
29. Horn, p. 30.
30. Brown, p. 13.
31. Bradley, pp. 32–35.
32. Ibid., pp. 32–35.
33. Brown, pp. 41–43.
34. Horn, p. 204.
35. Ibid., pp. 102–5.
36. Ibid., p. 105.
37. Bradley, p. xi.
38. Ibid., p. 17.
39. Ibid., p. 29.
40. Ibid., p. 32.
41. Ibid., pp. 32–35.
42. *Lumber and Coal Resources of the West*, reprint of November 1, 1902, edition of the *American Lumberman* (Chicago: The American Lumberman, 1902), pp. 5–6.
43. Ibid., pp. 19–21.
44. Bradley, p. 31.
45. Brown, pp. 34–38.
46. Bradley, p. 121.
47. Brown, pp. 19–20.
48. Horn, p. 77.
49. Ibid., p. 176.
50. Ibid.
51. Leonard J. Arrington, *David Eccles, Pioneer Western Industrialist* (Logan: Utah State University, 1975), pp. 85–89.
52. Clem Pope, *Switchback to the Timber* (Parkdale, Ore.: Old Forester Publishing Company, 1992), p. 19.
53. Horn, p. 76.
54. Ibid., pp. 181–84.
55. Ibid., pp. 181–205.

THE ROAD TO VERNONIA

1. *Vernonia Eagle*, October 5, 1923.
2. Leonard J. Arrington, *David Eccles, Pioneer Western Industrialist* (Logan: Utah State University, 1975), p. 119.
3. Ibid., pp. 15–16, 193.
4. Ibid., Appendixes 1 and 2.
5. Ibid.
6. Ibid., pp. 88, 119.
7. Ibid., p. 108.
8. Ibid., p. 254.
9. Ibid., pp. 240–41.
10. Ibid., Appendixes 1 and 2.
11. Ibid.
12. Ibid., pp. 89, 92.
13. Ibid.
14. Ibid., p. 228.
15. Ibid., p. 145.
16. Ibid., pp. 145, 63–65, 141.
17. Ibid., p. 164.
18. Ibid., p. 40.
19. Ibid., p. 41.
20. Ibid., pp. 40–41.

21. *Lumber and Coal Resources of the West* (Chicago: The American Lumberman, n.d.), p. 9.
22. John T. Gaertner, *North Bank Road—The Spokane, Portland & Seattle Railway* (Pullman: Washington State University Press, 1990), p. vii.
23. Ibid., p. vii.
24. Ibid.
25. Ibid., p. viii.
26. Ibid.; and Lorenz P. Schrenk and Robert L. Frey, *Northern Pacific Classic Steam Era* (Mukilteo, Wash.: Hundman Publishing, Inc., 1997), pp. 18–30.
27. Ibid., p. 6.
28. Ibid.
29. Ibid.
30. Ibid.
31. Ibid., pp. 6, 16, 22–23.
32. *Vernonia Eagle*, October, 6, 1922.
33. Nelson Courtland Brown, *Logging—Principles and Practices in the United States and Canada* (New York: John Wiley & Sons, Inc., 1934), p. 128.
34. *Oregon-American Lumber Company Articles of Incorporation*; and Arrington, Appendixes 1 and 2, p. 145.
35. Arrington, p. 252; and Gaertner, pp. 131–32.
36. Gaertner, pp. 131–32.
37. Arrington, p. 252.
38. Gaertner, pp. 177–82.
39. Ibid., p. 182.
40. Ibid., pp. 182–86.
41. Ibid., p. 182; and Ed Austin and Tom Dill, *The Southern Pacific in Oregon* Edmonds, WA.:Pacific Fast Mail, 1987), p. 185.

42. Gaertner, p. 184.
43. Ibid., p. 187.
44. Ibid., p. 189.
45. Ibid., pp. 187–89.
46. Ibid., p. 188.
47. Ibid., pp. 188–89.
48. *Portland, Astoria & Pacific Railroad Company Articles of Incorporation*.
49. Ibid.
50. Gaertner, p. 190.
51. *Portland, Astoria & Pacific Railroad Company Articles of Incorporation*.
52. Gaertner, p. 190.
53. Ibid.
54. Audio tape: *All Change Here*, produced by Northwest Public Affairs Network.
55. Gaertner, p. 185.
56. Ibid., p. 190; and *American Lumberman*, June 14, 1919.
57. *Nehalem Boom Company Articles of Incorporation*.
58. Ibid.; and Gaertner, p. 190.
59. Gaertner, p. 190.
60. *Nehalem Boom Company Articles of Incorporation*.
61. Gaertner, pp. 190 and 187.
62. *American Lumberman*, June 14, 1919, and August 23, 1919.
63. Gaertner, p. 190.
64. Marriner S. Eccles, *Beckoning Frontiers, Public and Personal Recollections* (New York: Alfred A. Knopf, 1966), pp. 42 and 45.
65. Ibid., pp. 45–46.
66. Ibid., pp. 46–47.
67. Ibid.
68. Gaertner, p. 190.
69. Ibid.
70. Ibid.
71. Ibid.
72. NP Pres. File 1404 C-7, PA&P 7/9/21 and 7/28/21.
73. Gaertner, p. 190.
74. Ibid.
75. Ralph W. Hidy, Frank Ernest Hill, and Allan Nevins, *Timber and Men: The Weyerhaeuser Story* (New York: The Macmillan Company, 1963), pp. 207–8, 212–13.
76. *Lumber and Coal Resources of the West*, pp. 47–49.
77. Gaertner, p. 191; and NP Pres. File 1404 C-7, PA&P 9/3/21.
78. Gaertner, p. 191.
79. Ibid.
80. Ibid.
81. Ibid.
82. Ibid.
83. Ibid.
84. Harley K. Hallgren and John F. Due, "United Railways of Oregon," *Pacific Railway Journal* (San Marino, Calif., 1962): 13 and 27.
85. NP Pres. File 1404 C-7, PA&P 8/6/21.
86. Gaertner, p. 192.
87. Ibid.
88. Ibid.; and NP Pres. File 1404 C-7, PA&P 7/10/22.
89. Ibid.; and PA&P 7/21/22.
90. Hallgren and Due, p. 23.
91. NP Pres. File 1404 C-7, PA&P 8/20/22.

BOOM TIMES ARRIVE

1. *Oregon-American Lumber Company Bond Issue Announcement*.
2. Ibid.
3. Ibid.
4. Audio tape: *All Change Here*, Northwest Public Affairs Network.
5. *The Log of Long-Bell*, various issues between 1953 and 1957.
6. Hank Johnston, *Rails to the Minarets, Timber Times* (1996): 118.
7. *Timberbeast* (spring 1989) 27.
8. John T. Gaertner, *North Bank Road—The Spokane, Portland & Seattle Railway* (Pullman: Washington State University Press, 1990), p. 195.
9. Ibid.
10. Ibid.
11. NP Pres. File 1661 W, PA&P 6/7/22 and 6/14/22.
12. *Portland, Astoria & Pacific Railroad Board Resolution*, December 1, 1923.
13. *Vernonia Eagle*, October, 15, 1923.
14. Ibid., March, 2, 1923.
15. Ibid., February 9, 1923.
16. Ibid., March 1, 1924.
17. Ibid., April 6, 1923; and December 14, 1923.
18. Ibid., February 22, 1924; March 21, 1924; July 11, 1924; and July 18, 1924.
19. Ibid.
20. Ibid.
21. Ibid., April 6, 1923.
22. Ibid., April 3, 1925.
23. Ibid.
24. Ibid., February 9, 1923; and equipment drawings on file at Columbia

County Historical Museum, Vernonia, Oregon.

25. *Vernonia Eagle*, December 12, 1924.
26. Ibid., March 21, 1924.
27. *The Log of Long-Bell*, May 1957.
28. *Vernonia Eagle*, July 18, 1924.
29. Ibid., July 10, 1924.
30. Ibid., July 18, 1924.
31. Ibid.
32. Michael Koch, *The Shay Locomotive, Titan of the Timber* (Denver, Col.: World Press, 1971), p. 438.
33. *Vernonia Eagle*, April 3, 1925.
34. Ibid.
35. Ibid., October 20, 1922.
36. Ibid., December 12, 1924.
37. Ibid., October 5, 1923.
38. Ibid., December 12, 1924.
39. Ibid., December 12, 1924; and September 1, 1922.
40. Ibid.
41. Ibid., December 12, 1924.
42. Ibid., February 16, 1923; and April 6, 1923.
43. Eckard V. Toy Jr., "The Ku Klux Klan in Tillamook, Oregon," reprinted from *Pacific Northwest Quarterly*, April, 1962, in *Tillamook History, Sequel to Tillamook Memories* (Tillamook Pioneer Association, 1975).
44. *Vernonia Eagle*, April 6, 1923; and September 7, 1923.
45. Ibid., June 5, 1925.
46. Ibid., June 12, 1925.

FROM THE ASHES

1. J. E. Lodewick, "Salvaging Fire Killed Timber," *West Coast Lumberman*.
2. Larry Fick and George Martin, *The Tillamook Burn—Rehabilitation and Reforestation* (Forest Grove, Ore.: Oregon Department of Forestry, 1992), pp. 88–89 and 260.
3. Lodewick.
4. *Oregon-American Lumber Corporation Articles of Incorporation*.
5. Walter R. Grande, *The Northwest's Own Railway*, vol. 1 (Portland, Ore.: Grande Press, 1992), p. 39.
6. Robert M. Hanft, *Red River* (Chico: Center for Business and Economic Research, California State University, Chico, 1981), p. 233.
7. Ibid., pp. 233–34.
8. Ibid., p. 234.

A NEW WORLD

1. Bert Webber, *Swivel-Chair Logger* (Fairfield, Wash.: Ye Galleon Press, 1976), p. 108.
2. *Timberbeast*, vol. 8, no. 3, 1994.
3. *Oregonian*, August 2, 3, 4, 5, 7, 8, and 22, 1939; and *Oregon Journal*, August 2, 3, 4, 5, 6, 7, 8, 10, 19, 22, and 29, 1939.
4. Ralph W. Hidy, Frank Ernest Hill, and Allan Nevins, *Timber and Men: The Weyerhaeuser Story* (New York: The MacMillan Company, 1963), pp. 429–30.
5. Ken Drushka, *Working in the Woods* (Madeira Park, B.C., Canada: Harbour Publishing, 1992), p. 244.

LUMBER GOES TO WAR

1. Ralph W. Hidy, Frank Ernest Hill, and Allan Nevins, *Timber and Men: The Weyerhaeuser Story* (New York: The MacMillan Company, 1963), pp. 446–48; and Ellis Lucia, *Head Rig* (Portland, Ore.: Overland West Press, 1965), pp. 199–206.
2. Bert Webber, *Silent Siege—III* (Medford, Ore.: Webb Research Group, 1992), pp. 26–27.
3. Ibid., pp. 171–95.
4. Ibid.
5. Ibid., pp. 163–70.
6. Ibid., p. 137, and numerous headlines contained in the work.
7. Ibid., pp. 171–95.
8. Various documents from court proceedings in *McKinney v. Oregon-American Lumber Corporation, et al.*
9. Larry Fick and George Martin, *Tillamook Burn, Rehabilitation and Reforestation* (Oregon Department of Forestry, 1992), p. 89.
10. J. E. Schroeder, State Forester, *From Tillamook Burn to Tillamook Forest* (Oregon State Forestry Department, May, 1979), pp. 9–10.
11. Oregon State Circuit Court Filing dated July 7, 1947, naming Oregon-American Lumber Corporation, et al.
12. *McKinney v. Oregon-American Lumber Company, et al.*
13. Telephone interview of August 24, 1998, with Carroll Bradley, esq. (retired), counsel for Carnation Lumber Company, a codefendant in *McKinney v. Oregon-American, et al.*
14. Webber, 171–95.
15. Ibid.

THE GLORY YEARS

1. *Atlas of Oregon* (Eugene, Ore.: University of Oregon Books, 1976), pp. 132–33 (in which the average rainfall for Astoria, Oregon, between 1900 and 1960 is plotted and indicates about 80 inches per year as the average rainfall); and *Webster's Ninth New Collegiate Dictionary* (Springfield, Mass.: Merriam-Webster, Inc., 1984), p. 973 (in which *rain forest* is defined as a tropical woodland with an annual rainfall of at least 100 inches of rain per year).

2. Ralph W. Hidy, Frank Ernest Hill, and Allan Nevins, *Timber and Men: The Weyerhaeuser Story* (New York: The MacMillan Company, 1963), p. 594.

3. *Central Coal & Coke Corporation 1952 Annual Report.*

4. Ibid.

THE LAST STAND

1. *The Log of Long-Bell*, December 1957.
2. *Central Coal & Coke Corporation 1952 Annual Report.*
3. *The Log of Long-Bell*, June–July 1960.
4. Ibid., May 1954.
5. Ibid., February 1960.
6. http://ci.longview.wa.us/information/tour/hist.html.
7. *The Log of Long-Bell*, June–July 1960.
8. See various issues of *The Log of Long-Bell* in which events in the Retail Division were reported. Also see http://ci.longview.wa.us/information/tour/hist.html.
9. *The Log of Long-Bell*, September 1954.
10. Ibid., July 1953; and *Central Coal & Coke Corporation 1953 Annual Report.*
11. *The Log of Long-Bell*, July 1953.
12. Ibid.
13. Ibid., July, August, and September 1956.
14. Ibid., November 1955.
15. Ibid., December 1955.
16. Ibid., January 1956.
17. Ibid., June 1956.
18. Ibid., August 1956.
19. Ibid., September 1956.
20. Ibid.
21. Ibid., August 1956.
22. Ibid., June 1955.
23. Ibid., November 1956.
24. Ibid., April 1960.
25. Telephone interview of March 4, 1999, with Larry Fick and George Martin, Oregon Department of Forestry, retired.
26. *The Log of Long-Bell*, December 1956.
27. Telephone interview of March 4, 1999, with Larry Fick and George Martin, Oregon Department of Forestry, retired.
28. *The Log of Long-Bell*, December 1956.
29. Telephone interview of March 4, 1999, with Larry Fick and George Martin, Oregon Department of Forestry, retired; and *The Log of Long-Bell*, December 1956.
30. *The Log of Long-Bell*, June 1957.
31. Ibid., July 1957.
32. Ibid., August 1957.
33. Ibid.
34. Ibid., April 1958, October–November 1957, and December 1957.
35. Ibid., January 1958.

EPILOGUE

1. *Vernonia Eagle*, January 2, 1958.
2. Ibid., April 24, 1958.
3. Ibid., June 19, 1958.
4. Ibid., July 17, 1958.
5. Ibid., November 6, 1958.
6. Ibid., November, 27, 1958.
7. Ibid., December 11, 1958.
8. Ibid., April 21, 1960, and September 1, 1960.
9. Ibid., August 25, 1960.
10. Ibid., September 1, 1960.
11. Ibid., July 28, August 4, 11, 18, September 1, 8, 15, and 22, 1960, March 30, April 4, and May 18, 1961.
12. Ibid., August 31, 1961.
13. Ibid., September 7, 1961.
14. Ann Fulton, *Vernonia, A Pocket in the Woods* (Portland, Ore.: n.p., 1997), p. 111.
15. Ibid.

INDEX

A. Guthrie & Company, 44, 50, 54, 68, 254
African American, 85, 86, 87, 329
A.G. Becker & Company, 109
Agriculture, 8, 247
Airplane factories, 213
Alaska, 233, 234
Alberni Pacific Lumber Company, 184
Aldrich, Ralph, Jr., 246
Alexander, A.C., "Chet," 185, 268
Allegheny Mountains, 6
Amalgamated Sugar Company, 26
American Federation of Labor (A F of L), 198–200, 202
American Goodwill Table, 101
American Land & Timber Company, 22
American Locomotive Company (Alco), 182, 184
Anderson, C. L., "Connie," 80, 117, 160, 174, 176, 246, 247, 250, 299–301, 328;
Anderson Park, 326
Anderson, Eric, 275
Anderson, Kenneth, 210
Anti-kickback fingers, 213
Antitrust laws, 212
Appledale Land Company, 55
Arch, cruiser, 320
Arkansas, 8, 11; Crosset, 81
Armstrong, Irvin, 303
Asiatics, 85
Assets, 105, 109, 112
Atkins, Bill, 60, 68
Atlantic Ocean, 14
Automobile, 83, 166
Auxiliary drum, 314

Backcut, 306
Bailey, Bill, 210

Baker, Fentress & Company, 111, 212, 240
Baldock, R.H., 166
Baldridge, Jack, 80
Baldwin Locomotive Works, x, 1, 43, 54, 60, 72, 274, 319
Ballast, 50, 54, 186, 227
Balmer, 231
Baltimore, 6
Bank, 83
Bankruptcy, 141, 145
Barker, Ezra, 223, 251, 253
Bars and taverns, 84
Bean, Judge, 125, 126
Beaver Creek Logging Company, 52, 57
Bee, beekeeper, bee rancher, 75, 76, 132, 133
Berger Engineering Works, 257, 305, 318
Bergerson, Harold, 287
Bergland, Frank, 286
Bergstrom, Delores, 247
Bernardin, J. M., "Joseph," 102, 103, 105, 110, 111, 113, 114, 116, 118, 138, 140, 141, 145, 160
Big Tree, 100-101
Bigelow, C.H., 68
Birkelund, George R., 111, 139, 141, 145, 181, 241, 250, 284
Blieile, Earl, 117
Block, 49, 177, 223
Blodgett, 141; John W., 90
Blount, Albert, 210; Forest, 71, 210
Board, board-feet, board-foot, 5, 9, 13, 36, 70, 92, 159, 169, 179, 205, 226, 227, 236, 249, 251, 258, 283, 289, 309
Boilers 70, 169, 172, 249, 276, 277
Bonds, bonded, bondholders, 37, 104, 109, 117; indebtedness, 93, 103, 111, 113, 143, 144, 160, 240

Bondholders, Central-Delta Protective Committee, 104, 111–113, 119, 138, 139, 140, 144; O-A Protective Committee, 111–13, 119, 138–41
Bonneville power system, 241
Booms, 17, 35, 55, 57, 211, 247–49, 256,
Booth-Kelly, 69
Borrow pit, 171
Bowerman, Todd, 74
Bowie County Lumber Company, 19
Bowman, 165
Boxing, 10, 13
Brake, 52, 217, 218, 220, 309; brakemen, 51, 220, 269, 270, 273, 298, 299, 301, 321
Brand, 94, 96
Breakage, 93
Bridges, Harry, 198
Brimmer, Andy, 210
British Columbia, 184
Browning, M. S., 21, 24
Brundage, Fred, 232
Buck, bucker, bucking, 94, 123, 221, 236, 258, 267, 294
Buda engine, 299
Budd, Ralph, 42, 52
Bulldozer, 44, 175, 177, 195, 224, 234, 272, 273, 277, 302, 320
Bunks, 51, 220, 256
Bunkhouse, 38, 68, 74, 75, 134, 150, 319
Burn See Fire
Burns-Briggs Lumber Company, v, 81
Burke, Milo, 326
Burlington Northern, 329
Burned Timber Tax Compromise Law, 145
Bus, 215
Butler, Irwin, 308
Byerly, 110; J.A., 110; Oliver, 110

Byers, William, "Bus," 221, 283

Caboose, 53, 187, 219, 283, 292, 325, 329
California, 14, 233, 247; Crescent City, 233; Fresno, 53; Los Angeles, 99, 326; Monterey, 90; Oroville, 17; San Francisco, x, 201; Sierra Nevada, 216; Weed, 54
Callan, A. C., 25, 26
Camp, Buster, 79; Divide, 123; Jap (See Japanese); McGregor, 35, 43, 44, 47, 53, 54, 74, 75, 77, 79, 97, 102–5, 109, 110, 123, 129, 133–35, 148, 149, 153, 163, 164, 166, 169, 171–73, 176, 178, 186, 194, 195, 196, 200, 214, 216, 235, 244, 245, 262, 263, 279, 280, 282, 293, 299, 300, 302, 303, 310, 318, 319, 321, 330; Number 1, 74, 79, 122, 124, 128, 129, 134, 150, 180, 195; Number 2, 74, 79, 97, 105, 106; Olson, x, 243, 245, 247, 249, 254, 262, 263, 267, 269–72, 274, 286, 288, 293, 298, 301, 302
Candle factory, 330
Cant, 1, 68, 69, 169
Car, 148; ballast, 189; box, 83, 298, 326; crummy, 298, 303, 308; dining, 298; flat, 163, 263; donkey-moving, 1, 6, 184, 256, 292; kitchen, 105, 298; line, 302; load, 15; rail, 69; snowplow, 299; tank, 184, 185, 270; water, 184; wood, 218, 247
Carco-matic, 253, 255, 257
Carpenters & Sawmill & Timber Workers, 197
Carriage, log, 61, 63, 71, 215; skyline, 223, 315
Carriers, 118, 145; Gerlinger, 84, 169; straddle, 84, 169; Willamette, 84, 169
Carrigan, Lee, 303

355

INDEX

Carts (horse-drawn), 70, 169
Cascade Mountain Range, 295
Cat, Caterpillar, 177, 213, 214, 222, 257, 267, 283, 284, 302, 312; skinner, 227
Caulked boots, 52
Cedar, Western Red, 96, 97, 147, 178, 182, 229, 231, 249, 286. *See also* Appendix E
Cedarwood Products (Timber) Company, 222, 250
Ceiling, 10; price, 245
Central Coal & Coke Company, Corporation, CC&CC, xiv, 2, 10, 11, 35–42, 44, 47, 53, 54, 60, 68, 69, 74, 75, 77, 79–81, 86, 89, 92, 93, 95–99, 102–4, 109, 118, 138–40, 144, 147, 148, 150, 155, 159, 182, 190, 191, 240, 287, 294, 295–97, 300, 323
Chaney, Henry., 144, 190, 226, 231, 233, 250
Chips, 13, 97, 249
Chlorinator, 267
Choker, 223, 303, 311
Christiansen, Ernie, 326
Christmas trees, 5
Chunk-out, 255
Churches, 83
Churchill, A., 188
Civil rights, 87
Civil War, 15
Civilian Conservation Corps (CCC), 132, 134, 135, 169, 194, 195, 196, 321
Clabaugh, R.R., 144
Clark & Wilson Lumber Company, 110, 152, 155, 196, 229, 230, 232, 233, 329
Clark, Weaver, 325
Clatsop/Columbia County line, 44, 54, 84, 145, 148, 150, 187, 222, 325
Clatsop County, 188, 272; School District Number 40, 75, 100
Clear-grained, 12, 101
Cletrac (Cleveland Tractor Company), 175, 194, 195, 222, 245, 255, 257, 312
C. N. Day Company, 253–56
Coal, 11, 86, 92
Coast Range, 42, 98, 163, 278, 280, 281, 310

Colorado, Edith, v, 81
Columbia & Nehalem Railway (Kerry Line), 77
Columbia Basin Loggers, v, 153, 154, 300;
Columbia Basin Sawmills, v, 154, 201, 300
Columbia County, 131, 145, 188; Historical Society Museum, xiii, 114, 328
Columbia River Gorge, 14
Columbia River Scaling Bureau, 35
Colvin, Howard, 268
Commissary, 105, 110
Committee for Industrial Organization (CIO), 152, 197–202, 261
Committee: "Retail Cooperation," 90; "Securing Orderly Control of Lumber Production and Distribution," 90
Common-Carrier, 52, 53, 185, 277
Communist Party, 201, 203
Competition, 14, 43, 55, 63, 89
Concrete, 37, 40, 42, 60, 61, 63
Congressional, 247; Joint Committee on Housing, 246
Connacher Logging Company, 57
Construction, 10, 37
Consume, consuming, 7, 13
Contractors (independent) 105, 149, 150, 223, 250. *Also see* Gyppo
Conversion, 113, 224, 253, 257
Cookhouse, 74, 105, 214, 224, 298
Coos Bay Lumber Company, 174
Copeland, J. W. , 109
Corey Brothers and Company. *See* Utah Construction Company
Corners (odd and short), 257, 312
Cougars, 234
Couplers, 52
Creditors, 104, 150
Creeks: Cow, 194, 195; Cronin, 178, 294, 311; North Fork Cronin, 130; Middle Fork Cronin, 130, 294, 295, 297, 303; South Fork Cronin, 130, 297; Ginger, 293, 300; Military, 130; Quartz, 321; Rock, 68, 73, 78, 84, 97, 102, 123, 127, 130, 197, 279, 283, 318, 321; North Fork Rock, 90, 132, 194, 195; Weed, 73, 176;

Wolf, 137, 148, 221
Cribbing, 96, 258
Cronwall & Company, 109, 144
Cronwall, Edward C., 109, 144, 146, 153, 160
Crosby, Frank B., 116, 117
Crosset, 12; Watzek-Gates, 81; Western, 138, 141
Crownsheets, 304
Crown Willamette Paper Company, 182, 183
Crown Zellerbach, 232, 233, 244, 245, 258, 261, 329
Cruise, 9, 35, 92, 93, 142, 292
Cummins, 175, 256
"Cut-out-and-get-out," xviii, 243, 291
Cutover land, 93, 121, 166, 291, 294, 296
Cutting circle, 35
Cutting crew, 225, 306. 307
Cyclone, 70, 112

Dalrymple, William, 201, 202
Daries, J. C., 228
David Eccles Company, 18, 25–27
Davies, David L., 250
Davis, Art, 246
Davis, Bill, 303, 318, 322
Davidson, Carl E., 116, 117, 123
Day, Clarence N., 254; Joe, 322
D. C., 122
Debt, 35, 38, 190, 287
Deck, decking, 44, 61, 69, 166, 185, 191, 206, 255, 282, 285, 320
Default, 91, 111
Defective, 93
Del Monte, 90
Delta Land & Timber Company, 36–39, 68, 74, 80, 102–4, 109, 112, 114, 139, 140, 143, 144, 147, 287, 323
Demand, 89, 91
Denny, Charles E., 228
Depletion, 12
Depreciation, 35, 43, 159, 289
Depression, 2, 57, 84, 105, 111, 116, 137, 138, 150, 151, 152, 181, 186, 227, 228, 299,

326
Detroit Trust Company, 58, 78, 121, 132, 133, 135, 161, 162, 179, 188, 189, 261, 283
DeVaney, Verle, 251
Devine, George, 322
Devine, J. H., 25
Dickson, Herman, 205, 246
Diesel, 193, 255, 302, 304, 305, 309
Dimension lumber, 13
Dining room, 68, 74, 75, 172, 173, 319
Disconnected logging trucks, 1, 50, 51, 55, 180, 185, 186, 245, 256, 258, 303, 314, 316, 317, 319, 321
Distribution, 7, 14, 15, 42
Dividend, 241, 266, 286
Dixon T., 52, 230, 231
Donkey 44, 51, 72, 98, 106, 123, 134, 135, 169, 172–74, 180, 184, 191, 193, 223, 240, 250, 255, 256, 301–3, 305, 313, 318, 319. *See also* Appendix A
Donnelly, Charles, 42, 52, 147
Dooley, Clay, 179; Spur, 292
Doyle & Rogers, 224, 251; Joe, 251, 264
Drawheads, 50, 52
Drying 37, 80; -kiln, xix, 14, 15, 41, 184. *See also* kiln
Dubendorf, Charles, 210
Dubois, 76, 77, 177
Dubois Lumber Company, 21
Dubois, Pennsylvania, 21
Dubois tract 37, 47, 55, 92, 110
Dunlap, "Red," 321
Dusenberry, Vern, 251
Dutch ovens, 40, 70

Early, Charles T., 21, 24; Ray B., 25
Easement, 286
East, Earnest, 71, 210; Thurman, 210
East Side Logging Company, 50, 52, 54, 57, 58, 78, 121, 123–27, 129, 132–35, 148, 161, 162, 172, 176, 179, 183, 189
Eastern & Western Lumber Company, 110, 258
Eccles, 44, 53, 55; David, 13, 54; David C., 2, 17, 18, 20, 21, 24, 26, 28; 26; Leroy, 20,

26; Marriner S., 18, 24; Royal, 21; Vivian, 20
Eccles Investment Company, 18, 24, 26
Edger, 69, 213
Efficiency, 205
Electrical, electricity, 41, 43, 47, 63, 66, 67, 115, 169, 171, 285
Elton, Jimmy, 321
Engineer, x, 44, 251, 269, 270, 272, 273, 280, 286, 298, 323
Erie Canal, 6
Estey, E. R., "Pooch," 80, 95, 128–130, 175
E.T. Chapin Company, 55

Fair Labor Standards Act, 261
Fairlead, 305
Faller, falling, 1, 47, 50, 93, 123, 221, 225, 236, 294
Family camp, 280, 319; housing, 47
Farlin, Oscar, 275
Farm, farmer, 6–8, 11, 17, 65, 95, 129, 181, 182, 248, 291, 294, 296, 297, 300, 326, 328, 329, 331
FBI, 235, 239
Federal Reserve Board, 103
Fentress, Calvin, 212
Fick, Larry, 311
Filer and Stowell, 63, 68
Filipino, 86
Finance, 25–27, 36, 37, 108, 240, 241, 287–89
Finish, 10
Finnell, Vera, 247
Fir (industry), 178, 190, 206, 243
Fir, Douglas (*Pseudotsuga Menziesii*) (Old-Growth Yellow), xi, xvi, xviii, xix, 1, 2, 7, 8, 13, 67, 71, 93, 98, 100, 137, 143, 183, 184, 190, 226, 227, 229, 231–33, 246, 247, 308, 313, 331; (*Pseudotsuga Taxifolia*), 101. *See also* Appendix E
Fir, Noble (*Abies procera*) (Larch) , 143, 231. *See also* Appendix E
Fir, White (*Abies concolor*), 229, 231, 143. *See also* Appendix E
Fires, 100, 121, 123, 233; 1932 Fire, 121, 126, 177; burned-over land, 142; Cochran, 126–28, 130, 190; Cow Creek, 191, 192, 193, 196, 200, 240; crown, 129, 133; damage, 124; Elsie, 189, 191, 192; fighting, 123, 124, 133, 194, 196, 276, 286; forestry laws, 121, 124, 135; hazard, 40, 121, 166, 326; K-P Timber Company, 122, 128; liability, 121; Music, 224, 240; Oregon-American, 122–24; patrol, 126, 129, 293; Patrol Associations, 121; 1945 Salmonberry Fire, 239, 243; 1956 Salmonberry Fire, 297; slashing 121, 122, 236; spot, 133, 310; Tideport, 127, 128; Tillamook, 131, 132, 138, 191, 192, 239, 243; Vernonia/Keasey 126; -weed, 75, 76, 132, 147; Wilson River, 239; Wolf Creek, 102, 103, 106, 121, 128, 134, 135, 138, 148, 159, 161, 162, 169, 177, 181, 187, 191, 192, 194, 195, 207
First-Aid, 225
Fitzloff, Leslie, 210
Fletcher, Dick, 247, 250
Flooring, 10, 13
Flora, Joe, 178
Fluke, Jim, 76
Forecast, 91
Freight, 13, 39
Fuel, 13, 40, 67, 70, 74, 98, 169, 185, 263, 302

Gales Creek and Wilson River Railroad (G. C. & W. R.), 42, 52
Galloway, Les, 76
Georgia-Pacific Lumber Company, 328
Gerlinger, 169, 214
Gibson, Claude, 210; Glen, 210; Will, 61
Ginger Creek Timber Unit, 283, 286, 291, 292, 301, 303–6, 308, 310, 318–20, 323. *See also* Keasey Timber Unit
Goodwin, H. S., 79
Grade, grading, 7, 69, 72, 75, 95, 96, 183, 250, 254; Number-Three-Common, 93, 98, 99, 129, 131, 132, 134
Grady, J. J., 80
Grand Coulee Dam, 17
Great Northern Railway (GN), xiv, xix, 2, 6, 42, 147, 148, 228, 231
Great Plains, 7, 8, 11
Greeley, Col. W. B., 155, 156
Green, E. A., 80
Green Mountain, 319
Greene and Landye, 261
Greenman Collection, xi, xii, xviii
Greenman, Judd, v, xi, xviii, 2, 81, 82, 92, 94, 95, 98, 99, 100, 102, 103, 104, 106, 109, 113–18, 123–25, 128, 131, 134, 140–42, 145, 146, 149, 150, 152–57, 159–61, 164, 179, 181–83, 185, 187, 189, 190, 198, 199, 201, 202, 211, 212, 222, 224–26, 228, 230–33, 239, 244, 246, 250, 261, 269, 272, 273, 275–79, 283, 284, 289, 296, 297, 299, 300
Ground leases, 166, 175
Grunden, Maynard, 80, 323
Gyppo, 166, 180, 232, 250, 251, 287, 292, 329

Hageman, Fred, "The Dutchman," 234, 250, 296, 302, 318, 321, 328
Hall, dance, 84
Hall, Ben, 210
Hammond, 41
Hammond Lumber Company, 144, 161, 162
Hammond/Tillamook, 161
Hammond-Winton, 42
Hardwood, 5
Hare & Hare, 295
Hare, Herbert S., 68
Harriman, Edward H., 19, 20
Hart, Charles, 143, 284
Hart, Carey, Spencer and McCulloch, 145, 284
Hart, Spencer, McCulloch and Rockwood, 143, 284
Hathaway, George L., 101
Haulback, 223
Haul (two, three, multiple-donkey), 166, 175, 319
Hausler, Fritz, 246

Hawaii, 234; Pearl Harbor, 212, 215, 225, 233, 235
Hawkins, Burt, 225
Hayes, E. E., "Edward," 68, 81, 86
Haymire, 74
Heenan, Jack, 221, 273, 283
Hemlock, Western (*Tsuga Heterophylla*), 10, 77, 96–98, 137, 142, 143, 160, 178, 181–83, 200, 229, 231, 232, 233, 246, 249, 261, 287. *See also* Appendix E
Hendrickson Lumber Company, 251
Hercules, 256
Hess, Ivan, 76
Highballing, 89, 106
High-climber, 48, 221
High-line, 258
Highways: State 47, 327; Sunset; 164, 169, 247, 321, 322; Wolf Creek, 110, 163–66, 169, 175–77, 179, 185, 187, 191, 206, 215, 221, 236, 263, 293, 296
Hill, James J., 17, 18, 20, 22
Hill Lines, Hill Roads. *See* Northern Lines, Northern Roads
Hindu, 86
Hines, Edward, 91
Holcomb, Holly, 80, 117, 246
Hollyfield, Herb, 116
Holt, W. E., 228, 229, 230, 231
Homestead Act of 1862, 7
Honey, fireweed, 76
Hooker, hooktender, 176, 321
Hoot-owl shift, 191
Hoover Dam, 17
Hotel, 83
House, housing, ix, 13, 37, 41, 86, 102, 105, 109, 149, 249; federal home-loan financing programs (FHA), 244, 245, 247, 287, 289; shortages, 244
Huber, William, 272
Hughes, Alfred J., "Paddy," ix, 80, 117, 246
Humboldt, 42, 44, 47, 93, 106, 122, 196
Hunteman, Albert, 210

Ice, 280
Idaho, Bovill, 55

357

INDEX

Illinois, 10; Chicago, 6, 13, 35, 109, 111, 140, 144
Incline, 127, 302
Indian, 100
Indiana, 10, 100
Industrial Workers of the World (IWW), (Wobblies), 151
Inman-Poulsen Lumber Company (I-P), xiii, 32, 44, 51, 54, 55, 57, 77, 79, 94, 103, 110, 120, 123, 131, 132, 135, 149, 150, 165, 173, 180, 183, 197, 226, 298; pond, 56, 131
Insurance, 40, 63
Integrated lumbering operation, 9
Interchange, 50
Intercoastal, 15
Interior, 13
International Paper Company, xiii, xviii, 296, 300, 303, 308, 309, 311, 326, 328, 329
International Woodworkers of America (IWA), 197, 200–202; Local 5-37, 198–200, 202, 215, 221
Interstate Commerce Commission (ICC), 52, 73, 185, 268, 277
Interstate Tractor and Equipment Company, 174
Interurban, 47
Iowa, 10, 247

Jacks, 96, 258
Jannsen, David, 327, 328
Japanese (Jap), 226, 234, 236, 261; balloon bombs, 233; bombardment, 233, 234, 235, 239, 240; Camp, 75, 91, 149; Colony, 86, 326; forces, 212; internment, 215, 225; nationals, 215, 225; Skidder, 163; Squares, 112; submarines, 233; workers, 75, 91, 92, 163, 194, 195
Jenkins, Dan, 327
Jet Stream, 234
Johnson, C. D., 12, 328
Johnson, Glenn, 302, 321
Johnson, Ted, 303
Johnston & McGraw Shingle Mill, 61, 96, 109, 182
Johnston Davis and Company, 182
Joint (maintenance)(use), 53, 54

Kansas, 10
Kansas City, Kansas, v, 35, 42, 81
Kansas City Star, 81
Kansas City Southern, 9
Kansas City Times, 157
Kansas & Texas Coal Company, 19
Kanzler, Julie, 247
Kaspar, Isabel, 247
Keasey Timber Unit, 176, 189, 231, 283, 286, 291, 301. *See also* Ginger Creek
Keith, Bill, 156; Charles, 2, 11, 12, 35, 36, 39, 40, 42, 43, 53, 59, 62, 82, 86, 89, 90, 93, 94, 100, 102, 103, 110, 111, 113, 114, 116–18, 125, 131, 138, 140, 142, 144, 146, 148, 152–57, 164, 183, 190, 243, 283, 289, 294, 297, 323; Lucille, 289; Richard H., 17
Keith & Hendry, 19
Keith & Perry, 11, 17, 157
Kendall, Harry T., 42, 91, 95, 98, 106, 154
Kenney, 147
Kerry, A.S., Line, 77, 79, 111, 177, 319
Kiln, 66, 68;-dry, 1, 43, 67, 73, 95, 98, 105; Drying Club, 182; internal circulation, 28; Simmons, 69
Kingsley, Ed, 177
Kinsey, Clark, 53, 95
Kitchen, 68
Klasson, Knut, 310, 329
Knapp-Peninsula (K-P) Timber Company, 78, 110, 122, 125, 126
Knauss, Archie, 80, 117, 184
Koster Products Company, 57, 127, 148, 179, 189

L&M Holding Company, 135; Logging Company, 187
LaBertew, M. C., 226–28
Labor, 86, 199, 258; convict, 311; organized, 223, 261, 297; skilled, 86, 198; shortages, 213, 244; strikes, 151, 169, 261; turnover, 215, 222; unrest, 151, 152, 169, 197; unskilled, 86. *See Also* Union
Laird, George, 101, 210, 246
Lake States, 7
Lakin, Jim, 174
Landing, 50, 106
Laramore, Louis, 210
Lath, 13, 69, 249
Lausmann, Antone, 58, 123, 124, 135
Layoffs, 103
Lease, 36, 44
Lee, Carol, 330; George, xiii, 67, 90, 171, 176, 177, 179, 195–97, 222, 224, 225, 227, 235, 247, 250, 257, 263, 267, 273, 283, 284, 286; Larry, 330
Leverman, 303, 309
Levy, 188
Lewis, John L., 197, 198, 201
Lewis and Clark, 99
Lilly, W. J., 80
Lima Locomotive Works, 74, 277; Shay, 74, 75, 184
Linn, Walter, 246
Lintner, G.V., 32
Liquidate, 9, 113, 140; self-, 155, 292
Livestock, 109, 186; Bob and Shorty, 169; Goats, 186
Loading Engine, 58, 180, 185, 196, 255, 257, 261, 309, 314, 318
Locomotives and speeders, 134; locomotive No. 2: 75, 91, 123, 149, 184, 217; speeder No. 10: 99, 184, 194, 299; speeder No. 11: 182, 183, 184, 185, 194, 244, 312; locomotive No. 100: 53; locomotive No. 101: 53; locomotive No. 102: 37, 43, 53, 60, 109, 184, 217, 303, 325; locomotive No. 103: 50, 55, 74, 122, 267, 268, 271, 283, 288, 296, 308, 325; locomotive No. 104: 54, 72, 221, 268–75, 279, 280, 292, 300, 301, 303, 304, 308, 318, 325, 329; locomotive No. 104 (wreck of): 269–76; locomotive No. 105: x, 60, 72, 123, 183, 185, 218, 219, 221, 264, 267–71, 273, 279, 280, 283, 292, 302, 303, 323, 325, 329; locomotive No. 106: 53, 74, 122, 194, 267–69, 273, 278, 280, 288, 299, 300, 303, 304, 325; locomotive No. 107: (U. P. No. 61): 275–77, 298; locomotive No. 116: xi, 74, 185; S. P. & S. No. 5: 268, 269, 276; S. P. & S. No. 156: 44, 53; S. P. & S. crane No. M-30: 55; Oregon-American crane: 38, 55, 58, 59, 104, 115, 182, 185, 211, 249, 302
Locomotive shed, 170
Lodges: American Legion, 85; Eastern Star, 85; Grange, 85; Knights of Pythias, 85, 188; Ku Klux Klan, 85, 86, 87; Maccabees, 85; Masonic, 85; Odd Fellows, 85, 235; Rebekkah, 85; Relief Corps, 85; Sons of Veterans, 85; Woodmen, 85
Log, logger, logging, xvi, xvii, xviii, 35, 47, 71, 76, 83, 104, 112, 121, 137, 155, 163, 180, 200, 216, 221, 250, 285, 298, 299, 308, 309, 313, 319, 329; chance, 8, 258; deck, decking, 73, 98, 115, 282, 285; dump, 36, 211, 212; hayrack boom, 97, 99; heel-boom, 99, 305, 309, 314, 317; high-lead, 104, 122, 253, 312; landing, 44; loading, 123, 200, 267; open-market supplies, 283; peeler, 181, 182, 208, 308; pulp, 208; salvage, 137, 140, 146; side, 51, 98, 301, 302, 305, 318; shortage, 244, 253; slip, 171, 289; train, ix, x, xi, 51, 145, 261; unloading, 59, 61, 220
Log of Long-Bell, 303, 318, 322, 323
Loggers & Contractors Machinery Company, 224, 255–57
Lone Pine Road, ix, x
Long-Bell Lumber Company, 10, 11, 19, 27, 43, 60, 142, 156, 182, 188, 256, 288, 296, 297, 298, 300, 302, 318; East mill, 296; West mill, 296; Vernonia division, 299
Long, R. A., 10, 11, 12, 19, 294
Long-side head rig, 63, 66, 69, 151, 205
Lost 40, 180, 263, 264, 298
Louisiana, 8, 10, 11, 294; Calcasieu Parish, 19; Carson, 68; Neame, 9, 74; Shreveport, 9; Vernon Parish, 19
Loyal Legion of Loggers and Lumbermen (4L), 151, 152

Ludwig, Mike, 246
Lumber, lumbering, lumberjack, lumbermen, xvi, xviii, 1, 7, 35, 37, 84, 87, 100, 181, 291, 325; buggies, 70, 84, 169; Code, 138; industry, xvii, 5; integrated, 9; retail yard 84, 85; rough, 251; storage sheds, 37, 66, 75, 78, 85; production, 6, 7, 10; seasoned, 27, 28, 43, 67; side, 10, 13, 14, 68–70, 72, 169, 209
Lumbermen's Industrial Relations Committee, Inc., v, 301

MacFarlane, Robert S., 231
Maine, 6
Manary Logging Company, 328
M&M Woodworking Company, 109
Mangat, Fred, 210
Manning, Jerry, 272
Marchuk, "Powder Bill," 225
Market, marketing, 15, 39, 42, 35, 105, 118, 160, 180–84, 206, 244–50
Marshall, Dave, 80, 117, 246, 272
Martin, Governor Charles, v, 300
McAllister, J. Vernon, 116
McDougall, Camp, 251; Natt, 44, 251, 252, 254
McGregor, Jeff, 272, 273; William H., "Bill," 47, 50, 57, 58, 59, 122, 132, 134, 318. *See also* Camp McGregor
McNary, Judge John H., 112; Senator, 211
McPhee & McGinnity, 81
McPherson, 58, 78, 121, 182; George, 162, 188; Jack, 162
Merchandising, 15
Meservey, M. C., 110
Mexico, 234; Temosachic, Chihuahua, 81
M. F. Brady Company, 53, 219, 276, 277
MGM Studios, 327, 328
Michigan, 6, 8, 10, 234; Detroit, 6
Midwest, xvi, 5, 6, 39, 181, 182, 247
Milan, Bill, 319
Mill, 233, 325; assorter, dry, 37, 40, 67, 69, 75, 105, 109, 182, 187; blowpiping, 171; capacity, 91, 99; dressed (slick) shed, 37, 67, 70, 78, 81, 106, 109; gang saw, 68, 70, 213; generators, 70; grinding room, 172; dust-collecting system, 172; head rigs, 61, 63, 67–69, 205, 206, 207; lease, 36, 112, 114, 116; Lindsay, 148; loading dock, 67, 109, 326; log washer, 171, 207; machine shop, 38, 42, 51, 67, 256, 272; open market, 95; planing, 15, 67, 68, 70, 77, 78, 105, 106, 109, 205, 327; molding, 70; office, 114, 287; pond, 36, 58, 67, 69, 70, 96, 97, 109, 115, 151, 182, 209, 232, 249, 281, 325, 328; powerhouse, ix, 40, 43, 67, 74, 109, 169; rail, 63, 283; rated, 61; refuse burner, 38, 40, 60, 67, 70, 112, 212; resaw, 69 72, 161; rough dock, 68, 70, 77, 78; rough shed; 68, 69, 70, 99, 109; shingle, 250; siting, 59; spur, 218, 219; stacker, 41, 67, 69, 150, 205; timber dock, 67, 69, 172; whistle, 1, 235, 323. *See also* Johnston & McGraw and Cedarwood Products (Timber) Company; Saw
Miller, Frank, 135, 189
Miller, Orville, 179, 182, 189
Milwaukee Bridge & Iron Company, 68
Minarets & Western Railroad, 53
Minger, Charles, 326
Minnesota, 7; Minneapolis, 6, 13; St. Paul, 35, 52, 230
Minorities, 85, 86, 153
Mississippi, 8; River, 6, 11, 60
Mississippi River Valley Lumberman, 289
Missouri, 7, 10, 11, Kansas City, 6–8, 59, 99, 109, 147, 156, 289, 294, 296; Keytesville, 155; St. Louis, 6
Missouri and Louisiana Railroad Company, 28
M. L. Stines Construction Company, 325
Molding, 13
Mole, 268, 269. *See also* S. P. & S. locomotive No. 5
Monaco, Vincent, "Shorty," 221, 283
Monoghan, John, 60
Monorail, 67, 68, 75, 77
Montana, Glendive, 99
Moore, John, 210
Mooter, Dan, 327
Mortgage, 112, 114, 140
Mother nature, 119, 280
Motive power, 43, 74, 267
Mt. Hood, 132, 321
Mt. Hood Lumber Company, 18
Mt. Hood Railway Company, 18
Mt. Jefferson, 321
Music, W. D., 188, 236

Nanson, Art, 326
National Lumber Manufacturers Association (NLMA), v, 89, 90, 156, 183, 301
National Model Railroaders' Association, 278
National Recovery Administration, 140
Natt McDougall Company, 252–54, 277
Nebraska, 10; Omaha, 6, 7
Negligence, 121, 123, 124, 161
Negro, 86
Nehalem Boom Company, xiv, 18, 25–28, 55
Nehalem Valley, 1, 85, 86, 110, 169, 171, 200, 222, 230, 241, 249, 329–31
New Deal, 119, 159
New Mexico, El Vado, 81
New York, 10; Albany, 6
New York Times, 101
Newton, Jim, 76
North Bend rigging system, 223, 315
North Coast Dry Kiln Company, 69, 91
North Dakota, Williston, 99
North River Insurance Company, 124
North Western Improvement Company, 228
Northern Lines, Northern Roads, xiv, 35, 39, 40, 41, 42, 52, 57, 58, 78, 111, 112, 145–47, 186, 187, 190, 227–31, 284
Northern Pacific Railway (NP), xiv, xix, 2, 42, 102, 228, 230, 231, 284
Northern Pacific Terminal Company, 20
Northwest, 225, 297
Northwest Oregon Forest Protection Association, v
Northwest Timber Unit, 79, 110, 176, 181, 300
Northwestern Equipment Company, 55

O-A (Oregon-American Lumber Company)(Oregon-American Lumber Corporation), v, x, ix, xii, xiv, xviii, 1, 35–44, 47, 50, 52–58, 67, 68, 72–83, 85–87, 89, 90, 92, 93, 96–99, 102 106, 109–14, 116–18, 121, 122, 124, 125, 127–33, 135, 137, 138, 140–49, 151, 153, 155, 156, 159–66, 169, 171–73, 175, 176, 179, 180, 182, 183, 186–88, 190, 191, 193, 196–98, 200–202, 205, 206, 208, 212–18, 221, 223–33, 236, 239–41, 243, 245, 248–58, 261, 263, 264, 267–69, 275–77, 279, 281, 283–89, 291–94, 297–301, 305, 309, 312, 315, 318, 319, 323, 325, 329, 330
O-A Hill, 68, 109, 113, 295, 326
Oak, 10
Office, 37
Ohio, 10; River Valley, 10, 181
Oil, 294
Oklahoma, 10, 11
Olin, Fred, R., 144, 145, 159, 181, 190, 223, 226, 228, 230, 231, 250
Olson, Andrew, "Andy," 171, 175, 176, 194, 195, 222, 225, 234, 245, 247, 257, 262, 267, 272, 273, 286, 296, 302, 321; Ole, 179, 234, 235
Orders, 208
Oregon, 1, 9, 13, 163, 199, 210, 216, 247, 280, 287, 294, 295; Astoria, 163; Banks, 22, 24, 326; Baker City, 13; Blue Mountains, 13; Bly, 234, 235; Brookings, 233; Burlington, 24, 25; Clatskanie, 240; Cochran, 126; Cornelius Pass, 47; Dee, 18; Fort Stevens, 233; Eastmann Spur, 222; Elsie, 189; Eugene, xii; Gardiner, 297; Glenwood, 191; Hamlet, 163; Hillsboro, 22; Homewood, 57, 58, 148; Houlton, 182; Hood River, 18; Keasey, ix, x, 57, 58, 84, 134, 148, 149, 176, 178, 183, 189, 215, 226, 227, 229, 236, 251, 258, 263, 264, 283, 299, 300, 301, 303, 304, 312, 318, 320, 321, 326; Lausmann, 58; Linnton, 58; McPherson, 57; Neahkahnie

INDEX

Mountain, 240; Portland, xvi, 53, 55, 57, 109, 110, 123, 137, 139, 144, 145, 147, 148, 164, 174, 182, 191, 199, 215, 224, 226, 230, 253, 261, 275, 276, 278, 286, 288, 311, 319, 327, 331; Poynter, 58, 148; Prescott, 230; Rafton, 47, 50, 52–55, 57, 70, 118, 181, 185, 200, 267; Salem, 164, 253; St. Helens Mountain, 230; St. Johns, 55; Saddle Mountain, 303; Seaside, 321; Scappoose, 110; Sherwood, 319; Sitts ranch, 50, 53, 55, 57, 58; Springfield, 69; Sunset Wayside and Spring, 321; Tara, 148; Three Sisters, 321; Tigard, 253; Tillamook, 137; Tophill, 277, 278; Tualatin Valley, 22; Twin Bridges, 79, 130, 132, 236, 268; Vaughn, 297; Vernonia, v, ix, x, 1, 2, 36, 38, 40, 41, 47, 53, 57–59, 61, 66–69, 72–74, 76, 82–84, 92, 95–97, 99, 103, 104, 106, 109, 110, 113, 114, 117, 127, 132, 141, 143, 144, 149, 150, 152, 153, 155, 160, 163, 165, 169, 181, 183, 185, 186, 199, 201–3, 215, 218, 219, 222, 225, 227, 229, 230, 233, 235, 236, 245, 249, 252, 255–57, 263, 264, 267–69, 274, 276–79, 281–83, 287, 289, 295, 297, 299–303, 309, 319, 323, 325–31; Viento, 18; Wauna, 286; Wedeberg, 126; Wheeler, 321; Willbridge, 221; Wilkesboro, 55, 58; Zan, 79, 149

Oregon Gas & Electric Company, 66, 169, 171, 241, 251

Oregon Lumber Company, 13, 18, 26

Oregon Railway & Navigation Company, 20

Oregon Short Line Railroad, 13

Oregon, State (of), 164; Board of Labor Conciliation, 202; Board (Department) of Forestry, xiii, 166, 239, 311; Forester, 135, 239; forestry statutes, 121, 124; Highway Commission (Department), 163, 164, 166, 188, 322; Welfare Committee, v, 300

Overhead Crossing, 164–66, 185, 215, 221, 263, 279, 292, 296, 298, 299, 322

Pace, Wesley, 247

Pacific Car and Foundry Company, 184
Pacific Coast, 318
Pacific Northwest, 51, 52, 60, 280, 281–83, 295
Pacific Ocean, 233, 234, 280, 295, 322
Pacific Slope, xvi, 9, 14, 311
Panama Canal, 14
Partnership, 39, 42; quasi, xix, 229
Pass line, 319
Paul H. Saunders and Son & Company, 144
Pawling & Harnischfeger Company (P&H), 68, 76, 90, 175, 263, 281, 282
Payroll, 9
Pebble Creek Tract, 230, 232, 233, 261, 280
Pennsylvania, 10, 164; Philadelphia, 6, 99
Pederson, Rueben, 326
Perry, John, 11, 19
Peterson, Erick, 310, 329
Petersson, Johan, 303
Pickard, Roland, 327
Pickering Lumber Company, 12
Pile-driver, 13, 258
Pine: Longleaf, 9, 10; Ponderosa, 8, 10; Shortleaf, 10; Southern, 11; White, 6, 8, 10
Pinkerton Agency, 122
Plant, shale processing, 330
Plywood, 181, 291, 297
Polygamy, 18
Poolroom, 84
Portland & Seattle Railway Company (P & S), 21; Astoria & Pacific Railroad (P A & P), xiv, 39, 40, 43, 44, 50, 52–54, 57, 58, 83, 254
Portland Journal, 70
Postal, 57, 58
Power, reverse gear, 276, 277; standby, 41, 66
Powder, blasting, 225, 234, 236
Prairie States, 14
Pritchett, Harold, 198, 201, 203
Product, production, productivity, 89, 91, 92, 160, 205, 206, 250; mix, 97; overrun, 93, 206; underrun, 93
Profit, 35

Pulp, paper mills, 5, 97, 181 232, 236, 249, 261, 267, 291
Pump, 217, 302, 308

Quality, 95

Rail, tonnage, 9; traffic, 9, 111
Railroad, 11, 43, 254; ties, 13, 134, 149, 251
Rain forest, 124, 280
Ratio of unfilled orders as a percent of lumber stocks, 207, 208, 244
Receivership, 99, 102, 103, 109, 112–14, 118, 119, 187
Reconstruction Finance Corporation (RFC), 144, 146, 147, 149, 150, 159, 160, 240
Recovery, 101, 142, 147, 152; accounting system, 93; grade-policy, 94
Recreation, 330
Rehabilitation, 148, 149
Reload, 185, 275; station, 236, 253–56, 302
Rengstorff, Erwin, H., 80, 122
Reorganization, 115, 138–43
Retail, retailers, retailing, 5, 95, 208, 247, 297; lumber yard, 15, 67, 70, 85, 109
Revis, Carl, 303
Reynolds, Ralph, "Boomer," 296
Richardson, Charles, 116
Rig, rigger, rigging, 44, 49, 72, 134; butt, 311
Right(s)-of-way, xiii, 39, 55, 79, 90, 104, 105, 162, 164, 165, 224, 250, 252, 254, 258, 281, 293, 318, 320, 321
Riley, Fred, 326
Riley, Gerald, 76
Ring of Fire, 327, 328
Rivers: Columbia, 43, 111, 138, 181, 230, 232, 295; Hudson, 6; Lewis and Clark, 22; Mississippi, 6, 14; Nehalem, 59, 73, 98, 130, 294; Salmonberry, 127, 129, 130, 254; North Fork Salmonberry, 78, 125, 132, 228, 236, 239, 252, 254, 322; West Fork of the North Fork Salmonberry, 228, 252, 297; Trask, 42; Willamette 43, 50; Willamette Slough, 55; Wilson 42,

141, 239
Roberson, Hamp, 80, 246
Robinson, Paul, 85
Rock, Crushed, 55
Rock Creek Logging Company, 52, 58; Rock Creek Timber Company, 77
Rocky Mountains, 10, 179
Roediger, Fred, xiii, 210, 215
Rogers, Nelson, 239
Roman Catholic, 85
Roofing, 13
Roth, Lester, 160
Routes, 13
Rowland, George, 326
Ruhl, F. "Merle," 80, 109, 116, 215, 247, 250
Rupp-Blodgett, 188
Rural Electrical Administration (REA), 241
Ruth Realty Company, 40, 41, 78, 121, 127, 130, 131, 134, 137, 145, 146, 206, 226, 229, 231, 239, 243, 245, 249, 252, 262, 283, 284, 286, 308

Saddle Mountain, 261, 322
Safety, 220, 221, 273, 274
Sales, salesmen, 8, 11, 14; commission, 15; network, 11; promotions, 95, 111
Salmonberry Timber Company (STC), 188–91, 227, 243, 254, 292, 302
Saunders, Paul, H., 144
Saw, crosscut, 94, 307; dust, 13, 249; kerf, 94; mill, ix, xviii, 5, 13, 38, 40–42, 67, 86, 105, 112, 114, 151, 205, 209, 224, 225, 251, 252, 283, 291, 306, 307; Reed-Prentice, gasoline, 224
Sawmill & Timber Workers Union (STWU), 153, 197; Local 2557, 198, 200; Sawyer, xvi, 63, 71, 198
Scale, scaler, scaling, 6, 93, 100
Schaffner, Robert C., 109
School, 75, 84, 102, 103, 169, 263
Schopflin, Frank, 43, 57
Scoggins, George, 28, 30, 32
Scott, Ulas, 116
Scowcroft, Joseph, 20, 24

Scraper, Fresno, 197
Second-growth, 12, 313
Section gang, 122
Self-regulate, 90
Shay, 50, 53, 74, 75, 149, 184, 276, 279, 296, 319, 322, 325. *See also* Locomotives
Sheathing, 10
Shields, 178–80, 221, 266, 268, 269, 273, 279, 284, 286, 291, 296, 299
Shifts, double (second), 61, 159, 160, 171, 185, 205; single (first), 161, 216, 285; one-and-a-half (shift-and-a-half), 205, 206
Shipyards, 213
Shoes, oxford, 311
Short Route to the Sea, 163–66
Short-side head rig, 66, 69, 71
Short-stake artists (boomers), 319
Shotgun-feed carriage, 1, 63
Shovel-runner (operator), 90, 223, 227
Shutdown, 43, 126, 148, 152, 199, 228, 245, 262, 280, 326
Siding, 10, 13
Silver Falls Timber Company vs. Eastern and Western Lumber Company, 161
Simmons, R.A., 69, 117, 246, 323
Skagit Steel & Iron Works, 173–75, 182, 184, 191, 224, 236, 240, 244, 257, 258, 299, 319
Skid, skidder, skidding, Lidgerwood, 257–79, 262, 294, 295, 299, 303, 308; road, 97, 223, 225, 309, 320; tree-rigged (unit), 72, 96, 97, 98, 104, 115, 134, 180, 185, 186, 208, 214, 222, 223, 258, 261, 282, 285, 301, 302, 305, 308, 309, 317, 319, 325
Skis, 286
Skuzi, Katherine, Hoffman, 247
Skyline, 97, 166, 223, 258
Slashing, 124, 126, 293, 310
Sled, 223
Sliffe, Arlie, 270, 272, 280, 299
Small, John, 210
Smith, Jim, 210
Smokestacks, 40, 209, 283
Snags, 195

Snoqualmie Falls Lumber Company, 283
Snow, 98, 280, 282, 283, 286
South, Deep, xvi, 80, 86
Southern Pine, 2, 5, 10, 36, 92, 99, 295; Association, 19
Southwest Timber Unit, 77, 121, 130, 164–66, 176, 177, 180, 186, 189, 226–28, 239, 252, 288, 293, 296, 297, 301, 308, 309
Species. *See* Appendix E
Speeders, 53, 148, 225, 299. *See also* Locomotives
Spencer, Omar C., 143, 145, 250, 284
Spokane, Portland & Seattle Railway (S P & S), ix, x, 42, 52–58, 145, 148–50, 163, 182, 185, 187, 189, 218, 226, 228–31, 236, 249, 258, 263, 267, 268–79, 282, 284, 286, 298, 300, 304, 325–27, 329
Sprague, Governor Charles A., 200, 202, 212
Spruce, Sitka, 231
Spurs, 54, 73, 74, 76, 78, 79, 90, 92, 97, 103, 104, 106, 110, 122–24, 128–30, 134, 148, 150, 159, 162, 169, 177, 179, 180, 194, 195, 221, 222, 251, 253–55, 258, 264, 270, 272, 275, 286, 292, 294, 295, 300–303, 305, 308, 312, 313, 321, 322
Squirrel, 305, 317
St. Paul & Tacoma Lumber Company, 261, 289
Stamm, E.P., 232
Stand, 142, 291
Station, 36, 58, 66, 172, 208, 215, 221, 227, 253, 302, 312
Statutes, forest, 12; of limitations, 125, 159
Steam, 6, 43, 255; -to-diesel conversion, 224
Steel, 40, 42, 60, 61, 63, 90, 255–57
Stern, Brothers & Company, 109, 147
Stern, Sigmund, 109, 147, 148, 155, 159, 160, 190, 191, 230, 250, 288, 294
Stimson Lumber Company, 326
Stith, L.C., 288
Stockholders, 38, 139, 140, 143, 159, 240, 241, 288, 294, 298
Stone, Andrew and Virginia, 327

Strategic, 35, 39, 40; partnership, 186; planning, 2, 283
Stumps, 177, 225
Stumpage, 113, 118, 289
Sumpter Valley Railway, 7, 13, 14, 18, 22
Supply, 7, 15; over-, 91
Sweden, 175, 302
Sweetwater Coal & Mining Company, 19
Swing, 44, 314; yarder, 318
Syndicates, 135, 162

Taft-Hartley Act, 203
Tallyman, 83
Taylor, Jack, 179
Taylor, Louis, 210
Taylor, Phil, 116
Taxes, 112, 118, 119, 293
Telephone, 83, 194, 300
Tennant, John, 296
Texas, 8, 10, 11, 47, 294; Conroe, 75, 323; El Paso, 80; Houston County, 19; Montgomery County, 19; Texarkana, 323; Walker County, 19
Theaters, 83
Thin-Barked (evergreen) species, 77, 142, 143, 160, 233, 249, 292. *See also* Appendix E
Thomas & Meservey (T&M), 35, 36, 92–94, 110, 177, 228, 292
Thompson, Paul L., 109
Tideport Logging Company, 127, 163
Ties, railroad, 263
Tillamook, 129, 131; County, 131, 138, 145, 303, 321
Timber, timbers, 13, 47, 67, 91, 103, 105, 209, 236; burned-over, 145, 146; exchanges, 76–79, 92, 166, 188; fire-killed, 143, 159, 178, 207; green, 292; stand, 142, 305; structural, 112
Tokens, 110
Tongs, 99
Tonty Lumber Company, 19
Toots-E whistle, 309
Torpedoes, 173
Tousley, Fred, 184, 246

Track, trackage, 44; agreement, 54, 218; layer (Clyde), 163; laying, 50; tail, 258, 314
Trademark, 95, 182
Trade, restraint of, 212
Transcontinental railroads, 12, 14, 99
Transportation, 9
Travel time lawsuit, 104, 245, 261, 262
Tree farm, 291, 296, 300
Tree, spar, 47, 50, 177, 261, 302, 305, 308, 317, 321; tail, 315
Trestles, 148, 165, 171, 253
Trimmer, trimmerman, 72, 86, 182
Truck, trucks, 258, 299, 308, 309; arch-bar type, 185; logging, 252–54, 257; motor, 166, 179, 232, 250; road, 251, 256, 262, 281; snap, 255
Trustee, 141
Tunnel, 47
Turner, W. F., 25
Turntable, 50, 57
Turrish, Henry, 50, 55, 110, 177

U. S. Epperson, 161
Undercut, 93, 306
Underweights, 63, 187
Union, 86, 153, 154, 203, 225; boycott, 152, 153; collective bargaining 154; jurisdictional dispute, 197, 198; shop (closed), 154, 198, 199, 201; shop (open), 198. *See also* Labor
Union Mills Lumber Company, 81, 225
Union Pacific Railroad, 13, 275–79; City of Portland, 278, 279
Union Wire Rope Company, 156
United Mine Workers, 86
United Railways, 47, 50, 52, 54, 55, 57, 58, 68, 72, 79, 112, 127, 148, 149, 181, 183, 186, 222
United States, 234; District Court for the District of Missouri, 141; District Court for the District of Oregon, 112; Forest Products Laboratory, University of Wisconsin, 27; Justice Department, 212, Spruce Production Corporation, 25

INDEX

University of Oregon, xi, xiii, 116, 247; Division of Special Collections and University Archives, xi, xii; Library System, xi xii; Map Library, xiii
Utah, 13; Ogden, 13, 17; Salt Lake City, 17; Tintic, 276; Weber County, 22
Utah Construction Company, 17, 22, 24, 26, 28, 30, 32, 33
Utah-Idaho Sugar Company, 17

Valpiani, Rose C., xiii, 247, 323
Van Vleet, George, 127, 178, 180
Vaughan, J. Walter, 151, 208, 247
Vernonia, Chamber of Commerce, 330; Friendship Jamboree, 330; Lake, 328; Light and Power Company, 66, 84; South Park & Sunset Steam Railroad (V. S. P. & S. S.), 328, 329; Tree Farm, 326, 328, 329. *See also* Oregon, Vernonia
Vernonia Eagle, xiii, 60, 70, 83, 85, 86, 87, 200, 225;
von Platen, 188
Voting trust, trustees, 144 159, 181,

Wagberg, John, 310, 329
Wage and Hour Administration, 261
Wagner Act (National Labor Relations Act), 152, 200
Wagner, Corydon, 289
Walker, Reverend Raymond, 202
Wall, Charles, 210, 246, 250
Washington, D.C., 138, 139, 164, 211, 245, 261
Washington County, 131
Washington, 9, 215, 247, 283; Cathlamet, 258; Chenowith, 18; Fallbridge, 57; Longview, 295–97, 308; Pasco, 20; Puget Sound, 14, 20; Tacoma, xvi; Seattle, xvi, 68; Spokane, 55; Union Mills, 81; Vancouver, 55, 274–76; Wishram, 57
Washington Iron Works, 174, 258
Waste, 13, 249
Water Tank, 304
Watzek, Aubrey R., 112, 114–17, 135, 138–41, 144, 164, 187, 288; C. H., "Harlan," 288; John W., 90
Waukesha, 174, 175, 299
Wedge, 306
Weed Creek Timber Unit, 176
Weed Lumber Company, 54
Weise, Larry, 247; Mary, 247
Wentworth & Irwin, Inc., 215
West, 12; Coast, 1, 43, 61, 97, 157, 180, 181, 233, 318
West Coast Bureau of Lumber Grades and Inspection, v, 300
West Coast Lumbermens Association (WCLA), v, 71, 89, 90, 95, 183, 184, 207, 208, 244, 297, 301; Code of Fair Competition, 117
West Oregon Lumber Company, 127, 189
West Oregon Electric Cooperative, 241
Western Loggers Machinery Company, 173, 196
Weyerhaeuser, F. E., 90
Weyerhaeuser Timber Company, 12, 43, 154, 247, 248
Wheelbase, 43
Wheeler, C. H., 78, 92, 177
Whistle, 321; punk, 309
White employees, 86
White, Lewis, 76, 133; Lloyd, 133
Whitten & Bryant, 68
Wholesale, 8, 14, 15, 85, 95, 159, 244, 247
Whorehouses, 84
Willamette, 47, 53, 224; Iron & Steel Works, 44, 61, 72, 97, 98, 115, 123, 169, 174, 180, 193, 222, 255, 257, 261, 274, 275, 278, 280, 282, 305, 319
Willamette Valley, 321
Williams Construction Company, 252–54
Wills, Frank, 272
Wilson & Reilly, 124, 125, 162
Wilson, James, 125
Windy, 222, 311
Windy-Gap, 284, 295, 322
Windy-Junction, 74, 106
Wire rope, 43, 72, 175, 223
Wisconsin, 6, 8; Milwaukee, 68
Witchel, A. J., 189
Wolff, Walter, 116, 117
Women workers, 215
Wood, Paul, 76
Woods, Bob, 272
Woods crew, 50
Wood products industry, 291
Wood, slab, 182
Works Progress Administration (WPA), 166
WWI, 8, 137, 151
WWII, x, 112, 169, 183, 184, 193, 205, 226, 233, 234, 236, 240, 243, 247, 252, 263, 285, 291, 292; allied, 205, 233; blackout, 235; civilian defense, 235; critical occupations, 215; Fir Lumber Advisory Committee, 207, 217; Food Distribution Administration, 214; Manpower Commission, 216; National Committee for the Conservation of Manpower, 221; Office of Price Administration (OPA), 207; Office of Production Management (OPM), 212–14; point-rationed commodities, 214; priorities, 205, 213; Production Board (WPB), 206, 215, 217, 232; rationing, 205, 213, 224; stamps, 222; Supply Priorities and Allocation Board (SPAB), 209, 211, 212; surplus equipment, 250, 252; United States Employment Service (USES), 216, 217, 220; victory gardens, 214; War Labor Board (WLB), 261; West Coast Lumber Administrator, 215; Western Log & Lumber Administor, 232
Worley, Frank, 76
Wornstaff, Joe, 90, 223, 224, 251, 253
Wye, 308
Wyoming, Granger, 20; Laramie, 99; Rock Springs, 19

Yarder, 1, 44, 47, 95, 106, 122, 123, 174, 175, 194, 223, 256, 257, 267, 314, 318, 320
Yellow Fir. *See* Fir, Douglas
Yeon Building, 30
Yerreck Tract, 77, 177, 178, 226–29, 231, 233, 245, 249, 252, 254, 258, 262, 267, 284
Young, Lowell, 94
Yukon Spur, 185–87, 236
Yunkers & Wiecks, 180, 188

Zaruk, Mike, 303
Zenger, Jack, 310, 329